CliffsNotes®

SAT® CRAM PLAN™

3rd Edition

William Ma and Jane R. Burstein

Houghton Mifflin Harcourt
Boston • New York

About the Authors

William Ma was chairman of the Math Department at the Herricks School District on Long Island for many years before retiring. He also taught as an adjunct math instructor at Baruch College, Columbia University, and Fordham University. He is the author of several other review books for subjects including AP Calculus, ACT, and GMAT. He is currently a math consultant.

Jane Burstein taught English at Herricks High School in New Hyde Park, New York, for 36 years. She has been an ACT and SAT tutor for 30 years, an instructor at Hofstra University, and a reader for AP exams. She is the author of several other review books including those for the ACT, GMAT, GRE, and ASVAB.

Acknowledgments

William Ma would like to thank his wife, Mary, and daughters, Janet and Karen, who gave him much help in putting the book together; Roberta Melendy, a retired math teacher from Herricks, who edited many parts of the book; and Christina Stambaugh for her patience and editorial assistance.

Jane Burstein would like to thank her husband, David, and children, Jessica, Jonathan, Beth, and Seth, for their encouragement and helpful suggestions. Many thanks also to Greg Tubach, Christina Stambaugh, and the technical editors for their editorial advice and expertise.

Editorial

Executive Editor: Greg Tubach
Senior Editor: Christina Stambaugh
Copy Editor: Lynn Northrup
Technical Editors: Barbara Swovelin, Mary Jane Sterling, and Tom Page
Production Editor/Proofreader: Erika West

CliffsNotes® SAT® Cram Plan™, 3rd Edition

Copyright © 2016 by Houghton Mifflin Harcourt Publishing Company
All rights reserved.

Library of Congress Control Number: 2015955428
ISBN: 978-0-544-57791-6 (pbk)

Printed in the United States of America
DOC 10 9 8 7 6 5 4 3 2 1

For information about permission to reproduce selections from this book, write to trade.permissions@hmhco.com or to Permissions, Houghton Mifflin Harcourt Publishing Company, 3 Park Avenue, 19th Floor, New York, New York 10016.

www.hmhco.com

Table of Contents

Introduction

That time in every high school student's life has arrived: The SAT hovers on the horizon. Your SAT score, along with your high-school transcript, your résumé of extracurricular activities, your letters of recommendation, and your application essays, is an important factor in the college admissions process, so you know how important it is to prepare. You're determined to do whatever it takes to get your best possible score on the test. All you need is a helpful study plan, one that's simple, organized, and doable—in other words, one you'll be able to stick to as you embark on the path to SAT success. No problem. Whether you have two months, one month, or one week, you can achieve your goals if you're organized and diligent.

About the Test

The SAT is comprised of five sections: one evidence-based reading section, one evidence-based writing and language section, two mathematics sections, and one optional essay section. The whole test (including the optional essay) takes 3 hours and 50 minutes.

Here is a sample test format. Section order may vary from what we show in the table below.

Section	Subject	Type of Questions	Time Allotted
1	Reading	52 evidence-based critical reading multiple-choice questions	65 minutes
2	Writing and Language	44 evidence-based writing and language multiple-choice questions	35 minutes
3	Mathematics (No calculator)	15 multiple-choice questions 5 student-produced response questions (grid-ins)	25 minutes
4	Mathematics (Calculator)	30 multiple-choice questions 8 student-produced response questions (grid-ins)	55 minutes
5	Optional Essay	1 analysis of an argument essay	50 minutes

Using a Graphing Calculator

The SAT Math Test is divided into two sections:

- No calculator: 25 minutes, 20 questions
- Calculator: 55 minutes, 38 questions

While all questions on the mathematics portion of the SAT can be solved without a calculator, using a calculator, particularly a graphing calculator, can help solve a problem more quickly and prevent careless errors. The TI-89 graphing calculator is one of the most versatile and easy-to-use calculators permitted for use on the SAT Math Test. In chapters IX–XII in this book, every question that can be solved with the help of a graphing calculator is indicated by a calculator icon. The appendix in this book explains how to use the TI-89 graphing calculator to solve SAT math questions.

Go to http://sat.collegeboard.org/register/calculator-policy for the latest information on which calculators are permitted on the SAT.

About This Book

The first step in getting ready for the SAT is to determine exactly how much time you have and then follow the appropriate plan: the two-month plan, the one-month plan, or the one-week plan. Each plan has a schedule along with the approximate time you'll need to allot to each task. In addition, each subject-review chapter gives you strategies for that part of the test. Included in each subject-review chapter are practice exercises to assist you in the areas in which you're weakest and to help you continue to maximize your strengths.

Once you determine which cram plan to follow, the next step is to take the Diagnostic Test. The answer key and answer explanations will guide you to the specific chapters or sections within the chapters that cover the topics in which you need the most help. At the end of the Diagnostic Test, you'll find a scoring guide that will give you an indication of your baseline score on each section of the SAT. Then you can begin to focus on the subject-review chapters. At the end of the book, you'll find a practice test, a simulated SAT with a scoring guide to give you an authentic test-taking experience.

General Test-Taking Strategies

- Become familiar with the format of the test. If you know what to expect, you will be less nervous and more confident on the day of the test.
- Use this book to familiarize yourself with the directions to each section of the test. Knowing the directions to each section ahead of time will save you precious minutes on the day of the test.
- Work at a steady pace. You do not have the time to get bogged down on any one question. If you are having difficulty with a question, take your best educated guess and move on. In most cases, it is better to answer a question than to return to an unanswered question later. The Diagnostic Test and the Practice Test will help you learn to pace yourself properly.
- There is no penalty for wrong answers. Never leave a question blank.
- Read each question very carefully, and be sure you know exactly what it asks. Many questions require you to note very specific details. Watch for **signal words** like *most, seldom, highest,* and *lowest.*
- Always read all the answer choices carefully, and use **POE** (Process of Elimination) to narrow down the answer choices.
- Use the answer choices to help you when you are unsure. On any multiple-choice question, the answer is always right in front of you.
- For the math sections, all figures are drawn to scale unless otherwise stated. (This means that you can often use the given figure to make an educated guess on the length of a line segment or the measure of an angle.)
- Make sure you completely fill in the corresponding circle on your answer sheet. Check yourself every five questions.
- Bring everything you will need with you on the day of the test: sharpened no. 2 pencils with good erasers, approved calculator, and tissues. It is a good idea to bring your own watch; you cannot be sure you will have a visible clock in the testing room. Cell phones are prohibited. Don't forget to have your admission ticket and photo ID with you.

I. Two-Month Cram Plan

	The Math Test	The Reading Test	The Writing and Language Test and The Essay
8 weeks before the test	**Study Time:** 3½ hours ❏ Take the **Diagnostic Test** and review answer explanations. ❏ Based on the questions you missed, identify difficult topics and their corresponding chapters. These chapters are your targeted chapters. ❏ Compare your SAT Essay to the rubric and the samples and target areas to improve.		
7 weeks before the test	**Study Time:** 3 hours ❏ **Heart of Algebra:** Chapter IX 　❏ Read sections A–F. 　❏ Do practice question 1 in each section. ❏ **Problem Solving and Data Analysis:** Chapter X 　❏ Read sections A–H. 　❏ Do practice question 1 in each section. ❏ **Passport to Advanced Math:** Chapter XI 　❏ Read sections A–L. 　❏ Do practice question 1 in each section. ❏ **Using the TI-89 Graphing Calculator:** Appendix 　❏ Do questions 1–2.	**Study Time:** 1½ hours ❏ **Reading:** Chapter V 　❏ Read sections A–C.1. 　❏ Do all practice questions in C.1. ❏ **Tier 2 Vocabulary:** Chapter VIII 　❏ Read aberration–comedic. 　❏ Highlight unfamiliar words; divide them into 5 equal groups, and study 1 group each night. 　❏ Review all 5 groups for 2 nights.	**Study Time:** 1 hour ❏ **Writing and Language:** Chapter VI 　❏ Read section A. 　❏ Read sections B.1.a–c. 　❏ Do half the practice questions in each section. 　❏ For targeted areas, do all the practice questions.
6 weeks before the test	**Study Time:** 3 hours ❏ **Heart of Algebra:** Chapter IX 　❏ Re-read sections A–F. 　❏ Do practice question 2 in each section. ❏ **Problem Solving and Data Analysis:** Chapter X 　❏ Re-read sections A–H. 　❏ Do practice question 2 in each section. ❏ **Passport to Advanced Math:** Chapter XI 　❏ Re-read sections A–L. 　❏ Do practice question 2 in each section. ❏ **Using the TI-89 Graphing Calculator:** Appendix 　❏ Do questions 3–4.	**Study Time:** 1½ hours ❏ **Reading:** Chapter V 　❏ Read sections C.2.a–d and C.3. 　❏ Do all practice questions in these sections. ❏ **Tier 2 Vocabulary:** Chapter VIII 　❏ Read compound–extinct. 　❏ Highlight unfamiliar words; divide them into 5 equal groups, and study 1 group each night. 　❏ Review all 5 groups for 2 nights.	**Study Time:** 1 hour ❏ **Writing and Language:** Chapter VI 　❏ Read sections B.1.d–g. 　❏ Do half the practice questions in each section. 　❏ For targeted areas, do all the practice questions. For those who plan to write the essay: ❏ **The Essay:** Chapter VII 　❏ Read section A.

continued

	The Math Test	The Reading Test	The Writing and Language Test and The Essay

5 weeks before the test	**Study Time:** 2½ hours
	❏ **Heart of Algebra:** Chapter IX
	  ❏ Review sections A–F.
	  ❏ Do practice question 3 in each section.
	❏ **Problem Solving and Data Analysis:** Chapter X
	  ❏ Review sections A–H.
	  ❏ Do practice question 3 in each section.
	❏ **Passport to Advanced Math:** Chapter XI
	  ❏ Review sections A–L.
	  ❏ Do practice question 3 in each section.
	❏ **Using the TI-89 Graphing Calculator:** Appendix
	  ❏ Do questions 5–6.
		Study Time: 1½ hours
		❏ **Reading:** Chapter V
		  ❏ Read section C.4.a–c.
		  ❏ Do practice questions in each section.
		❏ **Tier 2 Vocabulary:** Chapter VIII
		  ❏ Read extol–lassitude.
		  ❏ Highlight unfamiliar words; divide them into 5 equal groups, and study 1 group each night.
		  ❏ Review all 5 groups for 2 nights.
			Study Time: 1 hour
			❏ **Writing and Language:** Chapter VI
			  ❏ Read sections B.2.a–c.
			  ❏ Do half the practice questions in each section.
			  ❏ For targeted areas, do all the practice questions.
			❏ **The Essay:** Chapter VII
			  ❏ Read section B.

4 weeks before the test	**Study Time:** 2 hours
	❏ **Heart of Algebra:** Chapter IX
	  ❏ Review sections A–F.
	  ❏ Do practice question 4 in each section.
	❏ **Problem Solving and Data Analysis:** Chapter X
	  ❏ Review sections A–H.
	  ❏ Do practice question 4 in each section.
	❏ **Passport to Advanced Math:** Chapter XI
	  ❏ Review sections A–L.
	  ❏ Do practice question 4 in each section.
	❏ **Using the TI-89 Graphing Calculator:** Appendix
	  ❏ Do questions 7–8.
		Study Time: 1 hour
		❏ **Reading:** Chapter V
		  ❏ Review sections A–C.1.
		  ❏ Review practice questions in each section.
		  ❏ Do additional practice questions 1–6 at the end of the chapter.
		❏ **Tier 2 Vocabulary:** Chapter VIII
		  ❏ Read laudable–recluse.
		  ❏ Highlight unfamiliar words; divide them into 5 equal groups, and study 1 group each night.
		  ❏ Review all 5 groups for 2 nights.
			Study Time: 1 hour
			❏ **Writing and Language:** Chapter VI
			  ❏ Read sections B.2.d–g.
			  ❏ Do half the practice questions in each section.
			  ❏ For targeted areas, do all the practice questions.
			❏ **The Essay:** Chapter VII
			  ❏ Read sections C–E.

	The Math Test	The Reading Test	The Writing and Language Test and The Essay

3 weeks before the test	**Study Time:** 2 hours
	 ❑ **Heart of Algebra:** Chapter IX
	    ❑ Review sections A–F.
	    ❑ Do practice question 5 in each section.
	 ❑ **Problem Solving and Data Analysis:** Chapter X
	    ❑ Review sections A–H.
	    ❑ Do practice question 5 in each section.
	 ❑ **Passport to Advanced Math:** Chapter XI
	    ❑ Review sections A–L.
	    ❑ Do practice question 5 in each section.
	 ❑ **Using the TI-89 Graphing Calculator:** Appendix
	    ❑ Do question 9.
		Study Time: 1 hour
		 ❑ **Reading:** Chapter V
		    ❑ Review sections C.2.–C.4.
		    ❑ Review practice questions in each section.
		    ❑ Do additional practice questions 7–12 at the end of the chapter.
		 ❑ **Tier 2 Vocabulary:** Chapter VIII
		    ❑ Read recuperate–zealous.
		    ❑ Highlight unfamiliar words; divide them into 5 equal groups, and study 1 group each night.
		    ❑ Review all 5 groups for 2 nights.
			Study Time: 3 hours
			 ❑ **Writing and Language:** Chapter VI
			    ❑ Read sections B.3.a–g.
			    ❑ Do half the practice questions in each section.
			    ❑ For targeted areas, do all the practice questions.
			 ❑ **The Essay:** Chapter VII
			    ❑ Read sections F–G.
			    ❑ Write the essay in the additional practice at the end of the chapter.

2 weeks before the test	**Study Time:** 5 hours ❑ Take the **Practice Test** and review answer explanations. ❑ Based on your errors on the Practice Test, identify difficult topics and their corresponding chapters. These chapters are your targeted areas.		

	Study Time: 2 hours
	 ❑ Based on the Practice Test, review topic summaries for all targeted areas.
	 ❑ Redo those questions that you answered incorrectly on the Practice Test.
	 ❑ **Heart of Algebra:** Chapter IX
	    ❑ Do practice question 6 in each section.
	 ❑ **Problem Solving and Data Analysis:** Chapter X
	    ❑ Do practice question 6 in each section.
	 ❑ **Passport to Advanced Math:** Chapter XI
	    ❑ Do practice question 6 in each section.
	 ❑ **Using the TI-89 Graphing Calculator:** Appendix
	    ❑ Do questions 10–11.
		Study Time: 1 hour
		 ❑ **Reading:** Chapter V
		    ❑ Do additional practice questions 13–17 at the end of the chapter.
		 ❑ **Tier 2 Vocabulary:** Chapter VIII
		    ❑ Divide all highlighted words into 5 equal groups, and study the first group of words.
			Study Time: 1 hour
			 ❑ **Writing and Language:** Chapter VI
			    ❑ Do additional practice questions 1–12 at the end of the chapter.
			 ❑ **The Essay:** Chapter VII
			    ❑ Review transitional words (see pages 127–128 in Chapter VI). Consider sentences in your essay that could be improved by the addition of these words and phrases.

continued

	The Math Test	The Reading Test	The Writing and Language Test and The Essay

7 days before the test	**Study Time:** 1 hour
	❏ **Additional Topics in Math:** Chapter XII
	  ❏ Read sections A–G.
	  ❏ Do practice questions 1–2 in each section.
	❏ **Using the TI-89 Graphing Calculator:** Appendix
	  ❏ Do questions 12–13.
		Study Time: 1 hour
		❏ **Reading:** Chapter V
		  ❏ Review all sections, including the practice questions in each section.
		❏ **Tier 2 Vocabulary:** Chapter VIII
		  ❏ Study the second group of highlighted words.
			Study Time: 1 hour
			❏ **Writing and Language:** Chapter VI
			  ❏ Based on results of the Practice Test, begin to review all targeted areas.
			  ❏ Divide targeted areas into 4 sections. For first targeted area, do all remaining practice questions.

6 days before the test	**Study Time:** 1 hour
	❏ **Additional Topics in Math:** Chapter XII
	  ❏ Re-read sections A–G.
	  ❏ Do practice questions 3–4 in each section.
	❏ **Using the TI-89 Graphing Calculator:** Appendix
	  ❏ Do questions 14–15.
		Study Time: 1 hour
		❏ **Reading:** Chapter V
		  ❏ Continue to review all sections.
		❏ **Tier 2 Vocabulary:** Chapter VIII
		  ❏ Study the third group of highlighted words.
			Study Time: 1 hour
			❏ **Writing and Language:** Chapter VI
			  ❏ For second targeted area, do all remaining practice questions.

5 days before the test	**Study Time:** 1 hour
	❏ **Additional Topics in Math:** Chapter XII
	  ❏ Review sections A–G.
	  ❏ Do practice question 5 in each section.
	❏ **Using the TI-89 Graphing Calculator:** Appendix
	  ❏ Do questions 16–17.
		Study Time: 1 hour
		❏ **Reading:** Chapter V
		  ❏ Continue to review all sections.
		❏ **Tier 2 Vocabulary:** Chapter VIII
		  ❏ Study the fourth group of highlighted words.
			Study Time: 1 hour
			❏ **Writing and Language:** Chapter VI
			  ❏ For third targeted area, do all remaining practice questions.
			❏ **The Essay:** Chapter VII
			  ❏ Review sections A–E.

4 days before the test	**Study Time:** 1 hour
	❏ **Additional Topics in Math:** Chapter XII
	  ❏ Review sections A–G.
	  ❏ Do practice question 6 in each section.
	❏ **Using the TI-89 Graphing Calculator:** Appendix
	  ❏ Do questions 18–20.
		Study Time: 1 hour
		❏ **Reading:** Chapter V
		  ❏ Continue to review all sections.
		❏ **Tier 2 Vocabulary:** Chapter VIII
		  ❏ Study the fifth group of highlighted words.
			Study Time: 1 hour
			❏ **Writing and Language:** Chapter VI
			  ❏ For fourth targeted area, do all remaining practice questions.
			❏ **The Essay:** Chapter VII
			  ❏ Review the model essay and its analysis and commentary in sections G.4–5.

	The Math Test	The Reading Test	The Writing and Language Test and The Essay

3 days before the test	**Study Time:** 1 hour
	 ❏ Re-read targeted areas from each chapter.
	 ❏ Redo practice question 5 from each chapter in the targeted areas.
	 ❏ Review calculator questions in Appendix.
		Study Time: 1 hour
		 ❏ **Reading:** Chapter V
		    ❏ Continue to review all sections.
		 ❏ **Tier 2 Vocabulary:** Chapter VIII
		    ❏ Review all highlighted words.
			Study Time: 1 hour
			 ❏ **Writing and Language:** Chapter VI
			    ❏ Review all sections.
			    ❏ Look over answers to targeted writing and language questions (Chapter VI) and review any issues that are still problematic
			 ❏ **The Essay:** Chapter VII
			    ❏ Review sections A–E.

2 days before the test	**Study Time:** 1 hour
	 ❏ Review targeted areas from each chapter.
	 ❏ Redo practice question 6 from each chapter in the targeted areas.
	 ❏ Review calculator questions in Appendix.
		Study Time: 1 hour
		 ❏ **Reading:** Chapter V
		    ❏ Re-read the general strategies in section A and strategies for the focus skills in section C of Chapter V.
		 ❏ **Tier 2 Vocabulary:** Chapter VIII
		    ❏ Review all highlighted words.
			Study Time: 1 hour
			 ❏ **The Essay:** Chapter VII
			    ❏ Review the model essays in Chapter VII, in the Diagnostic Test, and in the Practice Test.

Night before the test	❏ Relax! You're well prepared for the test. Have confidence in your ability to do well. ❏ Exercise. It helps to relieve stress, improve sleep quality, and boost brain performance. ❏ Get a good night's sleep. Try to unplug from electronic devices at least 30 minutes before bedtime, and remove any distractions that might wake you during the night.		

Morning of the test	**Reminders:**
	 ❏ Eat a well-balanced, nutritious breakfast.
	 ❏ Take the following items with you on test day:
	    ❏ Your admission ticket and photo ID
	    ❏ Several no. 2 pencils and erasers
	    ❏ A calculator with fresh batteries
	    ❏ A watch
	 ❏ Try to go outside for a few minutes and walk around before the test to relieve stress.
	 ❏ **Most important:** Stay calm and confident during the test. Take slow, deep breaths and think positive thoughts if you feel at all nervous. You can do it!		

II. One-Month Cram Plan

One-Month Cram Plan			
	The Math Test	**The Reading Test**	**The Writing and Language Test and The Essay**
4 weeks before the test	**Study Time:** 3½ hours ❑ Take the **Diagnostic Test** and review answer explanations. ❑ Based on the questions you missed, identify difficult topics and their corresponding chapters. These chapters are your targeted chapters. ❑ Compare your SAT Essay to the rubric and the samples and target areas to improve.		

	Study Time: 3 hours
	❑ **Heart of Algebra:** Chapter IX
	  ❑ Read sections A–F.
	  ❑ Do practice questions 1–2 in each section.
	❑ **Problem Solving and Data Analysis:** Chapter X
	  ❑ Read sections A–H.
	  ❑ Do practice questions 1–2 in each section.
	❑ **Passport to Advanced Math:** Chapter XI
	  ❑ Read sections A–L.
	  ❑ Do practice questions 1–2 in each section.
	❑ **Using the TI-89 Graphing Calculator:** Appendix
	  ❑ Do questions 1–3.
		Study Time: 1½ hours
		❑ **Reading:** Chapter V
		  ❑ Read sections A–C.1.
		  ❑ Do all practice questions in C.1.
		❑ **Tier 2 Vocabulary:** Chapter VIII
		  ❑ Read aberration–eclectic.
		  ❑ Highlight unfamiliar words; divide them into 5 equal groups, and study 1 group each night.
		  ❑ Review all 5 groups for 2 nights.
			Study Time: 1 hour
			❑ **Writing and Language:** Chapter VI
			  ❑ Read section A.
			  ❑ Read sections B.1.a–c.
			  ❑ Do half the practice questions in each section.
			  ❑ For targeted areas, do all the practice questions.
			
			For those who plan to write the essay:
			❑ **The Essay:** Chapter VII
			  ❑ Read section A.

continued

	The Math Test	The Reading Test	The Writing and Language Test and The Essay

3 weeks before the test	**Study Time:** 3 hours
	❏ **Heart of Algebra:** Chapter IX
	  ❏ Re-read sections A–F.
	  ❏ Do practice questions 3–4 in each section.
	❏ **Problem Solving and Data Analysis:** Chapter X
	  ❏ Re-read sections A–H.
	  ❏ Do practice questions 3–4 in each section.
	❏ **Passport to Advanced Math:** Chapter XI
	  ❏ Re-read sections A–L.
	  ❏ Do practice questions 3–4 in each section.
	❏ **Using the TI-89 Graphing Calculator:** Appendix
	  ❏ Do questions 4–6.
		Study Time: 1½ hours
		❏ **Reading:** Chapter V
		  ❏ Read sections C.2.a–d and C.3.
		  ❏ Do all practice questions in these sections.
		  ❏ Do additional practice questions 1–6 at the end of the chapter.
		❏ **Tier 2 Vocabulary:** Chapter VIII
		  ❏ Read effrontery–nefarious.
		  ❏ Highlight unfamiliar words; divide them into 5 equal groups, and study 1 group each night.
		  ❏ Review all 5 groups for 2 nights.
			Study Time: 2 hours
			❏ **Writing and Language:** Chapter VI
			  ❏ Read sections B.1.d–g and B.2.a–c.
			  ❏ Do half the practice questions in each section.
			  ❏ For targeted areas, do all the practice questions.
			❏ **The Essay:** Chapter VII
			  ❏ Read section B.

2 weeks before the test	**Study Time:** 2½ hours
	❏ **Heart of Algebra:** Chapter IX
	  ❏ Review sections A–F.
	  ❏ Do practice questions 5–6 in each section.
	❏ **Problem Solving and Data Analysis:** Chapter X
	  ❏ Review sections A–H.
	  ❏ Do practice questions 5–6 in each section.
	❏ **Passport to Advanced Math:** Chapter XI
	  ❏ Review sections A–L.
	  ❏ Do practice questions 5–6 in each section.
	❏ **Using the TI-89 Graphing Calculator:** Appendix
	  ❏ Do questions 7–9.
		Study Time: 1½ hours
		❏ **Reading:** Chapter V
		  ❏ Read section C.4.a–c.
		  ❏ Do practice questions in each section.
		  ❏ Do additional practice questions 7–12 at the end of the chapter.
		❏ **Tier 2 Vocabulary:** Chapter VIII
		  ❏ Read negligent–zealous.
		  ❏ Highlight unfamiliar words; divide them into 5 equal groups, and study 1 group each night.
		  ❏ Review all 5 groups for 2 nights.
			Study Time: 2½ hours
			❏ **Writing and Language:** Chapter VI
			  ❏ Read sections B.2.d–g and B.3.a–g.
			  ❏ Do half the practice questions in each section.
			  ❏ For targeted areas, do all the practice questions.
			❏ **The Essay:** Chapter VII
			  ❏ Read sections C–G.
			  ❏ Write the essay in the additional practice at the end of the chapter.

7 days before the test	**Study Time:** 5 hours ❏ Take the **Practice Test** and review answer explanations. ❏ Based on your errors on the Practice Test, identify difficult topics and their corresponding chapters. These chapters are your targeted areas.		

	The Math Test	The Reading Test	The Writing and Language Test and The Essay
6 days before the test	**Study Time:** 2 hours ❑ Based on the Practice Test, review topic summaries for all targeted areas. ❑ Redo those questions that you answered incorrectly on the Practice Test. ❑ **Additional Topics in Math:** Chapter XII 　❑ Read sections A–G. 　❑ Do practice questions 1–2 in each section. ❑ **Using the TI-89 Graphing Calculator:** Appendix 　❑ Do questions 10–12.	**Study Time:** 1 hour ❑ **Reading:** Chapter V 　❑ Review sections A–C.1. 　❑ Do additional practice questions 13–17 at the end of the chapter. ❑ **Tier 2 Vocabulary:** Chapter VIII 　❑ Divide all highlighted words into 4 equal groups, and study the first group of words.	**Study Time:** 1 hour ❑ **Writing and Language:** Chapter VI 　❑ Based on results of the Practice Test, begin to review all targeted areas. 　❑ Do additional practice questions 1–12 at the end of the chapter. ❑ **The Essay:** Chapter VII 　❑ Review transitional words (see pages 127–128 in Chapter VI).
5 days before the test	**Study Time:** 1½ hours ❑ **Additional Topics in Math:** Chapter XII 　❑ Review sections A–G. 　❑ Do practice questions 3–4 in each section. ❑ **Using the TI-89 Graphing Calculator:** Appendix 　❑ Do questions 13–15.	**Study Time:** 1 hour ❑ **Reading:** Chapter V 　❑ Review sections C.2–C.3. ❑ **Tier 2 Vocabulary:** Chapter VIII 　❑ Study the second group of highlighted words.	**Study Time:** 1 hour ❑ **Writing and Language:** Chapter VI 　❑ Based on results of the Practice Test, begin to review all targeted areas. ❑ **The Essay:** Chapter VII 　❑ Review sections A–G.
4 days before the test	**Study Time:** 1½ hours ❑ **Additional Topics in Math:** Chapter XII 　❑ Review sections A–G. 　❑ Do practice questions 5–6 in each section. ❑ **Using the TI-89 Graphing Calculator:** Appendix 　❑ Do questions 16–20.	**Study Time:** 1 hour ❑ **Reading:** Chapter V 　❑ Review sections C.4.a–c. ❑ **Tier 2 Vocabulary:** Chapter VIII 　❑ Study the third group of highlighted words.	**Study Time:** ½ hour ❑ **Writing and Language:** Chapter VI 　❑ Based on results of the Practice Test, continue to review all targeted areas.
3 days before the test	**Study Time:** 1 hour ❑ Re-read targeted areas from each chapter. ❑ Redo practice question 5 from each chapter in the targeted areas. ❑ Review calculator questions in Appendix.	**Study Time:** 1 hour ❑ **Reading:** Chapter V 　❑ Review any sections that were targeted in the Practice Test. ❑ **Tier 2 Vocabulary:** Chapter VIII 　❑ Study the last group of highlighted words.	**Study Time:** ½ hour ❑ **Writing and Language:** Chapter VI 　❑ Based on results of the Practice Test, continue to review all targeted areas.

continued

	The Math Test	The Reading Test	The Writing and Language Test and The Essay

2 days before the test	**Study Time:** 1 hour
	❑ Re-read targeted areas from each chapter.
	❑ Redo practice question 6 from each chapter in the targeted areas.
	❑ Review calculator questions in Appendix.
		Study Time: 1 hour
		❑ **Reading:** Chapter V
		  ❑ Continue to review any sections that were targeted in the Practice Test.
		❑ **Tier 2 Vocabulary:** Chapter VIII
		  ❑ Review all highlighted words.
			Study Time: ½ hour
			❑ **Writing and Language:** Chapter VI
			  ❑ Based on results of the Practice Test, continue to review all targeted areas.

Night before the test	❑ Relax! You're well prepared for the test. Have confidence in your ability to do well. ❑ Exercise. It helps to relieve stress, improve sleep quality, and boost brain performance. ❑ Get a good night's sleep. Try to unplug from electronic devices at least 30 minutes before bedtime, and remove any distractions that might wake you during the night.		

Morning of the test	**Reminders:**
	❑ Eat a well-balanced, nutritious breakfast.
	❑ Take the following items with you on test day:
	  ❑ Your admission ticket and photo ID
	  ❑ Several no. 2 pencils and erasers
	  ❑ A calculator with fresh batteries
	  ❑ A watch
	❑ Try to go outside for a few minutes and walk around before the test to relieve stress.
	❑ **Most important:** Stay calm and confident during the test. Take slow, deep breaths and think positive thoughts if you feel at all nervous. You can do it!		

III. One-Week Cram Plan

	The Math Test	The Reading Test	The Writing and Language Test and The Essay
One-Week Cram Plan			
7 days before the test	**Study Time:** 3½ hours ❑ Take the **Diagnostic Test** and review answer explanations. ❑ Based on the questions you missed, identify difficult topics and their corresponding chapters. These chapters are your targeted chapters. ❑ Compare your SAT Essay to the rubric and the samples and target areas to improve.		

6 days before the test	**Study Time:** 3 hours
	❑ **Heart of Algebra:** Chapter IX
	  ❑ Read sections A–F.
	  ❑ Do practice questions 1–2 in each section.
	❑ **Problem Solving and Data Analysis:** Chapter X
	  ❑ Read sections A–H.
	  ❑ Do practice questions 1–2 in each section.
	❑ **Passport to Advanced Math:** Chapter XI
	  ❑ Read sections A–L.
	  ❑ Do practice questions 1–2 in each section.
	❑ **Using the TI-89 Graphing Calculator:** Appendix
	  ❑ Do questions 1–5.
		Study Time: 1½ hours
		❑ **Reading:** Chapter V
		  ❑ Read sections A–C.1.
		  ❑ Do all practice questions in C.1.
		❑ **Tier 2 Vocabulary:** Chapter VIII
		  ❑ Read aberration–eclectic.
		  ❑ Highlight unfamiliar words; divide them into 3 equal groups, and study first group.
			Study Time: 1 hour
			❑ **Writing and Language:** Chapter VI
			  ❑ Read section A.
			  ❑ Read sections B.1.a–c.
			  ❑ Do half the practice questions in each section.
			  ❑ For targeted areas, do all the practice questions.
			
			For those who plan to write the essay:
			❑ **The Essay:** Chapter VII
			  ❑ Read section A.

5 days before the test	**Study Time:** 3 hours
	❑ **Heart of Algebra:** Chapter IX
	  ❑ Re-read sections A–F.
	  ❑ Do practice questions 3–4 in each section.
	❑ **Problem Solving and Data Analysis:** Chapter X
	  ❑ Re-read sections A–H.
	  ❑ Do practice questions 3–4 in each section.
	❑ **Passport to Advanced Math:** Chapter XI
	  ❑ Re-read sections A–L.
	  ❑ Do practice questions 3–4 in each section.
	❑ **Using the TI-89 Graphing Calculator:** Appendix
	  ❑ Do questions 6–10.
		Study Time: 1½ hours
		❑ **Reading:** Chapter V
		  ❑ Read sections C.2.a–d and C.3.
		  ❑ Do all practice questions in these sections.
		  ❑ Do additional practice questions 1–6 at the end of the chapter.
		❑ **Tier 2 Vocabulary:** Chapter VIII
		  ❑ Read effrontery–nefarious.
		  ❑ Study second group of highlighted words.
			Study Time: 2 hours
			❑ **Writing and Language:** Chapter VI
			  ❑ Read sections B.1.d–g and B.2.a–c.
			  ❑ Do half the practice questions in each section.
			  ❑ For targeted areas, do all the practice questions.
			❑ **The Essay:** Chapter VII
			  ❑ Read section B.

continued

	The Math Test	The Reading Test	The Writing and Language Test and The Essay

4 days before the test	**Study Time:** 2½ hours
	❏ **Heart of Algebra:** Chapter IX
	  ❏ Review sections A–F.
	  ❏ Do practice questions 5–6 in each section.
	❏ **Problem Solving and Data Analysis:** Chapter X
	  ❏ Review sections A–H.
	  ❏ Do practice questions 5–6 in each section.
	❏ **Passport to Advanced Math:** Chapter XI
	  ❏ Review sections A–L.
	  ❏ Do practice questions 5–6 in each section.
	❏ **Using the TI-89 Graphing Calculator:** Appendix
	  ❏ Do questions 11–15.
		Study Time: 1½ hours
		❏ **Reading:** Chapter V
		  ❏ Read section C.4.a–c.
		  ❏ Do practice questions in each section.
		  ❏ Do additional practice questions 7–12 at the end of the chapter.
		❏ **Tier 2 Vocabulary:** Chapter VIII
		  ❏ Read negligent–zealous.
		  ❏ Study third group of highlighted words.
			Study Time: 2½ hours
			❏ **Writing and Language:** Chapter VI
			  ❏ Read sections B.2.d–g and B.3.a–g.
			  ❏ Do half the practice questions in each section.
			  ❏ For targeted areas, do all the practice questions.
			❏ **The Essay:** Chapter VII
			  ❏ Read sections C–G.
			  ❏ Write the essay in the additional practice at the end of the chapter.

3 days before the test	**Study Time:** 5 hours ❏ Take the **Practice Test** and review answer explanations. ❏ Based on your errors on the Practice Test, identify difficult topics and their corresponding chapters. These chapters are your targeted areas.		

2 days before the test	**Study Time:** 2½ hours
	❏ Based on the Practice Test, review topic summaries for all targeted areas.
	❏ Redo those questions that you answered incorrectly on the Practice Test.
	❏ **Additional Topics in Math:** Chapter XII
	  ❏ Read sections A–G.
	  ❏ Do practice questions 1–6 in each section.
	❏ **Using the TI-89 Graphing Calculator:** Appendix
	  ❏ Do questions 16–20.
		Study Time: 2 hours
		❏ **Reading:** Chapter V
		  ❏ Based on Practice Test, review sections that still need attention.
		  ❏ Do additional practice questions 13–17 at the end of the chapter.
		❏ **Tier 2 Vocabulary:** Chapter VIII
		  ❏ Review all highlighted words.
			Study Time: 1½ hours
			❏ **Writing and Language:** Chapter VI
			  ❏ Based on results of the Practice Test, begin to review all targeted areas.
			  ❏ Do additional practice questions 1–12 at the end of the chapter.
			❏ **The Essay:** Chapter VII
			  ❏ Review transitional words (see pages 127–128 in Chapter VI).

1 day before the test	**Study Time:** 1 hour
	❏ Re-read targeted areas from each chapter.
	❏ Redo practice question 6 from each chapter in the targeted areas.
		Study Time: 1 hour
		❏ **Tier 2 Vocabulary:** Chapter VIII
		  ❏ Review all highlighted words.
			Study Time: ½ hour
			❏ **Writing and Language:** Chapter VI
			  ❏ Based on results of the Practice Test, continue to review all targeted areas.

	The Math Test	The Reading Test	The Writing and Language Test and The Essay

Morning of the test	**Reminders:**
	❑ Eat a well-balanced, nutritious breakfast.
	❑ Take the following items with you on test day:
	    ❑ Your admission ticket and photo ID
	    ❑ Several no. 2 pencils and erasers
	    ❑ A calculator with fresh batteries
	    ❑ A watch
	❑ Try to go outside for a few minutes and walk around before the test to relieve stress.
	❑ **Most important:** Stay calm and confident during the test. Take slow, deep breaths and think positive thoughts if you feel at all nervous. You can do it!		

IV. Diagnostic Test

This Diagnostic Test, excluding the essay, is half the length of a full-length SAT Test. The Diagnostic Test has five sections—Reading Test, Writing and Language Test, Math Test – No Calculator, Math Test – Calculator, and the Essay (optional). The tests are designed to measure your ability in these five areas and to predict your success in college. Each question is numbered. Choose the best answer for each question and fill in the corresponding circle on the answer sheet provided.

When you take the Diagnostic Test, try to simulate the test conditions by following the time allotments carefully. On the actual SAT, if you finish a section before the allotted time runs out, you may not work on any other section. You may not go back to a previous section. For sections 1–4 of this Diagnostic Test, you'll need 1 hour and 32 minutes; you'll need an additional 50 minutes for the essay (the full amount of time given on the actual test):

- Reading Test: 33 minutes
- Writing and Language Test: 18 minutes
- Math Test – No Calculator: 13 minutes
- Math Test – Calculator: 28 minutes
- The Essay (optional): 50 minutes

Answer Sheet

Section 1: Reading Test

1	Ⓐ Ⓑ Ⓒ Ⓓ
2	Ⓐ Ⓑ Ⓒ Ⓓ
3	Ⓐ Ⓑ Ⓒ Ⓓ
4	Ⓐ Ⓑ Ⓒ Ⓓ
5	Ⓐ Ⓑ Ⓒ Ⓓ
6	Ⓐ Ⓑ Ⓒ Ⓓ
7	Ⓐ Ⓑ Ⓒ Ⓓ
8	Ⓐ Ⓑ Ⓒ Ⓓ
9	Ⓐ Ⓑ Ⓒ Ⓓ
10	Ⓐ Ⓑ Ⓒ Ⓓ
11	Ⓐ Ⓑ Ⓒ Ⓓ
12	Ⓐ Ⓑ Ⓒ Ⓓ
13	Ⓐ Ⓑ Ⓒ Ⓓ
14	Ⓐ Ⓑ Ⓒ Ⓓ
15	Ⓐ Ⓑ Ⓒ Ⓓ
16	Ⓐ Ⓑ Ⓒ Ⓓ
17	Ⓐ Ⓑ Ⓒ Ⓓ
18	Ⓐ Ⓑ Ⓒ Ⓓ
19	Ⓐ Ⓑ Ⓒ Ⓓ
20	Ⓐ Ⓑ Ⓒ Ⓓ

21	Ⓐ Ⓑ Ⓒ Ⓓ
22	Ⓐ Ⓑ Ⓒ Ⓓ
23	Ⓐ Ⓑ Ⓒ Ⓓ
24	Ⓐ Ⓑ Ⓒ Ⓓ
25	Ⓐ Ⓑ Ⓒ Ⓓ
26	Ⓐ Ⓑ Ⓒ Ⓓ

Section 2: Writing and Language Test

1	Ⓐ Ⓑ Ⓒ Ⓓ
2	Ⓐ Ⓑ Ⓒ Ⓓ
3	Ⓐ Ⓑ Ⓒ Ⓓ
4	Ⓐ Ⓑ Ⓒ Ⓓ
5	Ⓐ Ⓑ Ⓒ Ⓓ
6	Ⓐ Ⓑ Ⓒ Ⓓ
7	Ⓐ Ⓑ Ⓒ Ⓓ
8	Ⓐ Ⓑ Ⓒ Ⓓ
9	Ⓐ Ⓑ Ⓒ Ⓓ
10	Ⓐ Ⓑ Ⓒ Ⓓ
11	Ⓐ Ⓑ Ⓒ Ⓓ
12	Ⓐ Ⓑ Ⓒ Ⓓ
13	Ⓐ Ⓑ Ⓒ Ⓓ
14	Ⓐ Ⓑ Ⓒ Ⓓ
15	Ⓐ Ⓑ Ⓒ Ⓓ
16	Ⓐ Ⓑ Ⓒ Ⓓ
17	Ⓐ Ⓑ Ⓒ Ⓓ
18	Ⓐ Ⓑ Ⓒ Ⓓ
19	Ⓐ Ⓑ Ⓒ Ⓓ
20	Ⓐ Ⓑ Ⓒ Ⓓ
21	Ⓐ Ⓑ Ⓒ Ⓓ
22	Ⓐ Ⓑ Ⓒ Ⓓ

CUT HERE

Section 3: Math Test – No Calculator

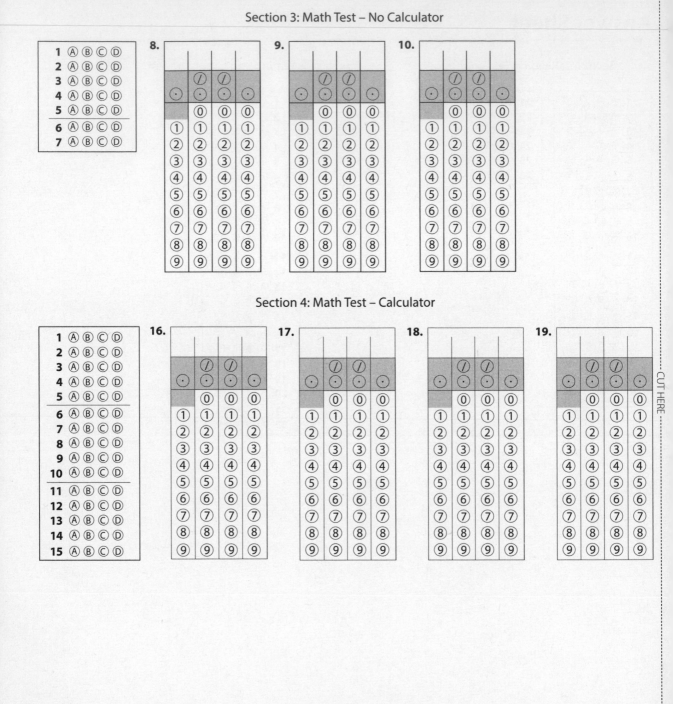

Section 4: Math Test – Calculator

Section 5: The Essay

CUT HERE

CUT HERE

CUT HERE

Section 1: Reading Test

33 Minutes—26 Questions

Directions: Carefully read the following passages and answer the questions that follow each passage. The questions after the pair of related passages may ask you about the relationship between the passages. Answer the questions based on the content of the passages: both what is stated and what is implied in the passages. Refer to the introductory material before each passage and any accompanying graphs and charts as needed to answer the questions.

Questions 1–9 are based on the following passage.

The following is an excerpt from the novel *The Beginning of Wisdom* written in 1921 by Stephen Vincent Benét.

There is another sound in the room now—a sound no one could have noticed before, it is so small and monotonous—the sound of even breathing. It comes from the great oak bed by
(5) the wall and the chair rocked close to the grate. Hearing it makes the room seem stiller and warmer. The fire shifts suddenly, throwing a gay flare on the face of the drowser before it, and the procession of dull-blue peacocks that
(10) parade the ivory chintz of the deep chairs and tall curtains. From the bed comes an indistinguishable sleepy sound that, finding itself nonsense, stops, and a little later begins again, this time enough waked up to be in words.
(15) "Nurse!" it says. "Oh, Nurse!"

The rumple of starched linen in the rocker moves infinitesimally and relapses without answering.

"Nurse!" repeats the voice from the bed,
(20) this time with a tickle of laughter in it. "Miss Hollis! Sorry to wake you!"

And now the linen hears and crackles. The figure in the chair rises, a tall strapping girl with a tumble of blond hair coming out from
(25) under her nurse's cap. She looks as vigorous and healthy as a young tree, but the pulled-down droop of the corners of her mouth shows that she recently has been thoroughly tired. She stands now with her arms over her

(30) head, yawning magnificently, and then suddenly realizing what she is doing, straightens and starts to look very professional. But the next minute her hands are at her eyes again, trying desperately to rub away the sleep.
(35) The voice from the bed is contrite.

"I'm awfully sorry. I know I shouldn't have waked you. I've been counting peacocks and peacocks getting the cruelty to. Because if you were as sleepy as I was—"
(40) "You should have waked me long ago, Mrs. Sellaby." The full dignity of an expert has been recovered. "I had no business to sleep like that. I don't know how I—" A yawn splits this in the middle, but she goes on determinedly, "I
(45) don't know what I—" Again the annihilating yawn. This time she gives up. "Oh, dear," she says frankly, "I *was* so tired …"

She busies herself with bottles and trays and pillows, hiding what yawns will come
(50) behind four fingers. The girl in the bed lies flat back, looking at the ceiling. Her hair, which is the color of pine smoke, is in thick, soft waves about her face.

It is a face with that delicate tense strength
(55) you may see in the hands of a great surgeon— the soul beneath it has been tempered steely, is as exquisitely balanced and direct as the long springing blade of an old rapier. And at present, in spite of the weight and heaviness of
(60) exhaustion upon it, so deep as to be almost visible and clinging like a netted veil, it is overwhelmed with peace, absorbed with peace.

1. The passage can primarily be described as

   A. a confrontation between two hostile characters.
   B. a reconciliation between previously estranged women.
   C. a narration that establishes a sympathetic relationship.
   D. an account of an employer reprimanding a lazy employee.

2. The first paragraph (lines 1–14) sets the mood of

   A. grandeur.
   B. quietude.
   C. disappointment.
   D. nostalgia.

3. The phrase "finding itself nonsense" (lines 12–13) suggests that

   A. the listener does not understand the speaker.
   B. the speaker does not understand herself.
   C. the speaker is unable to hear the listener.
   D. the noise of the fire drowns out the speaker's words.

4. The second call to the nurse suggests that the speaker is

   A. impatient with the lack of response.
   B. amused that the nurse is sleeping.
   C. dissatisfied with the nursing care she receives.
   D. experiencing severe pain and needs attention.

5. Which choice provides the best evidence for the answer to the previous question?

   A. Lines 19–20 ("'Nurse!' repeats … in it.")
   B. Line 22 ("And now … crackles.")
   C. Line 35 ("The voice … contrite.")
   D. Lines 41–42 ("The full dignity … recovered.")

6. The word "annihilating" (line 45) most nearly means

   A. killing.
   B. colliding.
   C. defeating.
   D. definitive.

7. The phrase "tempered steely" (line 56) refers to

   A. the volatile anger of the girl in the bed.
   B. the weapons displayed on the wall of the room.
   C. the heaviness of the illness that weighs upon the patient.
   D. the patient who, although ill, has inner strength.

8. The language of the last paragraph (lines 54–62) is best described as

   A. objective.
   B. metaphorical.
   C. histrionic.
   D. sardonic.

9. This passage reveals all of the following emotions EXCEPT

   A. enervation.
   B. contrition.
   C. serenity.
   D. indignation.

Questions 10–19 are based on the following passages and supplementary material.

Adapted from U.S. Fish and Wildlife Service.

Passage 1

The magnificent polar bear, the world's largest terrestrial carnivore, lives most of its life on the ice floes in the Arctic cap and feeds mostly on seals. Recently, the United States
(5) government has listed the polar bear as a "threatened species." Under the Endangered Species Act, the designation "threatened" indicates that, without some form of protection, this species likely faces extinction.

(10) The threat to these bears does not come from predators, but from global climate changes. Increased burning of fossil fuels has caused an unprecedented warming, which in turn has caused a loss of sea ice. As their habitat

(15) shrinks, the polar bears follow the retreating ice; some bears then find themselves stranded on land. Many animal lovers are disturbed by reports that this awesome, and for thousands of years self-sufficient, creature has been

(20) forced to rummage around garbage pails and camp sites for scraps of food. According to the U.S. Fish and Wildlife Service, "In the declining polar bear population of Canada's Western Hudson Bay, extensive scientific stud-

(25) ies have indicated that the increased observation of bears on land is a result of changing distribution patterns and a result of changes in the accessibility of sea ice habitat." Clearly, to ensure the survival of these beloved sym-

(30) bols of the Arctic, we must take action to prevent the diminution of their habitat.

Passage 2

Some climatologists investigating the claim that global warming threatens to cause polar bear extinction find little basis for fear. The

(35) study finds that for the most part, polar bear populations are intact. The polar bear population in the southern Beaufort Sea off Alaska's North Slope, for example, has been relatively stable for 20 years, according to a federal anal-

(40) ysis. Some government agencies fear that environmentalists are using the polar bear as an excuse to influence policy. One government official states, "While the legal standards under the ESA compel me to list the polar

(45) bear as threatened, I want to make clear that this listing will not stop global climate change or prevent any sea ice from melting. Any real solution requires action by all major economies for it to be effective. That is why I am tak-

(50) ing administrative and regulatory action to make certain the ESA isn't abused to make global warming policies." Moreover, since Earth has undergone climatic fluctuations for thousands of years and the polar bears have

(55) survived, there is insufficient evidence that polar bears are in danger of becoming extinct within the foreseeable future.

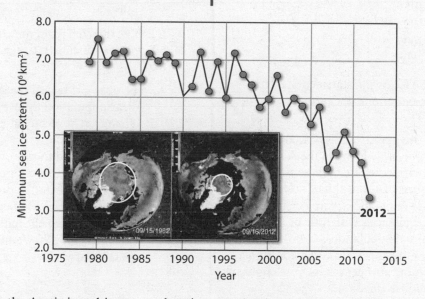

Summer sea ice in the Arctic is melting at an alarming rate. Arctic sea ice extent (circled in white in the map insets) declined to an all-time low on September 16, 2012. (Data courtesy of the National Snow and Ice Data Center; maps courtesy of University of Illinois.)

10. According to the author of Passage 1, the greatest threat faced by polar bears is

    A. the increased population of large predators that prey on polar bears.
    B. the encroachment of human settlements into the territories previously inhabited solely by the polar bears.
    C. the declining herds of seals that provide the major food source to the polar bears.
    D. the diminishment of the ice shelves.

11. The "animal lovers" in Passage 1 (line 17) are most likely "disturbed" because

    A. they are afraid that the hungry polar bears might attack people.
    B. they see the food-scavenging behavior as demeaning to the polar bears.
    C. they believe the change in diet may cause physiological damage to the polar bears.
    D. they believe the natural world and the modern world have reached an accommodation.

12. According to the information in the graph, the extent of sea ice fluctuated the least in the years

    A. 1980–1985.
    B. 1985–1990.
    C. 1995–2000.
    D. 2000–2005.

13. Which of the following statements, if true, would most undermine the primary argument of Passage 1?

    A. There are approximately 20,000 polar bears currently living in the Arctic cap.
    B. Large carnivores are often sensitive indicators of the health of an ecosystem.
    C. Climate fluctuations have occurred at regular intervals with little or no effect on animal populations.
    D. Environmentalists want the government to be more stringent in its restrictions on greenhouse emissions.

14. The word "basis" in Passage 2 (line 34) most nearly means

    A. core.
    B. foundation.
    C. beginning.
    D. center.

15. The word "abused" in Passage 2 (line 51) most nearly means

    A. treated harshly.
    B. overstepping limits.
    C. strictly prevented.
    D. taken advantage of.

16. The author of Passage 1 would most likely respond to the position stated in Passage 2 ("Some … policy"; lines 40–42) by stating that

    A. the continuation of an endangered species warrants a change in policy.
    B. the climate of the Arctic has natural fluctuations that are not influenced by human actions.
    C. the policies of the government are subject to the will of the populace.
    D. each state should make its own laws regarding the protection of indigenous species.

17. It can be inferred from the government official's comments (Passage 2, lines 43–52) that

    A. he does not regard the state of the polar bear population as justification for a change in government position on global warming.
    B. he feels forced to rely on insufficient data to make necessary policy changes.
    C. he believes we do the polar bears an injustice by our reliance on fossil fuels.
    D. the economy of the nation will suffer if we no longer allow humans to hunt polar bears.

18. The information in the graph most directly supports which assertion from the passages?

    A. For the most part, polar bear populations are intact.

    B. Under the Endangered Species Act, the designation "threatened" indicates that, without some form of protection, this species likely faces extinction.

    C. Increased burning of fossil fuels has caused an unprecedented warming, which in turn has caused a loss of sea ice.

    D. The polar bear population in the southern Beaufort Sea off Alaska's North Slope, for example, has been relatively stable for 20 years, according to a federal analysis.

19. Compared with the tone of Passage 1, the tone of Passage 2 is

    A. less objective.
    B. more detached.
    C. more impassioned.
    D. less satirical.

Questions 20–26 are based on the following passage.

In his annual messages to Congress in 1904 and 1905, President Theodore Roosevelt commented on and expanded the position of the U.S. regarding Latin America as stated in the Monroe Doctrine. His statements were aligned with his policy of "speak softly, and carry a big stick."

(Note: This is an abridged version of the complete text.)

The steady aim of this Nation, as of all enlightened nations, should be to strive to bring ever nearer the day when there shall prevail throughout the world the peace of justice.
(5) There are kinds of peace which are highly undesirable, which are in the long run as destructive as any war. Tyrants and oppressors have many times made a wilderness and called it peace. Many times peoples who were sloth-
(10) ful or timid or shortsighted, who had been enervated by ease or by luxury, or misled by false teachings, have shrunk in unmanly fashion from doing duty that was stern and that needed self-sacrifice, and have sought to hide
(15) from their own minds their shortcomings, their ignoble motives, by calling them love of peace. The peace of tyrannous terror, the peace of craven weakness, the peace of injustice, all these should be shunned as we shun
(20) unrighteous war. The goal to set before us as a nation, the goal which should be set before all mankind, is the attainment of the peace of justice, of the peace which comes when each nation is not merely safe-guarded in its own
(25) rights, but scrupulously recognizes and performs its duty toward others. Generally peace tells for righteousness; but if there is a conflict between the two, then our fealty is due first to the cause of righteousness....
(30) It is not true that the United States feels any land hunger or entertains any projects as regards the other nations of the Western Hemisphere save such as are for their welfare. All that this country desires is to see the neigh-
(35) boring countries stable, orderly, and prosperous. Any country whose people conduct themselves well can count upon our hearty friendship. If a nation shows that it knows how to act with reasonable efficiency and
(40) decency in social and political matters, if it keeps order and pays its obligations, it need fear no interference from the United States. Chronic wrongdoing, or an impotence which results in a general loosening of the ties of
(45) civilized society, may in America, as elsewhere, ultimately require intervention by some civilized nation, and in the Western Hemisphere the adherence of the United States to the Monroe Doctrine may lead the United States,
(50) however reluctantly, in flagrant cases of such wrongdoing or impotence, to the exercise of an international police power.... If every country washed by the Caribbean Sea would show the progress in stable and just
(55) civilization which with the aid of the Platt amendment Cuba has shown since our troops left the island, and which so many of the

republics in both Americas are constantly and brilliantly showing, all question of interfer- (60) ence by this Nation with their affairs would be at an end. Our interests and those of our southern neighbors are in reality identical. They have great natural riches, and if within their borders the reign of law and justice (65) obtains, prosperity is sure to come to them. While they thus obey the primary laws of civilized society they may rest assured that they will be treated by us in a spirit of cordial and helpful sympathy. We would interfere with (70) them only in the last resort, and then only if it became evident that their inability or unwillingness to do justice at home and abroad had violated the rights of the United States or had invited foreign aggression to the detriment of (75) the entire body of American nations. It is a mere truism to say that every nation, whether in America or anywhere else, which desires to maintain its freedom, its independence, must ultimately realize that the right of such inde- (80) pendence cannot be separated from the responsibility of making good use of it.

In asserting the Monroe Doctrine, in taking such steps as we have taken in regard to Cuba, Venezuela, and Panama, and in endeavoring to (85) circumscribe the theater of war in the Far East, and to secure the open door in China, we have acted in our own interest as well as in the interest of humanity at large. There are, however, cases in which, while our own interests are not (90) greatly involved, strong appeal is made to our sympathies…. In extreme cases action may be justifiable and proper. What form the action shall take must depend upon the circumstances of the case; that is, upon the degree of the atroc- (95) ity and upon our power to remedy it. The cases in which we could interfere by force of arms as we interfered to put a stop to intolerable conditions in Cuba are necessarily very few….

A great free people owes it to itself and to (100) all mankind not to sink into helplessness before the powers of evil.

20. The main purpose of this document is to

   A. prohibit U.S. military action in the Caribbean.

   B. establish the role of the U.S. as "policeman" for Latin America.

   C. encourage Europeans to support democracy in the region.

   D. support independence movements in many Latin American countries.

21. It can be inferred from this document that President Theodore Roosevelt believed in

   A. noninvolvement in world affairs.

   B. the sovereign rights of all nations.

   C. intervention when American interests are threatened.

   D. the need for a joint American-European effort to prevent the spread of Communism.

22. The "peoples" in line 9 are characterized as

   A. lazy and myopic.

   B. timid and dutiful.

   C. stern and selfish.

   D. ignoble and sharp-sighted.

23. In the first paragraph, Roosevelt establishes a contrast between

   A. the peace of terror and the peace of freedom.

   B. the peace of the individual and the peace of the nation.

   C. the peace of the weak and the peace of the strong.

   D. the peace of injustice and the peace of justice.

24. In line 27, the phrase "tells for" most nearly means

   A. reveals to.

   B. confides in.

   C. indicates.

   D. advocates.

25. Which of the following sentences provides evidence to support the assertion that Roosevelt believed the independence of a nation is not an inalienable right unencumbered by obligation?

   A. It is not true that the United States feels any land hunger or entertains any projects as regards the other nations of the Western Hemisphere save such as are for their welfare.

   B. If every country washed by the Caribbean Sea would show the progress in stable and just civilization which with the aid of the Platt amendment Cuba has shown since our troops left the island, and which so many of the republics in both Americas are constantly and brilliantly showing, all question of interference by this Nation with their affairs would be at an end.

   C. It is a mere truism to say that every nation, whether in America or anywhere else, which desires to maintain its freedom, its independence, must ultimately realize that the right of such independence cannot be separated from the responsibility of making good use of it.

   D. All that this country desires is to see the neighboring countries stable, orderly, and prosperous.

26. In line 85, the word "circumscribe" most nearly means

   A. confine.
   B. surround.
   C. demarcate.
   D. delineate.

IF YOU FINISH BEFORE TIME IS CALLED, CHECK YOUR WORK ON THIS SECTION ONLY. DO NOT WORK ON ANY OTHER SECTION IN THE TEST.

Section 2: Writing and Language Test

18 Minutes—22 Questions

Directions: Read the following passages carefully. Then consider the underlined words and phrases or the questions asked to determine the best answer to each question. Fill in the corresponding circle on your answer sheet. Some questions may refer to a whole paragraph or to the whole passage. Some questions may refer to graphs or charts that accompany a passage.

The evidence-based Writing and Language Test tests your ability to apply your knowledge of words, phrases, and language. You will be asked to recognize correctness and effectiveness of expression, organization, and sentence structure. In each passage, questions will ask you to make language choices; some questions give you the option of NO CHANGE. Choose NO CHANGE if you think the underlined portion is best as it is. If not, carefully consider choices B, C, and D, and select the one you think is the best.

In making your selection, follow the requirements of standard written English. Carefully consider the grammar, diction (word choice), sentence construction, and punctuation of each sentence. When you make your choice, select the most effective choice, the one that is clear and precise, without any awkwardness or ambiguity.

Questions 1–11 are based on the following passage.

Hiding in Plain Sight

The art of concealment or camouflage is one of the newest and most highly developed techniques of modern warfare. [1] Because the animals have been masters of it for ages. The lives of most of them are spent [2] in constantly conflict. Those that have enemies from which they cannot escape by rapidity of motion must be able to hide or disguise themselves. Those [3] hunting for a living must [4] being able to approach their prey without unnecessary noise or attention to themselves. It is very remarkable how Nature helps the wild creatures to disguise themselves by coloring them with various shades and tints best calculated [5] for enabling them to escape enemies or to entrap prey.

The animals of each locality are usually colored according to their habitat, but good reasons make some exceptions advisable. Many of the most striking examples of this protective resemblance among animals are the result of their very [6] indistinct association with the surrounding flora and natural scenery. There is no part of a tree, including flowers, fruits, bark, and roots, that is not in some way copied and imitated by these clever creatures. Often this imitation is astonishing in its faithfulness of detail. [7] Bunches of cocoanuts portrayed by sleeping monkeys, the leaves are copied by certain tree toads, and many flowers are represented by monkeys and lizards. The winding roots of huge trees are copied by snakes that twist themselves together at the foot of the tree.

In the art of camouflage—an art that affects the form, color, and attitude of [8] animals, Nature has worked along two different roads. One is easy and direct, the other circuitous and difficult. The easy way is that of protective resemblance pure and simple, where the animal's color, form, or attitude becomes like that of its habitat. In these cases, the animal becomes one with its [9] environment. It is enabled to go about unnoticed by its enemies or by its prey. The other way is that of bluff, and it includes all inoffensive animals that are capable of assuming [10] attitudes and colors that terrify and frighten. The colors in some cases are really of warning pattern, yet they cannot be considered mimetic unless [11]it is thought to resemble the patterns of some extinct model of which we know nothing; and since they are not found in present-day animals with unpleasant qualities, they are not, strictly speaking, warning colors.

1. **A.** NO CHANGE
   B. However, animals have been masters of it for ages.
   C. Since, the animals have been masters of it for ages.
   D. Animals have been masters of it for ages.

2. **A.** NO CHANGE
   B. for constant conflict
   C. in constant conflict
   D. on constantly conflicting

3. All of the following choices are acceptable EXCEPT
   A. hunting (as it is now)
   B. that are hunters
   C. that hunt
   D. whom hunt

4. **A.** NO CHANGE
   B. be able to approach
   C. have the ability of approaching
   D. have been able to approach

5. **A.** NO CHANGE
   B. to enabling them
   C. to enable those
   D. to enable them

6. **A.** NO CHANGE
   B. insensate
   C. intimate
   D. indefinable

7. **A.** NO CHANGE
   B. Bunches of cocoanuts portraying by sleeping monkeys
   C. Bunches of cocoanuts are portrayed by sleeping monkeys
   D. Bunches of cocoanuts being portrayed by sleeping monkeys

8. **A.** NO CHANGE
   B. animals. Nature
   C. animals—Nature
   D. animals; Nature

9. Which choice most effectively combines the sentences at the underlined portion?
   A. environment, and it is also
   B. environment; thus, it is
   C. environment, yet it is
   D. environment, in order to allow it to be

10. **A.** NO CHANGE
    B. those attitudes and colors which are to terrify and frighten
    C. terrifying attitudes and colors which are to frighten
    D. the attitudes and the colors which are terrifying and frightening

11. **A.** NO CHANGE
    B. they are
    C. it's
    D. they were

Questions 12–22 are based on the following passage and supplementary material.

Why Are Teenagers Always Tired?

Along with food, water, and air, sleep is necessary to life. But, for American teenagers, finding the time to get enough sleep is a serious issue. Almost half of all young people between the ages of 12 and 18 [12]reports that they don't get enough sleep during the week. By the time they come home from extracurricular activities or team [13]practices; and then begin what could be several hours of homework, it is often well past midnight before **14** they shut their eyes. Parents and teachers often maintain that staying up late is responsible for everything from sleepiness in class, to risk-taking behavior, to falling asleep at the wheel of a car. But, how much scientific evidence **15** is their to back up their claims? **16**

(1) Studies show that teenagers optimally need between 9 and 9½ hours of sleep a night. (2) Assuming that bedtime is about 11:00 p.m., teens should sleep until 8:00 a.m. (3) **17** Therefore, many high schools start as early as 7:30 a.m., and given that students have to be up and ready earlier, most teenagers are getting about 7 hours of sleep per night. (4) Over a period of time, this noticeable sleep deficit can lead to psychological and physical impairment. (5) Knowing the dangers of sleep **18** deprivation, fights often occur as parents try to force them to go to sleep by 10:00 p.m. (6) But, is getting teenagers to bed earlier the answer? **19**

Current evidence demonstrates that factors beyond socialization, homework, and the lure of technology **20** accounts for the adolescent delayed sleep onset. Recent experiments and sleep studies show that during the teenage years, the circadian rhythm (the technical term for the internal biological clock) shifts **21** as shown in recently conducted experiments. During adolescence the urge to sleep is triggered later in the evening, making it difficult for teens to fall asleep before 11:00 p.m. Called "sleep phase delay," this biological phenomena provides support to the teenagers' cry, "I can't fall asleep before midnight!" But, because schools start so early, there doesn't appear to be an answer to the sleep deprivation dilemma.

In fact, some school districts, recognizing the need to offset the irritating (and possibly dangerous) effects of sleep deprivation, have changed their start time from 7:30 to 8:30. The results have ranged from improved attendance to **22** decreased teenage traffic accidents. This adjustment would seem to be a simple solution to a serious problem. School administrators need to respond to the clinical and biological evidence and help teenagers decrease sleep deficits.

How High School Students Spend the Day: Self-Reported Data

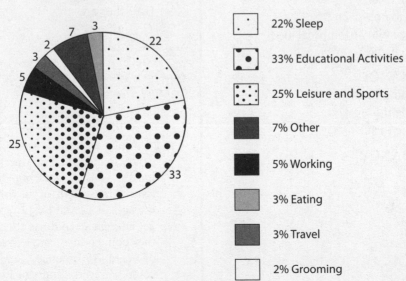

- 22% Sleep
- 33% Educational Activities
- 25% Leisure and Sports
- 7% Other
- 5% Working
- 3% Eating
- 3% Travel
- 2% Grooming

12. **A.** NO CHANGE
    B. report
    C. reporting
    D. is reporting

13. **A.** NO CHANGE
    B. practices, and then, begin
    C. practices and then, begin
    D. practices, and then begin

14. **A.** NO CHANGE
    B. shutting their eyes
    C. their eyes shut closed
    D. they are shutting their eyes

15. **A.** NO CHANGE
    B. are there
    C. is there
    D. was there

16. Could the information presented in the pie chart be used as evidence to support this paragraph?

    A. No, because the evidence in the pie chart is self-reported and not the result of a scientific study.
    B. No, because the information in the pie chart contradicts the information in the paragraph.
    C. Yes, because the scientific evidence later in the passage supports the data in the pie chart.
    D. Yes, because the information in both the paragraph and the pie chart is based on data reported by students.

17. **A.** NO CHANGE
    B. However,
    C. Although,
    D. Furthermore,

18. **A.** NO CHANGE
    B. deprivation, parents often fight with their teens
    C. deprivation, fighting ensues as parents try
    D. deprivation, with fights breaking out as parents try

19. For the sake of the cohesion of this paragraph, Sentence 4 should be placed

    A. where it is now.
    B. before Sentence 3.
    C. after Sentence 6.
    D. before Sentence 1.

20. **A.** NO CHANGE
    B. accounts to
    C. account to
    D. account for

21. **A.** NO CHANGE
    B. as recently conducted experiments show
    C. based on the results of recently conducted experiments
    D. Omit the underlined portion.

22. **A.** NO CHANGE
    B. a decreasing amount in the number of teenage traffic accidents
    C. a less in teenage traffic accidents
    D. having less teenage traffic accidents

IF YOU FINISH BEFORE TIME IS CALLED, CHECK YOUR WORK ON THIS SECTION ONLY. DO NOT WORK ON ANY OTHER SECTION IN THE TEST.

Section 3: Math Test – No Calculator

13 Minutes—10 Questions

Directions: For questions 1–7, choose the best answer from the choices given. Use of a calculator is not permitted.

Unless otherwise indicated:

- All figures are drawn to scale.
- All figures lie in a plane.
- All variables used represent real numbers.
- The domain of a given function f is the set of all real numbers x such that $f(x)$ is a real number.

Reference

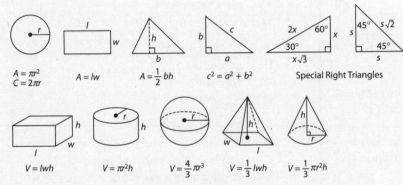

$A = \pi r^2$
$C = 2\pi r$

$A = lw$

$A = \frac{1}{2}bh$

$c^2 = a^2 + b^2$

Special Right Triangles

$V = lwh$

$V = \pi r^2 h$

$V = \frac{4}{3}\pi r^3$

$V = \frac{1}{3}lwh$

$V = \frac{1}{3}\pi r^2 h$

The complete arc of a circle measures 360°.

Also, the complete arc of a circle measures 2π radians.

The sum of the measures of the angles of a triangle is 180°.

1. At a bakery, the price of a doughnut is $0.80. After the first doughnut, each additional doughnut is $0.40. If Mary paid $4.00 for doughnuts, how many doughnuts did Mary buy?
   A. 5
   B. 6
   C. 8
   D. 9

2. There are 10 members on the Washington Middle School basketball team. The scatterplot in the accompanying figure shows the length of each player's right foot and the height of the player. The line of best fit is also shown. For the player whose right foot measures 11 inches, his actual height is how many inches greater than the height predicted by the line of best fit?

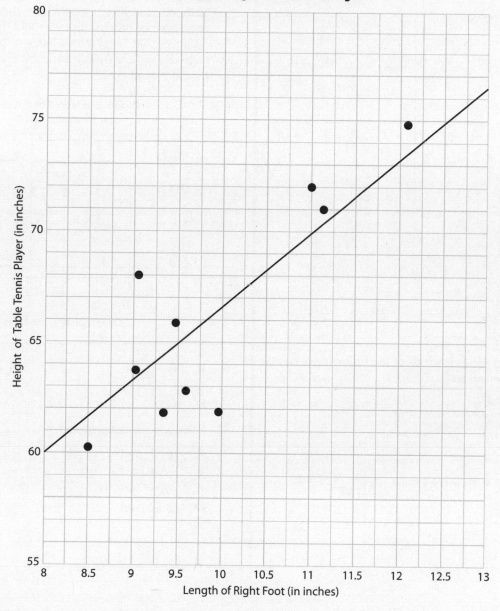

Length of Right Foot Versus Height

A. 0
B. 1
C. 2
D. 3

3. In the accompanying figure, the graphs of $p(x)$ and $q(x)$ are shown. What is the value of $p(q(2))$?

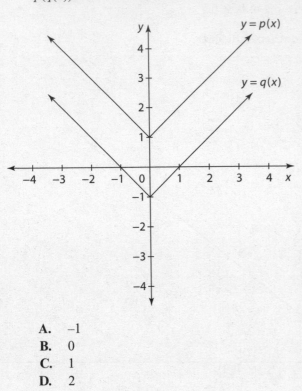

A. −1
B. 0
C. 1
D. 2

4. Given $i = \sqrt{-1}$, which of the following is equivalent to $2i(i^3 - 4i)$?

A. −6
B. $-6i^2$
C. 6
D. 10

5. If x is a negative integer, and $xy = -2$ and $y + x = 1$, what is the value of x?

A. −2
B. −1
C. 0
D. 1

6. Janet and Karen are meeting at a library to work on their math project. Because there are four libraries in town, they have decided to choose the library that would result in their traveling the smallest total distance. The accompanying scatterplot graph shows the distances that Karen would have to travel to go to each of the four libraries and the distances that Janet would have to travel to go to each of the four libraries. Which library should they choose?

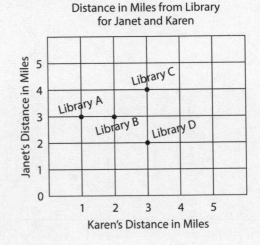

Distance in Miles from Library for Janet and Karen

A. A
B. B
C. C
D. D

7. What are the zeros of $f(x) = x^3 + 2x^2 - x - 2$?

A. 0, −1, and 1
B. −2, 1, and 2
C. −2, −1, and 1
D. 0, −2, and 2

Directions for Student-Produced Response Questions (grid-ins): Questions 8–10 require you to solve the problem and enter your answer by carefully making the circles on the special grid. Examples of the appropriate way to mark the grid follow.

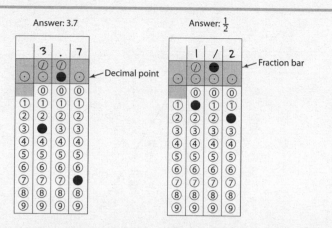

Do not grid in mixed numbers in the form of mixed numbers. Always change mixed numbers to improper fractions or decimals.

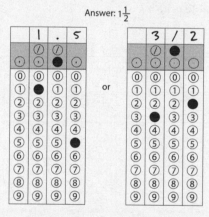

Space permitting, answers may start in any column. Each grid-in answer below is correct.

Answer: 123

Note: Circles must be filled in correctly to receive credit. Mark only one circle in each column. No credit will be given if more than one circle in a column is marked. Example:

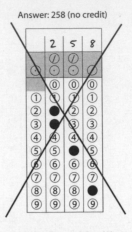

Always enter the most accurate decimal value that the grid will accommodate. For example, an answer such as .8888 … can be gridded as .888 or .889. Gridding this value as .8, .88, or .89 is considered inaccurate and, therefore, not acceptable. The acceptable grid-ins of $\frac{8}{9}$ are:

Answer: $\frac{8}{9}$

Be sure to write your answers in the boxes at the tops of the circles before doing your gridding. Although writing out the answers above the columns is not required, it is very important to ensure accuracy. Even though some problems may have more than one correct answer, grid only one answer. Grid-in questions contain no negative answers.

8. Karen gets a fixed allowance for lunch and entertainment every week. The accompanying bar graph shows the amount she spent on lunch for the past five weeks. If she spent 60% of her allowance on lunch during the second week, what percent of her allowance did she spend on lunch during the fourth week?

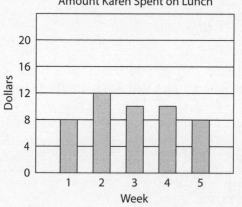

Amount Karen Spent on Lunch

Use the following information to answer questions 9 and 10.

There are 20 students on a school bus. Every one of the 20 students takes either algebra or geometry and no student takes both. The partially completed table in the accompanying figure shows the relative frequencies of algebra and geometry students on the bus by gender.

Relative Frequency of Table			
	Algebra	Geometry	Total
Male	0.4		0.6
Female		0.15	
Total			1

9. If a student is picked at random from the school bus, what is the probability that the student is a male and taking geometry?

10. How many students taking algebra are female?

IF YOU FINISH BEFORE TIME IS CALLED, CHECK YOUR WORK ON THIS SECTION ONLY. DO NOT WORK ON ANY OTHER SECTION IN THE TEST.

Section 4: Math Test – Calculator

28 Minutes—19 Questions

Directions: For questions 1–15, choose the best answer from the choices given. Use of a calculator is permitted.

Unless otherwise indicated:

- All figures are drawn to scale.
- All figures lie in a plane.
- All variables used represent real numbers.
- The domain of a given function f is the set of all real numbers x such that $f(x)$ is a real number.

Reference

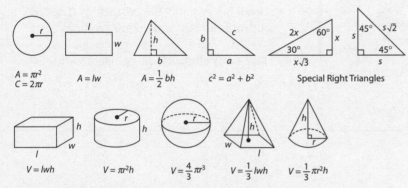

$A = \pi r^2$
$C = 2\pi r$

$A = lw$

$A = \frac{1}{2}bh$

$c^2 = a^2 + b^2$

Special Right Triangles

$V = lwh$

$V = \pi r^2 h$

$V = \frac{4}{3}\pi r^3$

$V = \frac{1}{3}lwh$

$V = \frac{1}{3}\pi r^2 h$

The complete arc of a circle measures 360°.

Also, the complete arc of a circle measures 2π radians.

The sum of the measures of the angles of a triangle is 180°.

1. Speedy Car Service charges customers per ride using the equation $c = 20 + 13.5x$, where c is the cost of the ride in dollars and x is the total number of miles of the ride. Which of the following best describes the meaning of the number 13.5 in the equation?

   A. The minimum number of miles per ride
   B. The maximum number of miles per ride
   C. An added charge if the number of miles of the ride is less than 20 miles
   D. The charge per mile in addition to an initial fee

2. A plane travels at 469 feet per second. At the same rate, which of the following is closest to the distance, in miles, the plane will travel in 2 hours 15 minutes?

   A. 338
   B. 469
   C. 720
   D. 1,055

3. Some of the values of the function *f* are shown in the accompanying table. If a function *h* is defined by $h(x) = 2f(x-1)$, what is the value of $h(2)$?

x	f(x)
−3	−1
−2	0
−1	4
0	2
1	−3
2	4
3	5

   A. −6
   B. −3
   C. 4
   D. 5

4. Bill paid $100 to rent a lawn mower for the weekend to mow lawns in his neighborhood for pay. He charges the same price for all his neighbors. If he mows 6 lawns, his net profit is $140. What is his net profit, in dollars, if he mows 12 lawns?

   A. 200
   B. 280
   C. 300
   D. 380

5. Set A = {−2, −1, 0, 2, 3, 4}. If set B contains only members obtained by multiplying each member of set A by −1, what is the median of set B?

   A. −2
   B. −1
   C. 0
   D. 1

6. If *n* is a positive integer and $\left(8^{\frac{2}{3}}\right)\left(n^{\frac{1}{4}}\right) = 16$, what is the value of *n*?

   A. 2
   B. 8
   C. 16
   D. 256

7. The following table summarizes the number of students having 1 to 4 calculators in a class of 20 students. What is the sum of the mode and the median number of calculators?

Number of Calculators per Student in Class	
Number of Calculators	Number of Students
1	12
2	4
3	3
4	1

   A. 1
   B. 2
   C. 3
   D. 4

8. In the accompanying figure, if $\overline{AB} \perp \overline{AC}$ and $\overline{DE}$ intersects $\overline{AB}$ and $\overline{AC}$ at *M* and *N*, respectively, what is the value of $x + y$, in degrees?

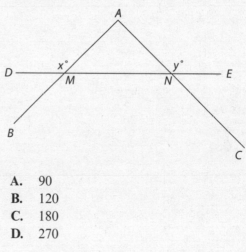

   A. 90
   B. 120
   C. 180
   D. 270

9. At 6 p.m., Karen and Janet are standing side by side in a park. Karen, who is 5 feet 6 inches tall, casts a shadow 11 feet long. Janet is 5 feet tall. How long is her shadow, in feet?

   A. 9
   B. 10
   C. 11
   D. 12

10. If $\dfrac{1}{6} < \dfrac{3}{n} < \dfrac{1}{4}$, how many integral values of n are possible?

 A. 1
 B. 3
 C. 5
 D. 6

11. In the accompanying diagram, $CB = 12$, $AB = 13$, and $m\angle C = 90$. What is the value of cos A?

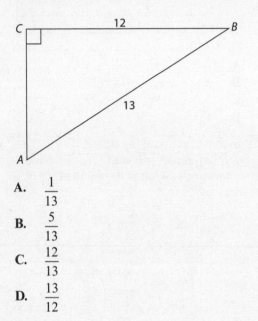

 A. $\dfrac{1}{13}$

 B. $\dfrac{5}{13}$

 C. $\dfrac{12}{13}$

 D. $\dfrac{13}{12}$

12. Which of the following points on the accompanying graph has coordinates that satisfy the equation $-|3x| + |y| = 2$?

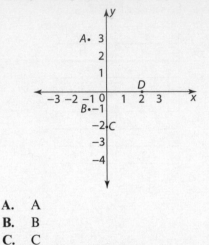

 A. A
 B. B
 C. C
 D. D

13. In a coordinate plane, an equation of line l is $y = 2x + 4$. If line m is the reflection of line l about the y-axis, which of the following is an equation of line m?

 A. $y = 2x - 4$
 B. $y = -2x + 4$
 C. $y = -2x - 4$
 D. $y = 4x + 2$

14. An equation of a circle is given as $x^2 + (y - 3)^2 = 1$. What is the area of this circle?

 A. π
 B. 2π
 C. 3π
 D. 9π

15. If $f(x) = x^2 + bx + c$, where b and c are positive integers and $c = \left(\dfrac{b}{2}\right)^2$, which of the following could be the graph of $f(x)$?

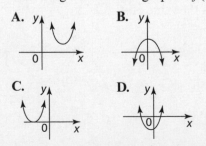

Directions for Student-Produced Response Questions (grid-ins): Questions 16–19 require you to solve the problem and enter your answer by carefully making the circles on the special grid. Examples of the appropriate way to mark the grid follow.

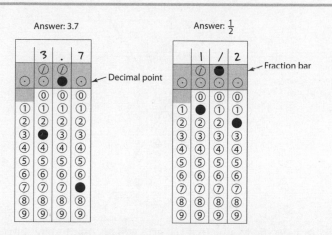

Do not grid in mixed numbers in the form of mixed numbers. Always change mixed numbers to improper fractions or decimals.

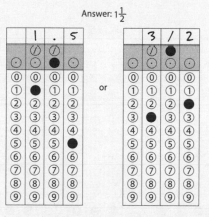

Space permitting, answers may start in any column. Each grid-in answer below is correct.

Note: Circles must be filled in correctly to receive credit. Mark only one circle in each column. No credit will be given if more than one circle in a column is marked. Example:

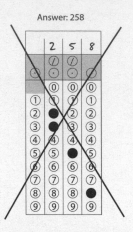

Answer: 258

Always enter the most accurate decimal value that the grid will accommodate. For example, an answer such as .8888 … can be gridded as .888 or .889. Gridding this value as .8, .88, or .89 is considered inaccurate and, therefore, not acceptable. The acceptable grid-ins of $\frac{8}{9}$ are:

Answer: $\frac{8}{9}$

Be sure to write your answers in the boxes at the tops of the circles before doing your gridding. Although writing out the answers above the columns is not required, it is very important to ensure accuracy. Even though some problems may have more than one correct answer, grid only one answer. Grid-in questions contain no negative answers.

16. Janet was saving a part of her salary every month so she could buy a house. In 4 months, she saved a total of $2,000. If the accompanying table shows the total amount of money that Janet had saved by the end of each month, how much did she save in March?

Janet's Savings	
Month	Total Amount in Dollars
January	500
February	800
March	1,400
April	2,000

17. A system of inequalities is given below.

$$y \geq x + 4$$
$$y \geq -2x + 7$$

In the xy-plane, if a point (p, q) lies in the solution set of the system, what is the value of p when q is the minimum possible value?

18. Given the system of equations below, h and k are constants and x and y are variables. If the system has infinitely many solutions, what is the value of $h + k$?

$$\frac{1}{2}x + \frac{1}{3}y = 5$$
$$3x - hy = k$$

19. A right circular cylinder with a radius of 2 centimeters and a height of 5 centimeters is inscribed in a right-circular cone as shown in the accompanying figure. The slant height of the cone is 10 centimeters and the diameter of the cone is 12 centimeters.

What is the volume, to the nearest cubic centimeter, of the space that is inside the cone and outside the cylinder?

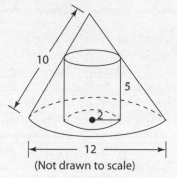

(Not drawn to scale)

IF YOU FINISH BEFORE TIME IS CALLED, CHECK YOUR WORK ON THIS SECTION ONLY. DO NOT WORK ON ANY OTHER SECTION IN THE TEST.

Section 5: The Essay

50 Minutes

Directions: You must write your essay in the space provided; you must use only the lines within the margin. You should write on every line (do not skip lines), avoid wide margins, and keep your handwriting to a reasonable size. You may write or print, but try to write as legibly as you can.

You will have 50 minutes for this section.

Read the following passage and consider the author's argument. Note how the author uses

- evidence, such as reasons, facts, or examples, to support his claim.
- logical reasoning to support and develop his ideas.
- stylistic elements such as diction and emotional appeals.

Adapted from *Birds and all Nature,* Vol. VII, No. 4, April 1900.

(1)   A comparatively untouched phase of the question of forest destruction is brought out in a book called *North American Forests and Forestry,* by Ernest Bruncken, a prominent western forester. The author incidentally discusses the part which our forests have had in shaping American character and our national history. This phase of the matter is interesting both as a historical study and as a suggestion of the moral as well as economic loss which must come with the denudation of our forest areas.

(2)   All thinking Americans know that the forests are an important factor in our commercial life, and Mr. Bruncken makes an impressive statement of the way in which the lumber industry permeates all the nation's activities. But the part played by the vast primeval forests in creating American character is not so generally realized. From the earliest colonial times the forests have had a moral and political effect in shaping our history. In the seventeenth century England was dependent upon Norway and the Baltic provinces for its timber for ships. This was in various ways disadvantageous for England, so the American colonists were encouraged with bounties to cut ship timbers, masts and other lumber for European export. This trade, however, was found to be unprofitable on account of the long ocean voyage, so the American lumbermen began to develop a profitable market in the West Indies. This was straightway interdicted by the short-sighted British government, and the bitter and violent opposition of the colonists against this tyrannical policy ceased only with the end of British dominion.

(3)   From that time to the present the forests of America have exercised a most important influence upon the nation, especially in creating the self-reliance which is the chief trait of the American character. The trappers, hunters, explorers and backwoods settlers who went forth alone into the dense forests received a schooling such as nothing else could give. As the forest closed behind the settler he knew his future and that of his family must henceforth depend upon himself, his ax, his rifle, and the few simple utensils he had brought with him. It was a school that did not teach the graces, but it made men past masters in courage, pertinacity, and resourcefulness. It bred a new, simple, and forceful type of man. Out of the midst of that backwoods life came Abraham Lincoln, the greatest example of American statesmanship the nation has produced. In him was embodied all the inherent greatness of his early wilderness surroundings, with scarcely a trace of its coarser characteristics.

(4)   As Mr. Bruncken says, mere remembrance of what the forests have given us in the past should be enough to inspire a wish to preserve them as long as possible, to stop wanton waste by forest fires, and even to repair our losses by planting new forests, as they do in Europe. The time has gone when the silence and dangers of the forest were our chief molders of sturdy character, but it is undeniable that the pioneer blood that still runs so richly in American veins has much to do with causing the idea of Philippine expansion to appeal so powerfully to the popular imagination. The prophets who see in the expansion idea the downfall of the nation forget that the same spirit subdued the American wilderness and created the freest government and some of the finest specimens of manhood the world has ever seen.

> Write an essay in which you analyze how the author builds an argument to convince the reader that American forests should be preserved rather than commercialized. Consider how the author uses evidence, such as reasons, facts, or examples, to strengthen the logic of his claim. As you write your essay, consider his reasoning and his use of stylistic elements such as word choice and appeals to emotion.
>
> In your essay, do not explain your position on this issue; rather, analyze how the author builds his argument to accomplish his purpose.

Be sure to write only in the space provided on your answer sheet.

IF YOU FINISH BEFORE TIME IS CALLED, CHECK YOUR WORK ON THIS SECTION ONLY. DO NOT WORK ON ANY OTHER SECTION IN THE TEST.

Answer Key

Section 1: Reading Test

1. C	8. B	15. D	22. A
2. B	9. D	16. A	23. D
3. B	10. D	17. A	24. C
4. B	11. B	18. C	25. C
5. A	12. B	19. B	26. A
6. C	13. C	20. B	
7. D	14. B	21. C	

Section 2: Writing and Language Test

1. B	7. C	13. D	19. A
2. C	8. C	14. A	20. D
3. D	9. B	15. C	21. D
4. B	10. A	16. D	22. A
5. D	11. B	17. B	
6. C	12. B	18. B	

Section 3: Math Test – No Calculator

1. D *(HA)*	6. A *(HA)*	*(HA)* – Heart of Algebra
2. C *(PSDA)*	7. C *(PAM)*	*(PSDA)* – Problem Solving and Data Analysis
3. D *(PAM)*	8. 50 *(PSDA)*	*(PAM)* – Passport to Advanced Math
4. D *(ATM)*	9. 0.2 *(PSDA)*	*(ATM)* – Additional Topics in Math
5. B *(PAM)*	10. 5 *(PSDA)*	

Section 4: Math Test – Calculator

1. D *(HA)*	5. B *(PSDA)*	9. B *(PSDA)*
2. C *(PSDA)*	6. D *(PAM)*	10. C *(HA)*
3. A *(PAM)*	7. B *(PSDA)*	11. B *(ATM)*
4. D *(HA)*	8. D *(ATM)*	12. C *(HA)*

13. B *(HA)*

14. A *(ATM)*

15. C *(PAM)*

16. 600 *(PSDA)*

17. 1 *(HA)*

18. 28 *(HA)*

19. 239 *(ATM)*

(HA) – Heart of Algebra

(PSDA) – Problem Solving and Data Analysis

(PAM) – Passport to Advanced Math

(ATM) – Additional Topics in Math

Answer Explanations

Section 1: Reading Test

1. **C.** Primary purpose: This primary purpose question asks you to consider the entire passage and characterize it as a whole. For this type of question, you should not focus on one small segment of the piece, but look at it in its entirety. The characters display no hostility (Choice A) toward each other, and there is no evidence that they've been estranged (Choice B). There is also no sense of reprimand (Choice D), so Choice C is the best answer.

2. **B.** Command of evidence/Tone: This tone question asks you to think about the atmosphere of the first paragraph of the passage and select the word that best describes the mood. ***Remember:*** This question asks you to look at the first paragraph *only,* not the whole passage. The words *stiller* and *sleepy sound* are keys to the quiet tone of the first paragraph. There is no evidence of grandeur (Choice A), disappointment (Choice C), or nostalgia (Choice D).

3. **B.** Interpreting words and phrases in context: To answer this question, you need to read closely and understand the context of the phrase *finding itself nonsense.* This is a line reference/purpose question. The source of the phrase is the voice from the bed. Therefore, it must emanate from the bedridden woman. That leaves only choices B and C. Since the voice in the bed is the speaker, it must be Choice B because the voice from the bed is the speaker, not the listener.

4. **B.** Inference: To answer this detail inference question, find the second call to the nurse and skim the lines that follow. The second call to the nurse is made by a voice "with a tickle of laughter in it." This clue should lead you to Choice B, because laughter suggests that the speaker is amused, not impatient (Choice A), dissatisfied (Choice C), or in pain (Choice D).

5. **A.** Command of evidence: The best evidence to support the answer to question 4 is the context clue that the speaker's voice has a "tickle of laughter in it." None of the other choices indicates amusement on the part of the speaker.

6. **C.** Words in context: Use the context to select the best meaning of the word as it is used in the passage. Immediately after the "annihilating yawn," the nurse "gives up." She tries to suppress the yawn, but she's too tired to hold it in. This suggests that the yawn is defeating (Choice C). While annihilating can mean killing (Choice A), that meaning doesn't fit the context. Choices B and D also don't fit the context of "giving up."

7. **D.** Words in context: This vocabulary question tries to trick you into missing the metaphorical use of the phrase *tempered steely*. The soul of the woman on the bed is compared to the blade of a *rapier,* a thin-bladed sword, which suggests her inner strength. There are no weapons (Choice B) in the room (as far as the passage indicates), and the woman is not angry (Choice A). Choice C is incorrect because although the woman is ill, the phrase is used to show her strength.

8. **B.** Analyzing language: This language question asks you to take note of the series of similes in this paragraph. The language is metaphorical (Choice B), not literal. For definitions of the words in choices A, C, and D, see Chapter VIII.

9. **D.** Understanding relationships: In an *except* question, you must remember that three of the answer choices will be correct. You're now looking for the incorrect one. It's also a vocabulary question; to answer correctly, you should know the meanings of all the words (see Chapter VIII). All the feelings are present in the passage except indignation (Choice D).

10. **D.** Command of evidence/Explicit meaning: If the question says, "According to the author," you should be able to find this detail in the text. The author specifically says: "The threat to these bears does not come from predators, but from global climate changes. Increased burning of fossil fuels has caused an unprecedented warming, which in turn has caused a loss of sea ice." Follow the logic of the two sentences. It should lead you to Choice D, the loss of the ice that is home to the polar bears. Choice A is contradicted by the passage. Choices B and C aren't mentioned in the passage.

11. **B.** Inference: This detail inference question requires you to do some interpretation. The animal lovers referred to in line 17 are disturbed by reports that "this awesome, and for thousands of years self-sufficient, creature has been forced to rummage around garbage pails and camp sites for scraps of food." This context clue should lead you to understand that the animal lovers are upset at the food-scavenging behavior of the bears. By describing the bears as "awesome" and previously "self-sufficient," the author suggests that they are no longer so, as evidenced by the fact that they're forced to eat garbage. This behavior has *demeaned* (lowered the status of) the bears (Choice B). There is no evidence of fear of attack (Choice A) or physiological damage (Choice C). Choice D is contradicted by the text.

12. **B.** Data interpretation: This statistical interpretation question requires you to refer to the graph and find the years of the LEAST fluctuation. Look for the points on the vertical axis (*y*-axis) that remain the steadiest, and, thus, represent the smallest changes in the extent of the sea ice. Then look on the horizontal axis (*x*-axis) for the corresponding years, in this case, 1985–1990 (Choice B).

13. **C.** Command of evidence/Main purpose: To find the correct statement that would *undermine* (weaken) the primary argument of Passage 1, you must first understand the main purpose of the passage. The primary argument of Passage 1 is that global climate changes have posed a danger to the polar bears that live on ice shelves in the Arctic. Thus, if it were discovered that climate fluctuation did not affect animal populations (Choice C), the argument of Passage 1 would be weakened.

14. **B.** Words in context: Try substituting each answer choice for the word in the passage. *Foundation* (meaning supporting evidence in this context), Choice B, makes the most sense in the sentence as it is used in the passage. The other choices don't fit in the context of the sentence.

15. **D.** Words in context: Follow the same technique as in question 14. Substitute the phrases in the answer choices for the word *abused* in the passage. Since the remarks in the passage refer to a government agency being used to make policy, the phrase *taken advantage of* (Choice D) best fits the meaning of the sentence in the passage. While Choice A, *treated harshly*, might be the meaning of *abused*, it doesn't fit this context. The other two choices don't fit the context either.

16. **A.** Synthesis: You must understand the position of the author of Passage 1 and consider how he would respond to the "fear that environmentalists are using the polar bear as an excuse to influence policy." Since you already know that the author of Passage 1 advocates a policy that helps the polar bears, you can safely assume he would welcome a change in policy (Choice A) that would secure the continuation of the polar bears. Based on the evidence in the text, he would not agree with choices B, C, or D.

17. **A.** Inference: You need to reread the government official's comments (Passage 2, lines 43–52) and think about his position. He makes a point to separate the "threatened" status for the polar bears from any government policy regarding global warming. He wants to make it clear that his action on the polar bears does not mean he believes global warming is the cause of the problem, nor does he want his position on the bears to be taken as a statement of policy. Choice B is incorrect because the comments don't make a point about insufficient data. Choice C is incorrect because there is no evidence in the comments that implies polar bears suffer injustice. Choice D is incorrect because the comments don't link polar bear hunting to the economy.

18. **C.** Data interpretation: This question asks you to find information on the graph to support one of the assertions from the passages. Neither the graph nor the included maps relay information on polar bear populations. Thus, choices A, B, and D aren't supported by the graphics. Choice C refers to the loss of sea ice shown on the graph.

19. **B.** Point of view/Tone/Vocabulary in context: This question tests both your ability to detect the author's attitude toward his subject and your vocabulary. It also amps up the difficulty by using the words *more* and *less* before the tone words and requires you to synthesize as you compare tones. Passage 1 is more subjective (*magnificent, awesome, beloved*) as it expresses great admiration for the polar bears and urges strong action to protect the species. Thus the tone of Passage 2 is *more detached* (impartial), Choice B, than the tone of Passage 1. Choice A is incorrect because the tone is more objective. Choice C is incorrect because the tone is less impassioned. The tone isn't satirical at all, so Choice D is incorrect.

20. **B.** Main purpose: This question asks you to understand what Roosevelt was attempting to accomplish in this document. In the first paragraph, Roosevelt delineates the conditions under which peace can be undesirable. In the second paragraph, he denies that any action on the part of the U.S. is based on imperialism: America is not seeking to add to its lands. Any intervention, therefore, would be done in the name of "friendship." However, he clearly states that the "police power" (Choice B) of the U.S. might become necessary if nations "washed by the Caribbean Sea" don't "obey the primary laws of civilized society." He doesn't prohibit U.S. military action (Choice A); in fact, he says it might be necessary. He doesn't encourage Europeans (Choice C) anywhere in the document. While he might support independence (Choice D), he doesn't express that as a goal of this document.

21. **C.** Inference: You have to consider Roosevelt's main purpose (stated in question 20) and extrapolate from that: Roosevelt believes that the U.S. must intervene when "our own interest as well as in the interest of humanity at large" is threatened. He might agree with the other choices, but only Choice C can be inferred from the evidence in the text.

22. **A.** Words in context/Textual reference: This question combines vocabulary with close reading. First, find the "peoples" in line 9. The passage states that the peoples "were slothful or timid or shortsighted." Now you need to know that *slothful* means lazy and *shortsighted* means myopic, Choice A (see Chapter VIII). Choice B is incorrect because the people may be timid, but they aren't dutiful. They also aren't characterized as stern, selfish, ignoble, or sharp-sighted, so choices C and D are incorrect.

23. **D.** Command of evidence/Text structure: This question requires careful examination of the first paragraph, looking for contrasting elements. Although many of the choices are mentioned in the paragraph, only *the peace of injustice and the peace of justice* (Choice D) are contrasted. Don't be tricked into choosing an answer only because the same words occur in the passage (as in *terror* or *weakness*).

24. **C.** Words in context: To answer this question, you must find the best meaning for the phrase "tells for." Although "tell" can mean *reveal* (Choice A) or *confide* (Choice B), neither meaning fits the context. Roosevelt doesn't mean that peace *advocates* righteousness (Choice D). The best answer for the context is that peace usually *indicates* righteousness (Choice C).

25. **C.** Command of evidence/Textual reference: This question requires you to find the sentence in the passage that supports the claim that "Roosevelt believed the independence of a nation is not an inalienable right unencumbered by obligation." Only Choice C carries the meaning that countries "must ultimately realize that the right of such independence cannot be separated from the responsibility of making good use of it."

26. **A.** Words in context: To answer this question, you must find the best meaning for the word *circumscribe*. Roosevelt wishes to *limit* the war; he makes it clear that any aggressive acts would be purely a "last resort." He would not want to *surround* (Choice B), *demarcate* (Choice C), or *delineate* (Choice D) war in this context (see Chapter VIII).

Section 2: Writing and Language Test

1. **B.** Sentence structure: You must recognize that the underlined portion is a sentence fragment. In addition, the introductory *Because* indicates a cause and effect relationship, which doesn't exist here. The best choice is *However, ...* (Choice B) for two reasons: First, it expresses the contrasting relationship between the first two sentences, and second, it creates a complete sentence.

2. **C.** Adjective/adverb confusion: The adverb *constantly* is used incorrectly to modify the noun *conflict*. The adjective *constant* is needed (Choice C). In addition, idiomatically, the correct preposition is *in* rather than *on*.

3. **D.** Pronoun case/Effectiveness of expression: Choice D is the unacceptable choice. The objective pronoun *whom* can't be used as the subject of the verb *hunt*.

4. **B.** Verb form/Wordiness: You need to choose the least wordy verb phrase that is idiomatically correct and effective. The helping verb *must* should be followed by the verb *be* as in Choice B. You can follow *must* with *have,* but choices C and D create unnecessary wordiness.

5. **D.** Idiom/Parallelism: The correct idiom is *to enable them* (Choice D). The pronoun *them* is preferable to *those* in this context to maintain the parallelism with *by coloring them.*

6. **C.** Diction: The point of the paragraph is the close association with background flora that enables animals to hide. Thus, *intimate* (Choice C) best expresses this close relationship.

7. **C.** Parallelism: This question addresses a series of parallel clauses in the sentence. Only Choice C has the verb form (*are portrayed*) that creates a clause parallel to the other clauses in the sentence (*leaves are copied* and *flowers are represented*).

8. **C.** Punctuation: Use the dash to set off an element in the sentence (Choice C). The dash after *camouflage* is the clue that a comma between *animals* and *Nature* is incorrect. You must complete the set-off element with another dash rather than a comma. The semicolon (Choice D) and the period (Choice B) are both incorrect because the first half of the sentence is not an independent clause.

9. **B.** Coordination: You must combine two sentences effectively. Choices A and D are unnecessarily wordy. Choice C incorrectly uses the conjunction *yet,* which sets up an illogical contrast.

10. **A.** Effectiveness of expression: No change. The sentence is most effectively worded as it is. All of the other choices are awkward and/or non-idiomatic.

11. **B.** Pronoun-antecedent agreement: The pronoun *it* is singular and can't be used to refer to the plural antecedent *colors,* making choices A and C incorrect. Choice B, *they are,* corrects the error. Choice D introduces a tense error by changing to past tense.

12. **B.** Subject-verb agreement: In this sentence, the subject of the singular form of the verb *reports* is *half,* a plural subject in this case because it refers to *people.* The correct verb form for a plural subject is *report.* (Choice B). Choice C incorrectly uses the *–ing* form of the verb without a helping verb. Choice D incorrectly uses the present progressive tense.

13. **D.** Punctuation: The first clause in this sentence has a compound predicate (*they come … and then begin*) so a semicolon is not necessary. A comma (not a semicolon) is used after the long introductory clause *By the time … practices* (Choice D). There is no need for a comma after *then* so choices B and C are incorrect.

14. **A.** Wordiness: No change. *They shut* is the most concise and effective wording here. The other choices are awkward (Choice B), have passive voice (Choice C), or incorrectly use the present progressive tense (Choice D).

15. **C.** Diction/Agreement: *Their* is a possessive pronoun used incorrectly here. The adverb *there* is needed, along with the singular form of the verb *is* to match the singular subject *evidence.* Choice C, *is there,* addresses both of these requirements.

16. **D.** Quantitative interpretation: The pie chart, which indicates that high schoolers report getting about 5½ hours of sleep per night (22% of 24 hours is approximately 5½ hours), is comprised of self-reported data from high school students. This supports the information in the passage that states: *Almost half of all young people between the ages of 12 and 18 report that they don't get enough sleep during the week.* Therefore, the data in the pie chart supports the evidence in the paragraph.

17. **B.** Transitional words: The information that follows *Therefore,* contrasts with the information in the preceding sentence. A transitional word that creates contrast is needed here. Of the choices, only Choice B, *However,* provides contrast.

18. **B.** Modification: The sentence begins with the participial phrase *Knowing the dangers of sleep deprivation,* which should modify *parents.* The only choice that places *parents* in the correct position immediately following the modifying phrase is Choice B.

19. **A.** Coherence: The logical sequence of sentences in the paragraph is correct as it is. It doesn't make sense to move Sentence 4 before Sentence 1 (Choice D) or Sentence 3 (Choice B) because the sleep deficit hasn't been mentioned in Sentence 1. It doesn't make sense to move Sentence 4 after Sentence 6 (Choice C) because Sentence 6 leads into the next paragraph.

20. **D.** Subject-verb agreement/Idiom: The plural subject *factors* requires the plural form of the verb *account.* The correct idiom is *account for,* (Choice D), not *account to* (Choice C).

21. **D.** Redundancy: The underlined portion should be omitted (Choice D) because the sentence begins with the information *Recent experiments and sleep studies show ….* To include *recently conducted experiments* is redundant.

22. **A.** Effectiveness of expression: No change. Of the choices, Choice A is the most effective expression of ideas in the sentence. Choices C and D use *less* incorrectly to refer to accidents (*fewer* would be correct). Choice B contains the unnecessarily wordy expression *amount in the number.*

Section 3: Math Test – No Calculator

1. **D.** Mary paid $0.80 for the first doughnut and had $3.20 left. Divide $3.20 by $0.40, and you have 8. Thus, Mary bought a total of $1 + 8 = 9$ doughnuts.

2. **C.** Inspecting the scatterplot and the line of best fit, the actual height of the player whose right foot measures 11 inches is 72 inches high, and the predicted height by the line of best fit is 70 inches. Thus, the difference is 2 inches.

3. **D.** Begin with $q(2)$, and you have $q(2) = 1$. Thus, $p(q(2)) = p(1) = 2$.

4. **D.** Applying the distributive property, you have $2i(i^3 - 4i) = 2i^4 - 8i^2$. Since $i^4 = 1$ and $i^2 = -1$, the expression $2i^4 - 8i^2$ becomes $2(1) - 8(-1) = 2 + 8$ or 10.

5. **B.** Since $y + x = 1$, you have $y = 1 - x$. Thus, $xy = -2$ becomes $x(1 - x) = -2$ and $x - x^2 = -2$ and $x^2 - x - 2 = 0$. Factor and you have $(x - 2)(x + 1) = 0$ and $x = 2$ or $x = -1$. Since x is negative, $x = -1$ is the only solution.

6. **A.** According to the scatterplot graph, the distance from library A to Karen's house is 1 mile and the distance to Janet's house is 3 miles. Thus, the total distance from library A to their houses is 4 miles, the smallest.

	A	B	C	D
Distance to Karen's house	1	2	3	3
Distance to Janet's house	3	3	4	2
Total Distance	4	5	7	5

7. **C.** Factor by grouping, and you have $x^2(x + 2) - 1(x + 2) = (x + 2)(x^2 - 1) = (x + 2)(x + 1)(x - 1)$. Set $(x + 2)(x + 1)(x - 1) = 0$, and obtain $x = -2$, $x = -1$, and $x = 1$. The zeros are -2, -1, and 1. This question could be given in either the no-calculator section or the calculator section. For steps on how to solve this problem using a calculator, see "Finding the Zeros of Polynomial Functions" in the Appendix.

8. **50** According to the bar graph, Karen spent $12 out of her allowance for lunch in the second week. Since $12 is 60% of her allowance, use the proportion $\dfrac{12}{\text{allowance}} = \dfrac{60}{100}$, which is equivalent to allowance $= \dfrac{100(12)}{60} = 20$. In the fourth week, Karen spent $10 on lunch. Therefore, $\dfrac{\$10}{\$20}$, which is $\dfrac{1}{2}$ or 50%.

9. **0.2** Inspecting the table, you note that the relative frequency of male students taking algebra is 0.4, and that the relative frequency of male students taking either algebra or geometry is 0.6. Therefore, the relative frequency of male students taking geometry is $0.6 - 0.4 = 0.2$. Thus, the probability of picking a male student taking geometry is 0.2.

10. **5**

Relative Frequency of Table			
	Algebra	Geometry	Total
Male	0.4	0.2	0.6
Female	0.25	0.15	0.4
Total	0.65	0.35	1

Complete the relative frequency table as shown above. Note that the relative frequency of female students taking algebra is 0.25. Since there are 20 students in total, the number of female students taking algebra is $(0.25)(20)$ or 5.

Section 4: Math Test – Calculator

1. **D.** The table below shows the relationship for the first 3 miles between the number of miles of a ride and its cost.

Miles	0	1	2	3
Cost	20	33.5	47	60.5

Note that for every 1-mile increase, the cost goes up by $13.50. Thus the number 13.5 in the equation $c = 20 + 13.5x$ is the charge per mile in addition to an initial fee of $20. Alternatively, the equation $c = 20 + 13.5x$ is a linear equation in the slope-intercept form of $y = mx + b$, where the slope $m = 13.5$. The slope of a line shows the change in the y value for every 1-unit change in x.

2. **C.** Note that 1 mile = 1,760 yards × 3 feet/yard = 5,280 feet, and 1 hour = 60 minutes = 60 × 60 seconds = 3,600 seconds. Therefore, 469 ft/sec $= \dfrac{469 \text{ ft}}{1 \text{ sec}} \cdot \dfrac{1 \text{ mile}}{5,280 \text{ ft}} \cdot \dfrac{3,600 \text{ sec}}{1 \text{ hr}} \approx 319.7727$ miles/hr. Note that 2 hours 15 minutes $= \left(2 + \dfrac{15}{60}\right) \text{hr} = 2\dfrac{1}{4} \text{hr} = 2.25$ hr. In 2.25 hours, the plane can travel (2.25) (319.7727) miles ≈ 719.4886 miles ≈ 720 miles.

3. **A.** Since $h(x) = 2f(x - 1)$, $h(2) = 2f(2 - 1)$ or $h(2) = 2f(1)$. The table shows that $f(1) = -3$. Thus, $2f(1) = 2(-3)$ or -6.

4. **D.** Let x be the price for mowing one lawn. Then $6x - 100 = 140$, or $6x = 240$ or $x = 40$. So, Bill charges $40 per lawn. Thus, 12 lawns = 12($40) = $480. His net profit is $480 - $100 = $380.

5. **B.** Set B = {2, 1, 0, -2, -3, -4}. The median is the middle number, and in this case, $\dfrac{(0 + -2)}{2}$ or -1.

6. **D.** Using your calculator, you have $\left(8^{\frac{2}{3}}\right) = 4$. Then, $4\left(n^{\frac{1}{4}}\right) = 16$ and $\left(n^{\frac{1}{4}}\right) = 4$. Raise both sides of the equation to the 4th power; you have $n = 256$. Alternatively, you could also solve this problem using the TI–89 calculator. See "Solving an Equation" in the Appendix.

7. **B.** The mode is the number that appears most often. In this case, the mode is 1. The median is the middle number, and in this case, it's also 1: 1, 1, 1, 1, 1, 1, 1, 1, 1, **1, 1**, 1, 2, 2, 2, 2, 3, 3, 3, 4. Note that the median is $\dfrac{1+1}{2} = 1$. Thus, the sum of the mode and median number of calculators is $1 + 1 = 2$.

8. **D.** If $\overline{AB} \perp \overline{AC}$, then $m\angle A = 90°$. Thus $m\angle AMN + m\angle ANM = 90°$. Note that $\angle AMD$ and $\angle AMN$ are supplementary. So are $\angle ANE$ and $\angle ANM$. Thus, $x + m\angle AMN + m\angle ANM + y = 360°$, or $x + y + 90° = 360°$ or $x + y = 270°$.

9. **B.** Note that 5 feet 6 inches is equivalent to 5.5 feet. Set up a proportion, $\dfrac{5.5}{11} = \dfrac{5}{x}$, where x is the length of Janet's shadow. Thus, $5.5x = 5(11)$ or $x = \dfrac{5(11)}{5.5}$ or $x = 10$.

10. **C.** The inequalities $\dfrac{1}{6} < \dfrac{3}{n} < \dfrac{1}{4}$ is equivalent to $\dfrac{1}{6} < \dfrac{3}{n}$ and $\dfrac{3}{n} < \dfrac{1}{4}$. Solving $\dfrac{1}{6} < \dfrac{3}{n}$, you have $n < 18$. Similarly, solving $\dfrac{3}{n} < \dfrac{1}{4}$, you have $12 < n$ or $n > 12$. Since $n > 12$ and $n < 18$, n must be 13, 14, 15, 16, or 17. Thus, there are 5 integral values for n.

11. **B.** The cosine function is defined as $\dfrac{\text{adjacent leg}}{\text{hypotenuse}}$. The adjacent leg to $\angle A$ is $\overline{AC}$. Using the Pythagorean theorem, you have $(AC)^2 + 12^2 = 13^2$ or $AC = 5$. Thus, $\cos A = \dfrac{5}{13}$.

12. **C.** A point satisfies an equation if substituting produces an equation that is true. Substitute the coordinates of each point into the equation $-|3x| + |y| = 2$. Only when the coordinates of $C\,(0, -2)$ are substituted is the resulting equation true: $-|3(0)| + |2| = 0 + 2 = 2$.

13. **B.** For a reflection about the y-axis, you substitute $-x$ for x. Thus, $f(-x) = 2(-x) + 4 = -2x + 4$.

14. **A.** The standard equation of a circle is $(x - h)^2 + (y - k)^2 = r^2$, where (h, k) is the center and r is the radius. In this case, $r^2 = 1$ and thus the radius is 1. Thus, the area of the circle is $\pi(1)^2$, or simply π.

15. **C.** The graph of the equation $y = ax^2 + bx + c$ is a parabola such that if $a > 0$, the parabola is concave up, and if $a < 0$, it is concave down. Given that $f(x) = x^2 + bx + c$, the coefficient of x^2 is 1, which means the graph of $f(x)$ is concave up. Also, $c = \left(\dfrac{b}{2}\right)^2$, so $f(x) = x^2 + bx + \left(\dfrac{b}{2}\right)^2$. Factor by completing the square, and you have $f(x) = \left(x + \dfrac{b}{2}\right)^2$. Set $f(x) = 0$, and you have $x = -\dfrac{b}{2}$, which means the function f has only one root and that the graph of f intersects the x-axis at only one point. Since b is positive, $x = -\dfrac{b}{2}$ is negative and that means the x-intercept is negative.

16. **600** The amount shown in the savings account is cumulative. In other words, the amount shown in March reflects what was saved in January, February, and March. Since Janet saved a total of $800 for January and February and a total of $1,400 for January, February, and March, she must have saved $1,400 - $800 = $600 for the month of March.

17. **1** Using your graphing calculator, graph inequalities as shown in the accompanying figure.

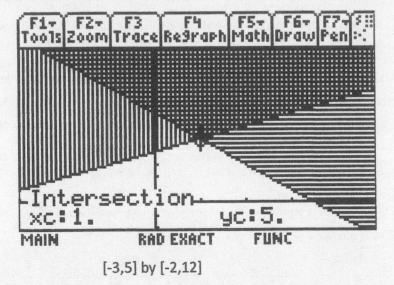

[-3,5] by [-2,12]

Note that the point of intersection of the lines $y = x + 4$ and $y = -2x + 7$ is $(1, 5)$. Also note that $(1, 5)$ is the lowest point in the intersection of the two inequalities. Thus, $p = 1$.

18. **28** Since the system has an infinite number of solutions, the two equations are equivalent. Multiply both sides of the equation $\frac{1}{2}x + \frac{1}{3}y = 5$ by 6, and obtain $3x + 2y = 30$. Comparing $3x + 2y = 30$ and $3x - hy = k$, you have $h = -2$ and $k = 30$. Thus, $h + k = 28$.

19. **239** Note that $\text{Volume}_{space} = \text{Volume}_{cone} - \text{Volume}_{cylinder}$. Find the height of the cone by using the Pythagorean theorem.

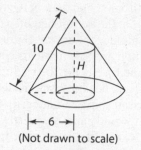

10

H

|← 6 →|
(Not drawn to scale)

Therefore, $6^2 + H^2 = 10^2$ and $H = 8$. Therefore $\text{Volume}_{cone} = \frac{1}{3}R^2H = \frac{1}{3}\pi(6)^2(8) = 96\pi \text{ cm}^3$, and $\text{Volume}_{cylinder} = \pi r^2 h = \pi(2)^2(5) = 20\pi \text{ cm}^3$. Thus, $\text{Volume}_{space} = 96\pi - 20\pi = 76\pi \text{ cm}^3 \approx 239 \text{ cm}^3$.

Section 5: The Essay

To score your essay: First, reread your essay. Then look at the sample essays below and compare your essay to the samples provided. (*Tip:* Because grading your own essay can be difficult, ask an English teacher at your school to grade it for you, based on the rubric on pages 141–142 in Chapter VII.) The numbers after the scores indicate the essay's scores on the three categories: Reading/Analysis/Writing.

Sample Essays

Advanced Response: 4/4/4

To begin his argument, the author immediately supports his position with reference to an authority, Ernest Bruncken, whom he identifies as "a prominent western forester." Bruncken suggests that forests have played an important role in creating the "American character" and in the history of this nation. Although the author offers no factual support for Bruncken's assertion, he links it to his primary claim: Forests are morally and economically essential to this nation. This claim leads to the logical, but so far unsubstantiated, conclusion that the destruction of the forest will have a detrimental effect on the nation.

The author continues his argument with the generalization that "All thinking Americans know that the forests are an important factor in our commercial life," a statement that causes the reader to accept the truth of the assertion or risk being categorized as a "non-thinking American." The author then references the historical significance of forests by presenting the background of the timber industry in colonial times. Moreover, he implies that this industry played a crucial role in bolstering the colonists' opposition to British tyranny. By thus linking the timber industry to the colonial rebellion against Britain, the author appeals to American nationalism and pride in our independence to support his position.

Continuing this appeal to the reader's nationalistic pride, the author links the forests to the essential quality of Americans: self-reliance. In a paragraph filled with dramatic language and images of courageous trappers, hunters, explorers, and settlers forging through the wilderness with only the basic necessities of life, the forest becomes the symbol that embodies American "courage, pertinacity, and resourcefulness." Strengthening his argument is the reference to possibly the most revered American president, Abraham Lincoln. The author links the image of this great hero with the forest from which Lincoln emerged as "the greatest example of American statesmanship the nation has produced." Again, the author supports his position that forests must be preserved with emotional tugs on the reader rather than with logical facts.

Finally, in the concluding paragraph, the author heightens his use of emotional appeals and dramatic diction by calling forests the "chief molders of sturdy character" and making the grand generalization that the advocates of forest preservation are "the finest specimens of manhood the world has ever seen." He maintains that we must honor the forests for their contribution to our heritage and protect them from "wanton waste." In his final appeal, he urges Americans to replant forests that have been destroyed and, in doing so, preserve our American spirit and integrity ("the pioneer blood that still runs so richly in American veins"), goals that most would agree are worthy ones.

While this argument is an attractive one, it doesn't offer much factual evidence or any specific examples of the specific economic value of forests. Nowhere does this author address how the denudation of forests has had a detrimental effect on the economy or on the daily lives of citizens. This is an argument that relies chiefly on pathos, on the emotional connection that readers feel to the history, on sweeping nationalistic generalities, and on sentimental language that reminds readers of their pride in their nation. In short, this argument forces readers to respond with their hearts rather than their brains.

Commentary

This **Advanced** response demonstrates a clear comprehension of the source text, insightfully analyzes the emotional power of the article, and provides abundant and effective textual evidence to support the writer's claims. The information is accurate, and while the organization is predictable (paragraph-by-paragraph), it is effective with a clear introduction, body, and conclusion. The writer uses transitions within paragraphs (*then, again, final*) and between paragraphs (*continues, Finally*). In addition, the writer skillfully weaves well-chosen textual references (*"the finest specimens of manhood the world has ever seen"*) into the response, referring to examples of dramatic language and images (Abraham Lincoln) to support assertions. The writer demonstrates an insight into the powerful appeal of national pride and a facility with language in the sentence variety (*In a paragraph filled with dramatic language and images of courageous trappers, hunters, explorers, and settlers forging through the wilderness with only the basic necessities of life, the forest becomes the symbol that embodies American "courage, pertinacity, and resourcefulness."*). The response is free of errors, and the tone is formal and objective.

Proficient Response: 3/3/3

This article presents a very passionate argument in favor of the preservation of American forests. The author has a clear agenda in that he sees the forests as totally essential to the history and culture of this country. He does make a strong argument, but he argues from the perspective of a patriotic person. He doesn't take the position of an economist discussing why forests are essential to the economy. He doesn't take the position of a scientist discussing why forests are a necessary part of the American ecosystem. Instead, he speaks in the passionate voice of a person who believes that American history and culture owe much to the forests. Thus, his supporting points are all about the history and culture of America.

The main point of this author's argument is that forests should be protected because they are an important part of the history of America. First pointing out "From the earliest colonial times the forests have had a moral and political effect in shaping our history," the author establishes this statement as the thesis of his argument. While it is true that he doesn't back this up with many particular details or facts, he does mention the timber industry, which supports the importance of wood from forests in the shaping of the early history of this country. In fact, he points out that this timber trade fanned the flames of rebellion when the colonies broke away from King George. By giving this, the author seems to assume that readers of his article will agree with this historical background as supporting evidence of his thesis, and so, he doesn't need to add more factual evidence.

Then, the author supports his position on forests by referring to forests as the source of a culturally defining characteristic of America. He equates the forests with American guts and grit in that they created the trait of self-reliance. To support this, he describes the settlers who went into the woods and carved out homesteads and farms and towns. These pioneers relied on themselves and on the forests that gave them food and shelter. The forests taught them "courage, pertinacity, and resourcefulness." Thus, the forests formed the cultural foundation of the American character. He uses an appeal to patriotism when he points out that Abraham Lincoln, one of our greatest presidents, was a "backwoods" person, implying that the woods made him into a strong and resourceful leader. All these great cultural qualities that the author discusses come from great forests, implying that the greatness of this nation is tied to the continuance of the forests.

The author makes a strong case that efforts should be made to preserve the American wilderness. Because his writing style is very eloquent and emotional, he keeps away from dry facts and examples and emphasizes patriotic words and phrases like "vast primeval forests" and "masters in courage." Without using series of facts about how much money and jobs the forests provide or their ecological importance to support his argument, he instead focuses on the role of forests in shaping our national character. With appeals to American patriotism and pride as the primary evidence to support his thesis, the argument is convincing to an emotional audience, but might be unconvincing to an audience that needs more evidence from facts and details.

Commentary

This **Proficient** response demonstrates that the writer understands the main point of the source text, interprets its sub-points, and analyzes the kind of evidence and rhetorical style of the author. The writer uses textual evidence to support the analysis by paraphrasing source material (*he points out that this timber trade fanned the flames of rebellion when the colonies broke away from King George*) and by quoting relevant information (*"From the earliest colonial times the forests have had a moral and political effect in shaping our history."*). The response is organized coherently with an introductory paragraph that states the main claim (*The author has a clear agenda in that he sees the forests as totally essential to the history and culture of this country.*). Each of the body paragraphs develops a point of his analysis. The concluding paragraph is effectively combined with the last body paragraph. The writer uses some sentence variety (*Without using series of facts about how much money and jobs the forests provide or their ecological importance to support his argument, he instead focuses on the role of forests in shaping our national character.*), and transitions within paragraphs (*Instead, While it is true, In fact*) and between paragraphs (*The main point, Then*). The essay is mostly free from mechanical errors, but has some repetitive wording (*history and culture*) and some vague pronouns (*By giving this*), but, for the most part, the language use is proficient.

Partial Response: 2/2/2

This article tries to convince the reader that it is important to preserve the American forests. The author actually is giving the argument of Ernest Bruncken, a forest expert who says that the forests are too important to the culture and history of America to be destroyed. The argument relies on pathos and some historical evidence to persuade the audience to accept its position.

Pathos is the primary tool this author uses to support his claim about the preservation of the forest. Pathos is the appeal to the emotions of the reader. The reader is most likely an American so the fact that the forest played a role in "shaping American character" will make the reader want to work to preserve the forests. Also, this is historically true. Even in colonial times, this author says, "the forests have had a moral and political effect." To back this claim up, he gives historical evidence about the colonishts who used the wood they cut from the forests to make parts for the ships. In this way, the forests were very important to the colonishts.

This author also uses historical evidence about Abraham Lincoln, who was very much in favor of protecting the forests. Lincoln was from the backwoods, so he knew that the forest made men self-reliant. They could go into the forest with an ax and a rifle and earn a living. If there were no forests, they couldn't feed their families and find food and build log cabins. This is a strong historical reason to save forests.

The forests are important, we need to save them and not have forest fires and not waste the forests by not replanting. The author uses the example of Europe to proves this point. In Europe no one replanted the forests so they are gone.

In conclusion, the article is a strong argument to save the forests. The author uses pathos and historical examples to prove his claim to the audience. He gets the Americans to want to save the forests because they are important to American history. He gives all the right reasons to protect the wilderness.

Commentary

This **Partial** response demonstrates some understanding of the reading and the task, but remains too general (*In this way, the forests were very important to the colonishts.*), contains errors in interpretation (forests in Europe **are** replanted), and repeats points several times. The writer comprehends the main sources of evidence, pathos and historical references, but shows little analysis of the ways these strategies are used to support the argument. The response uses some textual evidence, but uses it without adequately explaining how the quotations provide evidence. The organization of the response is uneven, with underdeveloped body paragraphs and very little conclusion. The writing is simplistic, with repetitive sentence structure (most sentences follow the subject-verb pattern). In addition, there are several grammatical errors, such as the run-on sentence that begins the fourth paragraph, awkward and ungrammatical phrasing (*The author uses the example of Europe to proves this point.*), and spelling errors (*colonishts*) that detract from the quality of the writing.

Inadequate Response: 1/1/1

This article by Ernest Brunken makes an argument that the forests are important to U.S. history. He uses reasons from U.S. history to make his case. He wants people to know that we need the forests to help keep the U.S. safe.

Ernest says that "All thinking Americans know that the forests are an important factor in our commercial life." This is his reason for saying that the need is for the forests to be saved. He has another reason for saving the forests. "From that time to the present the forests of America have exercised a most important influence upon the nation, especially in creating the self-reliance which is the chief trait of the American character." This quote means that people rely on the forests. We need to build houses out of wood and for using the forests to help get money for the economy.

This is why Ernest uses facts and reasons to say that the forests are very important to every person in the U.S.

Commentary

This **Inadequate** response demonstrates little understanding of the source, almost no analysis of the argument, and inadequate control of the conventions of standard written English. While there is an attempt to respond to the controlling idea, the importance of the preservation of the forest, the writer misunderstands much of the task. He or she attributes the authorship of the article to "Ernest Brunken" (note the writer's misspelling of Bruncken's last name) and seems to understand that Bruncken argues for the importance of the forests. Then the writer simply repeats his or her one point (*that the forests are very important to every person*). Although the writer does include two quotations from the text, he or she doesn't provide any sense that he or she understands the relationship of these quotations to the argument. In addition, there is little attempt at analysis in this response. The writer vaguely states that the argument is supported by facts and reasons, but this assertion is never supported by evidence. The writer fails to recognize the main emotional appeal of the argument and the historical and cultural references that support this appeal. The language of the response is vague (*This is why …*) and somewhat awkward (*This is his reason for saying that the need is for the forests to be saved.*). While there are paragraphs, they are brief and underdeveloped; there is no internal or external coherence and no use of transitional words.

Score Sheet for Diagnostic Test

Section 1: Reading Test

Section 2: Writing and Language Test

To calculate your Reading and Writing score:

1. Count the number of correct answers you got on Section 1: Reading Test. This is your raw score.
2. Using the Raw Score Conversion table, locate your raw score and match it to the number in the Reading Test score column.
3. Do the same with your Section 2: Writing Test score.
4. Add the two scores together (Reading Test score and Writing Test score).
5. Multiply that number by 10 to get your Reading and Writing score.

	Raw Score	Scaled Score
Section 1: Reading	(0–28)	(10–40)
Section 2: Writing and Language	(0–22)	(10–40)
Total of Reading and Writing Scaled Scores		(20–80)
Multiply Scaled Scores × 10		(200–800)

Reading Raw Score = Number right (Section 1) _____

Reading Scaled Score _____

Writing Raw Score = Number right (Section 2) _____

Writing Scaled Score _____

(Remember that there is no penalty for incorrect answers.)

Reading and Writing Scaled Score: _____ × 10 = _____

Note: To find your scaled score, use the following chart.

	Reading and Writing Raw Score Conversion				
Raw Score	Reading Section Score	Writing Section Score	Raw Score	Reading Section Score	Writing Section Score
1	10	10	15	25	30
2	11	11	16	27	31
3	12	12	17	29	33
4	13	13	18	30	35
5	14	14	19	31	37
6	15	15	20	32	38
7	16	17	21	33	39
8	17	19	22	34	40
9	18	21	23	35	
10	19	23	24	36	
11	20	25	25	37	
12	22	26	26	38	
13	23	27	27	39	
14	24	28	28	40	

Section 3: Math Test – No Calculator

Section 4: Math Test – Calculator

	Number Right
Section 3: Math Test – No Calculator	
Section 4: Math Test – Calculator	
TOTAL (Section 3 + Section 4)	

Raw score = Number right (Section 3 + Section 4) _____

(Remember that there is no penalty for incorrect answers.)

Raw score × 2 = _____

Math scaled score range: _____

Note: To find your scaled score range, use the following chart.

Mathematics Raw Score Conversion					
Raw Score	Scaled Score Range	Raw Score	Scaled Score Range	Raw Score	Scaled Score Range
58	800	38	600–640	18	430–480
57	770–800	37	600–630	17	420–470
56	760–780	36	590–620	16	410–460
55	730–760	35	580–620	15	400–440
54	720–750	34	580–610	14	380–420
53	710–740	33	570–600	13	360–400
52	700–740	32	570–600	12	350–390
51	690–730	31	550–590	11	340–380
50	680–720	30	550–580	10	330–370
49	680–710	29	540–570	9	320–360
48	670–710	28	550–570	8	310–350
47	660–700	27	540–570	7	300–340
46	660–690	26	520–560	6	290–330
45	650–690	25	510–550	5	280–320
44	640–680	24	500–540	4	260–300
43	640–670	23	480–530	3	240–280
42	630–670	22	480–520	2	220–260
41	630–660	21	460–510	1	200–220
40	620–650	20	450–500	0	200
39	610–650	19	440–490		

V. Evidence-Based Reading and Writing: The Reading Test

A. Overview: The Reading Test

The Reading Test consists of 52 questions designed to assess your reasoning and comprehension skills. You're presented with a series of passages, ranging in content and complexity, each followed by a set of questions. To answer the questions, you must refer to what the passages state **explicitly** and draw conclusions from information that is presented **implicitly**. On paired passages, you must understand each writer's point of view as well as the connections and dissimilarities. Some of the passages will be accompanied by informational graphics (charts, graphs, diagrams) for reference when you're answering specific questions.

Guessing strategy: There is no penalty for incorrect answers on the SAT. This means that you should answer every question on the test. First, eliminate any answer choices that appear to be irrelevant or incorrect; then, take an educated guess. If you have no idea, just fill in a circle on your answer sheet.

Here are some general strategies for successfully reading the passages:

- **Always read actively.** Focus on what the author is trying to tell you. Think as you read—don't allow your mind to drift. Have a mental dialogue with the text. Sometimes it's helpful to visualize the passage unfolding in front of your eyes, like a movie, or to annotate (mark up the passage by underlining or starring key points, and/or take brief notes) as you read. Just don't get so involved with underlining that you slow down and lose the sense of the passage.

- **Always read any introductory material given before the passage or passages carefully.** These notes may give you important literary, historical, or scientific background.

- **If you're confused by a sentence or a paragraph, don't reread.** The sentence or paragraph may become clearer as you read, or there may not be any questions about that part of the passage. If you have to reread, do so as you answer the questions.

- **Psych yourself up and try to be interested in the passage.** Link the passage in your mind to a topic that interests you. This strategy will help you stay focused.

- **Don't allow your personal feelings or your own knowledge about the topic to influence your answers.** Always go back to what is stated in or implied by the text to support your answer.

- **Always read *all* the answer choices before you select an answer.** Use the process of elimination as you read the answer choices. If you are sure an answer choice is wrong, cross out the letter of the choice. If you think it could be right, leave it alone. When you have read all the answer choices, look again only at the ones that are not crossed out, and evaluate their accuracy. Don't be fooled by an answer choice that makes a correct statement but does not answer the specific question. A statement may be true based on the information in the passage, but it may still be the wrong answer because it doesn't answer the question you're being asked.

- **Be on the lookout for EXCEPT questions.** For EXCEPT questions, three of the answer choices will be true. In these questions, you're looking for the answer choice that is false. Circle the word *EXCEPT* in your test booklet so you won't look for answer choices that are true.

■ **Pay particular attention to the ends of the answer choices.** Many of the answer choices start out right, but then the last word or phrase is incorrect. These are set up to trick you if you're rushing through the answer choices.

B. Content

The reading passages on the Reading Test cover the range of content areas that comprise most rigorous secondary school curricula. They are designed to evaluate your ability to understand and respond to the different reading requirements of different fields of study. The questions on each passage are crafted to reflect the varying subject-specific approaches to literacy that you're expected to demonstrate on the test. In other words, you don't read a chapter in a novel the same way that you read an analysis of a scientific experiment. You focus on a distinct set of reading techniques as you switch from subject to subject. On each test, at least one or two of the passages are accompanied by graphically represented data that you must interpret as you answer the related questions.

1. U.S. and World Literature

These passages are taken from previously published works of fiction or literary criticism. The questions address your understanding of such important literary elements as theme, characterization, and tone.

2. Analysis in History/Social Studies

These passages are drawn from important documents in U.S. history or those that are considered part of the "Great Global Conversation," documents that consider such topics as freedom and human rights. The passages cover political developments, global issues, environmental issues, and critical moments in history, and may be accompanied by graphically represented data.

3. Science

These passages are drawn from scientific writings. The questions address your ability to understand an experiment, to analyze research findings, to compare/contrast scientific approaches, or to determine logical conclusions. The passages may be accompanied by graphically represented data.

See the skills in Section C.4, "Disciplinary Literacy," for practice in specific content areas.

C. Focus Skills

The Reading Test passages are designed to be interesting and informative, but quite challenging. The questions following each passage cover a wide range of reading skills. Questions require you to recognize the main idea and/or the writer's main purpose, summarize text, identify rhetorical strategies, analyze the organization of the passage and/or the relationship of a paragraph to the whole, relate graphically presented data, and determine the meaning of words in context. These skills can be organized into four main categories:

- Words in Context
- Command of Evidence
- Analysis of Data in Graphics
- Disciplinary Literacy

1. Words in Context

The link between vocabulary and reading comprehension is documented in research. It is logical that if you can't understand the key words of a passage, you'll have difficulty comprehending what you're reading. By the time you're ready to take the SAT, the several years of language arts instruction you have completed should have helped you acquire a reasonably well-developed vocabulary. If not, Chapter VIII can help. It contains a list of Tier 2 words, those words that have been found to be most useful across a variety of subjects. These aren't obscure words that no one ever uses. They are words that are found frequently in written texts with a complexity on par with that of the SAT reading passages. The words on the SAT are all presented within the context of a passage; thus, you have textual support to help you determine the meaning of the word as it is used in the passage.

Don't rely on *denotation* (the dictionary meaning of a word) alone. The correct response often requires you to consider *connotation* (the suggested meanings or implications of a word).

The best approach to the vocabulary-in-context questions is to follow this method:

- Circle the word in the text.
- Reread the sentence before the one containing the word, the sentence with the word, and the following sentence.
- In your head, think of a word you know that could replace the word and still make sense in the context.
- Replace the word in the text with each of the words in the four choices.
- Select the choice that is most like the one you thought of and that makes the most sense based on the use of the word in the context.
- *Note:* Some of the choices may fit the context, but they aren't acceptable definitions of the word.
- *Note:* Some of the choices are synonyms for the word, but they don't fit in the context of the sentence.

For example, consider the word "common" in the excerpt below:

Upon entering the room, Lady Mary surveyed the inhabitants with a frosty stare. In very little time, she established that they were far too **common** for her to engage in conversation. She selected a chair somewhat removed from the others and, with ramrod straight back, seated herself.

The word "common" has several meanings; the most common meaning (pun intended) is familiar or ordinary. But, it also means uncouth, uncivilized, or unrefined. Ask yourself: Which one of these meanings fits best in the context of the passage? The context clues—"Lady Mary," "frosty stare," "chair somewhat removed from others"—suggest that Lady Mary considers the others in the room unworthy of her. Thus, the best meaning for the word "common" in this passage is uncouth or unrefined.

Practice

(*Note:* These practice passages are shorter than the passages on the actual SAT.)

(*Note:* The words are printed in bold text in this practice. On the actual SAT, they will not be printed in bold, but you will be given a line reference.)

Question 1 is based on the following passage.

Anthropology is a vast field that studies the past and present of human society. It encompasses the study of the social and cultural qualities of societies, investigating such aspects of society as language, religion, and social customs. More specific study of relationships between human beings and ecology is the **domain** of ecological anthropologists who focus on how cultures respond to the demands of the environment.

1. As it is used in the passage, the word "domain" most nearly means

   A. land area or territory.
   B. website authority.
   C. sphere of expertise.
   D. governmental jurisdiction.

Question 2 is based on the following passage.

The actual tomb of the great Duke is in the Crypt of the Cathedral, a massive sarcophagus **wrought** from a boulder of porphyry found in Cornwall, resting upon a granite base. The simple grandeur of the monument is admirably in keeping with the character of the man whom it commemorates. The mortal remains of England's greatest General lie close to those of England's greatest Admiral.

2. As it is used in the passage, the word "wrought" most nearly means

   A. fashioned.
   B. acted.
   C. twisted.
   D. produced.

Question 3 is based on the following passage.

For the purpose of enabling others to pursue a similar course of studies, I shall take especial pains to point out my course of proceeding as plainly as I can—such course with me having been entirely rational, positive, and direct, and without in any sense disturbing my ordinary **mode** of existence. The course pursued in physiological-psychological studies, in fact, does not differ greatly from that pursued in the study of purely psychological subjects, which is also carried on by means of introspection, though it is of a more positive nature.

3. As it is used in the passage, the word "mode" most nearly means

 A. mood.
 B. manner.
 C. genre.
 D. trend.

Question 4 is based on the following passage.

During all these years of unrequited labor, which extend far beyond the day on which I made my memorable discovery, my personal affairs meanwhile constantly suffering, with but one notable exception *no* hand was held out to me in **succor.** In view of this fact (and it is the experience of many who, in the privacy of their souls, are struggling after the light), I want to ask this question: With all the noble institutions for *learning,* why are there none to assist those who are attempting to solve questions *to be taught* for the benefit and advancement of mankind?

4. As it is used in the passage, the word "succor" most nearly means

 A. generosity.
 B. sweetness.
 C. friendship.
 D. aid.

Question 5 is based on the following passage.

My cry is not for recognition. My personality might be blotted out, like that of millions of others, without its being noticed, yet, by virtue of this trust which has been **reposed** in me, what a loss it would be! My cry is for investigation and the cooperation of others, so that this work may be carried on independent of myself. Meantime, I cannot transfer this task to others. I must first explain all that it is in my power to explain. I can then shift it from my shoulders onto theirs. They must be educated up to it before they can take hold of it as I have taken hold of it.

5. As it is used in the passage, the word "reposed" most nearly means

 A. repositioned.
 B. placed.
 C. rested.
 D. implanted.

Answers

1. **C.** *Domain* can mean area or territory, governmental jurisdiction, sphere of expertise, or website authority. Choice C, *sphere of expertise,* best fits the context of the passage, which is a explanation of anthropology and its sub-field, ecological anthropology. Thus, ecological anthropology is the area in which ecological anthropologists are expert. Choice A is not a logical choice because the passage isn't about a physical area or territory. Choices B and D are incorrect because the passage isn't about website authority or governmental jurisdiction.

2. **A.** *Wrought* means shaped or fashioned. The sarcophagus (coffin) was shaped or *fashioned* from a large boulder of porphyry (reddish purple rock). Wrought can mean *twisted* (Choice C), as in wrought iron, but that meaning doesn't fit the context of the sentence. Choice D, *produced,* is close, but *fashioned* from rock is more logical than *produced* from rock. Choice B, *acted,* doesn't fit the context.

3. **B.** Depending on the context, *mode* can mean manner, style, or genre. In this context, the *mode of existence* most nearly means the *manner* or style of existence (Choice B). It doesn't mean *genre* (Choice C), or a specific category or type of artistic expression in this context. Choice A is meant to distract because *mood* looks like *mode*. Choice D, *trend,* is not a meaning of *mode*.

4. **D.** *Succor* means support, assistance, or aid. The context clue in the last sentence, *none to assist,* can help lead you to the best choice. All the other choices—*generosity, sweetness, friendship*—are words that might go along with holding out a hand, but no context clues support these positive choices.

5. **B.** *Reposed* can mean Choice A, *repositioned* (as in the girl reposed her doll so that it held the bottle), or Choice C, *rested* (as in Daisy *reposed* on the sofa), but neither of those meanings fits the context *of trust … reposed in me.* Trust would more likely be *placed* in another person (Choice B) rather than the more illogical *implanted* (Choice D).

2. Command of Evidence

Command of evidence refers to your ability to understand the passages, to analyze the ideas, to make inferences, and to apply an idea to a similar situation. To answer these questions, you need the following skills:

- Comprehend the information in the passage.
- Identify main ideas and supporting details and determine the primary purpose.
- Infer from what is implied.
- Locate the evidence for an author's conclusion.
- Find relationships.
- Synthesize (combine various elements into a new whole).
- Extend reasoning to an analogous (similar) situation.
- Understand the structure of a text.
- Evaluate the persuasiveness of an argument.

a. Skills: Comprehend, Find the Main Idea, Determine the Primary Purpose

To find the **main idea** of a passage, first ask yourself, "What is this passage about? If I had to summarize it in one sentence, what would I say?" Your answer to these questions is the main idea. If the passage is long and dense and contains several major points, pay particular attention to the topic sentence of each paragraph and the last sentence of the passage. These sentences will frequently give you a good sense of the main, or most important, idea.

Primary purpose questions ask you to figure out what the writer is trying to accomplish. Think about the writer's presentation of ideas. Ask yourself, "Does this passage present a distinct point of view, either supporting, qualifying, or refuting a position?" In these cases, if the writer's purpose is positive, it may be to defend, to advocate, to support, or to justify; if it's negative, it may be to challenge, to refute, or to question. If the position is mixed—that is, the writer defends under some circumstances and challenges under others—the purpose may be to qualify. A passage may also be objective, simply presenting the ideas without taking a stance. In these cases, the writer's purpose may be to explain, to clarify, or to explicate.

Practice

Questions 6–8 are based on the following passage.

This passage is adapted from a work about travel published in 1814.

> In the early period of human history, when voyages and travels were not undertaken from the view of amusement or instruction, or from political or commercial motives, the discovery of adjacent countries was chiefly affected by war, and of distant regions by commerce.
>
> (5) The wars of the Egyptians with the Scythians, mentioned in the pristine pages of history, must have opened faint sources of information concerning the neighboring tribes. Under the Grecian empire of Alexander and his successors, the progress of discovery by war is first marked on the page of history; and science began to attend the banners of victory.
>
> The opulence of nature was now to be disclosed; and Greece was astonished at the miracles of India. The Romans not only inherited the Grecian knowledge, but, extending their arms to the North and (10) West, accumulated discoveries upon regions dimly descried by the Greeks, through the obscurity in which the Phoenicians enveloped their commercial advantages.

6. The primary purpose of this passage is to

   A. criticize a strategy.
   B. justify an undertaking.
   C. explain a phenomenon.
   D. defend an approach.

7. The main idea of this passage is

   A. the search for scientific information engendered the desire to travel.
   B. the wealth of the western world was mostly derived from looting conquered regions.
   C. the systematic conquest of weaker tribes decimated the ancient world.
   D. an increase in knowledge was a positive result of warfare.

8. The author of this passage would agree that science and warfare

   A. are equally important motivations for nations to undertake exploration.
   B. are mutually exclusive.
   C. are painful reminders of mankind's desire to destroy that which is unfamiliar.
   D. are related in that scientific knowledge is increased by contact predicated on conquest.

Answers

6. **C.** This primary purpose question asks you to think about why the author wrote the passage. Try to eliminate the most obviously incorrect answer choices first. Is the author criticizing anything? He is not, so cross out Choice A. Is there an undertaking that the author must justify? The author states his

points regarding the relationship between war and discovery, but he does not attempt to justify them, so Choice B is incorrect. Choice D is incorrect because the author does not defend; he merely asserts. That leaves Choice C, which is the correct answer. Don't be misled by the word *phenomenon;* it is sometimes used to mean any incident, occurrence, or observable fact. In fact, the author is explaining an occurrence in this passage.

7. **D.** To find the main idea, try to summarize the passage in a few words. The author is trying to show that exploration and an increase in knowledge were natural consequences of war. As nations conquered other territories, they absorbed the scientific and cultural discoveries of the lands. Notice that each of the incorrect choices contains a word or phrase that echoes a point made in the passage (Choice A mentions scientific information; Choice B mentions wealth; Choice C mentions conquest). If you are not reading carefully, it's easy to be tricked into selecting a choice that "looks" right. Always look beyond the words of an answer choice to determine its meaning.

8. **D.** This question asks you to draw a conclusion about the relationship between war and knowledge based on the author's main point in the passage. He says, *science began to attend the banners of victory* and *The Romans … accumulated discoveries.* These statements imply that, through conquest, invaders absorbed the knowledge of the conquered territories. Thus, warfare led to an increase in scientific knowledge. The passage doesn't indicate that science and warfare were equally important motivations (Choice A) or that they are mutually exclusive (Choice B). Choice C is incorrect because the author makes no reference to mankind's desire to destroy the unfamiliar.

b. Skills: Make Inferences, Locate Evidence, Find Relationships

Inference questions ask you to understand what the author suggests or implies. The answer will not be directly stated in the passage, so you have to "read between the lines." Some questions give you line references for a phrase. For example, a question may ask, "The claim in lines 22–25 suggests primarily that … ."

Here are some strategies for answering inference questions:

- First, underline, bracket, or circle the lines. Then, read around the point (the sentences before and after the specific point).
- Don't be tricked into thinking the answers will always be in those lines. Often, the best clue to the answer will be in the line just *before* the lines referred to; sometimes the best clue will be just *after* the lines referred to.
- Try to *paraphrase* the lines (put them in your own words) to be sure you understand the gist of the lines.

Locate evidence questions ask you to find the lines that best support (or refute or undermine) a given statement. For example, a question may ask, "Which of the following lines is the best evidence to support the claim that string theory is only demonstrable through mathematical equations?" First, be sure to keep in mind exactly what you're looking for: lines that support or lines that disprove. You have to evaluate the sentences in the choices and select the one that provides the best evidence.

Find relationship questions ask you to analyze and find connections between ideas. Transitional words can provide you with clues by setting up cause and effect (*because, since, as a result, consequently, therefore*) or comparison/contrast (*unlike, similarly, in contrast*) or order of importance (*primarily, most important, significantly*). Relationship questions may also ask you to determine the function of a sentence or phrase in relation to the topic as a whole. For example, "In relation to the passage as a whole, the last paragraph serves to … ."

Practice

Questions 9–11 are based on the following passage.

The following passage is an excerpt from a nineteenth-century essay entitled "Self-Reliance."

I read the other day some verses written by an eminent painter which were original and not conventional. The soul always hears an admonition in such lines, let the subject be what it may. The sentiment they instill is of more value than any thought they may contain. To believe your own thought, to believe that what is true for you in your private heart is true for all men,—that is genius. Speak your latent con-
(5) viction, and it shall be the universal sense; for the inmost in due time becomes the outmost,—and our first thought is rendered back to us by the trumpets of the Last Judgment. Familiar as the voice of the mind is to each, the highest merit we ascribe to Moses, Plato, and Milton is, that they set at naught books and traditions, and spoke not what men but what they thought. A man should learn to detect and watch that gleam of light which flashes across his mind from within, more than the lustre of the firma-
(10) ment of bards and sages. Yet he dismisses without notice his thought, because it is his. In every work of genius we recognize our own rejected thoughts: they come back to us with a certain alienated majesty. Great works of art have no more affecting lesson for us than this. They teach us to abide by our spontaneous impression with good-humored inflexibility then most when the whole cry of voices is on the other side. Else, to-morrow a stranger will say with masterly good sense precisely what we have thought
(15) and felt all the time, and we shall be forced to take with shame our own opinion from another.

9. The author refers to Moses, Plato, and Milton (line 7) in order to

   A. argue that only the ancient sages had real genius.
   B. suggest a chronological pattern to the development of thoughtful meditation.
   C. refute the notion that these men were individual thinkers rather than reflections of the current thinking of their times.
   D. cite examples of men who rejected conventional thought in favor of individual insight.

10. It can be inferred from the passage that the author would agree that

   A. ordinary people should seek to emulate the extraordinary artists, writers, and thinkers.
   B. great works of art are useless unless they provide inspiration to private hearts.
   C. individuals should recognize the worth of flashes of personal insight.
   D. the greatest praise a man may receive is that he is original and unconventional.

11. Which of the following lines from the passage best reflects the theme of self-reliance stated in the title of this excerpt?

   A. I read the other day some verses written by an eminent painter which were original and not conventional.

   B. The soul always hears an admonition in such lines, let the subject be what it may. The sentiment they instill is of more value than any thought they may contain.

   C. Familiar as the voice of the mind is to each, the highest merit we ascribe to Moses, Plato, and Milton is, that they set at naught books and traditions, and spoke not what men but what they thought.

   D. A man should learn to detect and watch that gleam of light which flashes across his mind from within, more than the lustre of the firmament of bards and sages.

Question 12 is based on the following passage.

   As a matter of personal gratification, I am indifferent to success; but I think the time has come when these matters should not continue to remain with me alone, but should become the property of all, not for my sake, nor simply for that of science, but for the sake of truth, and the benefit of mankind. Had my previous statements been given the consideration they deserved, other persons, in all probability, would have made *some* of the many discoveries, at least, that it has now been my privilege to make single-handed. Still, the field is inexhaustible; that which I have discovered being but an index hand to that which is still to be discovered. Having no reason to doubt but that I am a properly organized member of the human family, I consider myself entitled to speak of my personal experience as in like manner applicable to every other member of that family.

12. It can be inferred from the passage that the writer believes that

   A. he is the only person who has the skill and knowledge to uncover essential truths.

   B. with foreknowledge of his work, other investigators would have been able to make the same discoveries he did.

   C. his discoveries will provide others with an inexhaustible supply of answers to key mysteries.

   D. his discoveries deserve universal recognition for their benefits to mankind.

Answers

9. **D.** This question requires that you consider *why* the author mentions these three historical figures. You must infer his purpose in referring to these three famous men. Choice A is incorrect because the author never says that only sages had genius; in fact, this contradicts his main idea that every person has a spark of genius within. Choice B is there as a trick: It's true that the men are listed in chronological order, but that is unrelated to the author's purpose—he isn't making a point about the historical development of thought. Choice C is the direct opposite of the main point of the passage; the author is not *refuting* (disproving) but advocating the innate value of individual insight. That leaves Choice D, which correctly states the author's purpose in referring to the three men: They are perfect examples of unconventional thinkers who had faith in their own insights.

10. **C.** This inference question asks you to find the idea in the text with which the writer would agree. As Choice C indicates, the writer discusses the importance of recognizing the *gleam of light* which flashes through a man's mind, allowing him to see *what is true for you in your private heart is true for all men*. Choice A is incorrect because the writer emphasizes self-reliance; he wouldn't encourage emulation of others. Choices B and D, while referenced in the passage, can't be supported as positions with which the writer would agree.

11. **D.** The sentence that best reflects the theme of self-reliance is Choice D. None of the other choices reflects the specific idea of relying on one's individual insight. Choice A refers to poetry written by a famous painter. Choice B refers to the emotional response to the verses of the painter. Choice C refers to men who were willing to challenge tradition.

12. **B.** In the sentence, *Had my previous statements been given the consideration they deserved, other persons, in all probability, would have made* some *of the many discoveries, at least, that it has now been my privilege to make single-handed*, the writer implies that other persons with knowledge of his previous statements would have been able to make the same discoveries he has made (Choice B). He never implies that he is the only person who could have uncovered this knowledge (Choice A), nor does he suggest his discoveries are the answers to key mysteries (Choice C). Indeed, he states they are only an index hand to that which is still to be discovered. Choice D is incorrect because he doesn't suggest his discoveries deserve universal recognition, only that they shouldn't remain unconsidered.

c. Skills: Synthesize, Extend Reasoning

Synthesis questions ask you to integrate information. You may be asked to draw on more than one source, perhaps from introductory material or from one passage to another in paired reading passages. A typical synthesis question might ask you to consider what the writer of Passage 1 would say about an idea in Passage 2. You might also be asked to find an idea with which both writers would agree or disagree.

Extended reasoning questions require you to extrapolate—that is, to use critical thinking to go beyond what is directly stated in the passage. You must draw conclusions from what you read. These questions will ask you to *infer* (to draw a conclusion from what the author implies). The question may ask you what the author *suggests* or may ask what you can *assume* from the passage. These questions may ask you to apply the reasoning in the passage to a new but analogous situation.

Here are some strategies to consider when answering extended reasoning questions:

- Although the answer will not be directly stated in the passage, always use textual evidence to support your answer.

- Be careful not to allow your own opinions to influence your answer to the question. There will be hints in the passage to guide you to the correct answer choice.

Practice

Questions 13–15 are based on the following passage.

The following passage is adapted from the National Aeronautics and Space Administration (NASA) website.

One of the most important ideas of Einstein's theory of relativity is that gravity is a property of space-time geometry. Rather than following straight lines with a constant velocity as might be expected, particles diverge from this constant path. Einstein theorized that some force must be acting on them to create this divergence.

In his general theory of relativity, Einstein explains that gravity and inertia are the same. The "force" of gravity pressing you down in a chair is the same force you feel when the automobile you are in quickly slows down, and you continue to move forward. Einstein says gravity, like inertia, doesn't pull. Instead,

anything in space that has mass will warp or curve space and time around it. Think of a pillow as space.
(5) If you place a heavy (massive) object on the pillow, the pillow will curve around the object. According to Einstein, the amount of the curvature relates directly to the mass of the object. This curvature of space is what curves the path of the ray of light from a distant star.

Einstein's theory, which is highly mathematical, predicts that the curvature of space caused by the Sun's mass should bend starlight twice as much as Newton's principles predict it should. He published
(10) his prediction in Germany in 1915 during the Great War between England and Germany. A Dutch astronomer smuggled a copy of Einstein's paper out of war-torn Europe into England, where it was read by Arthur Stanley Eddington, Plumian Professor of Astronomy and Experimental Philosophy at Cambridge University.

Other astronomers had read earlier versions of Einstein's paper and tried to test his prediction during
(15) total solar eclipses in 1912 and 1914, but they were not successful in their attempts due to cloudy weather. When astronomers studied the conditions of the 1919 eclipse, it appeared the Sun would be well placed in a group of bright stars. Professor Eddington decided to lead a group to the island of Principe near the western coast of Africa, where the eclipse could be photographed. He also convinced Sir Frank Dyson, Director of the Royal Observatory, to send another group to a different location to reduce the chance
(20) that clouds might block the eclipse and prevent photographing the Sun. This other group, led by Dr. Andrew Crommelin from the Royal Observatory, traveled to northern Brazil to view the eclipse.

13. The scientists most likely prefer to test Einstein's predictions during a solar eclipse because

   A. during the eclipse, the curvature of the surface of the Sun would be clearly visible behind the moon.

   B. the eclipse would negate the effect of the mass of the Sun.

   C. the light of the Sun would be obscured, allowing the photographers to capture the curvature of the starlight.

   D. as the stars become better illuminated, their effects on the Sun would be more detectable.

14. Which of the following is most analogous to the 1919 actions of Eddington, Dyson, and Crommelin?

   A. To analyze the quality of light, three different artists paint the same scene at three different times of the year.

   B. To capture a strategic mountaintop location, infantry troops simultaneously approach the summit from three sides of the mountain.

   C. To perform an operation on a patient with multiple tumors, three teams of surgeons operate one after another.

   D. To investigate a murder, three different CSI teams meet at one location and combine their findings.

15. What aspect of this passage does the introductory material help to explain?

   A. The pull of inertia

   B. The effect of clouds on light

   C. The velocity of light rays

   D. The curvature of the path of light

Answers

13. **C.** The passage implies that normally it is difficult to see the curvature of the starlight because it is obscured by the brightness of the Sun. Therefore, a solar eclipse (in which the moon covers the disc of the Sun) would create optimal conditions: It would block the Sun's light, but allow the starlight to be measured (Choice C). Choice A is incorrect because the scientists aren't trying to measure the curvature of the Sun. Choice B is scientifically inaccurate; nothing in the passage suggests this is true. Choice D is incorrect because the scientists are trying to ascertain the effect of the mass of the Sun on starlight.

14. **B.** The situation that is most analogous is one in which three different approaches or positions are taken to increase the chances of success (Choice B). Choice A adds the variable of the time of year. Choice C has the surgeons operating sequentially (one after another). Choice D includes only one location.

15. **D.** To answer this synthesis question, you must take the information provided in the introductory material and link it to some idea in the passage. The introductory material explains that particles don't follow a straight path, but instead follow a curved trajectory. This is the explanation for the "pillow effect," or the bending of light rays, the impetus for the test of the starlight described in the passage (Choice D). The introductory material doesn't explain the pull of inertia (Choice A); in fact, Einstein's theory states that inertia doesn't pull. It also doesn't explain the effect of clouds on light, which is irrelevant to the passage (Choice B). Choice C (velocity) is mentioned in the introductory material, but not in the passage.

d. Skills: Understand Structure, Evaluate Persuasiveness

Understand structure questions ask you to recognize the author's organizational plan. The plan will vary according to the author's purpose. Here are some examples:

- In a narrative passage, the author might tell a linear story—chronologically recounting events—or he or she might use flashbacks or flash forwards to reveal the plot.
- In an expository passage (one that explains), an author might compare and contrast or use a cause-and-effect structure.
- In a persuasive passage, an author might make an assertion, defend the assertion, challenge other points of view, and defend his/her position.

Evaluate persuasiveness questions ask you to ascertain the effectiveness of the author's argument. Ask yourself these questions:

- Is the argument convincing?
- Is the reasoning logical?
- Has the author provided adequate evident for his or her conclusions?
- Does the argument remain general or are there specific and appropriate examples to prove the claim?
- How does the author make his or her case?

Practice

Questions 16–17 are based on the following passage.

Adapted from *History of the Peloponnesian War* by Thucydides.

According to the Athenian historian Thucydides, Pericles, an eminent Athenian politician, presented this funeral oration at the end of the first year of the Peloponnesian War (431–404 B.C.E.).

     Most of those who have spoken here before me have commended the lawgiver who added this oration to our other funeral customs. It seemed to them a worthy thing that such an honor should be given at their burial to the dead who have fallen on the field of battle. But I should have preferred that, when men's deeds have been brave, they should be honored in deed only, and with such an honor as this public
(5) funeral, which you are now witnessing. Then the reputation of many would not have been imperiled on the eloquence or want of eloquence of one, and their virtues believed or not as he spoke well or ill. For it is difficult to say neither too little nor too much; and even moderation is apt not to give the impression of truthfulness. The friend of the dead who knows the facts is likely to think that the words of the speaker fall short of his knowledge and of his wishes; another who is not so well informed, when he
(10) hears of anything which surpasses his own powers, will be envious and will suspect exaggeration. Mankind are tolerant of the praises of others so long as each hearer thinks that he can do as well or nearly as well himself, but, when the speaker rises above him, jealousy is aroused and he begins to be incredulous. However, since our ancestors have set the seal of their approval upon the practice, I must obey, and to the utmost of my power shall endeavor to satisfy the wishes and beliefs of all who hear me.

16. Which of the following is the most accurate description of the structure of the passage?

    A. The speaker presents the action with which he disagrees; he gives the reasons he disagrees; he agrees to take the action anyway.

    B. The speaker gives his position on an action; he gives the reasons for his actions; he gives the reasons why some might disagree with his actions.

    C. The speaker presents the action with which the he disagrees; he presents the reasons he disagrees; he refuses to take the action with which he disagrees.

    D. The speaker gives his position on an action; he gives the reasons for his actions; he refutes the reasons given by those who disagree with him.

17. The speaker tries to persuade his audience to understand his position by

    A. denigrating the position of those who disagree with his position.

    B. explaining that words are far more important than deeds.

    C. presenting his position while understanding the antithetical position.

    D. refusing to acknowledge the legitimacy of any position other than his own.

Answers

16. **A.** The speaker states that most people praise the person who decreed that a speech be given at a funeral. He explains that he disagrees because a speech might not give all the recognition that is due to those who died. He then states that he will obey the custom and do all he can to honor the dead. Choice A provides the most accurate description of the structure of the passage. All the other choices present the structure in the incorrect order or contain inaccurate interpretations of the speaker's persuasive techniques.

17. **C.** As stated in Choice C, the speaker presents himself as a reasonable man who understands the position of those who believe that it is important to speak in praise of those who sacrificed their lives

in war. Although this position is antithetical to his own position, he can sympathize with the need for a funeral oration. He doesn't denigrate the opinions of others (Choice A). He doesn't say that words are more important than deeds (Choice B); he says deeds are more important. He accepts the legitimacy of other positions so, Choice D is incorrect.

3. Analysis of Data in Graphics

So much information in today's highly technological world is presented quantitatively in the form of charts, graphs, or diagrams that statistical interpretation skills are deemed essential for college readiness. You're expected to be able to read and interpret statistical data that accompanies the reading passages. To do this, you must carefully examine the graph or chart, not only the data represented on the graph or chart, but also (and equally important) the title, the *x*-axis, and the *y*-axis.

Practice

Questions 18–19 are based on the following passage and supplementary material.

The following passage is adapted from the National Parks website.

Once common throughout the southeastern United States, fewer than 100 Florida panthers (*Puma concolor coryi*) are estimated to live in the wilds of south Florida today. The current range of Florida panthers is less than five percent of their original range across Florida, Georgia, Alabama, Mississippi, Louisiana, Arkansas, and parts of Tennessee and South Carolina. Florida panthers were heavily hunted
(5)   after 1832 when a bounty on panthers was created. Perceived as a threat to humans, livestock, and game animals, the species was nearly extinct by the mid-1950s.

Today, the primary threats to the remaining panther population are habitat loss, fragmentation, and degradation. Urban sprawl, the conversion of once-diversified agricultural lands into intensified industrial farming uses, and the loss of farmland to commercial development combine to reduce the amount
(10)   of suitable panther habitat. Other factors include mortalities from collisions with automobiles, territorial disputes with other panthers, inbreeding, disease, and environmental toxins. All these other factors, however, also are related to habitat reduction.

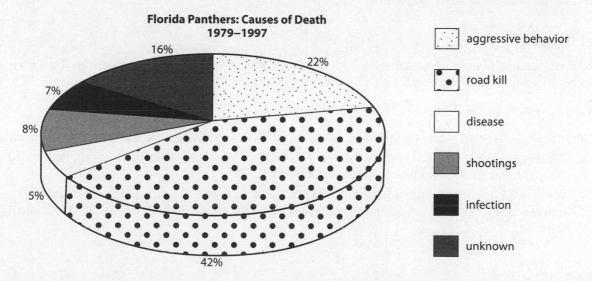

**Florida Panthers: Causes of Death
1979–1997**

- aggressive behavior
- road kill
- disease
- shootings
- infection
- unknown

16% 22% 7% 8% 5% 42%

18. Which of the following statements does the evidence in both the passage and the chart support?

    A.   The bounty on panthers has caused the rapid decline in panther population.

    B.   The agricultural development of unused land has contributed to the dwindling numbers of panthers.

    C.   Human encroachment forms the greatest threat to the survival of the panthers.

    D.   The loss of range land has limited breeding land for the panthers.

19. Which of the following details is NOT supported by information in either the passage or the chart?

    A.   Aggressive behavior among panthers is exacerbated by inbreeding.

    B.   More than 10% of panther deaths can be attributed to disease and infection.

    C.   Panthers have suffered a loss of more than 95% of their original ranging land.

    D.   More panther deaths are caused by human beings than by other panthers.

Answers

18. **C.** According to the passage, habitat loss and collisions with automobiles are the greatest threats to panthers. According to the chart, road kill (42%) and shootings (8%) combine to cause more panther deaths than any other factor. The chart doesn't support choices A, B, or D.

19. **A.** Neither the passage nor the chart links aggressive behavior to inbreeding (Choice A). Choice B is supported by the chart. Choice C is supported by the passage. Choice D is supported by both the chart and the passage.

4. Disciplinary Literacy

Disciplinary literacy is the ability to read, write, listen, speak, think critically, and perform in different ways and for different purposes. Each discipline has a specific vocabulary (think "metaphorical language" in literature; "claims," "premises," and "factions" in history/social studies; and "hypothesis formation" and "variables" in science. Thus, while you may be reading to understand character motivation in a fictional excerpt, you're reading to evaluate multiple sources of information in science and social studies. Some of the passages will be paired readings, and some of the history/social studies or science passages will contain information in chart, table, or graph form.

a. Literature

The literature selections will be taken from both classic and contemporary works of literature. They may also be from works of literary criticism (informational writing about works of literature).

Here are some strategies for reading literature passages:

- If the passage is an excerpt from a novel or a short story, try to envision the scene in your imagination.
- Picture the characters, and try to get inside their minds to understand their motivations, their moods, their attitudes, and their interaction with other characters.
- As you read, take note of the author's diction (choice of words). The word choice will reveal the author's tone or attitude toward the characters. Does he/she admire them? Despise them? Remain objective?

Practice

Questions 20–21 are based on the following passage.

The following passage is from the opening chapter of *The Age of Innocence* written in 1920 by Edith Wharton.

When Newland Archer opened the door at the back of the club box, the curtain had just gone up on the garden scene. There was no reason why the young man should not have come earlier, for he had dined at seven, alone with his mother and sister, and had lingered afterward over a cigar in the Gothic library with glazed black-walnut bookcases and finial-topped chairs which was the only room in the
(5) house where Mrs. Archer allowed smoking. But, in the first place, New York was a metropolis, and perfectly aware that in metropolises it was "not the thing" to arrive early at the opera; and what was or was not "the thing" played a part as important in Newland Archer's New York as the inscrutable totem terrors that had ruled the destinies of his forefathers thousands of years ago.

The second reason for his delay was a personal one. He had dawdled over his cigar because he was at
(10) heart a dilettante, and thinking over a pleasure to come often gave him a subtler satisfaction than its realization. This was especially the case when the pleasure was a delicate one, as his pleasures mostly were; and on this occasion the moment he looked forward to was so rare and exquisite in quality that— well, if he had timed his arrival in accord with the prima donna's stage-manager he could not have entered the Academy at a more significant moment than just as she was singing: "He loves me—he loves
(15) me not—HE LOVES ME!—" and sprinkling the falling daisy petals with notes as clear as dew.

20. The author's attitude toward Newland Archer is

   A.   indulgently amused.
   B.   scornfully mocking.
   C.   markedly hostile.
   D.   appropriately adulatory.

21. In the passage, Newland Archer's reasons for delaying his departure for the theater are motivated by

   A.   snobbery and artistic ineptitude.
   B.   inbred laziness and inscrutability.
   C.   social awareness and personal pleasure.
   D.   filial obligation and genteel delicacy.

Answers

20. **A.** The author is indulgently amused by Newland Archer (Choice A). To understand the author's attitude toward her character, you must look at the language she uses to describe him. There are no harsh or unpleasant adjectives describing Newland Archer in the passage. He arrives late to the opera because it is the right thing to do according to the rules of his society; thus, he is somewhat superficial and concerned about appearances. You also learn that most of his pleasures are delicate. True, the author appears to find him a bit self-involved and self-important, but the positive descriptive language (*the pleasure was a delicate one* and *the moment he looked forward to was so rare and exquisite in quality*) suggests she sees him as likeable. Use the process of elimination to eliminate choices B and C because they're too negative. Choice D doesn't allow for the author's obvious awareness of Archer's faults.

21. **C.** Archer decides to be fashionably late to the theater because he is aware that it is not socially correct to be prompt and because he wishes to time his entrance to the exquisite moment when the diva sings, "He loves me" (Choice C). In Choice A, snobbery could be an acceptable answer, but artistic ineptitude is not supported by the passage. Both descriptions in Choice B cannot be supported by the passage. Choice D would be correct if the passage stated that Archer doesn't want to leave his mother, but the text doesn't support that interpretation.

b. History/Social Studies

The history/social studies selection will be taken from important documents in U.S. history and/or writings about important issues in politics and the social sciences. For example, you may read Lincoln's Gettysburg Address, an anthropological discussion of tribal rituals, a linguistic analysis of gender differences, a study of conflicting educational practices, or an economic analysis of inflation.

Here are some strategies for reading history/social studies passages:

- Look for the writer's point of view. Try to ascertain any bias.
- Find the writer's purpose. What is he/she trying to accomplish?
- Evaluate the evidence in the passage: Does it support the writer's claims?
- Consider what information the writer has left out.
- If you're reading a historical document, consider the events at the time of the writing.

Practice

Questions 22–24 are based on the following passage and supplementary material.

The following passage is adapted from an article by the Bureau of Economic Analysis.

"Government consumption expenditures and gross investment," or "government spending," consists of two components: (1) consumption expenditures by federal government and by state and local governments and (2) gross investment by government and government-owned enterprises.

(5) Government consumption expenditures consist of the goods and services that are produced by general government (less any sales to other sectors and investment goods produced by government itself). Governments generally provide services to the general public without charge. The value of government production—that is, government's gross output—is measured as spending for labor and for intermediate goods and services and a charge for consumption of fixed capital (which represents a partial measure of the services provided by government-owned fixed capital).

(10) Gross investment consists of new and used structures (such as highways and dams), of equipment, and of intellectual property products purchased or produced by government and government-owned enterprises.

Government consumption expenditures and gross investment exclude current transactions of government-owned enterprises, current transfer payments, interest payments, subsidies, and transac-
(15) tions in financial assets and nonproduced assets, such as land.

**Real Government Consumption Expenditures
and Gross Investment**

Percent change from the preceding quarter

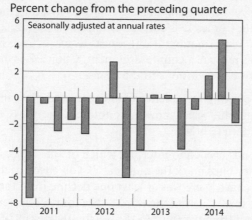

Source: U.S. Bureau of Economic Analysis, "GDP and the Economy,"
Second Estimates for the Fourth Quarter of 2014, news release (March 2015).

22. Which of the following choices best describes the relationship of the second and third paragraphs to the first paragraph?

   A. The first paragraph provides background information necessary to understand the terms in the second and third paragraphs.

   B. The second and third paragraphs provide a counterargument to terms used in the first paragraph.

   C. The second and third paragraphs illustrate and provide examples of exclusions to the terms listed in the first paragraph.

   D. The second and third paragraphs clarify and expand on terms used in the first paragraph.

23. Which of the following best represents the information in the graph?

   A. The reasons for the pronounced decline in government expenditures and gross investments from 2011 to 2013

   B. The steady growth in government expenditures and gross investments over the past four years and reasons for that growth

   C. The four-year fluctuations in government expenditures and gross investments and the sources of the changes

   D. The repetitive seasonal patterns in government expenditures and gross investments and the underlying reasons for those repetitive patterns

24. According to the graph, which of the following statements is true?

   A. Government expenditures and gross investments underwent a decline from the previous quarter in at least one quarter of every year represented by the chart.

   B. Government expenditures and gross investments increased the greatest amount from the previous quarter three of 2012.

   C. Government expenditures and gross investments declined the greatest amount from the previous quarter in the second quarter of 2011.

   D. The least change in government expenditures and gross investments from the previous quarter occurred in the first quarter of 2011.

Answers

22. **D.** The first paragraph introduces government consumption expenditures and gross investment; the second paragraph explains what *government consumption expenditures* are, and the third paragraph explains what *gross investment* is. Thus, Choice D is correct. Choice A is incorrect because the first paragraph doesn't provide background information; it introduces terms. Choice B is incorrect because the second and third paragraphs don't provide a counterargument. Choice C is incorrect because the second and third paragraphs don't present exclusions to the terms.

23. **C.** The graph represents the fluctuations in government expenditures and gross investments and where these changes arise (Choice C). The graph doesn't show a pronounced decline (Choice A), a steady growth (Choice B), or a repetitive pattern (Choice D).

24. **A.** A careful examination of the graph is needed to interpret which of the choices is true. On the *x*-axis, longer lines mark the years and shorter lines mark the quarters. If you check each quarter, you find that in every year represented by the chart, there was at least one decline from the previous quarter (from the second to the third quarter in 2011, from the third to the fourth quarter in 2012, from the third to the fourth quarter in 2013, and from the third to the fourth quarter in 2014).

c. Science

Science selections may address historical foundations for scientific knowledge or current explorations in biology, chemistry, physics, or Earth science. Many science readings will be accompanied by graphs or charts. Some passages may describe experiments or contrast theories.

Here are some strategies for reading science passages:

- Distinguish between fact and opinion in the presentation of information.
- Evaluate the effectiveness of a conclusion based on the evidence in the passage.
- Be able to cite evidence from the text to support an assertion.
- Read the title of any accompanying graphic and consider what information it relays.
- Look carefully at the labels on the *x*-axis and the *y*-axis of a graph to be sure you are aware of the variables.
- Use context clues to identify critical information.

Here are some words that signal contrast:

    although
    but
    despite
    even though
    however
    in spite of
    instead
    nevertheless
    rather than
    yet

Here are some words that signal ideas that are similar:

> and
> for example
> furthermore
> in addition
> likewise
> moreover

Here are some words that signal a cause-and-effect relationship:

> as a result
> because
> consequently
> hence
> since
> therefore

Practice

Questions 25–26 are based on the following passage and supplementary material.

Many technologies have been developed to take advantage of geothermal energy—the heat from the earth. Geothermal reservoirs are formed when hot water and steam are trapped in cracks or pores under a layer of impermeable rock. This energy is a renewable resource that can be drawn from several sources: hot water or steam reservoirs deep in the earth that are accessed by drilling; geothermal reservoirs
(5)   located near the Earth's surface, mostly located in the western U.S., Alaska, and Hawaii; and the shallow ground near the Earth's surface that maintains a relatively constant temperature of 50° to 60°F. All a geothermal system needs is heat, permeability, and water.

This variety of geothermal resources allows them to be used on both large and small scales. A utility can use the hot water and steam from reservoirs to drive generators and produce electricity for its cus-
(10) tomers. Other applications apply the heat produced from geothermal directly to various uses in buildings, roads, agriculture, and industrial plants. Still others use the heat directly from the ground to provide heating and cooling in homes and other buildings.

Geothermal Heat Pump Shipments, 2004–2009

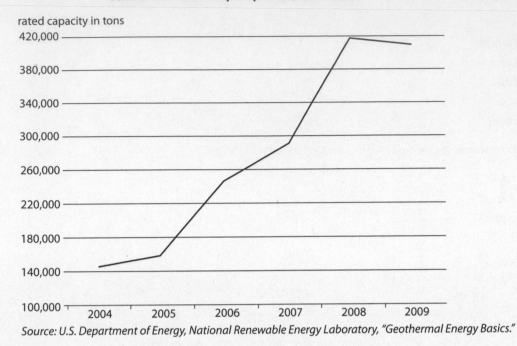

Source: U.S. Department of Energy, National Renewable Energy Laboratory, "Geothermal Energy Basics."

25. It is reasonable to conclude that the main goal of the writer of this article is to

    A. explore a variety of alternative energy resources.
    B. explain renewable energy and its advantages.
    C. compare the advantages of geothermal energy to those of fossil fuels.
    D. contrast the methods of obtaining trapped water and steam from under the Earth's surface.

26. According to the graph, which of the following statement is true?

    A. Shipments of geothermal pumps increased steadily from 2004 to 2009.
    B. Beginning in 2004, shipments of geothermal pumps increased every year except 2009.
    C. The increase in shipments of geothermal pumps was greater in 2006 than in 2007.
    D. Shipments of geothermal heat pumps decreased approximately 2% from 2008 to 2009.

Answers

25. **B.** The writer is giving some general information to explain what geothermal energy is and how it can be used as an energy source (Choice B). The writer doesn't explore any other energy sources, so Choice A is incorrect. He doesn't compare geothermal energy to any other energy (Choice C) or contrast methods of obtaining it (Choice D).

26. **D.** In 2009, shipments decreased to about 407,000 from a high of about 416,000 in 2008, approximately a 2% decrease (Choice D). Choice A is incorrect because the graph doesn't show a steady increase. Choice B is incorrect because the graph shows a decrease in 2008. Choice C is incorrect because the increase was greater in 2007 than in 2006.

D. Additional Practice

Directions: Carefully read the passages below and answer the questions that follow each passage. The questions after the pair of related passages may ask you about the relationship between the passages. Answer the questions based on the content of the passages: both what is stated and what is implied in the passages, as well as any introductory material before each passage.

Note: These practice passages are shorter than the passages on the actual SAT.

Questions 1–6 are based on the following passage.

The following passage is adapted from a letter written by George Washington in 1790.

The reflection on the days of difficulty and danger which are past is rendered the more sweet, from a consciousness that they are succeeded by days of uncommon pros-
(5) perity and security. If we have wisdom to make the best use of the advantages with which we are now favored, we cannot fail, under the just administration of a good Government, to become a great and happy
(10) people. The Citizens of the United States of America have a right to applaud themselves for having given to mankind examples of an enlarged and liberal policy: a policy worthy of imitation. All possess alike liberty of con-
(15) science and immunities of citizenship. It is now no more that toleration is spoken of, as if it was by the indulgence of one class of people, that another enjoyed the exercise of their inherent national gifts. For happily the
(20) Government of the United States, which gives to bigotry no sanction, to persecution no assistance, requires only that they who live under its protection should demean them-
selves as good citizens, in giving it on all
(25) occasions their effectual support. It would be inconsistent with the frankness of my character not to avow that I am pleased with your favorable opinion of my Administration, and fervent wishes for my felicity.

1. According to Washington, "reflection on the days of difficulty and danger which are past is rendered the more sweet" (lines 1–3) because

   A. these days follow times of peaceful coexistence with other nations.
   B. the development of a new nation is in danger.
   C. of awareness that they have led to a period of safety and richness.
   D. pleasant days spent thinking about the past are so rare in a world of turmoil.

2. Which of the following statements would most undermine Washington's assertion that "All possess alike liberty of conscience and immunities of citizenship" (lines 14–15)?

   A. The Declaration of Independence adopted in 1776 states "All men are created equal."
   B. Before the adoption of the Fourteenth Amendment, citizens of the states were automatically considered citizens of the United States.
   C. The Expatriation Act states "the right of expatriation is a natural and inherent right of all people, indispensable to the enjoyment of the rights of life, liberty, and the pursuit of happiness."
   D. Slavery continued to exist in the United States until the institution was ended by the sufficient states' ratification of the Thirteenth Amendment on December 18, 1865.

3. In the context of the passage, the statement "It is now no more ... national gifts." (lines 15–19) suggests

   A. at one time, some groups believed they had the inherent right to extend to or withhold privileges from other groups.

   B. some citizens are more indulgent than others in their interpretation of their natural rights.

   C. all citizens have the inalienable right to enjoy the natural resources of this great nation.

   D. this nation is founded on principles of toleration of diversity and belief in individual freedom.

4. The word "exercise" (line 18) most nearly means

   A. vigorous activity.

   B. training.

   C. goal.

   D. use.

5. The word "sanction" (line 21) most nearly means

   A. veto.

   B. consent.

   C. restriction.

   D. injunction.

6. In the last sentence of the passage, Washington

   A. implies that he is not usually a frank man.

   B. fears that he must admit to an inconsistency of character.

   C. admits that he relishes the admiration of his correspondent.

   D. wishes that he could be happier with his administration.

Questions 7–12 are based on the following passages and supplementary material.

Passage 1

On every worker's desk in every worker's cubicle in every major corporation in the United States, there sits a computer. To many

of us, it is inconceivable that having a computer
(5) was once considered a luxury. Now we cannot imagine doing business without data programs, e-mails, video conferencing, and the Internet. Along with this boon in technology, however, has arisen a rather surprising issue: privacy in
(10) the workplace. With easy access to the Internet, many workers cannot resist the temptation to send personal e-mails, do some Internet browsing, and maybe even shop a bit on company time. Concerned by this use of company tech-
(15) nology and waste of employee time, corporations are fighting back by installing monitoring devices. In 1986, Congress passed the Electronic Communications Privacy Act, which gave employers the right to monitor electronic com-
(20) munications in the workplace. Now companies can be sure all the "work" employees are doing on their computers is truly work related.

Passage 2

I love my job. I get to sit on an ergonomi-
cally designed chair in my own little private
(25) cubicle with a brand-new state-of-the-art computer on my sleek and shiny desk. The work is
not too demanding; my responsibility is to
check the financial records of the local stores.
These tend to come into the central office in
(30) waves: There are peaks and troughs. During a
peak, I am swamped and work nonstop to
keep up. But, then come the troughs ... a bliss-
ful hour or so of inactivity. While I wait for the
next batch of receipts to come in, I catch up on
(35) my e-mails and even do some of my holiday
shopping. This is such a great timesaver for
me. Since I can't afford my own computer, I
can keep up with friends and family while I'm
at my desk. But, recently, some of my col-
(40) leagues have heard rumors of corporate snoop-
ing. They say the company is going to install
monitoring devices to make sure we use our
computers only for company business. I can't
believe they would invade our privacy like that!
(45) I love this company and am a very loyal
employee. If the rumor proves true, I can't
imagine I will feel the same way about going to
work each day.

Forms of Workplace Monitoring

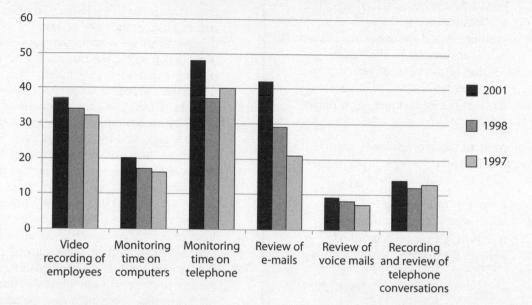

7. The author of Passage 1 repeats the word "every" (lines 1–2) in order to

   A. indicate the value of up-to-date equipment.

   B. underscore the ubiquity of computers.

   C. disparage modern society's reliance on technology.

   D. comment on the accuracy of machines versus human calculations.

8. The author of Passage 1 would most likely respond to the last sentence of Passage 2 by

   A. suggesting that computers have dramatically improved the productivity and accuracy of workers.

   B. noting that some companies have given their employees laptops to take home with them.

   C. observing that company loyalty should be based on brand loyalty.

   D. arguing that work time is just that: time to work.

9. Unlike Passage 1, Passage 2 makes use of

   A. statistical evidence.

   B. technological terminology.

   C. anecdote.

   D. historical evidence.

10. The authors of both passages would agree that

   A. corporations should prevent employees from using technology for non-work-related activities.

   B. monitoring the use of computers is an invasion of an employee's right to privacy.

   C. technology has engendered unforeseen personal rights issues.

   D. good business practices demand the involvement of employees in policy decision-making.

11. The two passages differ most in their

 A. knowledge of the technical aspects of modern technology.
 B. attitude toward the use of time in a work environment.
 C. opinion of the value of Internet shopping.
 D. sense of the importance of employee loyalty.

12. According to the Workplace Monitoring graph, the greatest increase in surveillance from 1997 to 2001 has been in

 A. telephone monitoring.
 B. video recording of employees.
 C. monitoring time on computers.
 D. review of e-mails.

Questions 13–17 are based on the following passage.

Adapted and reprinted with permission of the author, Jonathan Rappe.

The following article was written by a graduate of the Columbia Business School.

If you interviewed a random sample of business school students in 1988, the concept of environmental markets would have been foreign to virtually everyone you spoke with. If you did
(5) the same in 1968, the concept of "environment" itself would have been foreign to most. As we look forward at the opportunities for growth and investment both in the U.S. and globally in the two decades ahead, the specter of the effects of
(10) global warming and the pressure placed on natural resources from an expanding global population with ever-increasing rates of per-capita consumption will result in increased value placed on any activities, which lessen the impact of
(15) development on natural systems, including climate, air, water, biodiversity, etc.
 So what exactly do we mean when we say "environmental markets" and how are these markets going to impact the business landscape?
(20) First, the basics: Any time a unit of exchange arises from an underlying activity that is perceived to benefit the environment by either the buyer of that unit or the governing body that created the units of exchange, the main ingredi-
(25) ents of an environmental market are present. In a cap-and-trade system, the governing body places a cap on the total amount of air or water pollution that may be emitted by issuing an equivalent number of allowances, denominated
(30) in units of pollution. These allowances may be issued by the government to the business entities that are regulated by the program in amounts similar to their expected production, to lessen the economic impact, or those entities may have
(35) to purchase the allowances from the government in an auction. At the end of each specified period, usually a year, the business entities will have to surrender a number of allowances, or permits, equal to their generation of pollution
(40) during the period. As the governing entity reduces the supply of allowances available to the market in each subsequent year, the price will go up unless the regulated businesses invest in technologies that will reduce their pollution per unit
(45) of output, thereby reducing their demand and the overall market demand for allowances. Environmental markets that are not set up as cap-and-trade markets in the U.S. include the state-level markets for renewable energy credits,
(50) which are granted to producers of renewable energy and given value because utilities must purchase an amount of these credits determined by the state, and the voluntary market for greenhouse gas emissions, in which credits arising
(55) from a unit of greenhouse gas emissions avoided are granted to owners of qualifying project activities by accredited third-party verifiers and sold to voluntary buyers, primarily to conform with the buyer's goals becoming "carbon neu-
(60) tral." Companies can claim to be carbon neutral if they purchase an amount of these credits for avoided greenhouse gas emissions equivalent to the total amount of emissions they produce. This is increasingly important from a public rela-
(65) tions and corporate responsibility perspective in the United States, even in the absence of federal legislation governing greenhouse gas emissions.

13. The first two sentences of the passage are reproduced below.

> If you interviewed a random sample of business school students in 1988, the concept of environmental markets would have been foreign to virtually everyone you spoke with. If you did the same in 1968, the concept of "environment" itself would have been foreign to most.

The purpose of these sentences is to

A. suggest that the environmental movement had its roots in the recent past.

B. give examples of years in which foreign markets were environmentally savvier than U.S. markets.

C. imply that astute business students need to recognize and capitalize on unanticipated trends.

D. chastise those leaders in business education who reject the implications of global warming.

14. According to the author's use of the term "cap" (line 27), all of the following would require a "cap" EXCEPT

A. a coal-burning power plant.

B. an automobile powered only by electricity.

C. a waste incinerator.

D. a farm in which fertilizer runs off into a stream.

15. The word "allowances" (line 29) refers to

A. the amount of pollution an entity is permitted to emit.

B. the funds a business must set aside to pay for pollution clean-up.

C. the total government penalty issued to those companies who pollute the air and water.

D. the economic impact of the reduction of emissions in a given year.

16. The author believes that it is important for a company to become "carbon neutral" (lines 59–60) because

A. the company will be complying with government regulations.

B. the company will increase its environmental impact on the development of natural systems.

C. the company's image will benefit from its awareness of accountability.

D. the company's profits from foreign markets will increase.

17. The author of this passage most likely would agree that

A. government regulations that control allowable greenhouse emissions are too stringent.

B. the U.S. has a history of refusing to address environmental problems, a position that will adversely affect the growth of business in this country.

C. renewable resources in the United States are so abundant as to make regulations that govern their use superfluous.

D. in the future, more value will be placed on any activities that lessen the impact of development on natural systems.

Answers

1. **C.** In this line reference/detail question, Washington states that thinking about the past, a time when this nation faced a time of danger, is *sweet*. It is sweet because this time has been succeeded (followed) by a time that is safe and secure, *a consciousness that they [past days] are succeeded by days of uncommon prosperity and security* (Choice C). Choice A confuses the time sequence (peaceful days follow dangerous days, not the other way around). There is no evidence to support Choice B. There is no mention of the rarity or value of time to think, so Choice D is incorrect.

2. **D.** Remember that *to undermine* means "to weaken." First consider what the line reference means, and try paraphrasing it. Washington asserts that *All possess alike* the rights and privileges of citizenship. Choices A and B are supported by Washington's comments, so eliminate these two. Choice C refers to the Expatriation Act of 1868, which concerns the rights of American citizens in foreign lands, so it is off-topic. Choice D, which clearly states that slavery was legal until 1865, specifically contradicts Washington's assertion that *All* had rights, making Choice D correct.

3. **A.** This extended reasoning question asks you to understand a rather difficult sentence and then consider what it suggests. First, paraphrase the sentence: "It is now no more that toleration is spoken of, as if it was by the indulgence of one class of people, that another enjoyed the exercise of their inherent national gifts." You might come up with something like this: "We no longer think that one class of people has the right to 'tolerate' another, as if it were their natural right to grant privileges on their whim to other groups." Once you have paraphrased, you can more easily see that Washington suggests that, at one time, this attitude was the popular thought; Choice A states this clearly. Choices B, C, and D all use words from Washington's assertion, but they don't convey the correct thought. Choice B makes an irrelevant comparison among citizens' interpretations of their natural rights. Choice C simply states that all citizens have the right to enjoy natural resources, a point that is off-topic. Choice D doesn't address Washington's point about toleration. One of the tricks of the SAT writers is to use specific words from the passages in the answer choices to mislead you into choosing the incorrect response. Be sure you understand the *meaning* of an answer choice. Don't pick it because some of the words are correct.

4. **D.** This vocabulary-in-context question is not a difficult one if you follow the substitution method. First, circle the word *exercise* in the text. Next, read the context. Finally, substitute all the words in the choices for the circled word. You'll recognize that *exercise* does not refer to vigorous activity or training in this context, so you can eliminate choices A and B respectively. Although national gifts may be a goal (Choice C), it does not fit in this context as well as use *of their inherent national gifts* does (Choice D).

5. **B.** This vocabulary-in-context question might be more difficult, but you can still get the correct answer if you follow the substitution method. First, circle the word *sanction* and consider the context: *the Government of the United States, which gives to bigotry no sanction.* Because Washington has been praising the fundamental belief in equality in the new nation, you know you're looking for a word that indicates that the government does not approve of *bigotry* (prejudice or intolerance). Because the word *no* precedes the word *sanction,* you need a positive word to convey the correct meaning. Choices A, C, and D are all negative words, so you can eliminate them. *Consent* (Choice B) conveys the meaning of approval and fits the context of the sentence.

6. **C.** This is a straight reading comprehension question. Again, it tests your ability to paraphrase. Think about what Washington is saying in the last sentence. Put it in your own words. He states that he is *pleased with your favorable opinion of my Administration,* so you know he feels good about the positive

feedback he has received. Choices A, B, and D try to trick you by using specific words from the passage. Choice C correctly interprets Washington's feelings.

7. **B.** The author repeats the word *every* to emphasize the point that computers are found everywhere in the work environment (Choice B). This question is a fairly straightforward reading question, but it does test your vocabulary. You're expected to know that to *underscore* is to emphasize and that *ubiquity* means "present everywhere." Choice A is incorrect because the author doesn't mention the value or importance of computers, just that they're present. He is not disparaging (Choice C). Choice D is never referred to in the passage.

8. **D.** Choices A, B, and C are off-topic; these issues are only tangentially related to the topics discussed in the passages. The authors differ in their attitudes about what constitutes the proper use of time and equipment in the office. In the last sentence of Passage 2, the author implies that his attitude toward his job is based on his ability to use his "free time" for personal tasks. On the other hand, the author of Passage 1 clearly states, *Now companies can be sure all the "work" employees are doing on their computers is truly work related.* Therefore, the author of Passage 1 would most likely respond to the last sentence of Passage 2 by arguing that *work time is just that: time to work* (Choice D).

9. **C.** Neither passage contains statistical or historical evidence, so choices A and D are incorrect. Choice B is incorrect because technological terminology is limited to references to the Internet and computers in both passages. Because Passage 2 is a personal narrative, it can be considered an *anecdote* (a personal story), making Choice C correct.

10. **C.** Because these passages disagree on choices A and B, these choices are incorrect. Neither passage really discusses Choice D. Choice C is correct. Passage 1 indicates that personal use of the computer during work has raised *surprising* privacy issues, and the author of Passage 2 *can't believe* the company would monitor his use of the computer. Thus, this issue is an unforeseen one.

11. **B.** The passages reveal a clear difference in attitude toward employee use of time and equipment in the work environment (Choice B). Passage 1 is sympathetic to the corporation that wants to be sure *all the "work" employees are doing on their computers is truly work related.* Passage 2 sees nothing wrong with using downtime to accomplish personal tasks on the company computer. Choices A, C, and D are not relevant to the content of the two passages.

12. **D.** To answer this question correctly, you must be sure you are answering what the question asks. It is easy to look at the graph and assume that the highest column (monitoring time on the telephone) is the correct response. However, the question asks for the greatest increase from 1997 to 2001. You are looking for the biggest difference between the light gray bar and the black bar, which is in *review of e-mails* (Choice D).

13. **C.** The author refers to 1988 and 1968 to show the radical changes in the realm of environmental markets and to predict that more changes are to come. To be successful in business, one must be alert to trends; the author believes an understanding of environmental markets will be critical to the business landscape (Choice C).

14. **B.** The author explains the cap-and-trade system as one that places *a cap on the total amount of air or water pollution that may be emitted* (lines 27–28). The only choice that does not emit air or water pollution is an electric car (Choice B).

15. **A.** According to the passage, an allowance is equivalent to *the total amount of air or water pollution that may be emitted* (lines 27 28), Choice A.

16. **C.** The author mentions both public relations and corporate responsibility as reasons for a company to become carbon neutral in the absence of government regulations. Choice A is incorrect because the regulations are voluntary. Choice B is incorrect because becoming carbon neutral will lessen (not increase) the impact on the development of natural systems. Choice D is incorrect because the passage doesn't discuss company profits.

17. **D.** The author would clearly agree with Choice D: *in the future, more value will be placed on any activities that lessen the impact of develowwpment on natural systems.* This is evidenced in lines 12–15: *… ever-increasing rates of per-capita consumption will result in increased value placed on any activities, which lessen the impact of development on natural systems ….* Nowhere in the passage does the author state or imply the regulations are too stringent (Choice A). The passage discusses what the U.S. is doing to address environmental problems, so Choice B is incorrect. Choice C is contradicted by the information that the U.S. faces *the specter of the effects of global warming and the pressure placed on natural resources from an expanding global population ….*

VI. Evidence-Based Reading and Writing: The Writing and Language Test

Your ability to write well is likely to play a role in your future as you continue your education and move on to the work world. The purpose of the SAT Writing and Language Test is to provide evidence of your readiness to handle college and career writing. This evidence takes the form of revision and editing of a variety of texts in several content areas. You won't be asked to identify such grammatical units as a participial phrase or a gerund; however, you will be asked to recognize correct and effective use of language.

A. The Format of the Writing and Language Test

The test consists of 44 questions on four passages in various content areas such as humanities, social science, and science. Each passage will have some portions underlined, and four alternative answer choices will be offered or questions will be asked about the underlined portion. Many questions offer you the choice of NO CHANGE; choose NO CHANGE if you think the text is correct as written. In some passages, questions will be asked about the order of sentences and/or paragraphs. In those cases, the sentences and/or the paragraphs will be numbered. Other questions will ask you about a single paragraph or the passage as a whole.

To do well on the Writing and Language Test, you must demonstrate your knowledge of the grammatical conventions of standard written English, your ability to punctuate text correctly, and your awareness of idiomatic English usage (English that is used and accepted as correct by well-educated people). In addition, you'll have to demonstrate your ability to make correct rhetorical decisions.

What is rhetoric and what is a rhetorical decision? Rhetoric is the art of speaking and writing effectively. It involves the tools of the effective writer: choosing just the right word, knowing when to give a detail and when to omit irrelevant information, arranging ideas in the most effective and logical order, and providing clear and appropriate transitions. A simple way to think of rhetoric is to define it as the decisions the writer makes to accomplish his/her purpose effectively.

B. Specific Skills Tested on the Writing and Language Test

1. Conventions of Punctuation

a. Apostrophes

An apostrophe is used with nouns to indicate possession and in place of letters in contractions.

i. To Indicate Possession

Singular nouns: The possessive form of singular nouns is made by adding 's to the word.

Example: today + 's = today's lecture

I am glad I was present for today's lecture.

Example: Sydney + 's = Sydney's

The blanket is tucked into Sydney's crib.

Singular nouns that end in s: In most cases, singular nouns that end in **s** follow the same rule. However, in some cases, it becomes difficult to pronounce the word in its possessive form. In these cases, just the apostrophe alone may be added after the last **s** in the word.

Example: Luis + 's = Luis's or Luis'

Luis's car is parked behind the school. (or: Luis' car is parked behind the school.)

Plural nouns: If the plural form of the noun does not end in **s,** form the plural by adding **'s.**

Example: women + 's = women's

The women's artwork decorated the museum.

Plural nouns that end in s: If the plural form of the noun ends in **s,** add only the apostrophe to make it possessive.

Example: workers + ' = workers'

The workers' day began at 7:00 a.m.

Joint ownership: When two people own something together, the apostrophe is used only with the name of the last person mentioned.

Example: Jess and Jon's house

Indefinite pronouns: The possessive form of indefinite pronouns is formed by adding **'s.**

Example: one + 's = one's

It is important to protect one's identity from theft.

IMPORTANT: The possessive forms of personal pronouns never require an apostrophe.

Never use the apostrophe with these pronouns: *my, his, hers, its, ours, yours, theirs, whose.*

This situation will appear frequently on the test, and you can quickly eliminate choices that contain *its', yours', theirs', ours', hers',* or *his'.*

Note: *Who's* is the contraction of *who is;* the possessive form of *who* is *whose. It's* is the contraction of *it is.*

Example: We should determine who's going on the field trip so we know whose car to take.

ii. In Contractions

The apostrophe indicates that one or more letters has been omitted in a contraction.

Example: it is = it's (***Note:*** This is not the possessive form of **its,** which has no apostrophe.)

Example: who is = who's (***Note:*** This is not the possessive of **who,** which is **whose.**)

Example: would have = would've (***Note:*** It is never correct to write **would of, could of,** or **should of.**)

Practice

Directions: For the following practice questions, choose the correct word.

1. The (book's, books, books') cover was so worn that we couldn't decipher the title.

2. When I open my computer, I often find (its, it's, its') not on the proper screen.

3. All four of my (grandparents, grandparent's, grandparents') hometowns are in Ireland.

4. After the teacher read the poem aloud, (it's, its, its') meaning became clear to me.

5. The scientists were elated when they realized (their's, theirs', theirs) was the winning proposal.

6. We never (would of, would've) known that Charlie played the role of the Flash.

Answers

1. **book's** The singular possessive of book is ***book's.***

2. **it's** The contraction of it is is ***it's.***

3. **grandparents'** The plural possessive of grandparent is ***grandparents'.***

4. **its** The singular possessive pronoun is ***its.***

5. **theirs** The plural possessive pronoun is ***theirs.*** (The other choices are never correct.)

6. **would've** The contraction of would have is ***would've.*** (*Would of* is never correct.)

b. Commas

Commas are used for many purposes:

- To separate items in a series
- Before a conjunction that joins main clauses
- To set off any expressions that interrupt the sentence
- With a direct quotation
- To set off an appositive
- With a non-restrictive clause or phrase
- To set off geographical names, addresses, and dates
- To separate two adjectives when the word ***and*** can be inserted between them
- To separate contrasting parts of a sentence
- After an introductory phrase or clause

i. Separate Items in a Series

Commas are used to separate items in a series.

Example: My favorite desserts are coffee ice cream, chocolate mousse, strawberry shortcake, and peach pie. (words in a series)

Example: At our campsite ants crept into the tent, into my sleeping bag, and into my pajamas. (phrases in a series)

Example: Alexis explained that she couldn't find the apartment, that she had the wrong keys, and that she had to go home alone. (clauses in a series)

ii. Join Main Clauses

Use a comma before a coordinating conjunction that joins main clauses. FANBOYS is an acronym that will help you remember the coordinating conjunctions: For, And, Nor, But, Or, Yet, So.

Example: *Furious 7* is my favorite movie, but my brother finds it too unoriginal.

iii. Set Off Expressions

Commas are used to set off expressions that interrupt the sentence. Parenthetical expressions are set off with commas.

Example: The basketball finals, I am sure, will be sold out before noon today.

Example: My hometown, for example, is the number one grower of daffodils.

Words used in direct address are set off with commas.

Example: Raj, your cell phone is ringing.

Introductory words are set off with commas.

Example: Well, there certainly are a lot of comma rules.

iv. Direct Quotation

Commas are used with a direct quotation.

Example: The baseball coach shouted, "Everyone on the field in five minutes!"

Example: "Breathe deeply," the yoga instructor murmured softly, "and clear your minds of any stray thoughts."

v. Set Off an Appositive

Commas are used to set off an appositive. An **appositive** is a word or phrase that follows a noun or pronoun to explain or identify it.

Example: Mr. Esposito, the high school principal, addressed all the students this morning. (*The high school principal* is the appositive phrase.)

Note: You do not have to use commas with a one-word appositive that is closely related to the word it modifies.

> **Example: My sister Beth wears sneakers every day.**

> **Example: The French novelist Balzac also wrote plays and short stories.**

vi. Non-Restrictive Clause or Phrase

Commas are used with non-restrictive clauses or phrases. A non-restrictive clause or phrase is not essential to the meaning of the sentence.

> Example: Cell phone texting, relatively unused until the twenty-first century, is the preferred form of communication for millions of Americans. (Commas needed because *relatively unused until the twenty-first century* is the non-restrictive phrase; it is not essential to the meaning of the sentence.)

> Example: All students who come late to class will receive detention. (No commas needed because *who come late to class* is a restrictive clause; it is essential to the meaning of the sentence.)

> Example: The orchestra, which had just begun to play, was comprised of students from all over the city. (Commas needed because *which had just begun to play* is a non-restrictive clause; it is not essential to the meaning of the sentence.)

If you are not sure if the clause or phrase is essential or non-essential, here are some clues to help you:

- Try leaving out the clause or phrase. Does the sentence still make sense?
- Try moving the clause or phrase to a different position in the sentence. Does the sentence still make sense?

If your answer is *yes* to one or both of these questions, then the clause or phrase is non-essential and should be set off with commas.

vii. Geographical Names, Addresses, and Dates

Use commas to set off geographical names, addresses, and dates.

> Example: The average temperature in Juneau, Alaska, is 42 degrees.

> Example: Our new store will be located at 123 First Street, Portland, Oregon.

> Example: George Washington was sworn into office on April 30, 1789, at Federal Hall, New York City.

viii. Separate Two Adjectives

Use a comma to separate two adjectives when the word *and* can be inserted between them.

> Example: The girls wore light, colorful dresses to the prom.

Note: Do not use a comma if you would not use the word *and* between the adjectives.

> **Example: The girls wore light, colorful summer dresses to the prom. (You would not say "colorful and summer dresses.")**

ix. Separate Contrasting Parts of a Sentence

Use a comma to separate contrasting parts of a sentence.

> Example: The reading assignment is optional, not mandatory.

x. Introductory Phrase or Clause

Use a comma after an **introductory adverb clause** that begins with a subordinating conjunction such as *after, although, as, because, before, if, since, though, until, unless, when, whenever, where,* or *while.*

> Example: Because I did all the research over the summer, writing the paper was easy.

Use a comma after a **participial phrase** (a participle is a form of a verb that functions like an adjective to modify a noun or pronoun).

> Example: Thinking all day about the incident, Ella realized that she was responsible for the whole drama. (The phrase *Thinking all day about the incident* is a participial phrase modifying *Ella.*)

Use a comma after an **infinitive phrase** (to + verb).

> Example: To determine the calorie count of a snack, simply read the nutrition label on the package.

Use a comma after a long prepositional phrase or a series of prepositional phrases.

> Example: In the middle of the long night on the road, my cell phone rang.

Practice

Directions: Punctuate the following sentences correctly.

1. On April 1 1961 the first manned spaceflight was launched from Baikonur Kazakhstan.

2. Yes the flight from Milwaukee Wisconsin to Newark New Jersey takes two hours.

3. My chemistry teacher a woman from Florida has two advanced degrees from M.I.T.

4. Sophie loved most of the movie but not the ending.

5. My mother uses saffron very sparingly in her recipes for it is quite expensive.

6. Until I tried out for the play last year I had never been on a stage.

7. "The dance competition is over" the judges announced "and the team from New City High School has won first prize."

8. On the day of the SAT exam be sure to bring no. 2 pencils an eraser an acceptable calculator your picture ID and your admission ticket.

9. Ms. North my third grade teacher was seated in the row in front of me.

10. Hoping to do well on the biology test Alexander studied all weekend.

Answers

1. On April 1, 1961, the first manned spaceflight was launched from Baikonur, Kazakhstan. (Use commas to set off geographical names, addresses, and dates.)

2. Yes, the flight from Milwaukee, Wisconsin, to Newark, New Jersey, takes two hours. (Use commas to set off geographical names, addresses, dates, and introductory words.)

3. My chemistry teacher, a woman from Florida, has two advanced degrees from M.I.T. (Use commas to set off appositives.)

4. Sophie loved most of the movie, but not the ending. (Use a comma to separate contrasting parts of a sentence.)

5. My mother uses saffron very sparingly in her recipes, for it is quite expensive. (Use a comma before a coordinating conjunction that joins main clauses.)

6. Until I tried out for the play last year, I had never been on a stage. (Use a comma after an introductory adverb clause that begins with a subordinating conjunction.)

7. "The dance competition is over," the judges announced, "and the team from New City High School has won first prize." (Use commas with direct quotations.)

8. On the day of the SAT exam, be sure to bring no. 2 pencils, an eraser, an acceptable calculator, your picture ID, and your admission ticket. (Use a comma after a long prepositional phrase or a series of prepositional phrases; use a comma between items in a series.)

9. Ms. North, my third grade teacher, was seated in the row in front of me. (Use commas to set off an appositive.)

10. Hoping to do well on the biology test, Alexander studied all weekend. (Use a comma after a participial phrase.)

c. Colons

A colon indicates a pause in the sentence. It is used before a list; before a long, formal statement; and before an explanatory statement.

i. Before a List

Use a colon before a list of items, including a list that is introduced by the words *the following* or *as follows*.

Example: Our tour included all of the following cities: London, Paris, Rome, and Florence.

Note: Do not use a colon right after a preposition or a verb.

Example: We traveled through Africa by van, motorbike, and elephant. (no colon after the preposition *by*)

Example: All campers are expected to bring a flashlight, canteen, and sleeping bag. (no colon after the verb *bring*)

ii. Before a Long, Formal Statement

Use a colon to introduce a formal quotation. In this case, begin the quotation with a capital letter.

> Example: President Clinton began his Inaugural Address with these words: "My fellow citizens, today we celebrate the mystery of American renewal. This ceremony is held in the depth of winter. But, by the words we speak and the faces we show the world, we force the spring. A spring reborn in the world's oldest democracy that brings forth the vision and courage to reinvent America."

iii. Before an Explanatory Statement

Use a colon after a main clause when it is followed by a second clause or phrase that offers an explanation or a restatement of the first clause. In this case, if the statement after the colon is a complete clause and is important, you may begin it with a capital letter. (This is not a hard and fast rule. You will see it both ways: both with and without the capital letter.)

> Example: My day was a complete disaster: I got a flat tire on the way to work, missed an important meeting, and spilled coffee all over my desk. (a complete clause after the colon)
>
> Example: The Joker was driven by one goal: to destroy Batman. (a phrase after the colon)

Practice

Directions: Rewrite the following practice questions, correcting the punctuation.

1. My English teacher suggested that I memorize Macbeth's final words "Come on, let's go at it, Macduff, and damn the first man who cries, 'Stop! Enough!'"

2. The seminar covered all the alternative forms of energy solar, wind, geothermal, and biofuels.

3. From 2011 to 2014, four women won the Nobel Peace Prize Tawakkol Karman, Leymah Gbowee, Ellen Johnson Sirleaf, and Malala Yousafzai.

4. My favorite cities to visit are: New York, Los Angeles, and Chicago.

5. Sports fans are notoriously loyal Most will root for the same team forever.

6. The first crew of the International Space Station was comprised of one American and two Russians William Shepherd, Sergei Krikalev, and Yuri Gidzenko.

Answers

1. My English teacher suggested that I memorize Macbeth's final words: "Come on, let's go at it, Macduff, and damn the first man who cries, 'Stop! Enough!'" (Use a colon before a long, formal statement.)

2. The seminar covered all the alternative forms of energy: solar, wind, geothermal, and biofuels. (Use a colon before a list.)

3. From 2011 to 2014, four women won the Nobel Peace Prize: Tawakkol Karman, Leymah Gbowee, Ellen Johnson Sirleaf, and Malala Yousafzai. (Use a colon before a list.)

4. My favorite cities to visit are New York, Los Angeles, and Chicago. (Don't use a colon after a verb.)

5. Sports fans are notoriously loyal: Most will root for the same team forever. (Use a colon before an explanatory statement.)

6. The first crew of the International Space Station was comprised of one American and two Russians: William Shepherd, Sergei Krikalev, and Yuri Gidzenko. (Use a colon before a list.)

d. Semicolons

A semicolon is used to join main clauses, between main clauses connected by a conjunctive adverb or a connecting phrase, between main clauses if there is a comma within one or both clauses, or between items in a series if there are commas within the series.

i. Join Main Clauses

Use a semicolon between closely related main clauses in a compound sentence when the main clauses are not connected by a conjunction.

Example: I found the music loud and annoying; my cousins loved every note.

ii. Connection between Main Clauses

A semicolon is used between main clauses connected by a conjunctive adverb or a connecting phrase.

Example: The critics thought the dances were awkward and the songs were trite; however, we thoroughly enjoyed the musical. (*Note:* Use a semicolon before the conjunctive adverb and a comma after it.)

Example: The movie theater offered a complete refund to all the patrons; in fact, we got enough money back to pay for everyone's dinner. (*Note:* Use a semicolon before the connecting phrase and a comma after it.)

Some common conjunctive adverbs: *indeed, furthermore, however, moreover, besides, consequently, nevertheless, therefore, yet,* and *instead.*

Some common connecting phrases: *in fact, for example, for instance, that is, at the same time,* and *on the other hand.* (*Note:* Use the semicolon only when these phrases connect two **main** clauses.)

iii. Separate Main Clauses

A semicolon is used between main clauses if there is a comma within one or both clauses, or between items in a series if there are commas within the series.

Use a semicolon for clarity between clauses when there are commas within a clause.

Example: If the download takes too long, I'll have to leave before it's done; but if you stay until it's finished, we will be able to complete the project.

Use a semicolon for clarity between items in a series that contains a comma.

Example: The highest scores on the SAT were as follows: Kamal, 1540; Maria, 1580; Young, 1590.

Practice

Directions: Punctuate the following sentences correctly.

1. Before you go hiking you should remember two rules carry water and bring a fully charged cell phone.

2. Increases in the cost of tuition say administrators are driven by the increases in operating expenses consequently tuition is rising at all state universities.

3. The series isn't over yet however the outcome is all but assured.

4. My tour out west took me to Denver Colorado Las Vegas Nevada and Sacramento California.

5. I left early for the concert nevertheless I had to walk in during the first set.

6. When I finish painting the bedroom and I will soon I'll help you with the dining room and I am sure we'll be done by midnight.

Answers

1. Before you go hiking, you should remember two rules: carry water and bring a fully charged cell phone. (Use a comma after an introductory adverbial clause and a colon before an explanatory statement.)

2. Increases in the cost of tuition, say administrators, are driven by the increases in operating expenses; consequently, tuition is rising at all state universities. (Use a comma to set off an interrupter, a semicolon before a conjunctive adverb, and a comma after the conjunctive adverb.)

3. The series isn't over yet; however, the outcome is all but assured. (Use a semicolon before a conjunctive adverb and a comma after the conjunctive adverb.)

4. My tour out west took me to Denver, Colorado; Las Vegas, Nevada; and Sacramento, California. (Use a semicolon for clarity between items in a series that contains a comma.)

5. I left early for the concert; nevertheless, I had to walk in during the first set. (Use a semicolon before a conjunctive adverb and a comma after the conjunctive adverb.)

6. When I finish painting the bedroom, and I will soon, I'll help you with the dining room; and I am sure we'll be done by midnight. (Use the semicolon for clarity between clauses when there are commas within a clause.)

e. Dashes

Use a dash to indicate an important or abrupt break in thought or before a summary.

i. Abrupt Break in Thought

A dash gives the information that is set off special emphasis or indicates a sudden change in thought.

Example: This study guide for the SAT is one of the few books—no, it's the only book—that provides many examples.

Example: When I finally got my new bedroom furniture—three months after it was supposed to come—it looked terrible in my room.

Tip: When a dash sets off a part of the sentence, unless the sentence ends with that part, be sure to use a second dash (not a comma, as you'll see in some incorrect answers).

Not acceptable: Three of the items on the menu—shrimp, tuna, and crabmeat, are foods I can't eat.

Acceptable: Three of the items on the menu—shrimp, tuna, and crabmeat—are foods I can't eat.

ii. Before a Summary

Use a dash before a summary. In these cases, the dash and the colon are interchangeable. The dash is used after items in a series to indicate a summarizing statement.

Example: Swimming, biking, hiking—the trip offered a great variety of activities.

f. Parentheses

Use parentheses to enclose additional material or explanatory information that might be interesting to know but is not of major importance to the text. Information that is enclosed in parentheses can usually be removed from the text without changing the meaning or losing any essential information.

Example: One of the challenges of moving to a different state is all the paperwork (driver's license, change of address forms, registration) needed to establish new residency.

You could use a colon here for more emphasis since it is a list, or use a dash for strong emphasis. In this sentence, the material is not essential to the main meaning of the sentence, so parentheses are the proper punctuation.

Punctuation of parentheses can be tricky. Periods and other end punctuation go outside the close of a parenthesis. When the information enclosed in the parentheses is a complete sentence, treat it as such: Start with a capital letter and end with a period. A question mark or exclamation point, if it is part of the parenthetical material, can go inside a parenthesis, but another punctuation mark is needed to close the sentence:

Example: I carefully replaced the bent spoon with a new one (Who else would care about it?).

Example: We had to purchase new tires for the car. (The old ones had very little tread left.)

Practice

Directions: Punctuate the following sentences correctly.

1. David his head down in embarrassment came very late to the meeting.

2. St. Petersburg previously called Leningrad is a beautiful Russian city.

3. The starring role in the musical I can hardly believe it went to a freshman.

4. All the women on the team amazingly including me made all-state.

5. The park cold and barren in the winter chill made an unwelcome sight for the visitors.

6. Pencils, eraser, photo ID, admission ticket bring everything you need to the SAT.

Answers

1. David (his head down in embarrassment) came very late to the meeting. (Use parentheses to enclose additional material or explanatory information. Or, if you want to emphasize his embarrassment: David—his head down in embarrassment—came very late to the meeting. You could also use commas to set off this non-restrictive phrase: David, his head down in embarrassment, came very late to the meeting.

2. St. Petersburg (previously called Leningrad) is a beautiful Russian city. (Use parentheses to enclose additional material or explanatory information.)

3. The starring role in the musical—I can hardly believe it—went to a freshman. (Use dashes to indicate an important or abrupt break in thought.)

4. All the women on the team—amazingly, including me—made all-state. (Use dashes to indicate an important or abrupt break in thought.)

5. The park—cold and barren in the winter chill—made an unwelcome sight for the visitors. (Use dashes to indicate an important or abrupt break in thought.)

6. Pencils, eraser, photo ID, admission ticket—bring everything you need to the SAT. (Use a dash after items in a series to indicate a summarizing statement.)

g. Question Marks and Exclamation Marks

Question marks and exclamation marks are end marks that indicate the writer's intention: to ask a question or to make a strong or startling statement.

i. Question Marks

Use a question mark at the end of an interrogative sentence. An interrogative sentence is one that asks a question.

Example: When do you plan to take the SAT?

Do not use a question mark with an indirect question.

Example: My guidance counselor wants to know when I am going to take the SAT.

ii. Exclamation Marks

Use an exclamation mark after a startling statement or at the end of an exclamatory sentence.

Example: Wow! I got a great score on the SAT!

Practice

Directions: Punctuate the following sentences.

1. What was the most difficult question on the math test

2. The movie was awesome

3. I asked Noah if he would go to the review session with me

4. We came in first place Is that what you expected

5. Has the date for the Super Bowl been set yet

Answers

1. What was the most difficult question on the math test? (Use a question mark at the end of an interrogative sentence.)

2. The movie was awesome! (Use an exclamation mark after a startling statement or at the end of an exclamatory sentence.)

3. I asked Noah if he would go to the review session with me. (Do not use a question mark with an indirect question.)

4. We came in first place! Is that what you expected? (Use an exclamation mark after a startling statement or at the end of an exclamatory sentence; use a question mark at the end of an interrogative sentence.)

5. Has the date for the Super Bowl been set yet? (Use a question mark at the end of an interrogative sentence.)

2. Conventions of Usage in Standard Written English

a. Pronoun Use

i. Pronoun-Antecedent Agreement

Pronouns are words that are used to replace nouns. The noun that the pronoun replaces is called the *antecedent.* Usually, but not always, the antecedent comes before the pronoun.

A pronoun must agree with its antecedent in gender and number. If the antecedent of a pronoun is singular, the pronoun must be singular; if the antecedent is plural, the pronoun must be plural. If the antecedent is feminine, the pronoun must be feminine; if the antecedent is masculine, the pronoun must be masculine. For example:

Debbie brought her laptop to the Math Challenge.

Debbie is the feminine singular antecedent for the feminine singular pronoun *her*.

The *students* brought *their* laptops to the Math Challenge.

Students is the plural antecedent for the plural pronoun *their*.

If the antecedent refers to both genders, the phrase *his or her* is acceptable to avoid sexist language. When this phrasing is repeated several times in a sentence or paragraph, it may become awkward, though; you can avoid the problem by changing the sentence to the plural form:

Awkward: Each student put his or her laptop on his or her desk.

Better: The students put their laptops on their desks.

When indefinite pronouns are antecedents, determine whether they are singular or plural. Here are some singular indefinite pronouns:

each	one	no one	anybody
either	everyone	nobody	someone
neither	everybody	anyone	somebody

Here are some examples:

Each of the boys on the team took his trophy home.

Everyone chooses his or her favorite novel.

Exceptions: Sometimes, with *everyone* and *everybody,* the sense of the sentence is compromised when the singular pronoun is used. In these cases, the plural form is acceptable.

Awkward: Everyone in the crowd stood and applauded when he or she saw the float.

Better: Everyone in the crowd stood and applauded when they saw the float.

Here are some plural indefinite pronouns:

several	few	both	many

Here are some indefinite pronouns that are either singular or plural, depending on how they're used:

some	most	any
all	none	

For example:

Some of the play has lost *its* meaning.   singular in meaning

Some of the houses have lost *their* roofs.   plural in meaning

Two or more singular antecedents joined by *or* or *nor* take the singular pronoun:

Either Marlee or Olivia will bring her car to the football game.

Neither Louie nor Jaxon has taken his road test.

Every pronoun must clearly refer to a specific antecedent. To avoid a vague pronoun reference, be sure you can pinpoint the antecedent of the pronoun. Remember that the antecedent *must* be a noun.

Vague: In the newspaper it says that more young people voted this year than last year. (The pronoun *it* has no antecedent.)
Better: The article in the *Tribune* states that more young people voted this year than last year.

Vague: Jessica wants to be a doctor because it is so rewarding. (The pronoun *it* has no antecedent.)
Better: Jessica wants to bc a doctor because the work is so rewarding.

Vague: Barbara came late to every meeting, which annoyed her supervisor. (The word *which* is a vague pronoun because it has no antecedent.)
Better: Barbara came late to every meeting, a habit that annoyed her supervisor.
Or even better: Barbara's chronic lateness annoyed her supervisor.

Vague: Students are coming to school on time, bringing their books to class, and taking notes regularly. This helps the school receive federal funds. (*This* is a vague pronoun because it has no antecedent.)

Better: Students are coming to school on time, bringing their books to class, and taking notes regularly. The improved attendance helps the school receive federal funds.

ii. Pronoun Case Errors

If you've ever wondered whether to write *I* or *me,* you've encountered a pronoun case problem. Pronouns change their form depending on how they're used. The different forms of the pronouns are called *cases.* Pronouns have three cases:

- **Nominative:** The nominative case of pronouns is used when the pronoun is the subject or the predicate nominative.
- **Objective:** The objective case is used when the pronoun is the object of a verb or the object of a preposition.
- **Possessive:** The possessive case is used to indicate possession.

Nominative	Objective	Possessive
I	me	my, mine
we	us	our, ours
you	you	your, yours
he	him	his
she	her	her, hers
it	it	its
they	them	their, theirs
who	whom	whose

First, look at the whole sentence and determine what role the pronoun plays in the sentence. Is it the subject? Then use the nominative case. Is it an object of a verb or the object of a preposition? Then choose the objective case. Is the pronoun showing ownership? Then use the possessive case.

Nominative case:

- The pronoun as subject:
  - *He* and *I* want to be lab partners in chemistry.
  - Judy and *she* went shopping for decorations for the prom.
  - *Who* is going to be class president next year?

- The pronoun as *predicate nominative* (a word in the predicate part of the sentence that is linked to the subject):

  - The winners must have been *they.*
  - The team captains are Latoya and *she.*

Objective case:

- The pronoun as *object of a verb* (direct object or indirect object):
  - Jana gave *her* the gift. (*Her* is the indirect object of the verb *gave.*)
  - Hayley invited Juan and *him* to the dance. (*Juan* and *him* are the direct objects of the verb *invited.*)

- The pronoun as object of a preposition:
  - The head of the committee wanted to share the responsibility with *them*. (*Them* is the object of the preposition *with*.)
  - To *whom* should I address the letter of recommendation? (*Whom* is the object of the preposition *to*.)

Possessive case:

- Use the possessive case to show ownership and before a *gerund* (*-ing* form of a verb used as a noun):
  - The director appreciates *your* being prompt for all rehearsals. (*Your* is the possessive pronoun used before the gerund *being*.)
  - *His* quick thinking saved the day. (*His* is the possessive pronoun used before the gerund *thinking*.)

Practice

Directions: Select the correct pronoun in the following sentences.

1. This birthday present is from Vivek and (I, me).

2. The Intel Corporation awarded Julia and (she, her) the prize.

3. No one objected to (he, him, his) bringing a date to the prom.

4. Neither the seniors nor (us, we) have won the play contest.

5. Neither of these journals has all (its, their) entries.

6. Each of the participants presented (his or her, their) experiments to the panel.

7. Joe and Marco brought (his, their) calculators to the exam.

8. It is silly to let this disagreement come between you and (she, her).

9. I can't wait to find out if the champion is (her, she).

10. (Who, Whom) do you think should lead the group?

Answers

1. **me** The pronoun *I* is incorrect because the nominative pronoun is used for the subject or the predicate nominative. In this sentence, the pronoun *me* is correct; it is the object of the preposition *from*.

2. **her** The pronoun *she* is incorrect because the nominative form is used for the subject or the predicate nominative. In this sentence, the pronoun *her* is correct; it is the object of the verb *awarded*.

3. **his** The pronoun *he* is incorrect because the nominative form is used for the subject or the predicate nominative. The pronoun *him* is incorrect because the objective form is used for an object of a verb or an object of a preposition. The pronoun *his* is correct because the possessive pronoun is used before a gerund.

4. **we** The pronoun *us* is incorrect because the objective form is used for an object of a verb or an object of a preposition. The pronoun *we* is correct because the nominative pronoun is used for the subject or the predicate nominative. In this sentence, *we* is part of the compound subject *the seniors* and *we*.

5. **its** The pronoun *neither* (the antecedent) is singular. The singular pronoun *its,* not the plural pronoun *their,* must be used to refer to a singular antecedent.

6. **his or her** The pronoun *each* (the antecedent) is singular. The singular pronouns *his or her,* not the plural pronoun *their,* must be used to refer to a singular antecedent.

7. **their** The compound subject *Joe and Marco* (the antecedents) is plural. The plural pronoun *their,* not the singular pronoun *his,* must be used to refer to a plural antecedent.

8. **her** The pronoun *she* is incorrect because the nominative pronoun is used for the subject or the predicate nominative. In this sentence, the pronoun *her* is correct because it is the object of the preposition *between.*

9. **she** The pronoun *her* is incorrect because the objective form is used for an object of a verb or an object of a preposition. The pronoun *she* is correct because the nominative pronoun is used for the predicate nominative.

10. **Who** The pronoun *whom* is incorrect because the objective form is used for an object of a verb or an object of a preposition. The pronoun *who* is correct because the nominative pronoun is used for the subject. In this sentence, *who* is the subject of the verb *should lead.*

b. Agreement

i. Agreement of Subject and Verb

A verb must agree with its subject in number. A singular subject takes the singular form of a verb; a plural subject takes the plural form of the verb.

Singular: The boy climbs into the bus.	one boy
Plural: The boys climb into the bus.	more than one boy

Note: While most nouns form the plural by adding the letter *s*, most verbs in their plural form do not end in the letter *s*.

Phrases may intervene between the subject and the verb. In most cases, ignore the intervening phrase:

The boy in the black pants climbs into the bus.

In the black pants is a prepositional phrase.

Intervening prepositional phrases do not affect agreement of subject and verb, so the best approach is to cross out or bracket intervening phrases. This will avoid confusion.

Note: The subject of a sentence is *never* part of a prepositional phrase.

The bookcase filled with books covers the back wall.

The bookcase [filled with books] covers the back wall.

Be sure to find the subject and match it with the verb:

Working with the animals gives me pleasure.

Bracket the intervening phrases:

Working [with the animals] **gives** me pleasure.

Working is the singular subject; *gives* is the singular form of the verb.

Sometimes multiple phrases intervene:

Cold, moist air drifting in from the clouds above the distant mountains brings rain.

Follow the same procedure and reread the entire sentence, bracketing the phrases:

Cold, moist air [drifting in from the clouds above the distant mountains] brings rain.

Air is the singular subject; *brings* is the singular form of the verb.

Intervening parenthetical or explanatory phrases also do not affect agreement of subject and verb, so the best approach is to cross out or bracket intervening phrases. This will avoid confusion.

Bracket the intervening phrase or phrases and match the subject with the verb:

Example 1: The captain, along with four other volunteers, works with at-risk teens.

The **captain,** [along with four other volunteers,] **works** with at-risk teens.

Example 2: The community service club, like many other clubs in nearby schools, helps elderly people during snowstorms.

The community service **club,** [like many other clubs in nearby schools,] **helps** elderly people during snowstorms.

ii. Agreement Problems with Indefinite Pronouns

Singular indefinite pronouns take the singular form of the verb; plural indefinite pronouns take the plural form of the verb.

Each of the games on the computer *requires* skillful manipulation.   singular

Both of the games on the computer *require* skillful manipulation.   plural

Singular subjects joined by the correlative conjunctions *either . . . or* and *neither . . . nor* are singular.

Either the *novel* or the *play is* acceptable.

Plural subjects joined by these correlative conjunctions are plural.

Neither the *trees* nor the *bushes were* damaged by the fire.

When one subject is singular and one subject is plural, the verb agrees with the closer subject:

Neither the *parents* nor the little *girl is* afraid of spiders.

Either the *coach* or my *parents are driving* to the game.

iii. Agreement Problems with Inverted Sentences

These sentences are tricky because you'll encounter the verb before the subject. Again, the key to success is to find the subject, wherever it is in the sentence.

Note: The words *here* and *there* are never subjects.

Two months before the hurricane there **were** warning **signs.**

The plural subject *signs* agrees with the plural form of the verb *were*.

There **are** many **problems** with the economy today.

The plural subject *problems* agrees with the plural form of the verb *are*.

Be sure to read the whole sentence through to find the subject:

Onto the field **march** the **band** and **the color guard**.

The plural subject *band* and *color guard* agrees with the plural form of the verb *march*.

Over the trees **flies** a small **bird.**

The singular subject *bird* agrees with singular form of the verb *flies*.

iv. Noun Agreement

Use a singular noun to refer to a singular noun and a plural noun to refer to a plural noun. Sounds logical, right? Yet, problems do arise:

People who wish to be a teacher should apply here.

This sentence is incorrect because the plural noun *people* requires the plural noun *teachers* to be logical.

Correct: **People** who wish to be **teachers** should apply here.

Here's another example:

Incorrect: Tourists with a visa must sign in at Passport Control.
Correct: **Tourists** with **visas** must sign in at Passport Control.

Practice

Directions: Select the best word in the following sentences.

1. Into every life (come, comes) some issues that perplex us.

2. A carton of books (is, are) ready to be opened and stacked on the shelves.

3. Neither the cats nor the dog (is, are) in the house.

4. Each of the sentences on the bulletin boards (is, are) written by a student.

5. (Does, Do) either of the maps show the Himalayan Mountains?

6. One of the puzzling aspects of the physics equations (is, are) the vector analysis.

Answers

1. **come** The subject of the verb *come* is the plural noun *issues*.

2. **is** The subject of the verb *is* is the singular noun *carton*.

3. **is** With two subjects joined by *neither . . . nor,* use the subject closer to the verb (*the dog is*).

4. **is** The singular indefinite pronoun *each* is the subject of the verb *is*.

5. **Does** The subject of the verb *does show* is the singular indefinite pronoun *either*.

6. **is** The subject of the verb *is* is the singular indefinite pronoun *one*.

c. Comparisons

i. Illogical Comparisons

Use the word *other* or the word *else* to compare one thing or person to the rest of the group.

Illogical comparison: Our debate team won more prizes than any team. (This is illogical because your team is one of the comprising teams.)

Logical comparison: Our debate team won more prizes than any *other* team.

ii. Unbalanced Comparisons

Comparisons must be balanced and parallel. Use the words *than* or *as* to balance the sentence.

Unbalanced: The mathletes won as many points, if not more than, their opponents.

Balanced: The mathletes won *as* many points *as,* if not more *than,* their opponents.

iii. Faulty Comparisons

You must compare like things—apples to apples, not apples to oranges.

Faulty: After tasting all the exotic dishes at the ethnic food fair, I found I like the foods from India better than China. (In this sentence, you're comparing *foods* to *China.*)

Correct: After tasting all the exotic dishes at the ethnic food fair, I found I like the foods from India better than the foods (or those) from China. (Here you're comparing *foods* to *foods.*)

Faulty: Our track star was more dominant than the previous years. (This sentence compares the *track star* to *years.*)

Correct: Our track star was more dominant than track stars in previous years. (Here you're comparing *track star* to *track stars.*)

Practice

Directions: Correct the comparison errors in the following sentences.

1. The music of Rascal Flatts is as good as Sugarland.

2. Rachel felt her poetry was better than any student in the writing class.

3. My car is cleaner than any car in the parking lot.

4. It was clear that the flowers from the local garden shop were fresher than the florist.

5. The movie *Furious 7* was as suspenseful, if not more suspenseful than, the prequel.

6. The Spanish restaurant on South Street is better than any restaurant in town.

Answers

1. The music of Rascal Flatts is as good as **that of** Sugarland. (Compare apples to apples: *music* to *that*.)

2. Rachel felt her poetry was better than **that of** any **other** student in the writing class. (Comparisons must be balanced and parallel.)

3. My car is cleaner than any **other** car in the parking lot. (Comparisons must be balanced and parallel.)

4. It was clear that the flowers from the local garden shop were fresher than **those** from the florist. (Compare apples to apples: *flowers* to *those*.)

5. The movie *Furious 7* was as suspenseful **as,** if not more suspenseful than, the prequel. (Use the words *than* or *as* to balance the comparison in the sentence.)

6. The Spanish restaurant on South Street is better than any **other** restaurant in town. (Comparisons must be balanced and parallel.)

iv. Comparison of Adjectives and Adverbs

Use the comparative form of the adjective to compare *two* nouns or pronouns. The comparative form is formed in two ways:

- **One-syllable adjectives:** Add *-er*. (This ending is also used for some two-syllable adjectives.) For example:
  - Of the two boys, Troy is the younger.
  - Samantha is the funnier of the two sisters.

- **Most two-syllable-or-more adjectives:** Put the word *more* in front of the adjective. For example:
  - My computer is more efficient than Herb's.

Use the superlative form of the adjective to compare *three or more* nouns or pronouns. The superlative form is formed in two ways:

- **One-syllable adjectives:** Add *-est*. (This ending is also used for some two-syllable adjectives.) For example:
  - Amy is the youngest girl in the class.
  - The happiest teacher in the district is Sarah.

- **Most two-syllable adjectives:** Put the word *most* in front of the adjective. For example:
  - Dina won the award for the most cautious driver.

Here are some irregular comparison forms:

	Comparative	Superlative
good	better	best
bad	worse	worst
little	less or lesser	least
much	more	most
far	farther or further	farthest or furthest

Some adjectives, such as the following, are absolute values and cannot be intensified with *more* or *most:*

complete	round	totally
correct	square	unique
perfect	superior	
preferable	supreme	

v. Adjective/Adverb Confusion

Use an adjective to modify a noun or a pronoun, and use an adverb to modify a verb, an adjective, or another adverb.

Incorrect: The children's choir sang so beautiful that the audience was moved to tears. (incorrectly uses the adjective **beautiful** instead of the adverb **beautifully** to modify the verb "sang")

Correct: The children's choir sang so beautifully that the audience was moved to tears. (correctly uses the adverb **beautifully** to modify the verb "sang")

Practice

Directions: Correct the errors in the following sentences.

1. Of the jaguar and the hyena, the jaguar is the fastest.

2. When she won the lottery, my neighbor was the most happiest woman in town.

3. The fire chief was impressed by how speedy we all exited the building during the fire drill.

4. I thought the stuffed animal I bought for my little sister was more cuter than the one she has on her bed.

5. When we measured all ten basketball players, Jamal was the taller.

6. Among all the pottery on display, Russell's was the most unique.

Answers

1. Of the jaguar and the hyena, the jaguar is the **faster.** (When you're comparing two things, use the comparative form, *faster*, rather than the superlative form, *fastest*.)

2. When she won the lottery, my neighbor was the **happiest** woman in town. (Don't modify the superlative form of an adjective, *happiest*, with *most*.)

3. The fire chief was impressed by how **speedily** we all exited the building during the fire drill. (Use an adverb, *speedily*, rather than an adjective, *speedy*, to modify a verb, *exited*.)

4. I thought the stuffed animal I bought for my little sister was **cuter** than the one she has on her bed. (Don't modify the comparative form of an adjective, *cuter*, with *more*.)

5. When we measured all ten basketball players, Jamal was the **tallest**. (When you're comparing three or more things, use the superlative form, *tallest*.)

6. Among all the pottery on display, Russell's was **unique**. (The word *unique* is an absolute and should not be modified with *more* or *most*.)

d. Verb Use

i. Tense

Verbs tell the action or state of being in a sentence. They also indicate time by using different tenses. As you read, be aware of the tense of the passage and note any inconsistencies.

The six tenses in English are as follows:

- **Present:** Action taking place in the present
- **Past:** Action that has already taken place in the past
- **Future:** Action that will take place in the future
- **Present perfect:** Action that began in the past and continues into the present or for an unspecified or indefinite time in the past
- **Past perfect:** Action that began in the past and was completed before some other action
- **Future perfect:** Action that occurs before another action in the future

Present Tense		
	Singular	**Plural**
First person	I walk.	We walk.
Second person	You walk.	You walk.
Third person	He/she/it walks.	They walk.

Past Tense		
	Singular	**Plural**
First person	I walked.	We walked.
Second person	You walked.	You walked.
Third person	He/she/it walked.	They walked.

Future Tense		
	Singular	**Plural**
First person	I will walk.	We will walk.
Second person	You will walk.	You will walk.
Third person	He/she/it will walk.	They will walk.

Present Perfect Tense

	Singular	Plural
First person	I have walked.	We have walked.
Second person	You have walked.	You have walked.
Third person	He/she/it has walked.	They have walked.

Past Perfect Tense

	Singular	Plural
First person	I had walked.	We had walked.
Second person	You had walked.	You had walked.
Third person	He/she/it had walked.	They had walked.

Future Perfect Tense

	Singular	Plural
First person	I will have walked.	We will have walked.
Second person	You will have walked.	You will have walked.
Third person	He/she/it will have walked.	They will have walked.

Perfect tenses are always formed by using *have, has,* or *had* plus the past participle form of the verb. You also have the option of using the progressive form (*-ing*) in each tense to show ongoing action:

- Present progressive: I am walking.
- Past progressive: I was walking.
- Future progressive: I will be walking.
- Present perfect progressive: I have been walking.
- Past perfect progressive: I had been walking.
- Future perfect progressive: I will have been walking.

The present participle is the *-ing* form of the verb. In the case of the verb *to walk,* it's *walking.* These *-ing* forms cannot be verbs alone; they need a helping verb.

The past participle is the *-ed, -d, -t, -en,* or *-n* form of the verb. In the case of the verb *to walk,* it's *walked.*

Many verbs have irregular forms:

Present	Past	Past Participle
arise	arose	(have) arisen
become	became	(have) become
bring	brought	(have) brought
catch	caught	(have) caught
do	did	(have) done
drink	drank	(have) drunk
drive	drove	(have) driven

Present	Past	Past Participle
eat	ate	(have) eaten
fall	fell	(have) fallen
fly	flew	(have) flown
lend	lent	(have) lent
ring	rang	(have) rung
sing	sang	(have) sung
swim	swam	(have) swum
write	wrote	(have) written

Often verbs occur in verb phrases with a helping verb and a main verb. Some verbs like *do, have,* and *be* can be either main verbs or helping verbs:

Roberto will **do** his homework.   main verb

Roberto and Anna **do need** to practice their duet.   helping verb

Watch for sentences that have illogical shifts in tense or that use incorrect verb forms.

Illogical shift: He **searched** for signs of deer when he **notices** the tracks.

Correct: He **is searching** for signs of deer when he **notices** the tracks.   present

Or: He **was searching** for signs of deer when he **noticed** the tracks.   past

Check the tense of the context to determine whether the sentence should be in the present or past.

Incorrect verb form: We were shocked that he **had drank** all the water in the canteen.

Correct: We were shocked that he **had drunk** all the water in the canteen.

ii. Voice

Verb tenses have active and passive forms.

In the **active voice,** the subject of the sentence performs the action.

Example: Priya will play the part of Juliet in the school play. (**Priya** is the subject; **part** is the object.)

In the **passive voice,** the object (the receiver of the action) becomes the subject of the sentence.

Example: The part of Juliet will be played by Priya. (**Part** is the subject; **Priya** is the object.)

As a general rule, active voice is preferred to passive voice in standard written English. The passive voice is often more awkward and wordy than active voice. Also, it is important to avoid shifts from active to passive within a sentence.

Example: Because he had managed the store for four years, its operations were understood by him. (Awkward shift from active to passive.)

Better: Because he had managed the store for four years, he understood its operations.

The passive voice is acceptable when the subject is unknown or irrelevant.

Example: The mouse is often used in medical research.

Practice

Directions: Write the correct form of the italicized verb in the blank.

1. I was pleased to discover that I had _____ a mile. *swim*

2. By the next meet, I will have _____ my own record. *beat*

3. When I woke up, I found that two inches of snow had _____. *fall*

4. At last week's meeting, I _____ a presentation. *give*

5. Joan _____ her dog to school yesterday. *bring*

6. After the bell has _____, we can leave for the beach. *ring*

Answers

1. **swum** To show action that took place before past action, use the past perfect tense.

2. **beaten** To show action that will occur before another action in the future, use the future perfect tense.

3. **fallen** To show action that took place before past action, use the past perfect tense.

4. **gave** This is the simple past tense.

5. **brought** This is the simple past tense.

6. **rung** Use the present perfect tense to indicate an action that occurs at an indefinite time in the past.

e. Modification

i. Misplaced Modifiers

Modifiers are words, phrases, or clauses that describe, change, or specify other parts of a sentence. Modifiers are often participial phrases. For example:

> Standing on the bridge, we looked out over the entire city.

Standing on the bridge describes *we*.

> As I walked into the gym, I saw my friend waving madly.

Waving madly describes *friend*.

Sometimes modifiers are infinitive phrases:

> To accomplish all the chores, Inez got up early and got right to work.

To accomplish modifies *Inez*.

In English, changes in word order (syntax) lead to changes in meaning. A modifier that is misplaced can cause confusion. For example:

- **Maria spotted an orange cat sitting on a bench eating a sandwich.** In this example, the cat is sitting and eating.

- **Sitting on a bench eating a sandwich, Maria spotted an orange cat.** Here, Maria is sitting and eating.
- **Sitting on a bench, Maria spotted an orange cat eating a sandwich.** Maria is sitting and the cat is eating.

To avoid confusion, always place modifying phrases and clauses as close as possible to the words they modify.

ii. Dangling Modifiers

Dangling modifiers have no word or phrase to modify. For example, the following sentence is confusing:

> Walking along the side of the road, a car almost hit me.

Who is walking? Certainly not the car. To correct dangling modifiers, add the missing words or revise the sentence. You might revise this sentence to be:

> Walking along the side of the road, I was almost hit by a car.

Or:

> As I walked along the side of the road, I was almost hit by a car.

Practice

Directions: Revise the following sentences to correct the modification errors. Your answers may vary, but be sure to eliminate all modification confusion.

1. Happening in July, we were surprised by the event.
2. To protect your identity, the Internet is not a safe place to order from.
3. Reaching for my money, my wallet was nowhere to be found.
4. While swimming in the lake, my arm got a cramp.
5. My mother was impressed by the wildflowers driving through the mountains.
6. The rental agent looked for a new house for a family of six with four bedrooms.

Answers

Your answers may vary, but be sure all modification confusion is corrected.

1. We were surprised by the event, which happened in July.
2. To protect your identity, you shouldn't order from the Internet.
3. Reaching for my money, I couldn't find my wallet.
4. While swimming in the lake, I got a cramp in my arm.
5. While driving through the mountains, my mother was impressed by the wildflowers.
6. The rental agent looked for a new house with four bedrooms for a family of six.

f. Parallelism

Parallel ideas should be in the same grammatical form.

When you join ideas using conjunctions, nouns should be joined with nouns, prepositional phrases joined with prepositional phrases, and clauses joined with clauses.

	Unparallel	Parallel
Nouns	Martin Luther King, Jr., was honored for his courage, faith, and he had a willingness to stick to his beliefs.	Martin Luther King, Jr., was honored for his courage, faith, and willingness to stick to his beliefs.
Verb phrases	I like to ski, to hike, and swimming.	I like to ski, to hike, and to swim. I like to ski, hike, and swim. I like skiing, hiking, and swimming.
Prepositional phrases	We left the party early because of the inclement weather, and it was late.	We left the party early because of the inclement weather and the lateness of the hour.
Clauses	Hamlet found it difficult to believe that his father had died of natural causes and in the innocence of his uncle.	Hamlet found it difficult to believe that his father had died of natural causes and that his uncle was innocent.

Correlative conjunctions (such as *both . . . and, either . . . or, neither . . . nor,* and *not only . . . but also*), which always occur in pairs, can be tricky: Be sure what comes after the first conjunction is parallel to what comes after the second conjunction.

Unparallel: The car wash *not only* did a great job on my car, *but also* on my brother's.

Parallel: The car wash did a great job *not only* on my car, *but also* on my brother's.

Unparallel: The general had *neither* the support of his troops *nor* did he have the loyalty of his officers.

Parallel: The general had *neither* the support of his troops *nor* the loyalty of his officers.

Practice

Directions: Revise the following sentences to correct the errors in parallelism.

1. Hemingway's short stories have action, suspense, and they have memorable characters.

2. The new cars have auto-park, side sensors, and they also have Wi-Fi.

3. Enrique either wants to be a policeman or to become a fireman.

4. Galileo not only believed that the earth was round but also that it rotated around the sun.

5. The researcher was not only interested in the analysis of the compound but also in the application of the results.

Answers

Your answers may vary slightly.

1. Hemingway's short stories have action, suspense, and memorable characters.

2. The new cars have auto-park, side sensors, and Wi-Fi.

3. Enrique wants to be either a policeman or a fireman.

4. Galileo believed not only that the earth was round but also that it rotated around the sun.

5. The researcher was interested not only in the analysis of the compound but also in the application of the results.

g. Sentence Structure

Sentence structure questions concentrate on your understanding of the formation of effective sentences. You must recognize run-on sentences, comma splice errors, and incomplete sentences (sentence fragments).

i. Run-On Sentences

Two or more complete thoughts joined in one sentence without proper punctuation constitutes a run-on sentence:

> The lecture was on the life cycle of the frog it seemed to go on for hours.

A run-on can be corrected in several ways:

- **Break the sentence up into separate sentences:** The lecture was on the life cycle of the frog. It seemed to go on for hours.

- **Join the main clauses with a semicolon:** The lecture was on the life cycle of the frog; it seemed to go on for hours.

- **Change one or more of the main clauses to a subordinate clause:** Because the lecture was on the life cycle of the frog, it seemed to go on for hours.

- **Use a comma and a conjunction:** The lecture was on the life cycle of the frog, and it seemed to go on for hours.

- **Use the semicolon and a conjunctive adverb:** The lecture was on the life cycle of the frog; consequently, it seemed to go on for hours.

The most common run-on occurs when a comma joins two sentences (in what's known as a *comma splice*):

> We learned about the fall of the ancient civilization, it seemed to be a mysterious event.

Correct the comma splice by any one of the run-on correction methods.

Here are some options:

> We learned about the fall of the ancient civilization; it seemed to be a mysterious event.
> We learned about the fall of the ancient civilization, which seemed to be a mysterious event.
> We learned about the fall of the ancient civilization. It seemed to be a mysterious event.

ii. Sentence Fragments

Most sentence fragments are phrases or subordinate clauses.

Being interested in setting up a charity auction.	participial phrase
To be interested in setting up a charity auction.	infinitive phrase
Since we are all interested in setting up a charity auction.	subordinate clause

To avoid fragments, remember:

- A sentence must have a subject and a verb and express a complete thought.
- No word ending in *-ing* can stand alone as a verb without a helping verb (except one-syllable verbs like *sing* and *ring*).

Practice

Directions: Correct the following sentences.

1. *To Kill a Mockingbird* being my favorite novel because of the character of Scout.
2. The meeting seemed to last for hours, nothing new was discussed.
3. Hoping to fill all the seats in the auditorium for the school musical.
4. Raghav loves to go Pennsylvania, he has a house with a small pond where he can fish.
5. Living in Rome in a villa near the Spanish Steps.
6. A gray haze settling over the city.

Answers

Answers may vary.

1. *To Kill a Mockingbird* is my favorite novel because of the character of Scout. (Sentence fragment is missing a verb.)
2. The meeting seemed to last for hours; nothing new was discussed. (This is a comma splice error.)
3. We are hoping to fill all the seats in the auditorium for the school musical. (Sentence fragment is missing a subject.)
4. Raghav loves to go Pennsylvania; he has a house with a small pond where he can fish. (This is a comma splice error.)
5. We are living in Rome in a villa near the Spanish Steps. (Sentence fragment is missing a subject.)
6. A gray haze settled over the city. (Sentence fragment missing the proper verb form.)

3. Rhetoric

Rhetoric questions focus on style, writing strategy, and organization. You are asked to make decisions similar to those writers make when they revise their work.

a. Style

The four passages on the SAT Writing and Language Test will vary in style. You are expected to note the style (sometimes referred to as the writer's voice) and take it into consideration as you answer questions about the writers' decisions. Many passages are objective and informational; these will have a straightforward and unemotional style. Some passages will refer to information in graphic form.

In answering style questions, keep in mind that active verbs are preferable to passive ones.

> Example: **He designed the posters**. (active verb) is preferable to **The posters were designed by him**. (passive)

Practice

Directions: Select the best version of the underlined portion from the choices given.

That which distinguishes astronomy from all the other sciences is this: It deals with objects that we cannot touch. The heavenly bodies are beyond our reach; we cannot tamper with them or subject them to any form of experiment; we cannot bring them into our laboratories to analyze or dissect them. We can only watch them and wait for such indications as their own movements may supply. But we $\boxed{1}$ are confined to this earth of ours, and they are so remote; we are so short-lived, and they are so long-enduring; that the difficulty of finding out much about them might well seem insuperable.

1. **A.** NO CHANGE
   B. are nailed down
   C. are stuck like glue
   D. are here for the duration

Answer

1. **A.** In this question, you should note that the excerpt is written in a formal style. Therefore, choices B and C are far too informal for this passage. Choice D, although more formal than choice B or C, doesn't fit well idiomatically: *But we are here for the duration to this earth of ours . . .* doesn't make sense. Choice A, NO CHANGE, is the best phrasing for the underlined words.

b. Writing Strategy

These questions ask you to consider the appropriateness of the writer's strategy in either a portion of the passage or the entire passage. As you read, consider the following questions: Which is the best choice for the writer to accomplish his or her purpose? Which choice shows his or her awareness of the audience? Which choice is more effectively written? Is every piece of information relevant to the focus of the passage?

Practice

Directions: Select the best answer from the choices given.

Australasia consists of islands, great, small, and very small. Australia is so large an island that it ranks as the fifth and smallest of the continents. The insular character of Australasia has caused most of the great adventures connected with its discovery and colonization to be extraordinary feats of ocean travel rather than of land travel. $\boxed{1}$ But when we consider the size of the sailing ships, or of the mere junks, boats, or canoes on which some of the journeys were made, and the fact that the home of the explorers was not two, three, or four thousand miles away across the sea (as in the discovery of America and the West African coast), but more than triple that distance; that these hardy adventurers had to reach the unknown islands of the Pacific either around the stormy Cape of Good Hope or the still more stormy Cape Horn 2 in ships on which we might hesitate to embark in order to cross the Bay of Biscay or the Irish Channel, the achievements of the Australasian pioneers in the sixteenth, seventeenth, eighteenth, and early nineteenth centuries become almost unbelievable in their heroism and power of endurance.

1. At this point, the writer is considering adding the following sentence:

   Land travel during that time period was mostly accomplished by means of horse-drawn wagons.

   Should the writer add this sentence here?

   A. Yes, because it would add a detail that isn't included anywhere in the passage.
   B. Yes, because land travel is contrasted with ocean travel in the passage.
   C. No, because land travel vehicles aren't relevant to the passage.
   D. No, because the writer doesn't mention the pioneers until later in the passage.

2. The writer is considering deleting the underlined portion. If he does so, the passage will primarily lose
   A. nothing that adds any depth or detail to the passage.
   B. a physical description of the ships that allows the reader to visualize them clearly.
   C. a detail that adds dramatic intensity to the point being made.
   D. a foreshadowing of the conclusion.

Answers

1. **C.** The writer shouldn't add the information because the passage is mainly about sea travel; thus, choices A and B are incorrect. Choice D is incorrect because the pioneers in this passage travel by sea, not by land.

2. **C.** If the writer deletes the underlined portion, he will lose an image that adds intensity to the point that the ships weren't particularly sturdy, Choice C. Choice A is incorrect because the underlined part does add depth to the passage. It isn't Choice B because the underlined part doesn't give a clear picture of what the ships looked like. In no way does the underlined part foreshadow a conclusion (Choice D).

c. Organization

Questions on organization deal with the order and coherence of ideas in the passages. One of the keys to achieving coherence is the effective use of transitional words and phrases.

i. Order and Coherence

You will notice as you take the SAT Writing and Language Test that sometimes the sentences in the passage are numbered, and sometimes the paragraphs are numbered. This numbering tells you that you will encounter questions about order. Use the context clues to help you determine the best order. For example, if a person or place is mentioned by name, ask yourself, "Has this name been introduced or identified?" If the introduction comes later in the passage, then you know you must logically rearrange the order of the sentences. The same holds true for paragraph order. Use logic and look for clues within the passage to what happens next.

Practice

Directions: Select the best answer from the choices given.

(1) First, be sure you have gathered all your supplies in one convenient place. (2) Water that is too hot may scald the puppy, and water that is too cold will give him a chill. (3) Brush the puppy thoroughly before putting him in the water to remove any loose hair. (4) Next, fill the sink or tub with water at the correct temperature. (5) Shampoo the head and face first. (6) Finally, wrap him in a soft towel and rub him gently until he is completely dry. (7) Get the puppy wet and then apply shampoo. (8) Then rinse all the soap out until the water runs clear. (9) Giving your puppy his first bath can be a daunting task, but if you complete the following steps in order, you'll be successful.

1. The passage is best organized in which order?

   A.   1, 4, 2, 3, 5, 6, 9, 8, 7
   B.   2, 8, 9, 1, 5, 4, 7, 3, 6
   C.   9, 2, 8, 1, 3, 7, 4, 5, 6
   D.   9, 1, 4, 2, 3, 7, 5, 8, 6

Answer

1. **D.** The logical order is Choice D. Use the clues in the paragraph to help you arrange the sentences. For example, Sentence 6 should be last because it begins with *Finally.* Sentence 1 might look like it should be first because it begins with *First,* but a careful look at Sentence 9 will help you see that it contains the phrase *complete the following steps in order.* That is your clue that it should be the first sentence. Use logic to arrange the other sentences: you can't shampoo him until you've filled the tub. You can't dry him until you've rinsed out the soap.

Here is the paragraph in logical order:

(9) Giving your puppy his first bath can be a daunting task, but if you complete the following steps in order, you'll be successful. (1) First, be sure you have gathered all your supplies in one convenient place. (4) Next, fill the sink or tub with water at the correct temperature. (2) Water that is too hot may scald the puppy, and water that is too cold will give him a chill. (3) Brush the puppy thoroughly before putting him in the water to remove any loose hair. (7) Get the puppy wet and then apply shampoo. (5) Shampoo the head and face first. (8) Then rinse all the soap out until the water runs clear. (6) Finally, wrap him in a soft towel and rub him gently until he is completely dry.

ii. Transitional Words and Phrases

Transitional words and phrases link ideas and indicate the relationship of ideas within a sentence, a paragraph, or a passage. They are essential tools for a writer who wants to achieve a clear and logical flow of ideas.

Important Transitional Words and Phrases			
Words Used to Indicate an Example		**Words Used to Show a Result**	
For example For instance	Specifically	Consequently Hence	Accordingly Therefore
Words Used to Indicate a Reason		**Words Used to Indicate More Information**	
As Because	Since Due to	Besides In addition	Moreover Furthermore
Words Used to Contrast		**Words Used to Show Similarity**	
Although But However In contrast Nevertheless Whereas	While Yet On the other hand Still Despite	Another Similarly Likewise Also	Again In the same way Too Equally
Words Used to Establish Time Relationships		**Words Used for Emphasis**	
Before During After At last At this point	Later Soon Next Until Recently	Then Then again Once At the same time Assuredly	Indeed Clearly To be sure Without doubt

Practice

Directions: Select the best transitional word or phrase to fit in the sentences.

1. There was a terrible accident on the highway this morning; _____, traffic was snarled for miles.
   A. however
   B. nevertheless
   C. in addition
   D. consequently

2. It is below zero in Green Bay today, _____ it is warm and mild here in Miami.
   A. then
   B. but
   C. likewise,
   D. similarly,

3. The new school building will have several well-equipped laboratories; _____, it will help alleviate overcrowding in the other school buildings.
   A. although
   B. furthermore
   C. likewise
   D. whereas

4. My brother didn't study for his written road test; _____, he failed and has to take it again.
   A. nevertheless
   B. however
   C. hence
   D. for example

Answers

1. **D.** Use consequently to show *as a result.*

2. **B.** Use *but* to show contrast.

3. **B.** Use *furthermore* to add information.

4. **C.** Use *hence* to show a result.

d. Redundancy

In standard written English, conciseness is a goal. It is best to express your ideas in as few well-chosen words as possible. Always be alert for repetitive and wordy expressions such as the following:

true fact	various different	new innovations
important essentials	extreme in degree	the future to come
two equal halves	large in size	due to the fact that
consensus of opinion	round in shape	ten years in age
unexpected surprise	close proximity	problem that needs a solution

For example:

At the present time, the problem the community is currently facing must be addressed.

At first reading, you may think the sentence is grammatically correct. You'd be almost right. However, if you reread the sentence from the beginning, you'll see the phrase *At the present time.* This phrase makes the word *currently* redundant. You'll have to find a choice that eliminates this redundancy.

Practice

Directions: Rewrite the following sentences to avoid redundancies and wordiness. Your answers might be slightly different. Do not worry if this is the case; your goal is to eliminate the redundant expressions.

1. By associating and connecting together, the two teams were able to come up with a new innovation.

2. We chose a sign that was large in size due to the fact that we hoped every person and all people would be able to see it.

3. Every year the teachers do an annual review of their classroom supplies.

4. I told you the reason why you should take the SAT is because it is a good test.

5. Larry will tell you the honest truth about his past experience.

6. It is the consensus of opinion that we should advance forward and join together to solve the problems that need solutions.

Answers

1. **By connecting, the two teams were able to come up with an innovation.** The words *associating* and *connecting* mean essentially the same thing, as do the words *new* and *innovation*. The sentence is more concise with these unnecessary words eliminated.

2. **We chose a large sign so everyone could see it.** The expression *large in size* is redundant; *large* obviously refers to size. *Due to the fact that* is another wordy expression, as is *every person and all people*.

3. **The teachers do an annual review of their classroom supplies.** *Annual* means "every year," so it is redundant to include both.

4. **I told you to take the SAT because it is a good test.** *The reason why . . . is because* is a wordy expression.

5. **Larry will tell you the truth about his experience.** The truth is by definition honest; it does not need to be qualified. In this sentence, the word *experience* does not need to be preceded by *past;* that point is implied by the sentence.

6. **The consensus is that together we should advance and solve the problems.** The word *consensus* means "agreement of opinion," so *of opinion* is unnecessary. An advance is always forward and problems always need solutions. Aim for conciseness and eliminate these unnecessary words.

e. Idioms

Idioms are expressions or verb phrases that are used in English. The problem frequently arises when the incorrect preposition is used with a verb. Unfortunately, there are no rules—you just need to know what is accepted as correct. Usually, you can trust your ears—go with what sounds right.

Here are some common idioms:

abide by	complain about	method of
agree to (something)	conform to	object to
agree with (someone)	consists of	opinion of
apply for	depend on	participate in
approve of	differ from	prefer to
argue about (something)	discriminate against	preoccupied with
argue with (someone)	escape from	prohibited from
arrived at	in contrast to	protect from
believe in	insensitive to	relevant to
capable of	insight into	subscribe to
comment on	insist upon	succeeded in

Practice

Directions: Correct the idiom errors in the following sentences.

1. Ignacio proved that he was capable to rebuild the engine on the '62 Chevy.

2. While I was reading *Macbeth,* I was amazed that Shakespeare had such insight on ambitious leaders who ruthlessly seize power.

3. Alex tried to get his mother's attention, but she was preoccupied on the complicated recipe she was preparing.

4. Contrasting with the ornate style of Gothic architecture, modern geometric buildings have clean lines and sharp edges.

5. Because my dad is such a great cook, my family prefers eating at home rather than eating in restaurants.

Answers

1. Ignacio proved that he was **capable of rebuilding** the engine on the '62 Chevy.

2. While I was reading *Macbeth,* I was amazed that Shakespeare had such **insight into** ambitious leaders who ruthlessly seize power.

3. Alex tried to get his mother's attention, but she was **preoccupied with** the complicated recipe she was preparing.

4. **In contrast to** ornate Gothic architecture, modern geometric buildings have clean lines and sharp edges.

5. Because my dad is such a great cook, my family **prefers** eating at home **to** eating in restaurants.

f. Diction and Vocabulary

Diction means "word choice." A diction error occurs when a word is used incorrectly or inappropriately.

On the SAT, diction errors often occur with words that look alike, such as *refer/infer, prospective/perspective, formally/formerly, defensible/defensive,* or *reliable/reliant.* Be alert and careful as you read the sentences.

Vocabulary questions on the Writing and Language Test will measure your ability to understand the meaning of words in context and to recognize words that aren't used correctly.

Here are some commonly misused words:

- *among/between:* Use *between* for two people or things ("between my brother and me"). Use *among* for three or more ("among all my friends").
- *fewer/less:* Use *fewer* for anything you can count or plural words ("fewer times at bat"). Use *less* for whole quantities or singular words ("less pain").
- *amount/number:* Use *amount* for whole quantities ("amount of homework"). Use *number* for things you can count ("number of math problems").
- *being as/being that:* Avoid both these phrases as they are almost never correct; use *because* or *since* instead.
- *irregardless/regardless: Irregardless* is nonstandard; use *regardless* instead.
- *off of/off:* Avoid using *of* with the preposition *off.*
- *reason . . . is because/reason . . . is that:* Avoid the expression *the reason* (for something) *is because.* It is a nonstandard expression. The preferable expression is *the reason* (for something) *is that.*

Practice

Directions: Select the best word in the following sentences.

1. The choice for the lead in the play is (between, among) Ella and Sophie.

2. The Battle of the Classes will be (between, among) all four grades in the high school.

3. Because of budget cuts, (less, fewer) awards will be given to athletes this year.

4. When he was accused of plagiarism, the student became quite (defensible, defensive), claiming his work was completely original.

5. A large (amount, number) of students attended the pep rally on the football field.

6. From the (perspective, prospective) of an incoming freshman, high school may seem overwhelming.

7. I am sure I took the book (off of, off) the desk and put it away.

Answers

1. **between** Use *between* to refer to two people or things.

2. **among** Use *among* to refer to more than two people or things.

3. **fewer** *Fewer* refers to a number of individual things. (You can count awards.)

4. **defensive** You're defensive when you try to avoid or deflect criticism. *Defensible* means capable of being explained or protected from attack.

5. **number** Number refers to individual things (such as students) that can be counted.

6. **perspective** *Perspective* refers to one's viewpoint or outlook; *prospective* refers to something likely to occur.

7. **off** The phrase *off of* is nonstandard.

g. Quantitative Literacy

The Writing and Language Test reinforces the SAT's emphasis on literacy across the curriculum by including information presented in graphic form and by asking graphic-based questions.

You might be asked to analyze graphically presented data as part of your rhetorical decision-making. For example: Should the writer include the information? Which wording choice is the most concise and appropriate? What is best way to synthesize the information from the passage and the chart or graph?

Example:

Many visitors come to refuges to enjoy the spectacular vistas in Red Rocks Lakes National Wildlife Refuge, part of the greater Yellowstone ecosystem. Unfortunately, these vistas are often obscured by haze caused by fine particles in the air. Each major chemical component that contributes to haze or visibility at Red Rocks Lakes NWR is shown in the pie chart below. Organic compounds, soot, and dust reduce visibility as well. Monitoring for particles has not been done at Red Rocks Lakes NWR, but is being conducted about 100 miles east of Red Rocks Lakes at Yellowstone National Park. Due to the close proximity, the conditions at Yellowstone National Park are considered representative of the conditions at Red Rocks Lakes NWR. The pie chart below shows the average percent contribution to haze at Yellowstone National Park by each major chemical component. The single primary contributor to the haze is the pollution caused by human industrialization. Elemental carbon (EC) and organic carbon (OC) contribute to about 30% of the haze, and sources include wildfires, energy development, and motor vehicles. Sulfate contributes to about 15% of the haze and is largely due to large industrial sources such as coal-fired power plants and oil and gas development. Nitrate is a significant contributor to haze in winter and is a result of many sources including power generation, oil and gas development, motor vehicles, fertilizers, and livestock. Fine soil and coarse mass (dust) contribute 7% of the haze. Rayleigh scattering is a natural optical phenomenon where light is deflected by matter. This optical phenomenon gives the atmosphere its blue color. The other contributors to visibility are a combination of man-made and natural elements.

Yellowstone National Park Visibility/Haze Contributions

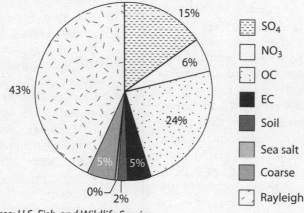

Source: U.S. Fish and Wildlife Service

Practice

Directions: Select the best answer from the choices given.

1. Which choice offers an accurate interpretation of the data on the pie chart?
   A. Less organic carbon than elemental carbon contributes to the haze.
   B. Man-made elements account for twice as much haze as a combination of natural elements.
   C. Using the data on the chart, it is difficult to determine what causes the haze at Red Rocks Lakes.
   D. While human beings are the major cause of the low visibility, a natural optical phenomenon accounts for a large portion of the haze.

Answer

1. **D.** According to the information in the chart and in the passage, Rayleigh, a natural optical phenomenon, causes 43% of the haze. Choices A and B are not accurate based on the statistics in the chart. Choice C is contradicted by the information in the chart.

C. Additional Practice

Directions: Select the best answer from the choices given.

Questions 1–12 are based on the following passage.

Featuring the Special Feature Article

A special feature article may be defined as a detailed presentation of facts in an interesting form adapted to rapid reading **1**for the purpose being to entertaining or informing the average person. It usually deals with (A) recent news that is **2**of sufficient importance to warrant elaboration; (B) timely or seasonal topics not directly connected with news; or (C) subjects of general interest that have no immediate connection with current events.

Although frequently concerned with news, the special feature article is more than a mere news story. It aims to supplement the bare facts of the news report by giving more detailed information **3**regarding, the persons, places, and circumstances that appear in the news columns. News must be published as fast as it develops, with only enough explanatory material to make it intelligible. The special article fills in the bare outlines of the hurried news sketch with the life and color that make the picture complete. The special feature article **4** must not be confused with the type of news story called the "feature," or "human interest," story. The latter **5**undertake to present minor incidents of the day's news in an entertaining form. Like the important news story, it is published immediately after the incident occurs. Its purpose is to appeal to newspaper readers by bringing out the humorous and pathetic phases of events that have little real news value. It exemplifies, **6**however, merely one distinctive form of news report.

The special feature article differs from the older type of magazine article **7**not so much in subject but in form and style. The most **8**marked difference lies in the fact that it

supplements the recognized methods of literary and scientific exposition with the more striking devices of narrative, descriptive, and dramatic writing.

The range of subjects for special articles is as wide as human knowledge and experience. Any theme is suitable that can be made interesting to a considerable number of persons. **9**A given topic may make either a local or a general appeal. If interest in it is likely to be limited to persons in the immediate vicinity of the place with which the subject is connected, the article is best adapted to publication in a local newspaper. If the theme is one that appeals to a larger **10**public, the article is adapted to a periodical of general circulation. Often local material has interest for persons in many other communities, and hence **11**is suitable for either newspapers or for magazines.

Some subjects have a peculiar appeal to persons engaged in a particular occupation or devoted to a particular avocation or amusement. Special articles on these subjects of limited appeal are adapted to agricultural, trade, or other class publications, particularly to periodicals that present **12**their material in a popular rather than a technical manner.

1. **A.** NO CHANGE
   B. for the purpose of entertaining and informing
   C. being to entertain and inform
   D. being entertaining and informing for

2. All of the following are acceptable substitutes for the underlined part EXCEPT:
   A. sufficiently important
   B. important enough
   C. sufficient enough
   D. of enough importance

3. **A.** NO CHANGE
   B. regarding; the persons, places, and circumstances
   C. regarding, the persons, places, and circumstances,
   D. regarding the persons, places, and circumstances

4. At this point, the writer is considering inserting the following information:

   , written with the perspective afforded by an interval of a few days or weeks,

   Should the writer make this addition here?

   A. Yes, because it demonstrates that the news article is written on timely topics rather than general-interest topics.
   B. Yes, because it clarifies the contrast between a news article and a feature article.
   C. No, because it is makes a point that has nothing to do with news articles.
   D. No, because it contains information that is explained later in the sentence.

5. **A.** NO CHANGE
   B. undertakes
   C. is undertaking
   D. have undertaken

6. **A.** NO CHANGE
   B. nevertheless,
   C. therefore,
   D. thereafter,

7. **A.** NO CHANGE
   B. not so much in subject but form and style
   C. not as much in subject but in form and style
   D. not so much in subject as in form and style

8. Which of the following is NOT an acceptable replacement for the underlined word?
   A. striking
   B. manifest
   C. stained
   D. obvious

9. Which choice provides a supporting example with details that reinforce the main point of the paragraph?
   A. NO CHANGE
   B. A given topic may be as local as improvements to the town pool or as general as Internet fraud.
   C. A given topic may have some things about it to appeal to local people and some things that have a broader audience.
   D. A given topic may give essential information about local issues or it may give specific information about larger, international events.

10. **A.** NO CHANGE
    B. public; the
    C. public: the
    D. public the

11. **A.** NO CHANGE
    B. is suitable either for
    C. are suitable for either
    D. is suitable to either

12. **A.** NO CHANGE
    B. its
    C. it's
    D. one's

Answers

1. **B.** Wordiness: You need to choose the least wordy verb phrase that is idiomatically correct and effective. In choices A, C, and D the word *being* is unnecessary. Also, the phrase *for the purpose* should be followed by the preposition *of*.

2. **C.** Redundancy: The phrase *sufficient enough* is redundant. Choices A, B, and D are all acceptable replacements because they are grammatically correct and aren't redundant.

3. **D.** Punctuation: Choice D correctly removes the comma after *regarding*. There is no need for any punctuation mark after *regarding* in this sentence, so choices A, B, and C are incorrect.

4. **B.** Rhetoric: Yes, the information should be included because it adds a necessary clarification of the difference between the news article and the feature article. It doesn't refer to the news article (Choice A); it refers to the special feature article. Choice C and D are incorrect because the addition is relevant and not redundant.

5. **B.** Subject-verb agreement: In this sentence, the subject is *latter;* it requires the singular form of the verb *undertakes.* Choice A is incorrect because *undertake* is the plural form of the verb. Choice C incorrectly changes the tense to the present progressive tense. Choice D is incorrect because *have undertaken* is the plural form of the present perfect tense.

6. **C.** Transitional words: Choice C, *therefore,* correctly provides the sense of *as a result,* which expresses the relationship between this sentence and the previous sentence. Choices A and B incorrectly suggest a contrast between the two sentences. Choice D, *thereafter,* incorrectly suggests a subsequent time relationship between the sentences.

7. **D.** Parallelism: Choice D correctly uses the parallel comparison *not so much in . . . as in . . . .* Choices A, B, and C incorrectly use the word *but* rather than *as* to express the comparison.

8. **C.** Diction: Choices A, B, and D are all acceptable alternatives to *marked* (meaning obvious or prominent) in this context. Choice C, *stained,* is not acceptable because it denotes blemished or discolored.

9. **B.** Rhetoric: Choice B is the best answer because it adds supporting examples (*improvements to the town pool* and *Internet fraud*). Choices A, C, and D are very general and don't contain specific examples to reinforce the main point that there is a large range of subjects.

10. **A.** Punctuation: The comma is the correct punctuation mark after an introductory adverbial clause. Choice B incorrectly uses the semicolon. Choice C incorrectly uses the colon. Choice D incorrectly omits the comma.

11. **B.** Agreement/Parallelism/Idiom: Choice B correctly uses the singular verb *is* to agree with the singular subject *material* and correctly places the preposition *for* after *suitable* and before *newspapers* (necessary because of the *for* before *magazines*). Choice A is not parallel because it places *either* after the preposition *for*. Choice C is incorrect because it is not parallel and lacks agreement (it uses the plural form of the verb *are* instead of the singular *is*). Choice D is not parallel and uses the incorrect idiom *suitable to.*

12. **A.** Pronoun agreement: Choice A correctly uses the plural pronoun *their* to agree with the plural antecedent *periodicals*. Choice B is incorrect because *its* is a singular pronoun. Choice C is incorrect because *it's* is the contraction of *it is*. Choice D is incorrect because *one's* is the possessive form of the singular indefinite pronoun.

VII. The SAT Essay

The SAT Essay is an optional component of the test. Some colleges require a score on the essay; others do not. Before you sign up for the SAT Essay, check the website or admissions material for the colleges to which you plan to apply to see if the essay is required for admission.

The purpose of the essay is to demonstrate your proficiency in reading, analysis, and writing. You have to read a presented argument, analyze the reasoning of the argument, and present your analysis of the evidence in a clearly written, well-reasoned essay. The topic of the argument will vary from test to test, but the arguments are drawn from such areas of general interest as the arts, the sciences, culture, politics, and current trends. You don't need any prior knowledge of the topic to write the essay.

A. Format of the Essay

You'll have 50 minutes to write the essay.

The essay portion of the test is set up as follows:

1. **First, you are given general directions:**

Read the following passage and consider the author's argument. Note how the author uses

- evidence, such as reasons, facts, or examples, to support his claim.
- logical reasoning to support and develop his ideas.
- stylistic elements such as diction and emotional appeals.

---

2. **Next, the source text will appear in the form of an essay arguing a claim.**
3. **The source text will be followed by the prompt:**

Write an essay in which you analyze how the author builds an argument to convince the reader that [the author's claim will be summarized here]. Consider how the author uses evidence, such as reasons, facts, or examples, to strengthen the logic of his claim. As you write your essay, consider his reasoning and his use of stylistic elements such as word choice and appeals to emotion.

In your essay, do not explain your position on this issue; rather, analyze how the author builds his argument to accomplish his purpose.

B. Critical Reading and Annotating

Critical reading and annotating (marking the text with notes) is the first (and a very important) step. You should spend at least 10 minutes reading critically and annotating. Annotating encourages you to think as you read and helps you engage with the text. As you read the essay, think about the claim the author makes and the evidence he provides in order to convince the reader to accept his claim as true. Annotate as you read, marking up your text to highlight main points, circle facts and examples used as evidence, underline effective word choice, and bracket appeals to emotion. Use any system that works for you; just maintain your focus on the evidence the writer uses to prove his claim.

C. Planning

It's helpful to begin by spending about 5 minutes writing a plan for your essay. Look over your annotated text and consider the main points you want to cover.

Remember: You aren't arguing **your** position on the topic; you are analyzing the effectiveness of the author's argument.

Begin by finding the author's thesis; exactly what is his claim?

Then consider: How does this author back up the claim? What form does the evidence take?

Here are some rhetorical strategies that an author might use to support a claim:

- Juxtaposition (author compares unlike ideas to make a point)
- Appeal to authority
- Statistical information
- Historical facts
- Diction—emotionally charged words
- Synthesis of multiple sources
- Comparison/contrast
- Figurative language (metaphors, similes, personifications)
- Allusions (biblical, mythological, pop culture)
- Assumptions (some logical; some not)
- Repetition
- Tone (sarcastic, humorous, accusatory, mournful)
- Irony

D. Writing

Spend about 30 minutes writing the essay.

1. State Your Analytical Thesis Clearly in the Introductory Paragraph

Having an original opening paragraph, one that will grab the attention of your readers, is always an advantage. However, in a timed analytical essay, you don't need a long introductory paragraph. Get to the point—the author's claim—quickly, so you have time to develop your analysis.

2. Develop Your Analysis

In the topic sentence of your first body paragraph, state the first technique the author uses to support his claim. Then explain how he uses it to support his argument. Evaluate its effectiveness as a rhetorical strategy. Cite specific examples from the text. If you have a second major point to make, begin a new paragraph. Use your concluding paragraph for a summative evaluation. Comment on the effectiveness or ineffectiveness of the author's argument in achieving his purpose.

3. Organize Coherently

As you develop your analysis, be sure to use transitional phrases. Transitional words and phrases link ideas and indicate the relationship of ideas within a sentence, a paragraph, or a passage. They are essential tools for a writer who wants to achieve a clear and logical flow of ideas.

See the table in Chapter 6 (page 128) for examples of transitional words and phrases.

These words and phrases are the key to coherence, and graders are trained to spot them. When you begin a new paragraph, use a phrase like "*Another* strategy . . ." or "She *also* cites statistics to . . . ." Use transitional phrases within the paragraph as well to help your ideas flow logically.

4. Use Active Verbs

To make your writing lively rather than flat, avoid state of being verbs (forms of the verb *to be*) and weak passive sentences. Also, avoid phrases like *I believe* and *I think,* as well as clichés.

- **Weak:** I think the author believes that no one reads newspapers anymore.
- **Strong:** The author generalizes when she argues that no one reads the newspaper anymore.
- **Weak:** The author uses some words with emotional appeal to show that government officials avoid making decisions.
- **Strong:** The author accuses bureaucrats of "dithering about" rather than making tough decisions.

5. Vary Your Sentence Structure

Most students have a tendency to write simple and compound sentences that follow the subject-verb pattern. Because you'll have very little time to revise your essay, be aware of sentence structure as you write.

- Start a sentence with a participial phrase:

  Instead of: The author chooses her words carefully to make her point about government spending.

  Write: Choosing her words carefully, the author makes a cogent point about government spending.

- Start with a subordinate clause:

  Because she addresses the counterargument, the author strengthens her claim that the current tax code is unfair.

- Start with an adverb:

  Consistently, the author cites statistics to prove her point about social media.

E. Proofreading

Try to allow 5 minutes to read over your essay. Be sure your writing is legible. If you see a mistake, change it by crossing out neatly or erasing carefully. You may insert a word or phrase above the line with a caret (^). *Remember:* Do not write outside the black lines.

F. The Essay Rubric

When you get your essay score, you'll see three scores: Reading (your ability to comprehend the source), Analysis (your ability to analyze the source and explain the author's presentation of the argument), and Writing (your ability to express yourself in standard written English). Two readers score the essay in each of the three categories, using a 4-point rubric. A score of **4** indicates the quality of the essay is **Advanced.** A score of **3** indicates the quality of the essay is **Proficient.** A score of **2** indicates the quality of essay is **Partial (uneven).** A score of **1** indicates the quality of the essay is **Inadequate.** The two readers' scores are then combined, with 8 being the highest score and 2 the lowest score. Therefore, you can receive scores ranging from 2 to 8 in each of the three scoring categories.

Essay Scoring Rubric

Score	Reading	Analysis	Writing
4	**Advanced:** ❏ The writer thoroughly understands the source text. ❏ The writer comprehends the main idea and the relevance and application of the details. ❏ The writer provides an accurate interpretation of the facts and inferences in the source text. ❏ The writer effectively uses textual evidence (both direct quotations and paraphrasing).	**Advanced:** ❏ The writer is insightful in analysis and comprehends the subtleties of the source text. ❏ The writer is thoughtful and critical in the analysis of the author's use of evidence, reasoning, and/or elements of style. ❏ The writer uses appropriate, ample, and considered textual support for claims. ❏ The writer considers all significant aspects of the source text.	**Advanced:** ❏ The writer organizes the response cohesively and demonstrates the ability to use language effectively and skillfully. ❏ The writer has a well-defined claim or thesis. ❏ The writer organizes the response effectively with a clear introduction, body, and conclusion. ❏ The writer demonstrates a skillful flow of ideas with effective transitions within paragraphs and between paragraphs. ❏ The writer uses sentence variety and effective diction. The tone of the response is appropriate and objective. ❏ The writer demonstrates a command of standard written English and makes few or no errors.
3	**Proficient:** ❏ The writer understands the source text. ❏ The writer comprehends the main idea and the importance of the details. ❏ The writer provides a mostly accurate interpretation of the facts and inferences in the source text. ❏ The writer appropriately uses textual evidence (both direct quotations and paraphrasing).	**Proficient:** ❏ The writer is effective in analysis and comprehension of the source text. ❏ The writer is proficient in the analysis of the author's use of evidence, reasoning, and/or elements of style. ❏ The writer uses appropriate and sufficient textual support for claims. ❏ The writer considers most significant aspects of the source text.	**Proficient:** ❏ The writer organizes the response competently and demonstrates the ability to use language effectively. ❏ The writer has a clear claim or thesis. ❏ The writer organizes the response coherently with a clear introduction, body, and conclusion. ❏ The writer demonstrates a competent flow of ideas with effective transitions within paragraphs and between paragraphs. ❏ The writer uses sentence variety and some effective diction. The tone of the response is appropriate and objective. ❏ The writer demonstrates a competent command of standard written English and makes no errors that detract from the clarity of the response.

continued

Score	Reading	Analysis	Writing
2	**Partial:** ❏ The writer demonstrates some understanding of the source text. ❏ The writer comprehends the main idea but not necessarily the importance of the details. ❏ The writer may have some inaccuracies in the interpretation of the facts in the source text. ❏ The writer makes some or uneven use of textual evidence (both direct quotations and paraphrasing).	**Partial:** ❏ The writer provides uneven evidence of analysis and incomplete comprehension of the source text. ❏ The writer shows limited awareness of the author's use of evidence, reasoning, and/or elements of style and doesn't explain their significance to the argument. ❏ The writer provides insufficient textual support for claims. ❏ The writer doesn't explain the most salient characteristics of the argument in the source text.	**Partial:** ❏ The writer shows little or no ability to organize the response competently and limited facility with language. ❏ The writer's claim or thesis is unclear. ❏ The writer fails to organize the response coherently; the introduction and conclusion are inadequate or unclear. ❏ The writer demonstrates little cohesive flow of ideas with uneven transitions within paragraphs and between paragraphs. ❏ The writer uses little sentence variety, and diction is vague or unoriginal. The tone of the response is uneven and somewhat inappropriate. ❏ The writer lacks a competent command of standard written English and makes some errors that detract from the clarity of the response.
1	**Inadequate:** ❏ The writer demonstrates little or no understanding of the source text. ❏ The writer shows little comprehension of the main idea and the relevance of details to that main idea. ❏ The writer may have an inaccurate understanding and interpretation of the facts in the source text. ❏ The writer makes little or no use of textual evidence (both direct quotations and paraphrasing).	**Inadequate:** ❏ The writer provides little or no evidence of analysis and inadequate comprehension of the source text. ❏ The writer shows little or no awareness of the author's use of evidence, reasoning, and/or elements of style and/or doesn't explain their significance to the argument. ❏ The writer provides little or no textual support for claims. ❏ The writer doesn't focus on the argument in the source text and may merely summarize or present a personal opinion.	**Inadequate:** ❏ The writer shows little or no ability to organize the response competently and inadequate facility with language. ❏ The writer's claim or thesis is unclear or missing. ❏ The writer fails to organize the response coherently; the introduction and conclusion are inadequate or missing. ❏ The writer demonstrates no cohesive flow of ideas with few or no transitions within paragraphs and between paragraphs. ❏ The writer uses little or no sentence variety, and diction is vague or inaccurate. The tone of the response is inappropriate. ❏ The writer shows poor command of standard written English and makes many errors that detract from the clarity of the response.

G. Sample SAT Essay, Annotation, Analysis, Response, Estimated Scores, and Commentary

To help you prepare for the test, a sample SAT Essay is presented below. It is followed first by an annotated version of the source text to demonstrate some of the ways that you might analyze the text in response to the prompt and then by a sample response with estimated scores and commentary.

1. Sample SAT Essay

Read the following passage and consider Theodore Roosevelt's argument. Note how he uses

- evidence, such as reasons, facts, or examples, to support his claim.
- logical reasoning to support and develop his ideas.
- stylistic elements such as diction and emotional appeals.

The following passage is the text of a speech Theodore Roosevelt gave in 1883. Entitled the "Duties of American Citizenship," the speech was intended to create awareness among Americans of their roles and responsibilities as citizens of this country.

(1)   Of course, in one sense, the first essential for a man's being a good citizen is his possession of the home virtues of which we think when we call a man by the emphatic adjective of manly. No man can be a good citizen who is not a good husband and a good father, who is not honest in his dealings with other men and women, faithful to his friends and fearless in the presence of his foes, who has not got a sound heart, a sound mind, and a sound body; exactly as no amount of attention to civil duties will save a nation if the domestic life is undermined, or there is lack of the rude military virtues which alone can assure a country's position in the world. In a free republic the ideal citizen must be one willing and able to take arms for the defense of the flag, exactly as the ideal citizen must be the father of many healthy children. A race must be strong and vigorous; it must be a race of good fighters and good breeders, else its wisdom will come to naught and its virtue be ineffective; and no sweetness and delicacy, no love for and appreciation of beauty in art or literature, no capacity for building up material prosperity can possibly atone for the lack of the great virile virtues.

(2)   But this is aside from my subject, for what I wish to talk of is the attitude of the American citizen in civic life. It ought to be axiomatic in this country that every man must devote a reasonable share of his time to doing his duty in the Political life of the community. No man has a right to shirk his political duties under whatever plea of pleasure or business; and while such shirking may be pardoned in those of small means it is entirely unpardonable in those among whom it is most common—in the people whose circumstances give them freedom in the struggle for life. In so far as the community grows to think rightly, it will likewise grow to regard the young man of means who shirks his duty to the State in time of peace as being only one degree worse than the man who thus shirks it in time of war. A great many of our men in business, or of our young men who are bent on enjoying life (as they have a perfect right to do if only they do not sacrifice other things to enjoyment), rather plume themselves upon being good citizens if they even vote; yet voting is the very least of their duties, Nothing worth gaining is ever gained without effort. You can no more have freedom without striving and suffering for it than you can win success as a banker or a lawyer without labor and effort, without

143

self-denial in youth and the display of a ready and alert intelligence in middle age. The people who say that they have not time to attend to politics are simply saying that they are unfit to live in a free community.

> Write an essay in which you analyze how Roosevelt builds an argument to convince his listeners to live up to their responsibilities as citizens. Consider how Roosevelt uses evidence, such as reasons, facts, or examples, to strengthen the logic of his claim. As you write your essay, consider his reasoning and his use of stylistic elements such as word choice and appeals to emotion.

2. Sample Annotated Source Text

(1)   Of course, in one sense, the [1]first essential for a man's being a good citizen is his possession of the home virtues of which we think when we call a man by the emphatic adjective of manly. No man can be a good citizen who is not a good husband and a good father, who is not [4]honest in his dealings with other men and women, [4]faithful to his friends and [4]fearless in the presence of his foes, who has not got a sound heart, a sound mind, and a sound body; exactly as no amount of attention to civil duties will save a nation if the domestic life is undermined, or there is lack of the rude military virtues which alone can assure a country's position in the world. [2]In a free republic the ideal citizen must be one willing and able to take arms for the defense of the flag, exactly as the ideal citizen must be the father of many healthy children. A race must be strong and vigorous; [2]it must be a race of good fighters and good breeders, else its wisdom will come to naught and its virtue be ineffective; and no sweetness and delicacy, no love for and appreciation of beauty in art or literature, no capacity for building up material prosperity can possibly atone for the lack of the great virile virtues.

(2)   But this is aside from my subject, for what I wish to talk of is the attitude of the American citizen in civic life. It ought to be axiomatic in this country that every man must devote a reasonable share of his time to doing his duty in the Political life of the community. [1]No man has a right to shirk his political duties under [6]whatever plea of pleasure or business; and while such shirking may be pardoned in those of small means it is entirely unpardonable in those among whom it is most common—in the people whose circumstances give them freedom in the struggle for life. In so far as the community grows to think rightly, it will likewise grow to regard [3]the young man of means who shirks his duty to the State in time of peace as being only one degree worse than the man who thus shirks it in time of war. [5]A great many of our men in business, or of our young men who are bent on enjoying life (as they have a perfect right to do if only they do not sacrifice other things to enjoyment), rather plume themselves upon being good citizens if they even vote; yet voting is the very least of their duties, [6]Nothing worth gaining is ever gained without effort. You can no more have freedom without striving and suffering for it than you can win success as a banker or a lawyer without labor and effort, without self-denial in youth and the display of a ready and alert intelligence in middle age. The people who say that they have not time to attend to politics are simply saying that they are unfit to live in a free community.

3. Source Text Analysis

Main argument: It is essential for every man to be a good citizen and not shirk his political responsibilities. Active participation in government is not a choice; it is a duty.

Primary technique: Emotional appeals

[1]Appeal to values: Roosevelt begins by an appeal to traditional values. He points out that being a good citizen is closely related to being a good husband and a good father. By making this connection, he shows his understanding of human psychology: no man wants to think of himself as a bad husband or a bad father. In the second paragraph he points out the shame of shirking civic responsibilities.

[2]Appeal to patriotism: Roosevelt connects being a good citizen to being willing to fight for one's country.

[3]Appeal to honor: Shirking political responsibilities is no different from being a coward in times of war.

Language Use

[4]Diction: Roosevelt uses words to characterize the good citizen that make an emotional appeal. Who would not want to be known as honest, faithful, and fearless?

Comparison/Contrast

[5]Young men are enjoying life rather than doing their duty.

Counterargument

[6]I know you're busy building a business or enjoying life.

4. Sample SAT Essay Response

Theodore Roosevelt gave this speech because of his concern that among Americans (he meant males), apathy was pervasive, and citizens weren't living up to their civic responsibilities. In this persuasive speech, Roosevelt tries to convince his listeners to become more actively involved in the political arena. He uses powerful emotional appeals and effective language rather than facts and statistics to convince his audience of the importance of active participation in government.

It is clear from the beginning of the speech that Roosevelt has a serious purpose: He believes that civic apathy poses a danger to freedom. Roosevelt concedes his awareness that Americans have busy lives; they get caught up in the day-to-day stresses and don't feel they have the time for political involvement. To make his case, however, he appeals to the traditional American values. A core value in this country is the responsibility a man has to his family. Roosevelt argues that it is impossible to be a good family provider without also being a good citizen. In fact, he states emphatically, "No man can be a good citizen who is not a good husband and a good father." This link he establishes impresses his listeners, most of whom consider themselves good family men. To further his argument, Roosevelt juxtaposes the example of active participation in civic duties with willingness to "take arms for the defense of the flag." In this appeal to the patriotism of his listeners, Roosevelt suggests a link between political activism and patriotism. He implies, by contrast, it is not patriotic to remain aloof from political involvement.

Roosevelt also uses persuasive language effectively in this speech to convince his audience to become more active in their political processes. Choosing his words carefully, he appeals to the emotions of his listeners, especially to the masculinity of his male listeners (this was 1883). In the very beginning of the speech he uses the word "manly" to describe a good citizen. He continues this connection between being a good citizen and being a good man by using a series of very powerful adjectives. Who would not want to be thought of as "honest," "faithful," and "fearless"? Yet, he implies, a person can't be honest, faithful, and fearless unless he is a good citizen. These virtues, so admired by many, are as important for a citizen as they are for a father. For Roosevelt's listeners, the point is very clear: If they want to consider themselves worthy men, they must become actively involved in politics.

In this speech, Roosevelt subtly addresses the counterargument that his listeners are too busy building their businesses or enjoying life. He acknowledges that work takes time and effort and that enjoyment is important, but he reiterates, "Nothing worth gaining is ever gained without effort." He urges his listeners to put the same effort into being a good citizen as they do into all their other endeavors. By appealing to their pride, their courage, and their family values, Roosevelt makes a very strong case for political involvement.

5. Sample Estimated Scores and Commentary

Advanced: 4 (Reading)/4 (Analysis)/4 (Writing)

Commentary

This **Advanced** response demonstrates a clear comprehension of the source text, insightfully analyzes the persuasive power of the speech, and provides effective textual evidence to support the writer's claims. The writer of this sample essay begins his analysis with a brief summary of the context for Roosevelt's speech (*apathy was pervasive, and citizens weren't living up to their civic responsibilities*) and ends the introductory paragraph with his thesis sentence: *He uses powerful emotional appeals and effective language rather than facts and statistics to convince his audience of the importance of active participation in government.*

The information is accurate, and while the organization is predictable (one paragraph on purpose and one paragraph on language use), it is effective with a clear introduction, body, and conclusion. The writer uses transitions within paragraphs (*To make his case, however, In fact, by contrast, He continues*) and between paragraphs (*It is clear, also*). In addition, the writer supports his assertions (*A core value in this country is the responsibility a man has to his family*) with well-chosen textual references (*"No man can be a good citizen who is not a good husband and a good father."*). In addition, the writer recognizes the rhetorical subtleties of Roosevelt's appeal designed to rouse his listeners to action: *it is not patriotic to remain aloof from political involvement.*

In his paragraph on language use, the writer demonstrates an insight into Roosevelt's powerful appeal to masculine pride and patriotism. Deftly acknowledging that Roosevelt was directing his remarks primarily to the men in the audience (*this was 1883*), the writer points out the specific words (*"manly," "honest," "faithful," "fearless"*) chosen to convince listeners of their responsibility to become involved in politics.

The response is well written with varied sentence structure [*Choosing his words carefully, he appeals to the emotions of his listeners, especially to the masculinity of his male listeners (this was 1883).*] and (*Who would not want to be thought of as "honest," "faithful," and "fearless"?*). There are no grammatical or usage errors, and the tone is formal and objective.

H. Additional Practice

Read the following passage and consider the John F. Kennedy's argument. Note how he uses

- evidence, such as reasons, facts, or examples, to support his claim.
- logical reasoning to support and develop his ideas.
- stylistic elements such as diction and emotional appeals.

The following is an excerpt from President John F. Kennedy's speech at Rice University in Texas on September 12, 1962, to counter the widespread perception that the U.S. was losing the "Space Race" to Russia. Kennedy felt strongly that a commitment to NASA's space program was essential to this country's security, prestige, and national identity, but the program was both costly and risky.

(1)   Those who came before us made certain that this country rode the first waves of the industrial revolutions, the first waves of modern invention, and the first wave of nuclear power, and this generation does not intend to founder in the backwash of the coming age of space. We mean to be a part of it—we mean to lead it. For the eyes of the world now look into space, to the moon and to the planets beyond, and we have vowed that we shall not see it governed by a hostile flag of conquest, but by a banner of freedom and peace. We have vowed that we shall not see space filled with weapons of mass destruction, but with instruments of knowledge and understanding.

(2)   Yet the vows of this Nation can only be fulfilled if we in this Nation are first, and, therefore, we intend to be first. In short, our leadership in science and in industry, our hopes for peace and security, our obligations to ourselves as well as others, all require us to make this effort, to solve these mysteries, to solve them for the good of all men, and to become the world's leading space-faring nation.

(3)   We set sail on this new sea because there is new knowledge to be gained, and new rights to be won, and they must be won and used for the progress of all people. For space science, like nuclear science and all technology, has no conscience of its own. Whether it will become a force for good or ill depends on man, and only if the United States occupies a position of pre-eminence can we help decide whether this new ocean will be a sea of peace or a new terrifying theater of war. I do not say that we should or will go unprotected against the hostile misuse of space any more than we go unprotected against the hostile use of land or sea, but I do say that space can be explored and mastered without feeding the fires of war, without repeating the mistakes that man has made in extending his writ around this globe of ours.

(4)   There is no strife, no prejudice, no national conflict in outer space as yet. Its hazards are hostile to us all. Its conquest deserves the best of all mankind, and its opportunity for peaceful cooperation may never come again. But why, some say, the moon? Why choose this as our goal? And they may well ask why climb the highest mountain? Why, 35 years ago, fly the Atlantic? Why does Rice play Texas?

(5)   We choose to go to the moon. We choose to go to the moon in this decade and do the other things, not because they are easy, but because they are hard, because that goal will serve to organize and measure the best of our energies and skills, because that challenge is one that we are willing to accept, one we are unwilling to postpone, and one which we intend to win, and the others, too.

(6)   It is for these reasons that I regard the decision last year to shift our efforts in space from low to high gear as among the most important decisions that will be made during my incumbency in the office of the Presidency.

(7)   The growth of our science and education will be enriched by new knowledge of our universe and environment, by new techniques of learning and mapping and observation, by new tools and computers

for industry, medicine, the home as well as the school. Technical institutions, such as Rice, will reap the harvest of these gains.

(8) And finally, the space effort itself, while still in its infancy, has already created a great number of new companies, and tens of thousands of new jobs. Space and related industries are generating new demands in investment and skilled personnel, and this city and this State, and this region, will share greatly in this growth. What was once the furthest outpost on the old frontier of the West will be the furthest outpost on the new frontier of science and space. Houston, your City of Houston, with its Manned Spacecraft Center, will become the heart of a large scientific and engineering community. During the next 5 years the National Aeronautics and Space Administration expects to double the number of scientists and engineers in this area, to increase its outlays for salaries and expenses to $60 million a year; to invest some $200 million in plant and laboratory facilities; and to direct or contract for new space efforts over $1 billion from this Center in this City.

(9) To be sure, all this costs us all a good deal of money. This year's space budget is three times what it was in January 1961, and it is greater than the space budget of the previous 8 years combined. That budget now stands at $5,400 million a year—a staggering sum, though somewhat less than we pay for cigarettes and cigars every year. Space expenditures will soon rise some more, from 40 cents per person per week to more than 50 cents a week for every man, woman and child in the United States, for we have given this program a high national priority—even though I realize that this is in some measure an act of faith and vision, for we do not now know what benefits await us.

(10) But if I were to say, my fellow citizens, that we shall send to the moon, 240,000 miles away from the control station in Houston, a giant rocket more than 300 feet tall, the length of this football field, made of new metal alloys, some of which have not yet been invented, capable of standing heat and stresses several times more than have ever been experienced, fitted together with a precision better than the finest watch, carrying all the equipment needed for propulsion, guidance, control, communications, food and survival, on an untried mission, to an unknown celestial body, and then return it safely to earth, re-entering the atmosphere at speeds of over 25,000 miles per hour, causing heat about half that of the temperature of the sun—almost as hot as it is here today—and do all this, and do it right, and do it first before this decade is out—then we must be bold.

(11) Many years ago the great British explorer George Mallory, who was to die on Mount Everest, was asked why did he want to climb it. He said, "Because it is there."

(12) Well, space is there, and we're going to climb it, and the moon and the planets are there, and new hopes for knowledge and peace are there. And, therefore, as we set sail we ask God's blessing on the most hazardous and dangerous and greatest adventure on which man has ever embarked.

Write an essay in which you analyze how John F. Kennedy builds an argument to convince the reader that the space exploration program should be expanded. Consider how Kennedy uses evidence, such as reasons, facts, or examples, to strengthen the logic of his claim. As you write your essay, consider his reasoning and his use of stylistic elements such as word choice and appeals to emotion.

In your essay, do not explain your position on this issue; rather, analyze how Kennedy builds his argument to accomplish his purpose.

VIII. Tier 2 Vocabulary

While the SAT doesn't have fill-in vocabulary questions, you will find many vocabulary-in-context questions on the Reading Test. In addition, the language used in the reading passages is fairly sophisticated and assumes a level of familiarity with vocabulary appropriate for a high school junior or senior. Your knowledge of these Tier 2 words will also help you find the right word choice in your own writing. For these reasons, you should expand your vocabulary by studying the Tier 2 vocabulary words.

aberration: An abnormality

abet: To aid in the commission (usually of a crime)

abrasive: Rough; coarse

abscond: To depart suddenly and secretly

abstemious: Characterized by self-denial or abstinence

abstruse: Difficult to understand

acquiesce: To comply; to agree; to submit

acumen: Quickness of intellectual insight

admonition: Gentle scolding or warning

adorn: To decorate or embellish

aerie: Bird's nest; place of sanctuary

aesthetic: Beautiful; relating to the appreciation of art or beauty

affable: Good-natured; easy to approach

agile: Able to move quickly (physically or mentally)

agitate: To move violently; to make someone anxious

alacrity: Cheerful willingness or promptness

alleviate: To relieve; to make less hard to bear

aloof: Reserved; distant

altruism: Unselfishness; charitableness

amalgamate: To mix or blend together

ambiguous: Having a double meaning

ambivalence: Uncertainty; mixed feelings

ameliorate: To relieve; to make better

amiable: Friendly

anecdote: A personal story (often short and humorous)

animosity: Hatred

apparition: Ghostly sight

appease: To soothe

approbation: Approval

arbiter: One who makes a judgment

arbitrary: Based on whim; random

arboreal: Pertaining to trees

arcane: Difficult to understand; known to only a few

ardor: Passion

articulate: Eloquent; able to express oneself well

ascetic: One who practices self-denial and excessive abstinence (n); characterized by severe self-discipline (adj)

ascribe: To assign as a quality or attribute

asperity: Harshness; roughness

assiduous: Unceasing; persistent

assuage: To relieve

astute: Keen in discernment

audacious: Bold; fearless

auspicious: Favorable

austere: Severely simple; strict; harsh

authoritarian: Demanding; despotic

avarice: Greed

banal: Commonplace; trite

belittle: To make seem less significant or worthy

bellicose: Warlike

belligerent: Displaying a warlike spirit

benefactor: One who does kindly and charitable acts

beneficent: Charitable

benevolence: An act of kindness or generosity

benign: Good and kind

berate: To scold severely

bewilder: To confuse

blithe: Carefree; joyous

boisterous: Lively; rowdy; overexcited

bolster: To support

bombast: Pompous or inflated language

boorish: Rude

brevity: Briefness

brusque: Curt; brief to the point of rude

burnish: To make brilliant or shining

cacophony: A disagreeable or discordant sound

cajole: To convince by flattering speech

calibrate: To standardize; to assess

callow: Young and inexperienced

capacious: Roomy

capitulate: To surrender

castigate: To punish

caustic: Sarcastic and severe

censure: To criticize severely

chagrin: Embarrassment or dismay

chicanery: The use of trickery to deceive

circumscribe: To limit or restrict

circumstantial: Based on inference rather than conclusive proof

cloying: Excessively sweet

coerce: To force

cogent: Strongly persuasive

collusion: A secret agreement for a wrongful purpose

comedic: Amusing

compound: To combine; to intensify

comprehend: To understand

comprehensive: All-inclusive; broad in scope

compromise: Meet halfway; expose to danger or disgrace

compunction: Uneasiness caused by guilt or remorse

concede: To admit or grant

conciliatory: Tending to reconcile

concord: Harmony

condescension: A snobby and pretentiously kind manner

conflagration: A great fire

congeal: To coagulate

congenial: Agreeable; friendly

connoisseur: An expert judge of art, especially one with thorough knowledge and sound judgment

consent: Agreement

console: To comfort

conspicuous: Clearly visible

constrict: To bind

contemplative: Calm and thoughtful

contemptuous: Scornful; disdainful

contrite: Remorseful

conventional: Usual; conservative

copious: Plentiful

corroboration: Confirmation

craven: Cowardly

credulous: Easily deceived

creed: Statement of beliefs; set of principles

curtail: To cut off; to cut short

dearth: Scarcity

decorum: Proper behavior

defame: To harm someone's reputation

defuse: To remove a threat

deleterious: Hurtful

delineate: To outline; to explain

demarcate: To define; to separate

denigrate: To belittle or defame

denounce: To condemn; to criticize harshly

deplete: To reduce; to lessen

depraved: Wicked; morally corrupt

deride: To ridicule

derivative: Coming from some origin; not original

deter: To frighten away

detrimental: Harmful

diatribe: A bitter or malicious criticism

didactic: Pertaining to teaching

diffidence: Shyness; lack of self-confidence

dilatory: Tending to cause delay

discern: To distinguish; to see clearly

disconsolate: Hopelessly sad

dissemble: To hide by putting on a false appearance

disseminate: To scatter; to distribute

dissent or dissension: Disagreement

distinctive: Different from others; typical

divulge: To tell something previously private or secret

docile: Quiet and easy to control

dogmatic: Stubbornly opinionated; making assertions without evidence

dotage: Old age

draconian: Very harsh or severe

dubious: Doubtful; skeptical; questionable

duplicity: Deceitfulness; dishonesty

eccentric: Odd; unconventional

eclectic: Coming from a variety of sources

effrontery: Boldness; audacity

effusive: Gushing; unrestrained in showing feelings

elucidate: To clarify

elusive: Tending to escape; hard to find or pin down

embellish: To add decoration

embezzle: To misappropriate secretly

encumbrance: A burden

enervate: To weaken

engender: To produce

enigma: A riddle or puzzle

enmity: Hatred

ephemeral: Short-lived

equanimity: Calmness; composure

equivocate: To be deliberately vague or misleading

eradicate: To destroy thoroughly

erratic: Irregular

erroneous: Incorrect

eschew: To avoid

evanescent: Existing briefly; ephemeral; fleeting

evoke: To call or summon forth

exacerbate: To make worse

exigent: Urgent; requiring action

expedient: Useful; advantageous

explicate: To explain; to clarify

explicit: Clear; unambiguous

extant: Still existing and known

extenuate: To make less severe

extinct: No longer in existence

extol: To praise in the highest terms

extraneous: Irrelevant

fabled: Legendary; famous

facetious: Amusing

facile: Easy

fallacious: Illogical

fathom: To understand (v); measurement of water depth (n)

flamboyant: Flashy; showy

flaunt: To show off

flout: To treat with contempt, disdain, or mockery

frenetic: Frantic; frenzied

frivolity: Silly and trivial behavior or activities

frugal: Economical

fundamentalism: A movement with a strict view of doctrine

gentility: Refinement; courtesy

germane: Relevant

gregarious: Sociable; outgoing

guile: Duplicity

gullible: Credulous

harbinger: First sign; messenger

hedonism: Pursuit of pleasure

heed: Pay attention to

heinous: Odiously sinful

heresy: An opinion or doctrine that opposes accepted beliefs or principles

histrionic: Dramatic; theatrical

hybrid: Crossbreed; mixture

hyperbole: Exaggeration

hypocrisy: Extreme insincerity

iconoclasm: A challenge to or overturning of traditional beliefs, customs, or values

idiosyncrasy: A habit peculiar to an individual; a quirk

ignoble: Low in character or purpose

ignominious: Shameful

illicit: Unlawful

illusory: Deceptive; misleading

immaculate: Clean; without blemish

imminent: About to occur

immutable: Unchangeable

impassive: Unmoved by or not exhibiting feeling

impede: To block; to obstruct

impermanence: Quality of not lasting (lacking permanence)

imperturbable: Calm

impervious: Impenetrable; to be unmoved or unaffected

implacable: Incapable of being pacified

implicate: To hint or suggest involvement

implicit: Implied

impromptu: Anything done or said on the spur of the moment

impugn: To oppose or attack; to suggest doubt

impute: To attribute

inadvertent: Accidental

inane: Silly

incessant: Unceasing

incipient: Initial; beginning of development

incisive: Sharp; perceptive

incite: To rouse to a particular action

incongruous: Unsuitable for the time, place, or occasion; inconsistent

incumbent: Obligatory (adj); one currently in office (n)

indelible: Permanent; unable to be removed

indigenous: Native

indignant: Angry at unfairness

indiscretion: An unwise action; a tactless lack of judgment

indolence: Laziness

indomitable: Unconquerable

inept: Not fit or suitable

inevitable: Unavoidable

inexorable: Unrelenting

inimical: Adverse

injunction: Court order; ban; command

innocuous: Harmless

inscrutable: Impenetrably mysterious or profound

insinuate: To imply

instigate: To start; to cause trouble

insurrection: Active resistance to authority

intrepid: Fearless and bold

introspection: The act of observing and analyzing one's own thoughts and feelings

inundate: To flood

inure: To harden or toughen by use or exposure

inveterate: Habitual; firmly established

invincible: Unable to be conquered, subdued, or overcome

iota: Small or insignificant amount

irate: Moved to anger

ire: Anger

irksome: Annoying

irrefutable: Certain; undeniable

irresolution: Indecisiveness

itinerant: Wandering

jeopardize: To put in danger

judicious: Prudent

juxtaposition: The act of putting side by side

lassitude: Lack of vitality or energy

laudable: Praiseworthy

legacy: A bequest

lethargic: Lacking energy; sluggish

libertarian: One who is tolerant or permissive (n); open-minded (adj)

listless: Inattentive

literal: Factual and unimaginative

lithe: Supple

ludicrous: Ridiculous

lustrous: Shining

malevolence: Ill will

malign: To speak evil of; to slander

malleable: Pliant

mediate: To arbitrate; to settle dispute

melancholy: Sad

mesmerize: To hypnotize

metaphorical: Non-literal; implicit comparison

meticulous: Careful; painstaking; fussy

mettle: Courage

microcosm: The world or universe on a small scale

misnomer: A name wrongly or mistakenly applied

mode: Style; method

modicum: A small amount

mollify: To soothe

momentous: Highly significant

morose: Gloomy

multifarious: Having great diversity or variety

mundane: Worldly; ordinary

mutability: Changeability

myopic: Short-sighted; near-sighted

myriad: A large indefinite number

mystical: Spiritual; magical

nadir: The lowest point

nefarious: Wicked or evil

negligent: Careless

negotiate: Discuss terms of agreement

neophyte: A beginner

nondescript: Having no distinguishing characteristics

noxious: Hurtful

objective: Impartial; neutral

obscure: Hard to understand; indistinct; not known

obstinate: Stubborn

obtrude: To push oneself on others

odious: Hateful

ominous: Threatening

onerous: Burdensome or oppressive

onus: A burden or responsibility

ostracism: Exclusion from society

pacifism: Belief in peace; nonaggression

panacea: A cure-all

paragon: A model of excellence

pariah: A social outcast

partisan: Showing partiality to a party or one side of an issue

passivity: Inactiveness; nonparticipation

pathos: The quality that arouses emotion or sympathy

peculiar: Odd; unique

pejorative: Expressing disapproval

perfunctory: Just going through the motions; mechanical

peripheral: Tangential; unimportant; minor

perjury: Lying under oath

permeate: To pervade

pernicious: Harmful; poisonous

pertinent: Relevant

pervasive: Widespread

pilgrimage: Journey (often religious)

placate: To calm or appease

plethora: Excess; abundance

pluralism: Different groups with different beliefs existing within one society

poignant: Emotionally painful

portray: Depict

pragmatic: Practical

precarious: Perilous; risky; unstable

preclude: To prevent

predominate: To be chief in importance

premature: Occurring too soon

prescience: Knowledge of events before they take place

prevalent: Widespread

primordial: Existing at the beginning of time

pristine: Pure; unspoiled

procrastination: Delay

prodigious: Immense

profound: Showing great perception; having deep meaning

profuse: Produced or displayed in overabundance

prosaic: Unimaginative

provincial: Unsophisticated; narrow-minded

prudence: Caution

pugnacious: Quarrelsome

punitive: As punishment

putative: Supposed; thought to exist

quandary: A puzzling predicament

quotidian: Of an everyday character; ordinary

ramify: To divide or subdivide into branches or subdivisions

recant: To withdraw formally one's belief (in something previously believed or maintained)

recidivism: The tendency to relapse into crime

recluse: One who lives apart from others or in seclusion

recuperate: To recover

relegate: To demote

renovate: To restore

repudiate: To refuse to have anything to do with; to reject

repulsive: Grossly offensive

repute: Reputation

reserve: To set something aside (v); distance or coolness of manner (n)

resilience: The ability to bounce back, cope, or adapt

respite: Interval of rest

reticent: Reserved; unwilling to communicate

revere: To respect highly; to worship

ritual: Established pattern of behavior, often ceremonial

salutary: Beneficial

sanction: To approve authoritatively (v); a threatened penalty for disobeying a law or rule (n)

sardonic: Scornfully mocking

secular: Nonreligious

self-effacing: Modest; humble

serenity: Calmness; peacefulness

shrewd: Characterized by skill at understanding and profiting by circumstances

solace: Comfort

solvent: Having sufficient funds

soporific: Causing sleep

sordid: Filthy; morally degraded

sparse: Thinly spread

specious: Something that has the appearance of truth but is actually false

spurious: Not genuine

squalid: Dirty and/or poverty-stricken

stingy: Cheap; unwilling to spend money

subsume: To include in something larger

subterfuge: A deceitful maneuver

subterranean: Underground

subtle: Slight; understated

succinct: Concise

supercilious: Haughty; arrogant

superfluous: More than is needed

suppress: To prevent from being disclosed or published

sycophant: A servile flatterer

tacit: Without words; unspoken

tangential: Not central; almost irrelevant

tedious: Boring; monotonous

temerity: Boldness; nerve

terse: Brief; concise

torpid: Dull; sluggish

tranquil: Calm; peaceful

transitory: Existing for a short time only

trepidation: Fear

trite: Made commonplace by frequent repetition

turbulent: Moving violently

ubiquitous: Being present everywhere

undermine: To subvert in an underhanded way; to weaken

underscore: To emphasize

understate: To devalue; to minimize

undulate: To move like a wave or in waves

unwarranted: Unjustified

vacuity: Lack of ideas; emptiness

vapid: Dull; uninteresting

vehement: Very eager or urgent

veracity: Truthfulness

verbose: Wordy

vestige: A remaining trace of something gone

veto: To reject (v); right to reject legislation (n)

vigilant: Alert and watchful

vigor: Energy

vital: Crucial; needed for life; lively

volatile: Unstable; explosive

voluminous: Large; long; prolific

whimsical: Fanciful; light-hearted; quirky

zealous: Passionate; very enthusiastic

IX. The Heart of Algebra

A. Linear Expressions and Linear Equations in One Variable

Linear equations are an important part of the SAT. When solving linear equations in one variable, you may have three possible outcomes:

- The equation has one solution. Example: $2n + 4 = 10$; thus, $n = 3$.
- The equation has no solution. Example: $k = k + 1$; in this case, there is no real value for k that can satisfy the given equation.
- The equation has infinitely many solutions. Example: $t + 3 = t + 3$; the value for t is the set of all real numbers.

Practice

1. Lara's Car Service charges an initial fee of $6, plus $2 for each $\frac{1}{2}$ mile. If the total charge for a ride is $38, how long is the ride, in miles?

   A. 8
   B. 16
   C. 32
   D. 44

2. If Janet is n years old, Karen is 2 years younger than Janet, and Mary is 4 years more than twice Janet's age, which of the following represents how many years older Mary is than Karen?

   A. $n + 6$
   B. $n - 2$
   C. n
   D. $n + 2$

3. The length of a rectangle is 5 feet, and its perimeter is p feet. Which of the following represents, in feet, the width of the rectangle?

   A. $\dfrac{p}{2}$
   B. $\dfrac{p+10}{2}$
   C. $\dfrac{p-5}{2}$
   D. $\dfrac{p}{2} - 5$

4. What is the value of k for the equation below?

$$\frac{k}{2} - \frac{k}{3} = 1 + \frac{k}{6}$$

A. 0
B. 1
C. 3
D. No solution

5. Ali wishes to mix two kinds of nuts together, some worth \$2 per pound and the rest worth \$8 per pound. If she wants to produce 12 pounds of mixed nuts worth \$6 per pound, how many pounds of the cheaper nuts should she use?

6. What is the value of x in the equation below?

$$\frac{15 - (4 + x)}{3} = 6$$

Answers

1. **A.** Let n represent the length of the ride, in miles. Since it's \$2 for each $\frac{1}{2}$ mile, the charge for each mile is (\$2)(2) = \$4. Therefore, $4n + 6 = 38$, which yields $n = 8$. The ride is 8 miles.

2. **A.** Since Janet's age is n, Karen's age is $(n - 2)$ and Mary's age is $2n + 4$. Since Mary is older than Karen, the difference in their ages is $(2n + 4) - (n - 2)$, which is equivalent to $2n + 4 - n + 2$ or $n + 6$, Choice A.

3. **D.** The perimeter of a rectangle p is $p = 2(\text{length}) + 2(\text{width})$. In this case, $p = 2(5) + 2(\text{width})$. Thus, $p = 10 + 2(\text{width})$ or width $= \frac{p - 10}{2}$ or width $= \frac{p}{2} - 5$, Choice D.

4. **D.** Multiply both sides of the equation by 6 and obtain $3k - 2k = 6 + k$. Combining like terms, you have $k = 6 + k$, and subtracting k from both sides of the equation, you have $0 = 6$, which is not possible. Thus, the equation has *no solution,* Choice D.

5. **4** Let x represent the number of pounds of the cheaper nuts (\$2 per pound), and, thus, $12 - x$ represents the more expensive nuts (\$8 per pound). See chart below.

Nuts	Pounds	Cost
Cheap (\$2)	x	$(2)(x)$
Expensive (\$8)	$(12 - x)$	$8(12 - x)$
Mixed (\$6)	12	$6(12)$

Since the total cost is the same, you have $2x + 8(12 - x) = 6(12)$. Applying the *distributive property*, you have $2x + 96 - 8x = 72$ or $-6x + 96 = 72$, which is equivalent to $-6x = -24$ or $x = 4$. Note that you could have also used two variables to solve this problem.

6. **−7** Simplify the numerator $15 - (4 + x)$ and obtain $\frac{11 - x}{3} = 6$. Multiplying both sides of the equation by 3, you have $11 - x = 18$. Thus, $-x = 7$ or $x = -7$.

B. Linear Inequalities in One Variable

Solving inequalities is part of the SAT. In general, you can solve a simple inequality the same way you would solve an equation, except when multiplying or dividing an inequality by a negative number. If you multiply or divide both sides of an inequality by a negative quantity, the direction of the inequality sign is reversed.

Practice

1. $1 - 2x < 13$

   For the inequality above, which of the following inequalities gives all values of x?

   A. $x > -7$
   B. $x > -6$
   C. $x < 6$
   D. $x < 7$

2. If $6 < 2x - 4 \le 10$, what is one possible value of x?

   A. -7
   B. 0
   C. 5
   D. 6

3. There are three tests for the fall semester for Karen's Algebra class. For the first two tests, Karen received an 88 and a 93. What is the minimum score that she must receive in order to have an average of 90 or more on the three tests?

   A. 87
   B. 89
   C. 90
   D. 92

4. Izzy has 40 feet of fencing material to create a rectangular garden with a width of 5 feet. If x represents the length of her garden in feet, which of the following inequalities gives all possible values of x?

   A. $x + 5 \le 40$
   B. $2x + 5 < 40$
   C. $2x + 10 < 40$
   D. $2x + 10 \le 40$

5. $1 - \dfrac{2}{3}x > \dfrac{1}{2}x - 4$

   What is the greatest integer that satisfies the inequality above?

6. Derek puts aside $900 for his entertainment budget for the next 6 months. During the first month, he buys concert tickets for $200 and spends nothing else on entertainment. What, in dollars, is Derek's maximum average monthly budget for entertainment for the remaining months?

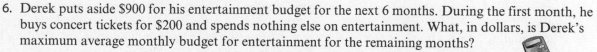

Answers

1. **B.** Subtract 1 from both sides of the inequality and obtain $-2x < 12$. Dividing both sides by -2, you have $x > -6$, Choice B. Note that when you multiply or divide both sides of an equality by a negative number, you must reverse the inequality sign. For steps on how to solve this problem using a calculator, see "Solving an Inequality" in the Appendix.

2. **D.** Adding 4 to all three parts of the compound inequality, you have $10 < 2x \le 14$. Divide the inequality by 2 and obtain $5 < x \le 7$. Thus, one possible value of x is 6, Choice D.

3. **B.** Let x represent Karen's score on the third test. Then the average for the three tests is $\dfrac{88+93+x}{3}$. You want the average to be greater than or equal to 90 (i.e., $\dfrac{88+93+x}{3} \ge 90$). Simplify the numerator, and then multiply both sides of the inequality by 3 to obtain $181 + x \ge 270$ or $x \ge 89$. Thus, the minimum score Karen must receive in order to have an average of 90 or more on the three tests is 89, Choice B.

4. **D.** Since the length of the garden is x feet and the width is 5 feet, the perimeter of the garden is $2(x) + 2(5)$. Izzy has 40 feet of fencing material. Thus, $2x + 2(5) \le 40$ or $2x + 10 \le 40$, Choice D.

5. **4** Multiply both sides of the inequality by 6 to obtain $6 - 4x > 3x - 24$. Subtracting $3x$ and 6 from both sides, you have $-7x > -30$. Divide both sides by -7 and you have $x < \dfrac{30}{7}$, or $x < 4.286\ldots$. Thus, the greatest integer that satisfies the inequality is 4.

6. **140** Let x be Derek's monthly budget for entertainment for the remaining 5 months. Therefore, his total entertainment budget for the next 5 months is $5x$, and $200 + 5x \le 900$ or $5x \le 700$. Solve the inequality, and you have $x \le 140$. Thus, Derek's maximum monthly entertainment budget for the remaining 5 months is $140.

C. Applications of Linear Functions

When solving problems involving linear functions, it is helpful to remember the following:

- A function f from *set A* to *set B* is a relation that assigns to each element in *set A* exactly one element in *set B*.
- Given a linear equation in two variables, you can always express one of the variables as a function of the other. For example, if $2m + 3n = 8$, then $m = -\dfrac{3}{2}n + 4$ or, in functional notation, $m = f(n)$ and $f(n) = -\dfrac{3}{2}n + 4$. In this case, n is known as the independent variable, and m is the dependent variable.
- When building a linear function to model a linear relationship between two quantities, always begin by determining which quantity is the independent variable and which is the dependent variable.

Practice

1. If the function f is defined by $f(x) = 2x - 6$, which of the following is equivalent to $5f(x) + 10$?

   A. $10x - 40$
   B. $10x - 20$
   C. $10x + 4$
   D. $7x + 4$

2. The rent for Donald's apartment in the year 2012 was $2,000 a month and in 2015 it was $2,195 a month. If his rent increases in a linear pattern, which of the following functions, r, models his monthly rent, in dollars, t years after 2012?

   A. $r(t) = 65t$
   B. $r(t) = 2,000 + 65t$
   C. $r(t) = 2,195 + 65t$
   D. $r(t) = 2,000 + 195t$

3. Aaron bought his computer in the year 2015 for $840. It is projected that in 4 years, his computer will become obsolete and have no value. Assuming that the value of his computer depreciates in a linear pattern, which of the following functions, h, models the value of his computer t years after 2015 with $0 \le t \le 4$?

   A. $h(t) = 210 + 4t$
   B. $h(t) = 210t$
   C. $h(t) = 840 - 4t$
   D. $h(t) = 840 - 210t$

4. In the coordinate plane, a line passes through the point $(1, 1)$ and intersects the x-axis and y-axis as shown in the accompanying diagram. Which of the following functions, $A(x)$, models the area of $\triangle ABC$?

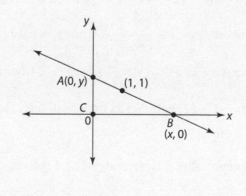

   A. $A(x) = \dfrac{1}{2}x^2$

   B. $A(x) = \dfrac{1}{2}(x)(x-1)$

   C. $A(x) = \dfrac{1}{2}(x)(x+1)$

   D. $A(x) = \dfrac{1}{2}(x)\left(1 + \dfrac{1}{x-1}\right)$

161

5. The relationship between degrees Fahrenheit, F, and degrees Celsius, C, is given by the equation $F = \frac{9}{5}C + 32$. If $F = 68$, what is the value of C?

6. If $y = f(x)$ is a linear function with $f(2) = 5$ and $f(-1) = 1$, what is the value of $f(0)$?

Answers

1. **B.** Since $f(x) = 2x - 6$, you have $5f(x) + 10 = 5(2x - 6) + 10$, which is equivalent to $10x - 20$, Choice B. (For steps on how to solve this problem using a calculator, see "Evaluating Algebraic Expressions Involving Functional Notations" in the Appendix.)

2. **B.** For the year 2012, $t = 0$ and the rent was \$2,000; you have the point $(0, 2{,}000)$. Similarly, for the year 2015, $t = 3$ and the rent was \$2,195; you have the point $(3, 2{,}195)$. Since the rent increases in a linear pattern, the slope of the line is $m = \dfrac{2{,}195 - 2{,}000}{3 - 0} = 65$. Using the equation $y = mx + b$, you have $y = 65x + b$. Substituting $(0, 2{,}000)$ into the equations, you have $b = 2{,}000$. Thus, the equation for Donald's rent is $y = 65x + 2{,}000$. Writing the equation as a function of t, you have $r(t) = 65t + 2{,}000$ or $r(t) = 2{,}000 + 65t$, Choice B.

3. **D.** Since this is a linear function with $t = 0$ for the year 2015, you have the points $(0, 840)$ and $(4, 0)$. The slope of the line is $m = \dfrac{0 - 840}{4 - 0} = -210$. Using the formula $y = mx + b$ and substituting the point $(0, 840)$ into the formula, you have $y = -210x + 840$. Thus, the function for the value of Aaron's computer is $h(t) = 840 - 210t$, Choice D.

4. **D.** The area of a triangle is $A = \frac{1}{2}(\text{base})(\text{height})$. Since $\triangle ABC$ is a right triangle, $A = \frac{1}{2}(x)(y)$. Now express y in terms of x. The slope of the line passing through $(x, 0)$ and $(0, y)$ can be obtained in two ways. Using the points $(x, 0)$ and $(1, 1)$, you have $m = \dfrac{-1}{x - 1}$, and using the points $(0, y)$ and $(1, 1)$, $m = \dfrac{y - 1}{-1}$. Since the slopes are the same, set $\dfrac{-1}{x - 1} = \dfrac{y - 1}{-1}$ and you have $(x - 1)(y - 1) = 1$ or $y - 1 = \dfrac{1}{x - 1}$ or $y = 1 + \dfrac{1}{x - 1}$. Thus, the area $A = \frac{1}{2}(x)(y)$ or $A = \frac{1}{2}x\left(1 + \dfrac{1}{x - 1}\right)$, Choice D.

5. **20** Since $F = 68$, you have $68 = \frac{9}{5}C + 32$. Subtract 32 from both sides to obtain $36 = \frac{9}{5}C$. Multiply both sides by $\frac{5}{9}$, and you have $C = 20$.

6. $\frac{7}{3}$ Since $y = f(x)$ is a linear function with $f(2) = 5$ and $f(-1) = 1$, you know that the points $(2, 5)$ and $(-1, 1)$ are on the graph of $y = f(x)$, and that the graph is a line. The slope of the line is $m = \dfrac{y_2 - y_1}{x_2 - x_1} = \dfrac{5 - 1}{2 - (-1)} = \dfrac{4}{3}$. Using the equation $y = mx + b$, you have $y = \frac{4}{3}x + b$. Substitute the point $(2, 5)$ into the equation and obtain $5 = \frac{4}{3}(2) + b$ or $b = \frac{7}{3}$. Thus, $y = \frac{4}{3}x + \frac{7}{3}$ or $f(x) = \frac{4}{3}x + \frac{7}{3}$; and $f(0) = \frac{7}{3}$.

D. Systems of Linear Equations in Two Variables

Given a system of two linear equations in two variables, the solution to the system is one and only one of the following:

- The solution has one ordered pair. The graphs of the two equations are straight lines with unequal slopes, and they intersect at one point.
- The system has no solution. The graphs are two parallel lines, which have equal slopes.
- The system has infinitely many solutions. The graphs are the same line. Their equations are equivalent.

Practice

1. What is the solution to the system of two linear equations whose graphs (lines l and p) are shown in the xy-plane below?

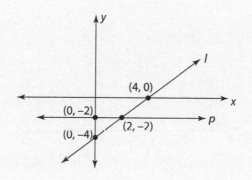

   A. $(0, -2)$
   B. $(0, -4)$
   C. $(2, -2)$
   D. $(4, 0)$

2. If the following ordered pair (p, q) satisfies the system of equations below, what is the value of $p + 2q$?

$$\frac{1}{2}x - \frac{1}{6}y = 7$$

$$\frac{1}{3}x + 2y = -8$$

   A. -18
   B. 0
   C. 6
   D. 28

3. If b is a constant, and the system of linear equations below has no solution, what is the value of b?

$$2x + 3y = 6$$
$$3x + by = 12$$

A. 2

B. 3

C. $\dfrac{9}{2}$

D. 6

4. Daryn has $2,000 to invest for her college fund. She invested part of the $2,000 in 2% bonds and the rest of the money in 3% stocks. Her total annual interest income from the two investments is $54. Solving which of the following systems of equations will reveal the amount of money, x, invested in bonds, and the amount of money, y, invested in stocks?

A.
$$x + y = 54$$
$$.02x + .03y = 2,000$$

B.
$$x + y = 2,000$$
$$.02x + .03y = 54$$

C.
$$x + y = 2,000$$
$$2x + 3y = 54$$

D.
$$x + y = 54$$
$$2x + 3y = 2,000$$

5. The system of linear equations that follows has infinitely many solutions. What is the value of the constant, c?

$$4x - 5y = 1$$
$$y = \frac{4}{5}x + c$$

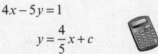

6. At the beginning of the school year, Drew paid $22 for 4 pens and 3 notebooks. Two days later, she decided to buy 6 more of the same pens and 5 more of the same notebooks before the price changed. If she spent $35 on these additional pens and notebooks, what was the cost, in dollars, of one notebook?

Answers

1. **C.** The solution to a system of linear equations in two variables is the intersection point of their graphs. Thus, the solution is (2, –2), Choice C.

2. **B.** Multiply both sides of the first equation by 12 to obtain $6x - 2y = 84$. Add this new equation with $\frac{1}{3}x + 2y = -8$ and you have $6\frac{1}{3}x = 76$, which is equivalent to $\frac{19}{3}x = 76$. Multiply both sides of the equation by $\frac{3}{19}$ to obtain $x = 12$. Substitute $x = 12$ in either one of the original equations; say, $\frac{1}{3}x + 2y = -8$, and you have $\frac{1}{3}(12) + 2y = -8$ or $y = -6$. Therefore, the solution to the system is $(12, -6)$ and $(p, q) = (12, -6)$. Thus, $p + 2q = 12 + 2(-6) = 0$, Choice B.

3. **C.** Since the system has no solution, the two lines, the graphs of the two equations, are parallel. Thus, the slopes of the lines are equal. Writing both equations in $y = mx + b$ form, you have $y = -\frac{2}{3}x + 2$ and $y = -\frac{3}{b}x + \frac{12}{b}$. Since the slopes are equal, set $-\frac{2}{3} = -\frac{3}{b}$ to obtain $b = \frac{9}{2}$, Choice C.

4. **B.** Since x is the amount invested in bonds and y is the amount invested in stocks, the total amount of the investment is $x + y = 2,000$. Bonds yield 2% interest and stocks, 3%. The total annual interest income is $.02x + .03y = 54$, Choice B.

5. $-\frac{1}{5}$ Since the system has infinitely many solutions, the graphs of the equations are the same line, which means the two equations are equivalent. Solve the equation $4x - 5y = 1$ for y, and you have $y = \frac{4}{5}x - \frac{1}{5}$. Thus, $c = -\frac{1}{5}$.

6. **4** Let p be the price of a pen and n be the price of a notebook, then $4p + 3n = 22$ and $6p + 5n = 35$. To solve for n, multiply the first equation by -3 and the second by 2 to find that $-12p - 9n = -66$ and $12p + 10n = 70$. Add the two equations, $-12p - 9n = -66$ and $12p + 10n = 70$, and you get $n = 4$. One notebook costs $4.

E. Linear Inequalities and Systems of Linear Inequalities in Two Variables

Knowing how to solve inequalities is essential to doing well on the new SAT. When working with inequalities in two variables, remember the following:

- You can solve for one of the variables in a linear inequality the same way you would solve a linear equation, except when multiplying or dividing an inequality by a negative number. In those cases, the direction of the inequality sign must be reversed.

- In the xy-plane, the graph of a linear inequality in two variables containing the symbol $\geq$ or $\leq$ is a region bordered by a solid line. If the symbol is $>$ or $<$, the region is bordered by a dotted line. The points on the dotted line are not part of the solution.

- In the xy-plane, the ordered pairs in the solution set of a system of linear inequalities must satisfy each and every one of the inequalities

Practice

1. Which of the following systems of inequalities is represented by the shaded region in the accompanying figure?

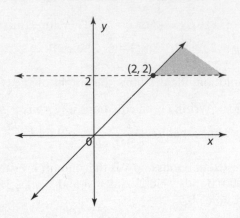

    A. $y \leq x$ and $y < 2$
    B. $y \leq x$ and $y > 2$
    C. $y < x$ and $y \geq 2$
    D. $y \geq x$ and $y > 2$

2. Which of the following ordered pairs is in the solution set of the system of inequalities below?

$$x + y < 2$$
$$2x - y \leq 4$$

    A. $(-1, 0)$
    B. $(0, 2)$
    C. $(1, 5)$
    D. $(3, 2)$

3. Five years ago, Mary was at least 3 years more than twice Karen's age. If k represents Karen's age now and m represents Mary's age now, which of the following describes the relationship of their ages 5 years ago?

    A. $m > 2k + 3$
    B. $m + 5 > 2(k + 5) - 3$
    C. $m - 5 \leq 2(k + 5) + 3$
    D. $m - 5 \geq 2(k - 5) + 3$

4. The approximate glycemic load for an apple is 6.2 and for an orange is 4. Bill wants to keep his total glycemic load from fruits to be no more than 30 a day, and he only eats apples and oranges. Which of the following inequalities represents the possible number of apples, h, and the number of oranges, k, that Bill can have in a day for him to meet his goal?

A. $(6.2 + 4)(h + k) \le 30$
B. $6.2h + 4k < 70$
C. $6.2h + 4k \le 30$
D. $\dfrac{6.2}{h} + \dfrac{4}{k} \le 30$

5. A stationery store is having a sale on pens and notebooks: All pens are \$2 each and all notebooks are \$1.50 each. Anna wants to spend at least \$20, but no more than \$30 total, for pens and notebooks, and she also wants to buy a minimum of four pens. Which of the following systems of inequalities solutions represents the possible number of pens, p, and the number of notebooks, n, that Anna can purchase and stay within her spending guidelines?

A. $2p + 1.50n < 30$
$p > 4$

B. $20 \le \dfrac{2}{p} + \dfrac{1.50}{n} \le 30$
$p \ge 4$

C. $20 < 2p + 1.50n < 30$
$p > 4$

D. $20 \le 2p + 1.50n \le 30$
$p \ge 4$

6. How many ordered pairs (x, y) are in the solution set of the system of inequalities below?

$$-4x + 2y \ge 1$$
$$y < 2x - 3$$

Answers

1. **B.** is correct. The solution sets of the system of inequalities for each of the four choices are shown here.

A.

B.

C.

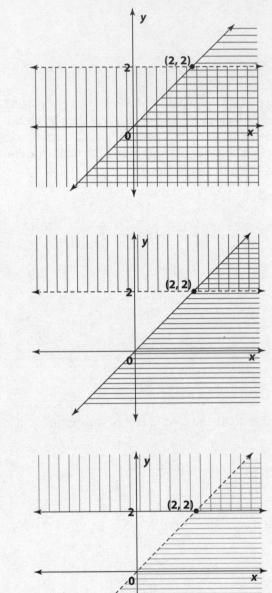

D.

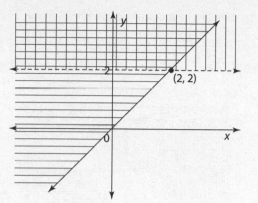

(2, 2)

Thus, the system of inequalities in Choice B is the correct choice.

2. **A.** An ordered pair is in the solution set of a system of inequalities if and only if the ordered pair satisfies each and every one of the inequalities in the system. In this case, the only ordered pair that satisfies both inequalities is $(-1, 0)$, Choice A. Substituting $x = -1$ and $y = 0$ in $x + y < 2$, and in $2x - y \leq 4$, you have $-1 + 0 < 2$ and $2(-1) - 0 \leq 4$ or $-1 < 2$ and $-2 \leq 4$, which are true. Thus, Choice A is correct.

Note that another way to solve this problem is to graph the two inequalities and see which point is in their intersection, the overlapping region.

3. **D.** Five years ago, Mary's age was $m - 5$ and Karen's age was $k - 5$.

	Current Age	Age 5 Years Ago
Mary	m	$m - 5$
Karen	k	$k - 5$

If 5 years ago Mary had been 3 years more than twice Karen's age, the relationship of their ages would have been described as $m - 5 = 2(k - 5) + 3$. Since 5 years ago Mary was at least 3 years more than twice Karen's age, the equation becomes an inequality instead: $m - 5 \geq 2(k - 5) + 3$, Choice D.

4. **C.** The glycemic load for an apple is 6.2; therefore, the glycemic load for h apples is $6.2h$. Similarly, the glycemic load for k oranges is $4k$. The daily total from apples and oranges is $6.2h + 4k$, for which Bill wants to be less than or equal to 30. Thus, $6.2h + 4k \leq 30$, Choice C, is correct.

5. **D.** Since pens are \$2 each and notebooks are \$1.50 each, the total cost for p pens and n notebooks is $2p + 1.50n$. To stay within Anna's spending guidelines, you have $20 \leq 2p + 1.50n \leq 30$. Note that it is inclusive of \$20 and \$30. Since Anna wants at least four pens, $p \geq 4$. Thus, Choice D is correct.

6. **0** Begin by examining the graphs of the inequalities. Rewrite $-4x + 2y \geq 1$ as $2y \geq 4x + 1$, which is equivalent to $y \geq 2x + \dfrac{1}{2}$. The graphs of the two inequalities are shown in the accompanying figure. Since the slopes of the lines $y = 2x - 3$ and $y = 2x + \dfrac{1}{2}$ are the same (the slope is 2), the two lines are parallel.

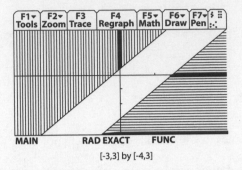

[-3,3] by [-4,3]

Note that the two regions do not intersect, which means there is no ordered pair satisfying both inequalities. Thus, the system has no solution.

F. Interpret the Meaning of a Variable, a Constant, or a Feature of the Graph of a Linear Function that Models a Context

When working with a linear function that models a context, it is important to keep in mind the following:

- The graph of a linear function in two *variables* is always a straight line, and all linear functions can be written in the form of $y = mx + b$, where m is the slope of the line and b is the y-intercept.
- Note that b, the y-intercept, is the y value when $x = 0$, and m, the slope, is the change in the y value for every one unit change in x. For example, the cost function of making pencils is $c(x) = 10 + 0.2x$, when x is the number of pencils made and c is the cost in dollars. The y-intercept is 10, which means the fixed cost of making pencils is \$10, regardless of the number of pencils made. The slope is 0.2, which means for each additional pencil made, the total cost goes up by 20 cents.

Practice

1. Zack, a cell phone sales representative, is paid $10 an hour and an additional $20 for each phone sold. Which of the following graphs best represents his hourly wages, y, for having sold x phones, $x \le 4$, in an hour?

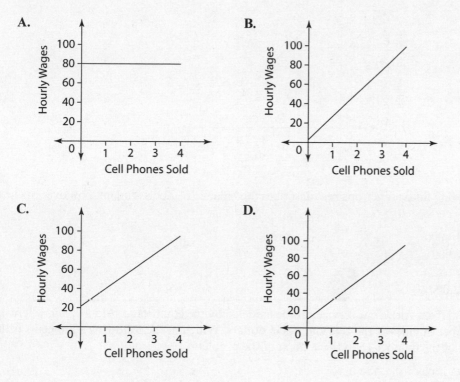

2. Zoe plans to pay off her student loan of $10,000 over the next 5 years, as illustrated in the accompanying figure.

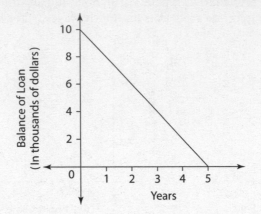

Which of the following linear functions best describes the balance of Zoe's student loan over the next 5 years?

A. $y = 2{,}000x - 10{,}000$
B. $y = 10{,}000 - 2{,}000x$
C. $y = 2{,}000x$
D. $y = 10{,}000 + 2{,}000x$

3. The cost of a ride, c, from Alex's car service can be modeled by the equation $c = 15 + 2.5m$, where m represents the number of miles of the ride and c is in dollars. Which of the following statements is the best interpretation of the number 15 in the context of the problem?

A. The charge per mile of the ride
B. The total charge for the ride
C. A fixed charge of the ride regardless of the number of miles of the ride
D. An additional charge if the ride is 2.5 miles

4. If c is a constant, which of the following could be the graph of the equation below in the xy-plane?

$$x - y = \frac{1}{c^2 + 1}$$

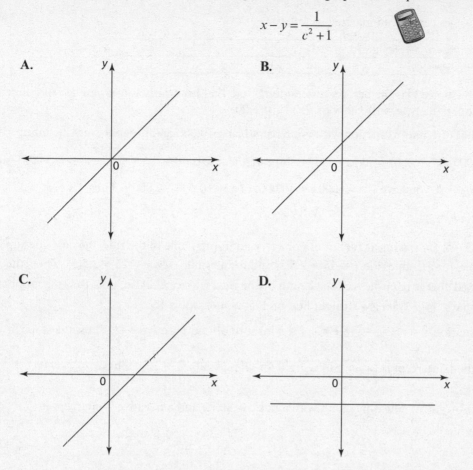

A.

B.

C.

D.

Use the following information to answer questions 5 and 6.

A manufacturing plant can produce 200 electronic tablets a day at a cost of $11,000 or 150 electronic tablets a day at a cost of $8,500. The cost is linearly related to the number of tablets produced a day.

5. What would be the total cost, in dollars, for manufacturing 120 tablets in a day?

6. What is the cost, in dollars, for running the manufacturing plant for a day, if no tablet was made for the day?

Answers

1. **D.** Zack's hourly wages can be summarized as follows:

Number of cell phone sold	0	1	2	3	4
Hourly wages	10	30	50	70	90

   Thus, the graph in Choice D is the best representation. Note that his hourly wages can be represented by a linear function; namely, $y = 10 + 20x$ or $f(x) = 10 + 20x$.

2. **B.** The graph is that of a linear function with y-intercept being 10,000 and ordered pairs including

   (0, 10,000), (1, 8,000), (2, 6,000), and so on. The slope of the line is $m = \dfrac{8,000 - 10,000}{1 - 0} = -2,000$. Using

   the formula $y = mx + b$, you have $y = -2,000x + 10,000$, or $y = 10,000 - 2,000x$. Thus, Choice B is correct.

3. **C.** The cost $c = 15 + 2.5m$ is a linear function. For every additional mile to the ride, the cost goes up by $2.50. For example, for a 2-mile ride, $c = 15 + 2.5(2)$ and for a 3-mile ride, $c = 15 + 2.5(3)$. Thus, the number 15 is a fixed charge regardless of the length of the ride, Choice C. Also, note that the graph of the linear function $c = 15 + 2.5m$ is a straight line, and its y-intercept is 15.

4. **C.** Rewrite the equation $x - y = \dfrac{1}{c^2 + 1}$ in $y = mx + b$ form to obtain $y = x - \dfrac{1}{c^2 + 1}$. Thus, the slope of

   the line is 1 and the y-intercept is $\dfrac{-1}{c^2 + 1}$. Since $c^2 \geq 0$ for all real values of c, you have $\dfrac{1}{c^2 + 1} > 0$.

   Therefore, $\dfrac{-1}{c^2 + 1}$ is negative. The only graph with a positive slope and a negative y-intercept is in

   Choice C.

5. **7,000** Since the cost is a linear function of the number of electronic tablets produced, use the formula

   $y = mx + b$, with y being the cost in dollars, and x being the number of tablets made. Using the ordered

   pairs (200, 11,000) and (150, 8,500), you have the slope $m = \dfrac{11,000 - 8,500}{200 - 150} = 50$, and $y = 50x + b$.

   Substitute the ordered pair (200, 11,000) in the equation to obtain $11,000 = 50(200) + b$ or $b = 1,000$. The cost function is $y = 50x + 1,000$. Thus, for 120 tablets, you have $y = 50(120) + 1,000$ or $y = 7,000$. The total cost for making 120 tablets is $7,000.

6. **1,000** The cost, y, of making x tablets in a day is $y = 50x + 1,000$. If no tablet was produced (i.e., $x = 0$), the cost of maintaining the manufacturing plant is $y = 50(0) + 1,000 = 1,000$. Note that $y = 1,000$ is the y-intercept of the graph of the cost function.

X. Problem Solving and Data Analysis

A. Percents

Percent means hundredths. One **percent** of a given number is the ratio of the number to 100 (i.e., the number divided by 100). When you have to find the percent of a number, always express the given percent as either a fraction or a decimal. For example, write 5% as 0.05 or $\frac{5}{100}$, and n% as $0.01n$ or $\frac{n}{100}$.

Practice

1. If n is a positive number, which of the following represents $2n$% of 150?

   A. $3n$
   B. $30n$
   C. $60n$
   D. $75n$

2. The graph below shows how Saree's salary was determined last year. If Saree earned a total of $18,000 in overtime pay last year, how much did she receive as bonuses?

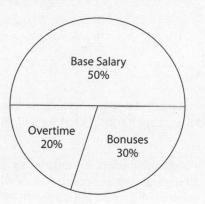

   A. $6,000
   B. $9,000
   C. $27,000
   D. $54,000

3. A chemist has two solutions, A and B, containing 10% and 20% acid, respectively. She wishes to mix 500 cc of solution A with a portion of solution B to produce a new solution that is 12% acid. Solving which of the following equations will yield x, the number of cc's of solution B needed to produce the new solution?

    A. $500(.10) + .20x = (500 + x)(.12)$
    B. $500(.10) = .20x$
    C. $(500 + x)(.20) = 1000(.10)$
    D. $(500 + x)(.30) = .12$

4. An investment portfolio begins with $11,000; its balance for a 3-year period is shown in the accompanying figure.

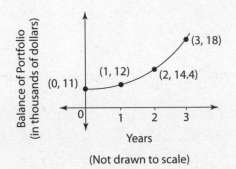

What is the growth, in percent, in the portfolio from the end of the first year to the end of the second year?

    A.   9.1%
    B.   20.0%
    C.   26.7%
    D.   30.9%

5. The list price for a certain graphing calculator was $84. Anna bought the calculator for $91.14, which included the local sales tax and no other charges. What was, in percent, the sales tax rate?

6. Two rounds of auditions were being held to select 40 students for a new chorus that was being formed. In the first round of auditions, 30 students were selected, 80% of whom were girls. If 25% of the members of the chorus had to be boys, how many boys had to be selected in the second round of auditions?

Answers

1. **A.** Because $2n\%$ is $\dfrac{2n}{100}$, then $2n\%$ of 150 is equivalent to $\dfrac{2n}{100}(150) = 3n$, Choice A.

2. **C.** Let x be Saree's annual salary last year. Because the overtime pay was 20% of Saree's salary, $0.2x = 18,000$ and $x = 90,000$. The bonuses were 30% of Saree's salary, so $0.3x = 0.3(90,000) = 27,000$. Thus, Saree's bonuses for last year totaled $27,000, Choice C. You can also do this problem by setting up a proportion to find the bonuses. Let y be the bonuses. Then $\dfrac{0.2}{18,000} = \dfrac{0.3}{y}$, $0.2y = (0.3)(18,000)$, and $y = 27,000$.

3. **A.** Since solution A contains 10% acid, 500 cc of solution A contains 500(0.10) cc acid. Similarly, x cc of solution B contains $(x)(0.20)$ cc acid. The volume of the new solution is $(500 + x)$ cc, and its acid content is $(500 + x)(0.12)$ cc. Thus, $500(0.10) + .20x = (500 + x)(0.12)$, Choice A.

4. **B.** Examining the graph, you see that the balance of the portfolio is $12,000 at the end of the first year, and $14,400 at the end of the second year. The growth is $2,400 or $\dfrac{2,400}{12,000} \times 100\% = 20\%$, Choice B.

5. **8.5** The amount of the sales tax was $91.14 – $84.00 = $7.14. Thus, the sales tax rate was $\dfrac{7.14}{84} \times 100\% = 8.5\%$.

6. **4** If 25% of the 40 chorus members must be boys, there must be a total of $0.25(40) = 10$ boys selected. In the first round, because 80% of the 30 students were girls, 20% of the 30 students were boys and 20% of 30 is $0.20(30) = 6$. Because 10 boys are needed and 6 were already selected in the first round, in the second round the number of boys selected must be $10 - 6 = 4$.

B. Ratios, Rates, and Proportions

A **proportion** is an equation that states that two ratios are equal. For example, $\dfrac{2}{3} = \dfrac{10}{15}$ or $3:6 = 4:8$. When setting up a proportion, make sure that you use the same unit of measurement for the corresponding quantities and write the ratios in the same order. For example, given the question "If five pens cost 60¢, how much will two dozen pens cost at the same rate?", you should express two dozen pens as 24 pens and use the proportion $\dfrac{5}{.60} = \dfrac{24}{x}$, where x represents the cost of 24 pens. Notice that the order of the proportion is $\dfrac{5 \text{ pens}}{\text{cost of 5 pens}} = \dfrac{24 \text{ pens}}{\text{cost of 24 pens}}$. You could also use other equivalent proportions such as $\dfrac{5 \text{ pens}}{24 \text{ pens}} = \dfrac{\text{cost of 5 pens}}{\text{cost of 24 pens}}$.

Practice

1. On a blueprint for an office building, 6 inches represents a height of 45 feet. Using this scale, how many inches on the blueprint will represent 30 feet?

   A. 1.5
   B. 2
   C. 4
   D. 5

2. Given a number such that $\dfrac{2}{5}$ of the number is 30, what is $\dfrac{1}{3}$ of the number?

   A. 4
   B. 10
   C. 12
   D. 25

3. The speed of light is 299,792,458 meters per second. The diameter of the earth at the equator is 12,742 kilometers. Traveling at the speed of light, approximately how many times can a particle go around the earth at its equator in 2 minutes?

   A.   0.14
   B.   8
   C.   16
   D.   899

4. Kaela is 5 feet 6 inches tall and casts a shadow that is 11 feet long. If Dan is standing behind Kaela and he is 6 feet tall, how long is his shadow?

   A.   10 feet
   B.   11 feet
   C.   11 feet 6 inches
   D.   12 feet

5. Saree and Lara were the only candidates running for president of the senior class. When the votes were tallied, the ratio of the number of votes that Saree received to the number of votes that Lara received was 3 to 2. If 60 students voted for Saree, how many students voted in the election?

6. Tom can paint a house in 12 hours, and Hunter can paint the same house in 6 hours. Working together, how many hours will it take for Tom and Hunter to paint the house?

Answers

1. **C.** To find the number of inches on the blueprint, x, use the proportion $\frac{6}{45} = \frac{x}{30}$. Then $45x = 6(30)$ and $x = 4$, Choice C.

   Notice that you do not have to convert inches to feet. When you set up a proportion, corresponding quantities must have the same unit of measurement. In this problem, you're comparing inches on the blueprint to height measured in feet. Both blueprint numbers are in the same units (inches), and both heights are in the same units (feet), so the proportion may be set up without converting. If the height of one building were given in feet and the height of the other building were given in inches, you would have to convert both to feet or both to inches before the proportion could be set up.

2. **D.** Let x be the number. Since $\frac{2}{5}$ of the number is 30, you have $\frac{2}{5}x = 30$ or $x = 75$. Thus, $\frac{1}{3}$ of the number is $\frac{1}{3}(75) = 25$, Choice D.

   You can also do this problem by using a proportion: $\frac{\frac{2}{5}}{30} = \frac{\frac{1}{3}}{x}$. Thus, $\frac{2}{5}x = \frac{1}{3}(30)$, or $x = 25$.

3. **D.** The diameter of the earth at the equator is 12,742 kilometers or $12{,}742 \times 1{,}000 = 12{,}742{,}000$ meters. Thus, its circumference at the equator is $C = \pi d = 12{,}742{,}000\pi$ meters. Since the particle is traveling at the speed of light (299,792,458 meters per second), the particle can go around the earth in

$\dfrac{\text{circumference}}{\text{speed}} = \dfrac{12{,}742{,}000\pi \text{ meters}}{299{,}792{,}458 \text{ meters per second}} \approx 0.133526 \text{ second}$. Thus in 2 minutes, which is

120 seconds, the particle can go around the earth in $\dfrac{120 \text{ sec}}{0.133526 \text{ sec}} \approx 898.699 \approx 899$ times, Choice D.

Note that another approach to solve the problem is as follows:

$\left(\dfrac{299{,}792{,}458 \text{ meters}}{1 \text{ sec}}\right)\left(\dfrac{1 \text{ revolution}}{12{,}742{,}000\pi \text{ meters}}\right)\left(\dfrac{60 \text{ sec}}{1 \text{ min}}\right) \times 2 \text{ min} \approx 898.699$ revolutions or 898.699 times.

Note: If you use $\pi = 3.14$ instead of the π key on your calculator, your answer is 899.155284, which still rounds to 899.

4. **D.**

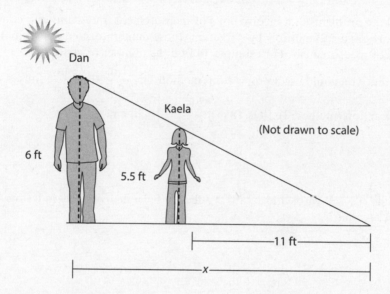

Dan

Kaela

(Not drawn to scale)

6 ft

5.5 ft

11 ft

x

Since each triangle has a right angle and the triangles share an angle, they are similar. As long as all numbers are expressed in the same units, with Kaela's height as 5.5 feet instead of 5 feet 6 inches,

Dan's height can be found using the equation $\dfrac{\text{Kaela's height}}{\text{length of Kaela's shadow}} = \dfrac{\text{Dan's height}}{\text{length of Dan's shadow}}$

or $\dfrac{5.5}{11} = \dfrac{6}{x}$ or $5.5x = 66$ or $x = 12$. Dan's shadow is 12 feet long, Choice D.

5. **100** To find the number of votes that Lara received, x, solve the proportion $\dfrac{3}{2} = \dfrac{60}{x}$ or $x = 40$.

Because 60 students voted for Saree and 40 voted for Lara, the number of students who voted is $60 + 40 = 100$.

6. **4** Tom can paint a house in 12 hours, so he can paint $\frac{1}{12}$ of the house in 1 hour. Similarly, Hunter can paint $\frac{1}{6}$ of the house in 1 hour. If they work together, in 1 hour they can paint $\frac{1}{12}+\frac{1}{6}=\frac{1}{12}+\frac{2}{12}=\frac{3}{12}$ or $\frac{1}{4}$ of the house. Tom and Hunter can paint $\frac{1}{4}$ of the house in 1 hour, so it will take them $1\div\left(\frac{1}{4}\right)$ or 4 hours to paint the whole house.

C. Unit Conversions

In general, when solving problems that involve units of measurement, rates, and unit conversions, you could either (1) use a proportion, or (2) multiply by a fraction whose numerator and denominator are equivalent, but in different units of measurement. For example, to find the number of centimeters in 8 inches given that 1 inch = 2.5 centimeters, you could use a proportion (method 1), $\frac{1 \text{ in}}{2.5 \text{ cm}}=\frac{8 \text{ in}}{x \text{ cm}}$; thus, $x = 20$ cm, or you could multiply by a fraction (method 2); thus, $(8 \text{ in})\left(\frac{2.5 \text{ cm}}{1 \text{ in}}\right)=20$ cm.

Practice

1. Given that 1 mile = 1,760 yards and 1 yard = 3 feet, if Tyler is driving 90 miles per hour, what is his speed in feet per second?

   A. 44
   B. 132
   C. 586.7
   D. 7,920

2. If Michael bought 2 gross of table tennis balls for $360, what is the cost, in dollars, per ball? (*Note:* 1 gross = 12 dozen.)

   A. 1.25
   B. 1.80
   C. 2.50
   D. 180

3. A tourist from China visiting New York brought with her 20,000 CNY (Chinese Yuan Renminbi). The exchange rate was 1.00 CNY = 0.159488 USD (U.S. dollars). She exchanged her 20,000 CNY to U.S. dollars. At the end of her visit, she had 450 U.S. dollars left, and she wanted to exchange the 450 U.S. dollars back to CNY. If the exchange rate was the same, how much money in CNY should she receive?

   A. 71.77
   B. 2,739.76
   C. 2,821.53
   D. 19,550.00

4. If milk costs $2 per quart in New York City, and the same milk costs 40 pesos per liter in Mexico City, and if the currency exchange rate is 1 peso = 0.0663841 U.S. dollar, which of the following statements is true? (Note that 1 liter ≈ 1.06 quarts.)

   A. Milk costs more in New York City than in Mexico City.
   B. Milk costs more in Mexico City than in New York City.
   C. Milk costs the same in New York City and in Mexico City.
   D. There is not enough information to determine whether milk costs more in either New York City or Mexico City.

5. The density of a liquid Z35 is approximately 2 kilograms/meter^3. A storage tank in the shape of a right circular cylinder has a diameter of 10 meters at its base, and a height of 6 meters. If the tank is completely filled with liquid Z35, what is the approximate weight to the nearest kilogram of all the liquid Z35 in the tank? Use $\pi = 3.14$.

6. Bill can run a mile in 15 minutes. If he could maintain this speed for an upcoming 5-kilometer race, what would be Bill's approximate time, in minutes, in completing the race? Round your answer to the nearest one hundredth. (1 mile ≈ 1.6 kilometers)

Answers

1. **B.** Since 1 mile = 1,760 yards and 1 yard = 3 feet, you have 1 mile = 1,760 × 3 = 5,280 feet. Thus,

$$\frac{90 \text{ mi}}{1 \text{ hr}} = \frac{90 \times 5,280 \text{ ft}}{1 \text{ hr}} = \frac{90 \times 5,280 \text{ feet}}{1 \times 60 \text{ min}} = \frac{90 \times 5,280 \text{ feet}}{60 \times 60 \text{ sec}} = 132 \text{ ft/sec}.$$ Note that you could have also used

a single expression to find the answer: $\frac{90 \text{ mi}}{1 \text{ hr}} \cdot \frac{5,280 \text{ ft}}{1 \text{ mi}} \cdot \frac{1 \text{ hr}}{60 \text{ min}} \cdot \frac{1 \text{ min}}{60 \text{ sec}} = 132 \text{ ft/sec}$, Choice B.

2. **A.** Note that 1 gross = 12 dozen, and 1 dozen = 12, and thus 2 gross = 2 × 12 × 12 = 288. Since the cost of

288 balls is $360, the price of one ball is $\frac{\$360}{288 \text{ balls}} = \$1.25$, Choice A. You could have also used a proportion

to find the answer: $\frac{360 \text{ dollars}}{288 \text{ balls}} = \frac{x \text{ dollar}}{1 \text{ ball}}$, which is equivalent to $288x = 360$ or $x = \frac{360}{288} = 1.25$.

3. **C.** Using a proportion $\frac{\text{CNY}_1}{\text{USD}_1} = \frac{\text{CNY}_2}{\text{USD}_2}$, you have $\frac{1 \text{ CNY}}{0.159488 \text{ USD}} = \frac{x \text{ CNY}}{450 \text{ USD}}$ or

$x = \frac{(1)(450)}{0.159488} = 2,821.53 \text{ CNY}$, Choice C.

4. **B.** Milk costs 40 pesos per liter in Mexico City. Begin by converting pesos to U.S. dollars, and you

have $\frac{40 \text{ pesos}}{1 \text{ liter}} = \frac{40 \text{ pesos}}{1 \text{ liter}} \left(\frac{0.0663841 \text{ U.S. dollars}}{1 \text{ peso}} \right) = \frac{2.65536 \text{ U.S. dollars}}{1 \text{ liter}}$, which means that milk

costs approximately $2.66 U.S. dollars per liter in Mexico City. Now convert liters to quarts, and you have $\left(\dfrac{2.65536}{1\text{ liter}}\right)\left(\dfrac{1\text{ liter}}{1.06\text{ quarts}}\right) = \dfrac{2.50506\text{ U.S. dollars}}{1\text{ quart}}$. Thus, milk costs approximately \$2.51 U.S.

dollars per quart in Mexico City. Therefore, milk costs more in Mexico City than in New York City, Choice B.

5. **942** The volume of the storage tank is $V = \pi r^2 h = \pi(5)^2(6)\text{m}^3 = 150\,\pi\text{m}^3$. Since the density of liquid Z35 is 2 kg/m^3, the approximate weight of all the liquid in the tank is $(150\pi\text{m}^3)(2\text{ kg/m}^3) = 300\pi$ kg ≈ 942 kilograms.

6. **46.88** Begin by converting miles to kilometers. A mile in 15 minutes is equivalent to 1.6 kilometers in 15 minutes. Thus, running 1 kilometer takes Bill $\dfrac{15\text{ min}}{1.6\text{ km}} = \dfrac{9.375\text{ min}}{1\text{ km}} = 9.375\text{ minutes}$. For the 5-kilometer race, his time would be 9.375 min $\times$ 5 = 46.88 minutes. Note that you can also use a proportion to solve the problem: $\dfrac{15\text{ min}}{1.6\text{ km}} = \dfrac{x\text{ min}}{5\text{ km}}$ or $x = 46.88$ minutes.

D. Scatterplots and a Line or Curve of Best Fit

When solving problems involving scatterplots or a line of best fit, it is helpful to remember the following:

- A **line or curve of best fit** is a line or curve that best describes a set of data points. Some of the common curves are those of quadratic, cubic, polynomial, logarithmic, and exponential functions.
- A **correlation coefficient, r,** indicates how strong the correlation is between two variables. The closer $|r|$ is to 1, the stronger the correlation. For example, $r = -0.9$ indicates a stronger correlation than $r = 0.8$.
- If $r > 0$, the slope of the regression line is positive, and if $r < 0$, the slope is negative.

Practice

1. Which of the following values of a correlation coefficient represents data with the strongest linear correlation between two variables?

   A. -0.92
   B. 0
   C. 0.85
   D. 1.2

Use the following information to answer questions 2–4.

Twenty students took a math test. The scatterplot in the accompanying figure shows, for ten students, the relationship between the number of hours a student studied for the test and the student's grade for the test. The figure also shows the line of best fit.

**Grades of 10 Students for a Math Test
and the Number of Hours They Studied for the Test**

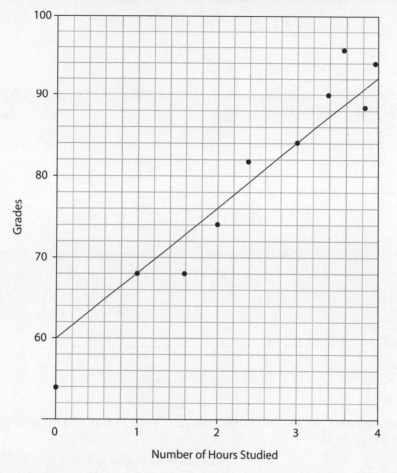

2. According to the line of best fit, which of the following is the predicted grade for a student who studied 2 hours for the test?

   A. 74

   B. 76

   C. 82

   D. 84

3. Based on the line of best fit, what was the minimum number of hours a student had to study in order to earn a grade of 96 or higher?

   A. 3.6

   B. 4.5

   C. 5

   D. 6

4. Of the ten students whose grades are on the scatterplot, how many have an actual grade within 4 points of the predicted grade by the line of best fit?

   A. 3
   B. 5
   C. 7
   D. 9

5. The scatterplot of a set of data points is shown in the accompanying diagram. Which of the following equations could best model the data?

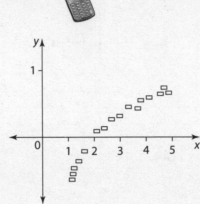

   A. $y = 2 - \sqrt{x}$
   B. $y = x + 2$
   C. $y = \log(x - 1)$
   D. $y = 2^x + 1$

6. The number of elephants in a region in Asia from 2010 to 2015 is shown in the scatterplot below. The line of best fit is also shown.

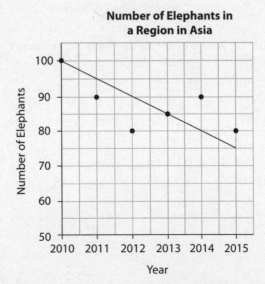

According to the line of best fit, what is the average annual decrease in the number of elephants in the region?

Answers

1. **A.** The correlation coefficient, r, is always $-1 \leq r \leq 1$. If $r > 0$, the slope of the regression line is positive, and if $r < 0$, the slope of the regression line is negative. To determine the strength of a linear relationship between the two variables, you look at $|r|$. The closer the $|r|$ is to 1, the stronger the linear relationship between the two variables. Among the choices given, $|-0.92| = 0.92$, Choice A, is the closest to 1.

2. **B.** Since the student studied 2 hours for the test, go to 2 on the x-axis and then go up to the point on the line of best fit. Notice that the corresponding y-value for $x = 2$ is 76, Choice B.

3. **B.** Begin by finding the slope of the line of best fit. Pick any 2 points on the line with integer coordinates; for example, $(4, 92)$ and $(3, 84)$. The slope is $\dfrac{92 - 84}{4 - 3} = 8$, which means that for every additional hour of study, a student's grade goes up 8 points. Remember, you already have the point $(4, 92)$, which means that a student studying 4 hours would receive a grade of 92. A grade of 96 is 4 more points than 92. Thus, a student needs to study an additional half-hour; that is, a student has to study a total of 4.5 hours in order to receive a grade of 96 or higher, Choice B.

4. **C.** Students who studied 0, 1.6, and 3.6 hours received grades of 54, 68, and 96, respectively. Their grades were more than 4 points from the predicted grades by the line of best fit. The other seven students had grades all within 4 points of their predicted grades, Choice C.

5. **C.** Enter the equation of each choice into the calculator and examine its graph. The graph of $y = \log(x - 1)$ best models the data, Choice C.

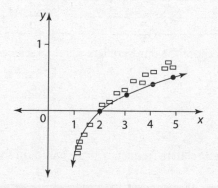

6. **5** From the line of best fit, select 2 points with integer coefficients; for example, $(2010, 100)$ and $(2013, 85)$. The slope of the line is $m = \dfrac{y_2 - y_1}{x_2 - x_1}$, and in this case, $m = \dfrac{100 - 85}{2010 - 2013} = -5$. Thus, the yearly decrease in the number of elephants in the region is 5.

E. Two-Way Tables, One-Way Tables, and Bar Graphs

Tables and bar graphs are used to show the relationship between two categorical variables. Data can be shown as frequency counts or as relative frequencies. Relative frequencies for two-way tables can also be displayed as relative frequencies for the entire table, for rows, or for columns. Try the following practice problems.

185

Practice

1. Two hundred and forty students signed up for an after-school sports program. Each student selected one and only one of four sports available: basketball, football, soccer, and tennis. Their selections are summarized in a relative frequency table below.

Relative Frequency Table				
Sports	Basketball	Football	Soccer	Tennis
Percent	45	12.5	35	7.5

How many students signed up for tennis?

A. 8
B. 15
C. 18
D. 32

Use the following information to answer questions 2–4.

Fifty third-graders were asked which subject they like more: math or science. Their responses are summarized in a two-way frequency table below.

Frequency Table			
	Math	**Science**	**Total**
Boys	13	10	23
Girls	9	18	27
Total	22	28	50

2. To the nearest tenth, what percent of the third-graders who like science more than math are girls?

A. 36.0
B. 54.0
C. 64.3
D. 66.7

3. Below is a partially constructed relative frequency table based on the information provided earlier on the fifty third-graders.

Relative Frequency Table			
	Math	**Science**	**Total**
Boys	0.26	0.20	0.46
Girls	x		
Total		y	1.00

What is the value of $x + y$?

A. 0.18
B. 0.74
C. 37
D. 74

4. Below is a partially constructed relative frequency of row table based on the information provided earlier on the fifty third-graders.

Relative Frequency of Row Table

	Math	Science	Total
Boys	56.5%	43.5%	100%
Girls		x	100%
Total			100%

What is the value of x in percent?

A. 33.3

B. 36

C. 56

D. 66.7

5. A furniture manufacturer has three factories that make tables and chairs. In the month of January, the three factories together produced 200 tables and 600 chairs. The production levels of the three factories are shown below in a relative frequency of column table.

Relative Frequency of Column Table

	Tables	Chairs	Total
Factory A	0.20	0.33	0.3
Factory B	0.50	0.40	0.425
Factory C	0.30	0.27	0.275
Total	1.00	1.00	1.00

How many chairs did Factory B produce in the month of January?

6. A baker asked 40 of her customers which pie they like more: apple or pumpkin. Their responses are summarized in a stacked bar graph below.

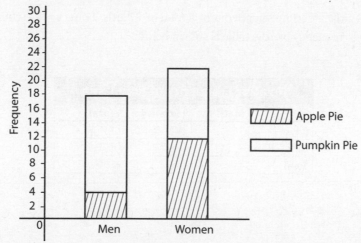

If one person is randomly selected from all the customers who prefer apple pie, what is the probability that the person selected is a woman?

Answers

1. **C.** The table shows that 7.5% of students signed up for tennis. Convert 7.5% to either a decimal, .075, or a fraction, $\dfrac{7.5}{100}$. Thus, the number of students who signed up for tennis is $(240)\dfrac{7.5}{100}$ or 18, Choice C. Note that you could also have used a proportion to solve the problem: $\dfrac{7.5\%}{100\%} = \dfrac{x}{240}$ or $x = 18$.

2. **C.** The science column shows that there are 28 students who prefer science, and of the 28 students, 18 are girls. Thus, the percent of the 28 students who are girls is $\left(\dfrac{18}{28}\right)(100\%) \approx 64.285\% \approx 64.3\%$, Choice C.

3. **B.** Remember that this is a relative frequency table. Based on the frequency table provided earlier, there are 9 girls who preferred math and there are 50 students total. Thus, $x = \dfrac{9}{50} = 0.18$. Similarly, there are 28 students who chose science out of 50; therefore, $y = \dfrac{28}{50} = 0.56$. The value of $(x + y)$ is $= 0.18 + 0.56 = 0.74$, Choice B. A completely constructed relative frequency table is shown below.

Relative Frequency Table			
	Math	**Science**	**Total**
Boys	0.26	0.20	0.46
Girls	0.18	0.36	0.54
Total	0.44	0.56	1.00

4. **D.** Remember that this is a relative frequency of row table. Based on the frequency table provided earlier, there are 18 girls preferring science out of a total of 27 girls. Thus, $x = \dfrac{18}{27}(100\%) \approx 66.7\%$, Choice D. A complete relative frequency of row table is shown below.

Relative Frequency of Row Table			
	Math	**Science**	**Total**
Boys	56.5%	43.5%	100%
Girls	33.3%	66.7%	100%
Total	44%	56%	100%

5. **240** The conditional frequency for Factory B under the chair column is 0.40, which means Factory B produced 40% of the total number of chairs made by the three factories. Since the three factories together produced 600 chairs, Factory B made (600)(0.40) or 240 chairs. (It might be helpful to see the complete relative frequency of column table as shown below. Please note that you do not need to construct a complete frequency table to answer the question.)

Relative Frequency of Column Table			
	Tables	Chairs	Total
Factory A	40	200	240
Factory B	100	240	340
Factory C	60	160	220
Total	200	600	800

6. $\frac{3}{4}$ The stacked bar graph shows that of the customers who prefer apple pie, 4 are men and 12 are women. The total number of customers who prefer apple pie is 16. Thus, the probability of a woman being picked from all the customers who prefer apple pie is $\frac{12}{16}$ or $\frac{3}{4}$. (It might be helpful to see a frequency table for the stacked bar graph. Please note that you do not need to construct a frequency table for the stacked bar graph to answer the question.)

Frequency Table			
	Apple Pie	Pumpkin Pie	Total
Men	4	14	18
Women	12	10	22
Total	16	24	40

F. Linear and Exponential Growth

A common formula for the **linear growth model** is $y = mx + b$, where b is the initial value of y and m is the rate of growth/decay for every one-unit change in x. (Note that $y = mx + b$ is also the slope-intercept form of a line.) If $m > 0$, y increases (grows); if $m < 0$, y decreases (decays).

Common formulas for the **exponential growth model** are:

$$y = ab^x \begin{cases} \text{if } a > 0 \text{ and } 0 < b < 1, \; y \text{ decreases} \\ \text{if } a > 0 \text{ and } b > 1, \; y \text{ increases} \end{cases}$$

$$A = P(1+r)^t \begin{cases} \text{if } r > 0, A \text{ increases} \\ \text{if } r < 0, A \text{ decreases} \end{cases}$$

For continuous growth/decay:

$$A = Pe^{rt} \begin{cases} \text{if } r > 0, A \text{ increases} \\ \text{if } r < 0, A \text{ decreases} \end{cases}$$

For compound interest:

$$A = P\left(1+\frac{r}{n}\right)^{nt}$$, compounding n times per year with r, the rate in decimal, and t in years

$$A = P(1+r)^t$$, compounding once per year with r, the rate in decimal, and t in years

Practice

1. Caitlyn wishes to buy a new set of speakers that costs $460. She has $120 for this purchase and plans to save an additional $20 a month until she has sufficient money for the speakers. If n represents the minimum number of months that Caitlyn needs to save until she can purchase the speakers, which of the following equations yields the correct answer for n?

   A. $120 + 20n = 460$
   B. $20n = 460$
   C. $20n = 460 + 120$
   D. $20n - 120 = 460$

2. A business office bought a new copying machine for $2,950. The depreciated value after n years is projected as $2,950 - 650n$ for $0 \le n \le 4$. What is the maximum number of years for the depreciated value of the copying machine to be greater than or equal to $1,000?

   A.   1
   B.   2
   C.   3
   D.   4

Use the following information to answer questions 3 and 4.

There are 60 bacteria in a culture initially, and the number of bacteria in the culture triples every 2 hours.

3. If N represents the number of bacteria in the culture and h represents the number of hours passed since the culture had 60 bacteria, which of the following equations models the number of bacteria in the culture over time?

   A. $N = 60h$
   B. $N = 60 + 3h$
   C. $N = 60(3)^{\frac{h}{2}}$
   D. $N = 60(3)^{2h}$

4. If h is an integer and h represents the number of hours passed since the culture had 60 bacteria, what is the minimum integer value of h for the culture to have more than 10,000 bacteria?

   A.   5
   B.   8
   C.   9
   D.   10

5. George bought a new set of headphones for $329. It is projected that the value of the headphones depreciates 20% per year. To the nearest dollar, what will be the value of the headphones in 3 years?

6. Mary invested $50,000 at an annual interest rate of 2.4% compounded quarterly. What is the minimum number of years, in integral years, for her initial investment to double?

Answers

1. **A.** Caitlyn saves $20 a month; in n months, she would have $20n$ dollars. Since she has set aside $120 initially for the purchase of the new speakers, she would have, in n months, a total of $120 + 20n$ dollars. The cost of the speakers is $460. Thus, $120 + 20n = 460$ is the correct equation, Choice A.

2. **C.** Since the depreciated value is greater than or equal to $1,000, you have $2,950 - 650n \geq 1000$, or $-650n \geq -1,950$ or $n \leq 3$. Thus, the maximum value for n is 3, Choice C. Note that when you divide both sides of an inequality by a negative number, you switch the inequality sign.

3. **C.** Since h represents the number of hours, $\dfrac{h}{2}$ represents the number of 2-hour periods. For example, if $h = 8$, then $\dfrac{h}{2} = 4$ (there are four 2-hour periods in 8 hours). Also, for every 2-hour period, the number of bacteria triples. For example, if $h = 8$, then $\dfrac{h}{2} = 4$, which means the number of bacteria will triple four times or 3^4. Thus, $N = 60(3)^{\frac{h}{2}}$ is the correct equation, Choice C.

4. **D.** The number of bacteria, N, over time, h, is represented by $N = 60(3)^{\frac{h}{2}}$, and in this case, $10,000 = 60(3)^{\frac{h}{2}}$.

   Enter this equation in your TI-89 graphing calculator: *Solve* $(10,000 = 60(3) \wedge (h/2), h)$, and obtain $h = 9.313560$. Since the number of bacteria is more than 10,000, $h = 10$, Choice D.

5. **168** This is an exponential decay problem. The formula is $A = P(1 - r)^t$, with P being the initial amount, r the depreciation rate in decimal, t the number of years, and A the balance. In this case, you have $A = 329(1 - 0.20)^3$ or $A = 168.448 \approx 168.45$. To the nearest dollar, $A = 168$.

6. **29** This is a compound interest problem. The formula is $A = P\left(1 + \dfrac{r}{n}\right)^{nt}$, where P is the principal (initial investment), r the annual interest rate in decimal, n the number of compoundings per year, and t the number of years. In this case, you have $2(50,000) = 50,000\left(1 + \dfrac{.024}{4}\right)^{4t}$. Enter this equation in your TI-89 calculator: *Solve* $\left(2(50,000) = 50,000\left(1 + \dfrac{.024}{4}\right) \wedge (4t), t\right)$, and you have $t = 28.9677$. Thus, $t = 29$.

G. Statistics: Mean, Median, Mode, Range, and Standard Deviation

Knowing the following definitions is essential to solving problems in statistics:

- The **mean** of a set of numbers or algebraic expressions is the average of the set. For example:
  - The average of 5, 6, and 10 is $\dfrac{5+6+10}{3}$ or 7.
  - The average of $x + 8$ and $5x - 4$ is $\dfrac{x+8+5x-4}{2}$ or $3x + 2$.

- The **median** of an ordered list of numbers is the middle value. For example:
  - The median of 2, 6, 10, 11, 14 is 10.
  - The median of 2, 6, 8, 20 is $\dfrac{6+8}{2}$ or 7.

- The **mode** of a list of numbers is the number that appears most often. For example:
  - The mode of 2, 3, 5, 5, 5, 6, 6, 8 is 5.
  - The **modes** of 2, 3, 6, 6, 8, 8, 12, 15 are 6 and 8.

- The **range** of a set of numbers is the difference between the maximum value and the minimum value. For example:
  - The range of 2, 6, 10, 11, 14 is 12.
  - The range of 2, 3, 5, 5, 5, 6, 6, 8 is 6.

Practice

1. Tommy's test grades in his math class for the first quarter are 90, 84, 80, 92, 84, and 98. Of the six grades in the first quarter, if p is the mean, q is the median, and r is the mode, which of the following inequalities is true?

   A. $r < q < p$
   B. $r < p < q$
   C. $p < r < q$
   D. $q < p < r$

Use the following information to answer questions 2 and 3.

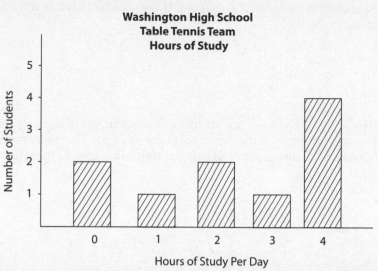

**Washington High School
Table Tennis Team
Hours of Study**

The accompanying graph shows the frequency distribution of the number of hours that members of the table tennis team at Washington High School study each day.

2. What is the median number of hours of study for the team?

   A. 2
   B. 2.5
   C. 3
   D. 3.5

3. If h is the mean number of hours of studying for the team, k is the mode, and p is the range, which of the following statements is true?

   A. $k < h < p$
   B. $h < k < p$
   C. $h < p < k$
   D. $h < k \leq p$

4. In a certain hospital, the salaries of surgeons and the salaries of pediatricians are both normally distributed. The mean salary of surgeons at this hospital is $400,000 a year with a standard deviation of $100,000. The mean salary of pediatricians at the same hospital is $250,000 a year with a standard deviation of $50,000. Dr. Smith, a surgeon, has an annual salary of $450,000, and Dr. Lee, a pediatrician, has an annual salary of $300,000. Which of the following statements is true?

   A. In the hospital, Dr. Smith's salary is in a higher percentile among all the surgeons than Dr. Lee's salary percentile among all the pediatricians.
   B. In the hospital, Dr. Lee's salary is in a higher percentile among all the pediatricians than Dr. Smith's salary percentile among all the surgeons.
   C. The salaries of both doctors are in the same percentile in their respective groups.
   D. There is insufficient information to determine which doctor's salary is in a higher percentile in their respective groups.

5. Set A contains ten real numbers with a standard deviation of h. Set B also contains ten real numbers generated by taking each number in Set A minus 4. If the standard deviation for Set B is k, which of the following statements is true?

   A. $k = h - 4$
   B. $k = h$
   C. $k = h + 4$
   D. $k = h + 6$

6. In the fall semester, Mary received a 77 on her first calculus test. She performed much better on the subsequent tests and her average for the subsequent tests was a 91. The final average for all her calculus tests was 87.5. What was the total number of calculus tests Mary took in the fall semester?

   A. 2
   B. 3
   C. 4
   D. 5

Answers

1. **A.** The mean is the average: $p = \dfrac{90 + 84 + 80 + 92 + 84 + 98}{6} = 88$. The median, q, is the middle value of

   80, 84, 84, 90, 92, 98 or $\dfrac{84 + 90}{2} = 87$. The mode, r, is the value that appears the most often: 84. Thus, $r < q < p$, Choice A. For steps on how to solve this problem using a calculator, see "Finding Mean, Median, Quartiles, and Standard Deviation of a Given Set of Data" in the Appendix.

2. **B.** Inspecting the graph, you see that there are a total of 10 students on the table tennis team: two studying 0 hours a day, one studying 1 hour, two studying 2 hours, one studying 3 hours, and four studying 4 hours a day. Listing the number of hours of studying, you have 0, 0, 1, 2, 2, 3, 4, 4, 4, 4. The

   median number is between the fifth and sixth numbers. Thus, the median is $\dfrac{2 + 3}{2} = 2.5$ hours, Choice B.

3. **D.** The total number of hours of study for the 10 members of the team is 2(0) + 1(1) + 2(2) + 1(3) +

   4(4) or 24. Therefore, the mean is $\dfrac{24}{10}$ or $h = 2.4$ hours. The range is the maximum minus the minimum number of hours of study, and thus, $p = 4 - 0$ or $p = 4$ hours. The mode is the most frequent number, and in this case $k = 4$ hours. Thus, $h < k \le p$, Choice D. Note that $h < p \le k$ is also a true statement since both k and $p = 4$, but $h < p \le k$ is not among the answer choices.

4. **B.**

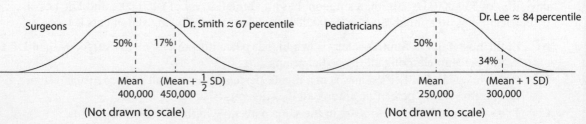

(Not drawn to scale)

Dr. Smith's salary is a half standard deviation above the mean, while Dr. Lee's salary is 1 standard deviation above the mean. Thus, Dr. Lee's salary is relatively higher among all the pediatricians in the hospital than Dr. Smith's salary among all the surgeons, Choice B.

5. **B.** The standard deviation is defined as $\sqrt{variance}$ or $\sqrt{\dfrac{\sum(x_i - \overline{x})^2}{n}}$, which is the square root of the sum of the squares of the deviations from the mean and divided by the number of data values. In this case, Set B contains numbers that are 4 less than the numbers in Set A. Therefore, the mean of Set B is also 4 less than the mean of Set A, and the deviations from the mean are the same in both sets or $k = h$, Choice B. Thus, the standard deviations for the two sets are identical. For example, if Set A = {6, 10}, then the mean is 8 and the standard deviation is $\sqrt{\dfrac{(6-8)^2 + (10-8)^2}{2}} = 2$. Set B = {2, 6}, the mean is 4, and the standard deviation is $\sqrt{\dfrac{(2-4)^2 + (6-4)^2}{2}} = 2$.

6. **C.** Let n be the total number of calculus tests Mary took during the fall semester. (Note that after the first test, she took $(n - 1)$ more tests.) The total number of points for all of Mary's tests is $77 + 91(n - 1)$, and the average of all her tests is $\dfrac{77 + 91(n - 1)}{n} = 87.5$. Solve the equation and you have $n = 4$. Therefore, there were 4 tests in the fall semester, Choice C.

H. Evaluating Graphs, Tables, and Data Collections

When solving problems involving graphs, charts, and tables, always remember to:

- Read the title of the figure, the labeling of the axes, and the legend if provided.
- Be careful of the scale for each axis. For example, one unit on the x-axis may equal to 2 hours, and one unit on the y-axis may represent 10 miles.
- Beware of change of units. For example, the question may ask for the area of a rectangle in square feet, but the dimensions could be given in inches.

Practice

1. A school district wishes to survey a sample of students to determine what kind of activities the district should offer to all students in a summer program. Which of the following is least likely to contain bias?

    A.   Surveying members of the basketball team
    B.   Surveying a sample of students in the computer room
    C.   Surveying a sample of students arriving at school in the morning
    D.   Surveying a sample of students taking honors chemistry

2. The accompanying line graph shows the number of books sold by Whitman's Bookstore in each month from January to May. What percent of the number of books sold in February is equal to the number of books sold in May?

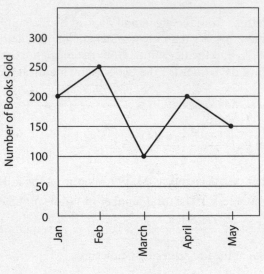

Whitman's Book Sales

A. 25%
B. 40%
C. 60%
D. 75%

3. In 2016, students who attended Washington High School or Adams High School were allowed to participate in only one sport for the year: tennis, soccer, swimming, or basketball. Based on the information provided in the accompanying bar graph, how many more students at Washington High School than at Adams High School participated in a sport in 2016?

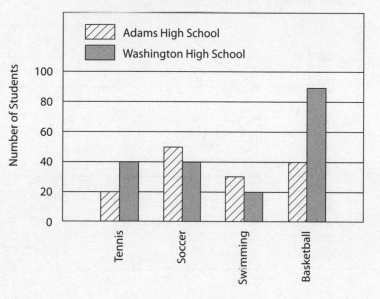

**Number of Students in Sports
at Washington High School and Adams High School**

A. 40
B. 50
C. 70
D. 140

4. In the accompanying diagram, the double line graph shows the revenues and expenses of Concord Electronics for the past 5 years. Which year had the greatest profit?

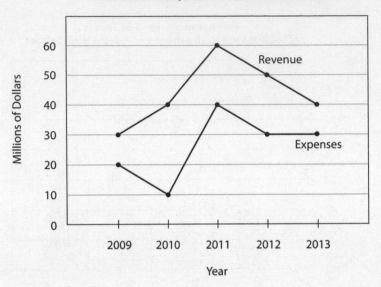

Revenue and Expenses of Concord Electronics

A. 2009
B. 2010
C. 2012
D. 2013

5. In a certain city, the temperatures in degrees Fahrenheit at 8:00 a.m. for the past 10 consecutive days are shown in the accompanying stem-and-leaf diagram. What is the median temperature in degrees Fahrenheit for the 10-day period?

Stem	Leaf
4	9
5	2 4 4 6
6	2 2 5
7	0 1

Key: 7|1 = 71°F

6. Each of the 24 students in Mr. Martin's class plays tennis, soccer, or both. If four students play both sports and eight play only tennis, how many students play only soccer?

A. 12
B. 14
C. 16
D. 18

Answers

1. **C.** Since the summer program is open to all students, the activities should reflect the interests of the entire student population. Students on the basketball team, in the computer room, or taking honors chemistry are likely to prefer activities not necessarily representative of all students. In addition, the selection of students should be random. Surveying a sample of students arriving at school in the morning is least likely to contain bias, Choice C.

2. **C.** According to the graph, you know that the number of books sold in February is 250 and the number of books sold in May is 150. Use the proportion $\frac{150}{250} = \frac{x}{100\%}$, which is equivalent to $x = \frac{100(150)}{250}\%$ or 60%, Choice C.

3. **B.** At Washington High School, 40 students played tennis, 40 played soccer, 20 swam, and 90 played basketball, totaling $40 + 40 + 20 + 90 = 190$ students who participated in a sport. At Adams High School, 20 students played tennis, 50 played soccer, 30 swam, and 40 played basketball, totaling $20 + 50 + 30 + 40 = 140$ students who participated in a sport. The difference between the number of students who participated in a sport at Washington High School and at Adams High School is $190 - 140 = 50$, Choice B.

4. **B.** Profit = Revenue − Expenses. According to the line graph, in 2010, revenue was $40 million and expenses were $10 million. Profit for 2010 was $30 million, the largest for the 5-year period, Choice B.

	2009	2010	2011	2012	2013
Revenue	30	40	60	50	40
Expenses	20	10	40	30	30
Profit	10	30	20	20	10

5. **59** According to the stem-and-leaf diagram, the temperatures for the past 10 days are 49, 52, 54, 54, 56, 62, 62, 65, 70, and 71. Since the median of a data set arranged in numerical order is the middle number, the median temperature is $\frac{56 + 62}{2}$ or 59°F.

6. **A.** Set up a Venn diagram with x representing the number of students who only play soccer.

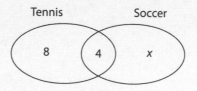

Because four students play in both sports and eight students play only tennis, the number of students who play only soccer is $24 - (8 + 4) = 24 - 12 = 12$, Choice A.

XI. Passport to Advanced Math

A. Arithmetic Operations on Polynomials

When performing arithmetic operations on polynomials, remember the following:

- Distribute the minus sign when subtracting polynomials. For example, $(x^2 - 3x + 4) - (4x^2 + 6x - 10) = x^2 - 3x + 4 - 4x^2 - 6x + 10 = -3x^2 - 9x + 14$.

- Add exponents when multiplying monomials of the same variable. For example, $(6x^8)(-2x^2) = -12x^{10}$.

- Subtract exponents when dividing monomials of the same variable. For example, $\dfrac{15x^6}{5x^2} = 3x^4$.

- Distribute the negative sign when dividing a polynomial by a monomial with a negative sign. For example, $\dfrac{6x^4 - 4x^2 + 6x}{-2x} = -3x^3 + 2x - 3$.

Practice

1. If $h = (x - 1)^2$ and $k = x + 1$, what is hk in terms of x?

   A. $x^2 - 1$
   B. $x^2 + 1$
   C. $x^3 + x^2 - x - 1$
   D. $x^3 - x^2 - x + 1$

2. What polynomial must be subtracted from $x^2 - 4$ so that the difference is $2x^2 - 3x + 1$?

   A. $-x^2 + 3x - 5$
   B. $x^2 - 3x + 5$
   C. $-x^2 - 3x + 1$
   D. $x^2 + 3x + 5$

3. If the length of a rectangle is represented by $2x$ and the width by $3x + 1$, what is the perimeter of the rectangle in terms of x?

   A. $x + 1$
   B. $5x + 1$
   C. $10x + 2$
   D. $10x + 4$

4. For all values of $x \neq 0$, which of the following is equivalent to $\dfrac{3x^6 - 2x^4 + x^2}{-x^2}$?

   A. $-3x^3 - 2x^2 + x$
   B. $-3x^3 - 2x^2 + 1$
   C. $3x^4 - 2x^2$
   D. $-3x^4 + 2x^2 - 1$

5. What is the remainder when $x^2 - 4x - 12$ is divided by $x - 2$?

6. If $(x - a)(x - b) = x^2 - 4x - 21$, what is the value of ab?

Answers

1. **D.** You are given $h = (x - 1)^2$ and $k = x + 1$. That means $hk = (x - 1)^2 \cdot (x + 1) = (x - 1)(x - 1)(x + 1)$. Since multiplication is commutative, first multiply $(x - 1)(x + 1)$ and obtain $(x^2 - 1)$. Next, multiply $(x - 1)(x^2 - 1)$, and you have $x^3 - x^2 - x + 1$, Choice D.

2. **A.** Subtract each polynomial in the four choices from $x^2 - 4$ and check the result. Starting with Choice A, you have $(x^2 - 4) - (-x^2 + 3x - 5) = x^2 - 4 + x^2 - 3x + 5$ or $2x^2 - 3x + 1$, the desired result. There is no need to check the other answer choices.

3. **C.** The perimeter of a rectangle equals twice the length plus twice the width. Thus, the perimeter is $2(2x) + 2(3x + 1)$, which is equivalent to $4x + 6x + 2$ or $10x + 2$, Choice C.

4. **D.** The expression $\dfrac{3x^6 - 2x^4 + x^2}{-x^2}$ is equivalent to dividing each term in the numerator by the denominator x^2. Thus, $\dfrac{3x^6}{-x^2} - \dfrac{2x^4}{-x^2} + \dfrac{x^2}{-x^2} = -3x^4 + 2x^2 - 1$, Choice D. Remember that when you divide monomials with the same base, you subtract exponents.

5. **−16** Using long division, you have

$$
\begin{array}{r}
x - 2 \\
x - 2 \overline{) x^2 - 4x - 12} \\
\underline{x^2 - 2x} \\
-2x - 12 \\
\underline{-2x + 4} \\
-16
\end{array}
$$

   Thus, the remainder is −16.

6. **−21** Begin by multiplying $(x - a)(x - b)$ and obtain $x^2 - ax - bx + ab$ or $x^2 - x(a + b) + ab$. Since $x^2 - x(a + b) + ab = x^2 - 4x - 21$, you have $-(a + b) = -4$ and $ab = -21$.

B. Arithmetic Operations on Rational Expressions

When performing arithmetic operations on rational expressions, remember the following:

- Find the **LCD** (lowest common denominator) when adding and subtracting rational expressions.
- Distribute the minus sign when subtracting an algebraic expression containing a set of parentheses.

  For example, $\dfrac{1}{x-3} - \dfrac{1}{x+1} = \dfrac{x+1-(x-3)}{(x-3)(x+1)} = \dfrac{4}{(x-3)(x+1)}$.

- Rewrite $\dfrac{a}{b} \div \dfrac{c}{d}$ as $\dfrac{a}{b} \cdot \dfrac{d}{c}$.

- Note that if $a \neq b$, then $\dfrac{a-b}{b-a} = -1$.

Practice

1. For all values of x not equal to 4, which of the following expressions is equivalent to $\dfrac{x^2-16}{2x-8}$?

   A. $\dfrac{x-4}{2}$

   B. $\dfrac{x}{2}+4$

   C. $x+2$

   D. $\dfrac{x+4}{2}$

2. For all values of x not equal to ± 2, which of the following is equivalent to the sum of $\dfrac{1}{x+2} + \dfrac{1}{2-x}$?

   A. $\dfrac{1}{x+1}$

   B. $\dfrac{2}{x+2}$

   C. $\dfrac{1}{x^2-1}$

   D. $\dfrac{-4}{x^2-4}$

3. If $y \neq -1$ and $y \neq 1$, which of the following is equivalent to $\dfrac{2}{y-1} - \dfrac{1}{y+1} - \dfrac{4}{y^2-1}$?

   A. $\dfrac{1}{y-1}$

   B. $\dfrac{1}{y+1}$

   C. $\dfrac{-1}{y^2-1}$

   D. $\dfrac{y-3}{y^2-1}$

4. If $n \neq 0$ and $n \neq 5$, which of the following is equivalent to $\left(n - \dfrac{25}{n} \right)\left(1 + \dfrac{5}{n-5} \right)$?

   A. -5
   B. 5
   C. $n-5$
   D. $n+5$

5. If $x \neq 0$, $y \neq 0$, and $y \neq \dfrac{3}{2}x$, which of the following is equivalent to $\dfrac{\dfrac{x^2}{4} - \dfrac{y^2}{9}}{\dfrac{y}{18} - \dfrac{x}{12}}$?

   A. $-3x - 2y$
   B. $-3x + 2y$
   C. $3x - 2y$
   D. $3x + 2y$

6. If $t \neq -5$ and $t \neq 3$, what is the value of $\dfrac{t^2-9}{t^2+2t-15} \div \dfrac{4t+12}{2t+10}$?

Answers

1. **D.** Factoring both the numerator and denominator of $\dfrac{x^2-16}{2x-8}$, you have $\dfrac{(x+4)(x-4)}{2(x-4)}$, which is equivalent to $\dfrac{x+4}{2}$, Choice D.

2. **D.** Multiply both the numerator and denominator of $\dfrac{1}{2-x}$ by -1 and you have $\dfrac{-1}{x-2}$. Now $\dfrac{1}{x+2} + \dfrac{1}{2-x}$ becomes $\dfrac{1}{x+2} - \dfrac{1}{x-2}$. The lowest common denominator (LCD) of $(x+2)$ and $(x-2)$ is $(x+2)(x-2)$. Therefore, $\dfrac{1}{x+2} - \dfrac{1}{x-2} = \dfrac{1(x-2)-1(x+2)}{(x+2)(x-2)} = \dfrac{x-2-x-2}{(x+2)(x-2)}$ or $\dfrac{-4}{x^2-4}$, Choice D.

3. **B.** Note that $y^2 - 1 = (y - 1)(y + 1)$ and that the LCD (lowest common denominator) of the three fractions $\dfrac{2}{y-1}$, $\dfrac{1}{y+1}$, and $\dfrac{4}{y^2-1}$ is $(y-1)(y+1)$. Rewrite $\dfrac{2}{y-1} - \dfrac{1}{y+1} - \dfrac{4}{y^2-1}$ as $\dfrac{2(y+1)-1(y-1)-4}{(y-1)(y+1)}$, which is equivalent to $\dfrac{2y+2-y+1-4}{(y-1)(y+1)}$ or $\dfrac{y-1}{(y-1)(y+1)}$ or $\dfrac{1}{(y+1)}$, Choice B. For steps on how to solve this problem using a calculator, see "Working with Rational Expressions" in the Appendix.

4. **D.** Express $n - \dfrac{25}{n}$ as a single fraction, and you have $\dfrac{n^2}{n} - \dfrac{25}{n} = \dfrac{n^2-25}{n}$. Similarly,

$1 + \dfrac{5}{n-5} = \dfrac{n-5}{n-5} + \dfrac{5}{n-5} = \dfrac{n}{n-5}$. The product $\left(n - \dfrac{25}{n}\right)\left(1 + \dfrac{5}{n-5}\right)$ becomes

$\left(\dfrac{n^2-25}{n}\right)\left(\dfrac{n}{n-5}\right) = \dfrac{(n-5)(n+5)}{n} \cdot \dfrac{n}{n-5}$ or $n + 5$, Choice D.

5. **A.** The LCD (lowest common denominator) of the fractions $\dfrac{x^2}{4}$, $\dfrac{y^2}{9}$, $\dfrac{y}{18}$, and $\dfrac{x}{12}$ is 36. Multiply each fraction by 36 and you have $\dfrac{9x^2 - 4y^2}{2y - 3x}$, which is equivalent to $\dfrac{(3x-2y)(3x+2y)}{(2y-3x)}$ or $-(3x + 2y)$

$= -3x - 2y$, Choice A. Note that $\dfrac{3x-2y}{2y-3x} = -1$.

6. $\dfrac{1}{2}$ Begin by rewriting the problem as $\dfrac{t^2-9}{t^2+2t-15} \cdot \dfrac{2t+10}{4t+12}$. Factoring each expression, you have

$\dfrac{(t+3)(t-3)}{(t+5)(t-3)} \cdot \dfrac{2(t+5)}{4(t+3)}$ or $\dfrac{1}{2}$.

C. Rational Exponents and Radicals

Common algebraic expressions containing rational exponents and radicals:

- $x^{-n} = \dfrac{1}{x^n}$, $x \neq 0$. For example, $3^{-2} = \dfrac{1}{3^2}$.

- $x^{\frac{m}{n}} = \sqrt[n]{x^m}$ or $\left(\sqrt[n]{x}\right)^m$ if $\sqrt[n]{x}$ exists. For example, $8^{\frac{2}{3}} = \sqrt[3]{8^2}$ or $\left(\sqrt[3]{8}\right)^2$.

- $\left(\dfrac{a}{b}\right)^{-n} = \left(\dfrac{b}{a}\right)^n$, $a \neq 0$ and $b \neq 0$. For example, $\left(\dfrac{3}{5}\right)^{-2} = \left(\dfrac{5}{3}\right)^2$.

- $\sqrt{x^2} = |x|$. For example, $\sqrt{(-5)^2} = |-5| = 5$.

- $\sqrt[3]{x^3} = x$. For example, $\sqrt[3]{(-2)^3} = -2$.

Practice

1. If $x \neq 0$ and $y \neq 0$, which of the following is equivalent to $\sqrt[3]{64x^6y^5}$?

   A. $8x^3y^2\sqrt{y}$

   B. $8x^2y^2\sqrt[3]{y}$

   C. $4x^3y^2\sqrt[3]{y}$

   D. $4x^2y\sqrt[3]{y^2}$

2. What is the value of $\sqrt{125}+10\sqrt{\dfrac{1}{5}}$?

   A. $3\sqrt{5}$

   B. $7\sqrt{5}$

   C. $15\sqrt{5}$

   D. $27\sqrt{5}$

3. Which of the following is equivalent to $\dfrac{2+\sqrt{2}}{2-\sqrt{2}}$?

   A. -1

   B. 4

   C. $3-2\sqrt{2}$

   D. $3+2\sqrt{2}$

4. Which of the following has the greatest value if $0 < x < 1$?

   A. $\sqrt[3]{x}$

   B. $\sqrt{x}$

   C. x

   D. x^2

5. What is the value of $36\left(\dfrac{4}{9}\right)^{-\frac{1}{2}}$?

6. What is the value of $x^2 + x^{\frac{1}{4}}$ if $\sqrt{x} = 4$?

Answers

1. **D.** $\sqrt[3]{64x^6y^5} = \sqrt[3]{64}\left(\sqrt[3]{x^6}\right)\left(\sqrt[3]{y^5}\right) = 4x^2\sqrt[3]{y^3}\sqrt[3]{y^2} = 4x^2y\sqrt[3]{y^2}$, Choice D.

2. **B.** Begin by simplifying $\sqrt{125}$ as $\sqrt{25}\sqrt{5} = 5\sqrt{5}$. Note that $\sqrt{\dfrac{1}{5}} = \dfrac{\sqrt{1}}{\sqrt{5}} = \dfrac{1}{\sqrt{5}}$. Rationalizing the

   denominator of $\dfrac{1}{\sqrt{5}}$, you have $\dfrac{1}{\sqrt{5}} \cdot \dfrac{\sqrt{5}}{\sqrt{5}} = \dfrac{\sqrt{5}}{5}$. Therefore, $10\sqrt{\dfrac{1}{5}} = \dfrac{10\sqrt{5}}{5} = 2\sqrt{5}$. Thus,

   $\sqrt{125} + 10\sqrt{\dfrac{1}{5}} = 5\sqrt{5} + 2\sqrt{5}$ or $7\sqrt{5}$, Choice B.

3. **D.** Rationalizing the denominator, you have $\dfrac{2+\sqrt{2}}{2-\sqrt{2}} \cdot \dfrac{2+\sqrt{2}}{2+\sqrt{2}}$. Note that

   $\left(2+\sqrt{2}\right)\left(2+\sqrt{2}\right) = 4 + 2\sqrt{2} + 2\sqrt{2} + 2 = 6 + 4\sqrt{2}$ and that $\left(2+\sqrt{2}\right)\left(2-\sqrt{2}\right) = 4 - 2\sqrt{2} + 2\sqrt{2} - 2 = 2$.

   Therefore, $\dfrac{2+\sqrt{2}}{2-\sqrt{2}} = \dfrac{6+4\sqrt{2}}{2}$ or $3 + 2\sqrt{2}$, Choice D.

4. **A.** One approach to the problem is to assign a numerical value to x. For example, let $x = 0.5$, then
   $\sqrt[3]{x} = \sqrt[3]{0.5} \approx 0.79$, $\sqrt{x} = \sqrt{0.5} \approx 0.71$, $x = 0.5$, $x^2 = (0.5)^2 = 0.25$, and $x^3 = (0.5)^3 = 0.125$. Therefore,
   $\sqrt[3]{x}$ has the greatest value, Choice A.

5. **54** Following the order of operations, you begin with $\left(\dfrac{4}{9}\right)^{-\frac{1}{2}}$, which is equivalent to $\left(\dfrac{9}{4}\right)^{\frac{1}{2}}$ or $\dfrac{3}{2}$. Thus,

   $36\left(\dfrac{4}{9}\right)^{-\frac{1}{2}} = 36\left(\dfrac{3}{2}\right) = 54$.

6. **258** Squaring both sides of the equation $\sqrt{x} = 4$, you have $x = 16$. Therefore,

   $x^2 + x^{\frac{1}{4}} = (16)^2 + (16)^{\frac{1}{4}} = 256 + 2$ or 258.

D. Creating Equivalent Forms of Algebraic Expressions

When creating equivalent algebraic expressions, try the following:

- Simplify an algebraic expression (e.g., $\dfrac{6x^8}{3x^2}$ is equivalent to $2x^6$).

- Combine into a single fraction (e.g., $\dfrac{1}{x-3} - \dfrac{1}{x+3}$ is equivalent to $\dfrac{6}{x^2-9}$).

- Divide using long division (e.g., $\dfrac{x^2}{x+3}$ is equivalent to $x - 3 + \dfrac{9}{x+3}$). See practice problem 5.

- Decompose into partial fractions (e.g., $\dfrac{2}{x^2-1}$ is equivalent to $\dfrac{1}{x-1} - \dfrac{1}{x+1}$). See practice problem 4.

Practice

1. If $a \neq 0$ and $b \neq 0$, which of the following is equivalent to $\dfrac{\left(2a^{-1}b^2\right)^3}{8a^{-6}b^3}$?

   A. $\dfrac{3}{4}a^3b^2$

   B. $\dfrac{3}{4a^{-9}b}$

   C. $\dfrac{b^3}{a^9}$

   D. a^3b^3

2. If $n \neq -1$, which of the following is equivalent to $n - 1 + \dfrac{1}{n+1}$?

   A. $\dfrac{1}{n^2-1}$

   B. $\dfrac{n}{n^2-1}$

   C. $\dfrac{n}{n+1}$

   D. $\dfrac{n^2}{n+1}$

3. If $2m + n - 6 = 0$, what is the value of $m + \dfrac{n}{2}$?

   A. -12
   B. -3
   C. 3
   D. 12

4. If $k \neq \pm 1$, which of the following is equivalent to $\dfrac{2}{k^2-1}$?

   A. $\dfrac{1}{k-1} - \dfrac{1}{k+1}$

   B. $\dfrac{1}{k+1} - \dfrac{1}{k-1}$

   C. $\dfrac{1}{k+1} + \dfrac{1}{k-1}$

   D. $\dfrac{2}{k^2} - 1$

5. If $t \neq -2$ and $\dfrac{t^2}{t+2}$ is written in an equivalent form $t - 2 + \dfrac{k}{t+2}$, what is the value of k?

6. If $(x + y)^2 = 4 + x^2 + y^2$, what is the value of xy?

Answers

1. **D.** Begin by simplifying $(2a^{-1}b^2)^3$, which is equivalent to $(2)^3(a^{-1})^3(b^2)^3$ or $8a^{-3}b^6$. Therefore,

   $$\frac{\left(2a^{-1}b^2\right)^3}{8a^{-6}b^3} = \frac{8a^{-3}b^6}{8a^{-6}b^3} = a^{(-3-(-6))}b^{(6-3)} \text{ or } a^3b^3, \text{ Choice D.}$$

2. **D.** Rewrite $n-1+\dfrac{1}{n+1}$ as $\dfrac{n}{1}-\dfrac{1}{1}+\dfrac{1}{n+1}$. Note that the LCD (lowest common denominator) is $n + 1$.

   Thus, $\dfrac{n}{1}-\dfrac{1}{1}+\dfrac{1}{n+1}$ is equivalent to $\dfrac{n(n+1)-1(n+1)+1}{n+1}$ or $\dfrac{n^2+n-n-1+1}{n+1}$ or $\dfrac{n^2}{n+1}$, Choice D.

3. **C.** Begin by dividing both sides of the equation by 2 and obtain $m+\dfrac{n}{2}-3=0$. Adding 3 to both sides, you have $m+\dfrac{n}{2}=3$, Choice C.

4. **A.** One approach is to decompose $\dfrac{2}{k^2-1}$ into a partial fraction. Begin by rewriting $\dfrac{2}{k^2-1}$ as

   $\dfrac{2}{(k-1)(k+1)}$. Set $\dfrac{2}{(k-1)(k+1)}=\dfrac{A}{k-1}+\dfrac{B}{k+1}$. Combine $\dfrac{A}{k-1}+\dfrac{B}{k+1}$ as a single fraction, and you have

   $\dfrac{A(k+1)+B(k-1)}{(k-1)(k+1)}$. Now you have $\dfrac{2}{(k-1)(k+1)}=\dfrac{A(k+1)+B(k-1)}{(k-1)(k+1)}$. Setting the numerators equal, you

   obtain $2 = A(k + 1) + B(k - 1)$. Letting $k = 1$, you have $2 = 2A$ or $A = 1$, and letting $k = -1$, you have

   $2 = -2B$ or $B = -1$. Thus, $\dfrac{2}{k^2-1}=\dfrac{1}{k-1}-\dfrac{1}{k+1}$, Choice A.

   Another approach is to combine the two given fractions in each of the four answer choices into a

   single fraction. For example, in Choice A, $\dfrac{1}{k-1}-\dfrac{1}{k+1}=\dfrac{(1)(k+1)-(1)(k-1)}{(k-1)(k+1)}=\dfrac{2}{k^2-1}$.

5. **4** Using long division, you have

   $$
   \begin{array}{r}
   t-2 \\
   t+2\overline{)t^2-0t+0} \\
   \underline{t^2+2t} \\
   -2t+0 \\
   \underline{-2t-4} \\
   4
   \end{array}
   $$

   Thus, $\dfrac{t^2}{t+2}=t-2+\dfrac{4}{t+2}$ and $k = 4$. Note that you could also use the TI-89 graphing calculator to do

   long division. For steps on how to solve this problem using a calculator, see "Working with Equivalent Forms of an Algebraic Expression" in the Appendix.

6. **2** Begin by expanding $(x + y)^2$, and you have $(x + y)^2 = (x + y)(x + y)$ or $x^2 + 2xy + y^2$. Therefore, $x^2 + 2xy + y^2 = 4 + x^2 + y^2$ or $2xy = 4$ or $xy = 2$.

E. Isolating a Variable or a Quantity of Interest in an Equation

When isolating a single variable in an equation that contains other variables, it is useful to compare the equation with a similar equation that has numerical values. For example, to solve for x in $ax + b = c$, it is helpful to examine the solution for $2x + 4 = 10$, and then follow similar strategies. Note that a solution for $2x + 4 = 10$ is as follows: $2x = 10 - 4$ and $x = \dfrac{10 - 4}{2}$. Similarly, a solution for $ax + b = c$ is $ax = c - b$ and $x = \dfrac{c - b}{a}$.

Practice

1. If $ax + by + c = 0$ and $b \neq 0$, what is the value of y in terms of a, b, c, and x?

   A. $\dfrac{ax - c}{b}$

   B. $\dfrac{-b}{ax + c}$

   C. $\dfrac{ax + c}{-b}$

   D. $\dfrac{ax + c}{b}$

2. The volume, V, of a right circular cone is given as $V = \dfrac{1}{3}\pi r^2 h$, with r being the radius of the base circle and h the height of the cone. Which of the following is the value of h in terms of r and V?

   A. $3\pi r^2 V$

   B. $\dfrac{V}{3\pi r^2}$

   C. $\dfrac{3V}{\pi r^2}$

   D. $\dfrac{3\pi r^2}{V}$

3. If $a \neq \pm c$ and $ax + b = d - cx$, what is the value of x in terms of a, b, c, and d?

   A. $\dfrac{b + d}{a - c}$

   B. $\dfrac{a + c}{d - b}$

   C. $\dfrac{d - b}{a + c}$

   D. $\dfrac{d + b}{a + c}$

4. The area of a trapezoid, A, is given as $A = \frac{1}{2}(b_1 + b_2)h$, with b_1 and b_2 the lengths of the two parallel sides and h the height of the trapezoid. What is the value of h in terms of b_1, b_2, and A?

A. $\frac{1}{2}A(b_1 + b_2)$

B. $A - \frac{1}{2}(b_1 + b_2)$

C. $\frac{A}{2(b_1 + b_2)}$

D. $\frac{2A}{b_1 + b_2}$

5. If 1 USD (U.S. dollar) is exchanged for 6.26934 CNY (Chinese Yuan Renminbi), how many USD, to the nearest hundredth, is equivalent to 1 CNY at the same rate?

6. If $x^2 + 6x = 9$, what if the value of $(x + 3)^2$?

Answers

1. **C.** Begin by subtracting the terms ax and c from both sides of the equation and obtain $by = -ax - c$.

   Dividing both sides by b, you have $y = \frac{-ax - c}{b}$ or $\frac{ax + c}{-b}$, Choice C. For steps on how to solve this problem using a calculator, see "Isolating a Variable in an Equation" in the Appendix.

2. **C.** Begin by multiplying both sides of the equation by 3 and obtain $3V = \pi r^2 h$. Divide both sides by (πr^2) and you have $\frac{3V}{\pi r^2} = h$, Choice C.

3. **C.** Begin by adding the term cx to both sides of the equation and obtain $ax + cx + b = d$. Subtracting b from both sides, you have $ax + cx = d - b$. Factor $ax + cx$ and you have $x(a + c) = d - b$. Finally, divide both sides by $(a + c)$ and obtain $x = \frac{d - b}{a + c}$, Choice C.

4. **D.** Begin by multiplying both sides of the equation by 2 and obtain $2A = (b_1 + b_2)h$. Divide both sides by $(b_1 + b_2)$ and you have $\frac{2A}{b_1 + b_2} = h$, Choice D.

5. **0.16** Since 1 USD = 6.26934 CNY, divide both sides of the equation by 6.26934 and you have 0.159506 USD = 1 CNY. To the nearest hundredth, 1 CNY = 0.16 USD.

6. **18** One way to solve this problem is by "completing the square." Begin by taking half of the coefficient of the linear term, which is $\frac{1}{2}(6)$ or 3. Squaring 3, you have $3^2 = 9$. Adding 9 to both sides of the equation, you have $x^2 + 6x + 9 = 9 + 9$ or $x^2 + 6x + 9 = 18$. Factor the trinomial on the left and obtain $(x + 3)^2 = 18$. Note that another approach is to solve for x by using the quadratic formula, and then evaluate the expression $(x + 3)^2$.

F. Solving Quadratic Equations

All quadratic equations can be written in the form of $ax^2 + bx + c = 0$. Below are several types of quadratic equations and their solutions. Note that not all quadratic equations are factorable.

- By factoring:

$$(a) \quad x^2 - 4x - 21 = 0 \qquad (b) \quad 3x^2 - 6x = 0$$
$$(x+3)(x-7) = 0 \qquad\qquad 3x(x-2) = 0$$
$$x = -3 \text{ or } x = 7 \qquad\qquad x = 0 \text{ or } x = 2$$

- By taking the square root: For example, if $(x-5)^2 = 7$, then $x - 5 = \pm\sqrt{7}$ or $x = 5 \pm \sqrt{7}$.

- By applying the quadratic formula: If $ax^2 + bx + c = 0$, then $x = \dfrac{-b \pm \sqrt{b^2 - 4ac}}{2a}$.

- By completing the square: For example, if $x^2 + 6x - 4 = 0$, then $x^2 + 6x = 4$ or $x^2 + 6x + \left(\dfrac{6}{2}\right)^2 = 4 + \left(\dfrac{6}{2}\right)^2$, which is equivalent to $x^2 + 6x + 9 = 13$ or $(x+3)^2 = 13$; thus, $x + 3 = \pm\sqrt{13}$ or $x = -3 \pm \sqrt{13}$.

Practice

1. If $6n^2 = 15n$ and $n > 0$, what is the value of n?

   A. $\dfrac{-5}{2}$

   B. 0

   C. $\dfrac{2}{5}$

   D. $\dfrac{5}{2}$

2. If $9k^2 + 1 = 6k$, what is the value of k?

   A. -3

   B. $-\dfrac{1}{3}$

   C. $\dfrac{1}{3}$

   D. 3

3. If the roots of a quadratic equation are $\dfrac{1}{2}$ and -2, which of the following could be the equation?

   A. $x^2 + 3x - 2 = 0$
   B. $2x^2 + 3x - 1 = 0$
   C. $2x^2 + 3x - 2 = 0$
   D. $2x^2 + 3x + 2 = 0$

4. If $t^2 - 2t = 2$ and $t > 0$, what is the value of t?

   A. $\sqrt{3} - 1$
   B. $\sqrt{3}$
   C. $1 + \sqrt{3}$
   D. 2

5. If x is a real number, how many values of x satisfy the equation $(x + 10)^2 = 25$?

6. If $p^2 + p = -\dfrac{1}{4}$, what is the value of $p + \dfrac{1}{2}$?

Answers

1. **D.** Rewrite $6n^2 = 15n$ as $6n^2 - 15n = 0$. Factoring, you have $3n(2n - 5) = 0$. Set each factor equal to zero and obtain $n = 0$ or $n = \dfrac{5}{2}$. Since $n > 0$, $n = \dfrac{5}{2}$, Choice D.

2. **C.** Rewrite $9k^2 + 1 = 6k$ as $9k^2 - 6k + 1 = 0$. Factoring, you have $(3k - 1)(3k - 1) = 0$. Set each factor equal to zero, and obtain $k = \dfrac{1}{3}$, Choice C.

3. **C.** Given a quadratic equation $ax^2 + bx + c = 0$ (which is equivalent to $x^2 + \dfrac{b}{a}x + \dfrac{c}{a} = 0$), the sum of the roots is $-\dfrac{b}{a}$ and the product of the roots is $\dfrac{c}{a}$. In this case, the sum is $\dfrac{1}{2} + (-2) = -\dfrac{3}{2}$ and the product is $\left(\dfrac{1}{2}\right)(-2) = -1$. Thus, an equation could be $x^2 - (-)\dfrac{3}{2}x + (-1) = 0$ or $x^2 + \dfrac{3}{2}x - 1 = 0$. Multiplying both sides of the equation by 2, you have $2x^2 + 3x - 2 = 0$, Choice C.

   Another approach to the problem is as follows: Since $x = \dfrac{1}{2}$ and $x = -2$, the factors of the equation are $\left(x - \dfrac{1}{2}\right)$ and $(x + 2)$, and the equation is $\left(x - \dfrac{1}{2}\right)(x + 2) = 0$. Expanding the left side of the equation and then multiplying both sides by 2, you will have the same result.

4. **C.** Rewrite $t^2 - 2t = 2$ as $t^2 - 2t - 2 = 0$. Applying the quadratic formula, you have $a = 1$, $b = -2$, $c = -2$, and $t = \dfrac{-(-2) \pm \sqrt{(-2)^2 - 4(1)(-2)}}{2(1)}$ or $t = \dfrac{2 \pm \sqrt{12}}{2} = \dfrac{2 \pm 2\sqrt{3}}{2} = 1 \pm \sqrt{3}$. Thus, $t = 1 + \sqrt{3}$ or $t = 1 - \sqrt{3}$, which is negative. Since $t > 0$, $t = 1 + \sqrt{3}$, Choice C. Another approach to this problem is to use "completing the square."

5. **2** Instead of multiplying $(x + 10)(x + 10)$ and then factoring to solve the quadratic equation $x^2 + 20x + 75 = 0$, keep the equation in its original form and find the square root of both sides. Thus, $(x + 10) = \pm 5$. Solving the equations $x + 10 = 5$ and $x + 10 = -5$, you have $x = -5$ or $x = -15$. Therefore, there are two values of x satisfying the given equation. For steps on how to solve this problem using a calculator, see "Solving an Equation" in the Appendix.

6. **0** One approach is to apply "completing the square." Begin by taking half the coefficient of p and obtain $\frac{1}{2}(1) = \frac{1}{2}$. Squaring $\frac{1}{2}$, you have $\left(\frac{1}{2}\right)^2 = \frac{1}{4}$. Add $\frac{1}{4}$ to both sides of the equation and obtain $p^2 + p + \frac{1}{4} = -\frac{1}{4} + \frac{1}{4}$ or $p^2 + p + \frac{1}{4} = 0$. Factoring, you have $\left(p + \frac{1}{2}\right)^2 = 0$. Taking the square root of both sides, you have $p + \frac{1}{2} = 0$.

Another approach is to rewrite $p^2 + p = -\frac{1}{4}$ as $p^2 + p + \frac{1}{4} = 0$. Either factoring or applying the quadratic formula will yield the same result.

G. Rational and Radical Equations

When solving rational equations,

- identify the LCD (lowest common denominator) of all fractions in the equation.
- multiply both sides of the equation by the LCD.
- solve the derived equation.
- check for extraneous roots.

When solving radical equations,

- isolate the radical.
- square both sides of the equation if the radical is a square root. Similarly, cube both sides if the radical is a cube root, and so on.
- solve the derived equation.
- check for extraneous roots.

Practice

1. Which of the following is the solution set of the equation $9 + \sqrt{2n-1} = 4$?

    A. $\{-13\}$
    B. $\{-12\}$
    C. $\{13\}$
    D. $\{\ \}$

2. If $k \neq 0$ and $h = \dfrac{1}{\sqrt[3]{k}}$, what is the value of k in terms of h?

    A. $\dfrac{1}{h^3}$

    B. $\dfrac{1}{\sqrt[3]{h}}$

    C. $\sqrt[3]{h}$

    D. h^3

3. If $\dfrac{3}{x+2} = \dfrac{2}{x-2}$, what is the value of x?

    A. -10
    B. -2
    C. 2
    D. 10

4. Which of the following is the solution set of the equation $\dfrac{x}{x-2} - \dfrac{5}{x} = \dfrac{2}{x-2}$?

    A. $\{2\}$
    B. $\{5\}$
    C. $\{2, 5\}$
    D. $\{\ \ \}$

5. If $3\sqrt{t-1} - \sqrt{t+1} = 0$, what is the value of t?

6. If $\dfrac{y+3}{y} = \dfrac{9}{y^2 + 3y}$, what is the value of y?

Answers

1. **D.** Isolate $\sqrt{2n-1}$ by subtracting 9 from both sides of the equation, and you have $\sqrt{2n-1} = -5$. This is

    not possible, since $\sqrt{2n-1}$ must be greater than or equal to zero. Thus, the equation has no solution,

    Choice D. Note that had you squared both sides of the equation $\left(\sqrt{2n-1}\right)^2 = (-5)^2$ and obtained $2n-1 = 25$, $n = 13$ would have been an extraneous root. For steps on how to solve this problem using a calculator, see "Solving Radical Equations" in the Appendix.

2. **A.** Rewrite $h = \dfrac{1}{\sqrt[3]{k}}$ as $h = k^{-\frac{1}{3}}$. Raise both sides of the equation to the -3 power, and you have

    $(h)^{-3} = \left(k^{-\frac{1}{3}}\right)^{-3}$ or $h^{-3} = k$, which is equivalent to $\dfrac{1}{h^3} = k$, Choice A.

3. **D.** The LCD (lowest common denominator) of the fractions $\dfrac{3}{x+2}$ and $\dfrac{2}{x-2}$ is $(x + 2)(x - 2)$.

Multiplying both sides of the equation by $(x + 2)(x - 2)$, you have $3(x - 2) = 2(x + 2)$ or $3x - 6 = 2x + 4$. Solve for x and obtain $x = 10$. Check for extraneous roots by substituting $x = 10$ in the original

equation, and you have $\dfrac{3}{x+2} = \dfrac{2}{x-2}$ or $\dfrac{1}{4} = \dfrac{1}{4}$. Thus, $x = 10$ is a root, Choice D.

4. **B.** The LCD (lowest common denominator) of the fractions $\dfrac{x}{x-2}$, $\dfrac{5}{x}$, and $\dfrac{2}{x-2}$ is $x(x - 2)$.

Multiplying both sides of the equation by $x(x - 2)$, you have $x(x) - 5(x - 2) = 2x$ or $x^2 - 5x + 10 = 2x$. Simplifying, you have $x^2 - 7x + 10 = 0$. Then factoring, you obtain $(x - 5)(x - 2) = 0$, which yields

$x = 5$ or $x = 2$. Checking for extraneous roots, note that when $x = 2$, $\dfrac{x}{x-2}$ becomes $\dfrac{2}{0}$, which is not

possible. When $x = 5$, you have $\dfrac{5}{5-2} - \dfrac{5}{5} = \dfrac{2}{5-2}$ or $\dfrac{2}{3} = \dfrac{2}{3}$. Thus, the only solution is $x = 5$, Choice B.

5. $\dfrac{5}{4}$ Isolate $3\sqrt{t-1}$ by rewriting the equation as $3\sqrt{t-1} = \sqrt{t+1}$. Squaring both sides, you have $9(t - 1)$

$= t + 1$ or $9t - 9 = t + 1$ or $t = \dfrac{5}{4}$. Check for extraneous roots by substituting $t = \dfrac{5}{4}$ into the equation

$3\sqrt{t-1} - \sqrt{t+1} = 0$. You have $3\sqrt{\dfrac{5}{4}-1} - \sqrt{\dfrac{5}{4}+1} = 0$ or $3\sqrt{\dfrac{1}{4}} - \sqrt{\dfrac{9}{4}} = 0$ or $\dfrac{3}{2} - \dfrac{3}{2} = 0$. Thus, $t = \dfrac{5}{4}$ is a root.

6. **−6** The LCD (lowest common denominator) of the two fractions is $y(y + 3)$. Multiplying both sides of the equation by $y(y + 3)$, you have $(y + 3)(y + 3) = 9$ or $(y + 3)^2 = 9$. Taking the square root of both sides, you have $y + 3 = \pm\sqrt{9}$, which yields $y = 0$ or $y = -6$. Check for extraneous roots: Note that when

$y = 0$, $\dfrac{y+3}{y}$ becomes $\dfrac{0+3}{0}$, which is not possible. When $y = -6$, you have $\dfrac{-6+3}{-6} = \dfrac{9}{(-6)^2 + 3(-6)}$ or

$\dfrac{1}{2} = \dfrac{1}{2}$. Thus, $y = -6$ is the only possible root.

H. Systems of Equations Consisting of One Linear and One Non-Linear Equation

To solve systems of equations consisting of one linear and one non-linear equation, if the use of a graphing calculator is allowed (e.g., TI-89), enter the equations in the calculator and solve. If the use of a graphing calculator is not allowed,

- solve the linear equation for one of the variables in terms of the other.
- substitute the derived expression in the non-linear equation and solve.
- find the value of the other variable using substitution.
- check solution(s) in the original equations.

Practice

1. If (x, y) is a solution to the system of equations below, what is a possible value of y?

$$\frac{x^2}{3} + \frac{y^2}{3} = 3$$
$$y = x + 3$$

   A. -6
   B. -3
   C. 0
   D. 6

2. If (x, y) is a solution to the system of equations below, what is the value of $4x^2$?

$$2x^2 + \frac{y^2}{2} = 8$$
$$y + 2x = 0$$

   A. 2
   B. 4
   C. 8
   D. 16

3. How many solutions does the system of equations below have?

$$y = 2x^2 + 5$$
$$y = 4$$

   A. 0
   B. 1
   C. 2
   D. 4

4. If (h, k) is a solution to the system of equations below and $h < 0$, what is the value of k?

$$y = x^2$$
$$y = \frac{1}{2}x + 3$$

   A. $-\dfrac{3}{2}$
   B. 2
   C. 4
   D. $\dfrac{9}{4}$

5. If (m, n) is a solution to the system of equations below, what is the value of $m + n$?

$$\frac{x^2}{2} + \frac{y}{2} = 2$$
$$2x + y = 5$$

6. The perimeter of a rectangular plot of land is 23.5 meters and its length is greater than its width. If the area of the land is 31.875 square meters, what is the length of the rectangular plot of land, in meters?

Answers

1. **C.** Multiply both sides of the equation $\frac{x^2}{3} + \frac{y^2}{3} = 3$ by 3 and obtain $x^2 + y^2 = 9$. Rewrite $y = x + 3$ as $y - 3 = x$ or $x = y - 3$. Substitute $(y - 3)$ for x in the equation $x^2 + y^2 = 9$ and obtain $(y - 3)^2 + y^2 = 9$. Expanding, you have $y^2 - 6y + 9 + y^2 = 9$ or $2y^2 - 6y = 0$. Factoring, you have $2y(y - 3) = 0$, which yields $y = 0$, Choice C, or $y = 3$. Note that you could also use the TI-89 graphing calculator to solve this problem. See "Solving a System of Equations" in the Appendix.

2. **C.** Multiply both sides of the equation $2x^2 + \frac{y^2}{2} = 8$ by 2 and you have $4x^2 + y^2 = 16$. Rewrite $y + 2x = 0$ as $y = -2x$. Substitute $-2x$ for y in the equation $4x^2 + y^2 = 16$ and obtain $4x^2 + (-2x)^2 = 16$ or $4x^2 + 4x^2 = 16$, which is equivalent to $8x^2 = 16$. Dividing both sides of the equation by 2, you have $4x^2 = 8$, Choice C.

3. **A.** Substitute 4 for y in $y = 2x^2 + 5$ and you have $4 = 2x^2 + 5$, which is equivalent to $-1 = 2x^2$ or $x^2 = -\frac{1}{2}$. This is not possible, since there is no real number whose square is negative. Thus, the system has no solution, Choice A.

4. **D.** Since $y = x^2$ and $y = \frac{1}{2}x + 3$, set $x^2 = \frac{1}{2}x + 3$, which is equivalent to $x^2 - \frac{1}{2}x - 3 = 0$ or $2x^2 - x - 6 = 0$. Factoring, you have $(2x + 3)(x - 2) = 0$, which yields $x = -\frac{3}{2}$ or $x = 2$. The corresponding y-values are $\left(-\frac{3}{2}\right)^2 = \frac{9}{4}$ and $(2)^2 = 4$, respectively. Since $h < 0$, $k = \frac{9}{4}$, Choice D.

5. **4** Multiply both sides of the equation $\frac{x^2}{2} + \frac{y}{2} = 2$ by 2 and obtain $x^2 + y = 4$. Rewrite $2x + y = 5$ as $y = -2x + 5$. Substitute $-2x + 5$ for y in the equation $x^2 + y = 4$ and you have $x^2 - 2x + 5 = 4$ or $x^2 - 2x + 1 = 0$. Factoring, you have $(x - 1)(x - 1) = 0$, which yields $x = 1$. Substitute $x = 1$ in either $\frac{x^2}{2} + \frac{y}{2} = 2$ or $2x + y = 5$ and obtain $y = 3$. Thus, the solution to the system is $(1, 3)$ and $m + n = 4$.

6. **7.5** Let x represent the length and y the width. See accompanying figure.

y

x

Since the perimeter is 23.5 meters, $2x + 2y = 23.5$, and since the area is 31.875 square meters, $xy = 31.875$. Enter the two equations into the TI-89 calculator and solve. (See "Solving a System of Equations" in the Appendix.) You have $x = 4.25$ and $y = 7.5$ or $x = 7.5$ and $y = 4.25$. Since the length is greater than the width, $x = 7.5$.

I. Zeros and Factors of Polynomials

Given that p is a polynomial function and that k is a constant, the following statements are equivalent:

- $x = k$ is a zero of the function p
- $x = k$ is a root of the equation $p(x) = 0$
- $x = k$ is a solution of the equation $p(x) = 0$
- $(x - k)$ is a factor of the polynomial $p(x)$
- $(k, 0)$ is an x-intercept of the graph of p

Practice

1. If $(k, 0)$ is an x-intercept of the graph of $g(x) = 5x^4 - 45x^2$, which of the following could be the value of k?

    A. -5
    B. -3
    C. 5
    D. 9

2. The graph of a polynomial function f is shown in the accompanying figure. Which of the following could be the function f?

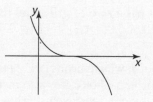

    A. $f(x) = (x - 1)^2$
    B. $f(x) = (x + 1)^2$
    C. $f(x) = (x - 1)(2x + 1)$
    D. $f(x) = -(x - 1)^3$

3. The zeros of a polynomial function f are $-2, \frac{1}{2}$, and 1. Which of the following could be the function f?

    A. $f(x) = \frac{1}{2}(x-2)(2x+1)(x-1)$

    B. $f(x) = \frac{1}{2}(x-2)(2x+1)(x+1)$

    C. $f(x) = \frac{1}{2}(x+2)(2x-1)(x+1)$

    D. $f(x) = -2(x+2)(2x-1)(x-1)$

4. If $\left(\frac{1}{2}, 0\right)$ is an x-intercept of the graph of the polynomial function $f(x) = 2x^3 - 3x^2 - tx + 2$ and t is a constant, what is the value of t?

    A. $-\frac{3}{2}$

    B. -1

    C. $\frac{3}{2}$

    D. 3

5. If $x = -2$ is a zero of the polynomial function $f(x) = x^3 + kx^2 - 4$ and the point $(2, h)$ is on the graph of f, what is the value of h?

6. If $h(x) = kx^3 - x^2 - 8x + 4$ with k a constant, and $h(x)$ is divisible by $(x + 2)$, what is the value of k?

Answers

1. **B.** Since $(k, 0)$ is an x-intercept, $x = k$ is a zero of g. To find the zeros of g, set $5x^4 - 45x^2 = 0$. Factoring the left side, you have $5x^2(x^2 - 9) = 0$ or $5x^2(x + 3)(x - 3) = 0$. Therefore, the zeros of g are 0, -3, and 3, and thus, k could be -3, Choice B.

2. **D.** Note that $x = 1$ is the only zero of f, which means $(x - 1)$ is the only factor of the polynomial $f(x)$. Therefore, choices B and C are incorrect. Choice A is also incorrect because the function in Choice A is a quadratic function and its graph is concave upward. Thus, the correct answer is Choice D. Note that the leading negative sign in the function $f(x) = -(x - 1)^3$ shows that the graph rises to the left and falls to the right. In addition, the exponent 3 in $-(x - 1)^3$ tells you that the zero $x = 1$ has a multiplicity of 3 and that the graph has a "terrace point" at $x = 1$.

3. **D.** Since the zeros of f are $-2, \frac{1}{2}$, and 1, the factors of the polynomial function f are $(x + 2)$, $\left(x - \frac{1}{2}\right)$,

    and $(x - 1)$. That means $f(x)$ could be $f(x) = (x+2)\left(x - \frac{1}{2}\right)(x-1)$. Note that the factor $\left(x - \frac{1}{2}\right)$ could

    be replaced by $(2x - 1)$ with no effect on the zeros of f. Therefore, $f(x)$ could also be $f(x) = (x + 2)(2x - 1)$ $(x - 1)$. Lastly, you could multiply the right side of the equation by any non-zero real number and the zeros of f will stay the same. Thus, $f(x)$ could be $f(x) = -2(x + 2)(2x - 1)(x - 1)$, Choice D.

4. **D.** Since $\left(\dfrac{1}{2}, 0\right)$ is an x-intercept, $x = \dfrac{1}{2}$ is a zero of the function f. Set $2\left(\dfrac{1}{2}\right)^3 - 3\left(\dfrac{1}{2}\right)^2 - t\left(\dfrac{1}{2}\right) + 2 = 0$

   and obtain $2\left(\dfrac{1}{8}\right) - 3\left(\dfrac{1}{4}\right) - \dfrac{1}{2}t + 2 = 0$, which is equivalent to $\dfrac{1}{4} - \dfrac{3}{4} - \dfrac{1}{2}t + 2 = 0$ or $\dfrac{3}{2} - \dfrac{1}{2}t = 0$ or $t = 3$,

   Choice D.

5. **16** Since $x = -2$ is a zero of the function f, set $(-2)^3 + k(-2)^2 - 4 = 0$ and obtain $k = 3$. Therefore, $f(x) = x^3 + 3x^2 - 4$. The point $(2, h)$ is on the graph of f. Substitute 2 for x and you have $(2)^3 + 3(2)^2 - 4 = h$ or $h = 16$.

6. **2** Since $h(x)$ is divisible by $(x + 2)$, $x = -2$ is a zero of $h(x)$. Substitute -2 for x in $h(x)$ and you have $k(-2)^3 - (-2)^2 - 8(-2) + 4 = 0$, which is equivalent to $-8k - 4 + 16 + 4 = 0$ or $k = 2$.

J. Quadratic and Exponential Functions

Equations of quadratic functions include:

- $f(x) = ax^2 + bx + c, a \neq 0$

  axis of symmetry is $x = \dfrac{-b}{2a}$

  $a > 0$, parabola opens upward

  $a < 0$, parabola opens downward
- $f(x) = a(x - h)^2 + k, a \neq 0$

  (h, k) is the vertex and $x = h$ is the axis of symmetry

Equations of exponential functions include:

- $f(x) = a^x, a > 0$ and $a \neq 1$.

  $f(x)$ increases if $a > 1$

  $f(x)$ decreases if $0 < a < 1$

Also see Chapter X, section F, "Linear and Exponential Growth."

Practice

1. Mary wishes to create a rectangular garden bounded by a fence on all four sides. If she uses 60 feet of fence, what is the maximum area of the garden in square feet?

   A. 225
   B. 400
   C. 900
   D. 3,600

Use the following information to answer questions 2 and 3.

A projectile is fired vertically upward from ground level with an initial velocity of 64 feet/second. The equation $s(t) = -\frac{1}{2}gt^2 + v_0 t + s_0$ describes the position of the projectile as a function of time, where s_0 is the projectile's initial position, v_0 is the initial velocity, t is the time elapsed since the projectile was fired, and g is the acceleration constant of 32 feet/second^2.

2. How long, in seconds, will it take for the projectile to first reach 48 feet?

   A. $\frac{3}{4}$

   B. 1

   C. 2

   D. 3

3. How long, in seconds, will it take for the projectile to hit the ground?

   A. 2
   B. 3
   C. 4
   D. 6

4. Saree bought a car for $30,000. It is projected that the value of the car will depreciate by 10% per year for the next 5 years. What will be the value of Saree's car, to the nearest dollar, in 3 years?

   A. 21,000
   B. 21,870
   C. 27,000
   D. 29,970

5. In the xy-plane, the vertex of a parabola is (1, 4). If the points (0, 6) and (3, t) are on the parabola, what is the value of t?

6. Lara invested $100 in a trust fund that manages to double her investment every 2 years. What will the balance of Lara's investment be in 8 years?

Answers

1. **A.** Let x represent the width of the rectangular garden. The length is $\frac{60 - 2x}{2}$ or $(30 - x)$.

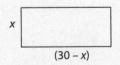

x | (30 – x)

Let y represent the area of the garden. Therefore $y = x(30 − x)$, or $y = −x^2 + 30x$. Note that the graph of the equation is a parabola, and that since the coefficient of x^2 is negative, the parabola is concave downward and has a maximum point. The axis of symmetry is $x = \dfrac{−b}{2a} = \dfrac{−30}{2(−1)} = 15$. At $x = 15$, $y = −(15)^2 + 30(15) = 225$. Thus, the maximum area of Mary's garden is 225 square feet, Choice A. Alternatively, you could use a graphing calculator and inspect the graph of $y = −x^2 + 30x$. Using the Maximum function, you will obtain the point (15, 225).

2. **B.** Note that the initial position is $s_0 = 0$, the initial velocity $v_0 = 64$ feet/second, and the acceleration constant $g = 32$ feet/second^2. Therefore, you have $s(t) = −\dfrac{1}{2}(32)t^2 + 64t + 0$ or $s(t) = −16t^2 + 64t$.

At $s(t) = 48$, set $48 = −16t^2 + 64t$ and you have $16t^2 − 64t + 48 = 0$. Factoring, you have $16(t^2 − 4t + 3) = 0$ or $16(t − 3)(t − 1) = 0$. Therefore, $t = 1$ or $t = 3$. Since the question asks for the time the projectile first reaches 48 feet, $t = 1$, Choice B. (Note that at $t = 3$, the projectile is on its way down, reaching a height of 48 feet for the second time.)

3. **C.** Note that when the projectile hits the ground, its position is $s(t) = 0$. Since $s(t) = −16t^2 + 64t$, set $0 = −16t^2 + 64t$. Factoring, you have $−16t(t − 4) = 0$. Therefore, $t = 0$ or $t = 4$. At $t = 0$, the projectile was on the ground ready to be fired. At $t = 4$, it returned to the ground. Thus $t = 4$, Choice C.

4. **B.** The value of Saree's car can be expressed as an exponential function $f(t) = 30{,}000(1 − 0.1)^t$, where t is the number of years since the car's purchase. At $t = 3$, $f(3) = 30{,}000(0.9)^3 = 21{,}870$, Choice B. Note that depreciating the car's value by 10% per year is equivalent to retaining 90% of its value per year.

5. **12** Begin with the equation $y = a(x − h)^2 + k$, where $a \neq 0$ and (h, k) is the vertex of the parabola. Since the vertex is (1, 4), you have $y = a(x − 1)^2 + 4$. Find the coefficient a by using the point (0, 6). Substituting $x = 0$ and $y = 6$, you have $6 = a(0 − 1)^2 + 4$ or $a = 2$. Therefore, an equation of the parabola is $y = 2(x − 1)^2 + 4$. At $x = 3$, you have $y = 2(3 − 1)^2 + 4 = 12$. Thus, the point $(3, t)$ is (3, 12); that is, $t = 12$.

6. **1,600** This is an exponential growth problem. Note that 8 years is equivalent to four 2-year periods. Therefore, the balance of Lara's investment in 8 years is $A = 100(2)^{\frac{8}{2}}$ or $A = 100(2)^4 = 1{,}600$.

The balance is $1,600.

K. Transformations and Compositions of Functions

When solving problems involving transformations and compositions of functions, it is important to look at the functional notations carefully. For example, $(f \circ g)(x)$ is equivalent to $f(g(x))$. Other functional notations are listed below.

- If $y = f(g(x))$, then y is a composition of f and g. Evaluating $y = f(g(x))$ for a given value of x requires first substituting x in $g(x)$ and then substituting the answer for $g(x)$ in f. The order of substitution may not be reversed since composition is generally not commutative.

■ Many of the problems involving functions can be solved by using a graphing calculator (see "Solving an Equation Involving a Function" in the Appendix).

Given the graph of $y = f(x)$:

■ Shifting vertically

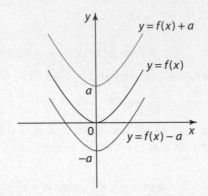

■ Shifting horizontally

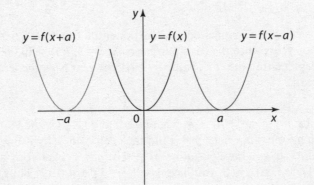

■ Reflecting about an axis

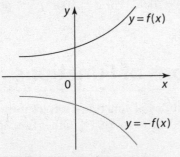

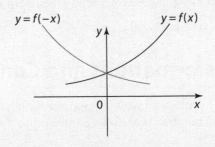

Reflecting over the x-axis   Reflecting over the y-axis

Practice

1. If $f(2x + 1) = 4x - 7$ for all values of x, what is the value of $f(5)$?

    A. -20
    B. 1
    C. 13
    D. 38

2. In the accompanying figure, the graph of $y = f(x)$ is shown. Which of the following could be the graph of $f(x + 2)$?

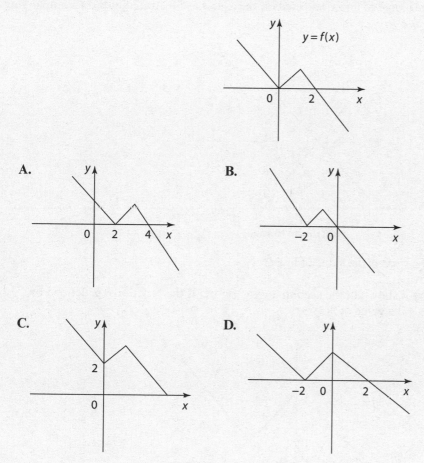

3. If $f(x) = \dfrac{1}{2x - 8}$ and $g(x) = \sqrt{x}$, which of the following is the domain of $f \circ g$?

    A. $x \neq 4$
    B. $x \geq 0$ and $x \neq 4$
    C. $x \neq 16$
    D. $x \geq 0$ and $x \neq 16$

4. The life expectancy of a certain virus is given by the function $L(t) = \dfrac{12t + 36}{t + 1}$, $t \le 120$, where t is the temperature, in Celsius, of the environment in which the virus is placed and L is the number of minutes that the virus will survive in that environment. What is the change in life expectancy, in minutes, if the temperature is raised from 7°C to 23°C?

A. −16
B. −2
C. 15
D. 16

5. In the xy-plane, line l is the image of line k reflected on the x-axis as illustrated in the accompanying figure.

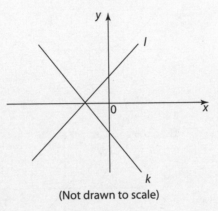

(Not drawn to scale)

If the slope of line k is $-\dfrac{3}{2}$, what is the slope of line l?

6. The graph of the function f is shown in the accompanying figure. If the function h is defined by $h(x) = 3f(x - 1) + 1$, what is the value of $h(3)$?

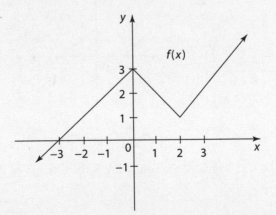

Answers

1. **B.** Set $2x + 1 = 5$ and obtain $x = 2$. Therefore, $f(5)$ can be rewritten as $f(5) = f(2(2) + 1)$. Evaluating $f(2(2) + 1)$, you have $f(2(2) + 1) = 4(2) - 7 = 1$, Choice B.

2. **B.** The graph of $f(x + 2)$ is the same as the graph of $f(x)$ shifted two units to the left. Therefore, $(0, 0)$ is shifted to $(-2, 0)$ and $(2, 0)$ becomes $(0, 0)$. Thus, Choice B is the graph of $f(x + 2)$.

3. **D.** Note that the notation $(f \circ g)(x)$ is equivalent to $f(g(x))$. Since $g(x) = \sqrt{x}$, the domain of g is $x \geq 0$.

   The composition function $f(g(x)) = f(\sqrt{x}) = \dfrac{1}{2\sqrt{x} - 8}$; therefore, the denominator $2\sqrt{x} - 8 \neq 0$ or $x \neq 16$.

   Thus, the domain for $f \circ g$ is $x \geq 0$ and $x \neq 16$, Choice D. Note that the domain of $f(x) = \dfrac{1}{2x - 8}$ is $x \neq 4$. However, this is not relevant to the domain of $f(g(x)) = \dfrac{1}{2\sqrt{x} - 8}$.

4. **B.** At 7°C, the life expectancy of the virus is $L(7) = \dfrac{12(7) + 36}{7 + 1} = \dfrac{120}{8} = 15$ minutes, and at 23°C $L(23) = \dfrac{12(23) + 36}{23 + 1} = \dfrac{312}{24} = 13$ minutes. Therefore, the change in life expectancy is $13 - 15 = -2$ minutes, Choice B.

5. $\dfrac{3}{2}$ One approach to the problem is to examine the x-intercept and y-intercepts of the two lines. Let the y-intercept of line l be point B with coordinates $(0, d)$, and let the y-intercept of line k be point C with coordinates $(0, -d)$. Let the x-intercept of both lines be point $A(-a, 0)$. See accompanying figure.

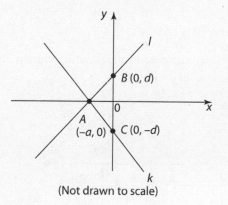

(Not drawn to scale)

   Note that point B is the image of point C and that point A is its own image. Also, note that the slope of line k is $\dfrac{-d - 0}{0 - (-a)} = \dfrac{-3}{2}$, which is equivalent to $\dfrac{-d}{a} = \dfrac{-3}{2}$, and that the slope of line l is $\dfrac{d - 0}{0 - (-a)}$, which is equivalent to $\dfrac{d}{a}$. Thus, the slope of line l is $\dfrac{3}{2}$.

6. **4** Substituting $x = 3$ in $h(x) = 3f(x - 1) + 1$, you have $h(3) = 3f(2) + 1$. The graph of $f(x)$ shows that $f(2) = 1$. Therefore, $h(3) = 3(1) + 1 = 4$.

L. Interpret the Meaning of a Constant, Variable, and Graph of Non-Linear Equations

When interpreting the meaning of different features of non-linear equations, it is important to remember the following:

- The solution to a system of equations, if it exists, is the intersection point of all the graphs of the equations in the system.
- For exponential growth and decay problems, the variables in the equation $A = pe^{rt}$ represent the following: t is time, r the rate, p the initial amount, and A the amount at a given time t. Note that when $t = 0$, $A = p$.
- For work-related problems:
  - For example, if Mary can complete a project in x hours, then in 1 hour, the fraction of the project that she can finish is $\dfrac{1}{x}$.
- Given a polynomial equation: $p(x) = a_n x^n + a_{n-1} x^{n-1} \ldots + a_1 x + a_0$ where $a_n \neq 0$ and a_0 is the y-intercept. Note that at $x = 0$, $p(x) = a_0$.

  - If n = odd and $a_n > 0$, the graph falls on the left and rises on the right.
  - If n = odd and $a_n < 0$, the graph rises on the left and falls on the right.
  - If n = even and $a_n > 0$, the graph rises on both the left and the right.
  - If n = even and $a_n < 0$, the graph falls on both the left and the right.

Practice

1. For $-8 \leq x \leq 3$, what is the maximum value of the function shown in the xy-plane below?

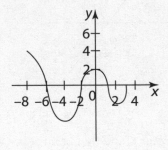

   A. -8
   B. -4
   C.   2
   D.   4

2.

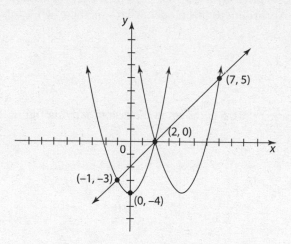

A system of three equations:

$$y = x - 2$$
$$y = x^2 - 4$$
$$y = x^2 - 8x + 12$$

and their graphs in the xy-plane are shown in the accompanying figure. Which of the following points is the solution to the system?

A. $(-1, -3)$
B. $(0, -4)$
C. $(2, 0)$
D. $(7, 5)$

3. George can paint a house in 10 hours. John can paint the same house in x hours. George paints the house alone for an hour and then John joins him to paint the house. Working together for 6 hours, they finish painting the house. Which of the following equations yields the correct answer for x?

A. $6(10 + x) = 100$

B. $6\left(\dfrac{1}{10} + \dfrac{1}{x}\right) = 1$

C. $6\left(\dfrac{2}{10} + \dfrac{1}{x}\right) = 1$

D. $\dfrac{1}{10} + 6\left(\dfrac{1}{10} + \dfrac{1}{x}\right) = 1$

4. The population of a town is given by $p = 3{,}500e^{0.025t}$, with $e \approx 2.71828$, and t is the time in years, with $t = 0$ corresponding to 2010. According to this model, what was the town's population in 2010?

   A.   0
   B.   2,640
   C.   3,500
   D.   3,589

5. The graph of $y = f(x)$ for $-2 \le x \le 5$ is shown in the accompanying figure. If $k < 0$ and $f(k) = 0$, what is the value of k?

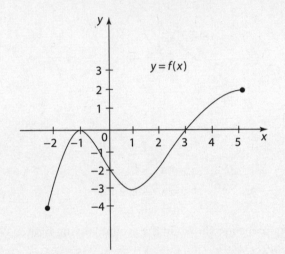

   A. -2
   B. -1
   C.   0
   D.   3

6.

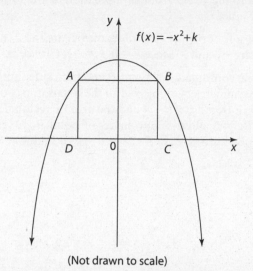

$f(x) = -x^2 + k$

(Not drawn to scale)

In the accompanying figure, $ABCD$ is a rectangle with vertices A and B on the parabola, $f(x) = -x^2 + k$, $k > 0$. If $AB = 4$ and the area of rectangle $ABCD$ is 32, what is the value of k?

Answers

1. **D.** The maximum value of a function is the y-coordinate of the highest point on the graph. In this case, the highest point is $(-8, 4)$. Thus, the maximum value is 4, Choice D.

2. **C.** The solutions to a system of equations are the points that are on the graphs of all the equations; in other words, the points where all the graphs intersect. In this case, there is only one *intersection* point for all three graphs, and the intersection point is $(2, 0)$, Choice C.

3. **D.** George can paint the house in 10 hours. Therefore, in 1 hour, he can complete $\dfrac{1}{10}$ of the house.

Similarly, in 1 hour, John can complete $\dfrac{1}{x}$ of the house. Working together, in 1 hour, they can finish $\left(\dfrac{1}{10} + \dfrac{1}{x}\right)$ of the house, and in 6 hours, $6\left(\dfrac{1}{10} + \dfrac{1}{x}\right)$ of the house. Since George worked alone for an hour, you have $(1)\left(\dfrac{1}{10}\right) + 6\left(\dfrac{1}{10} + \dfrac{1}{x}\right) = 1$, Choice D.

4. **C.** Since $t = 0$ corresponds to the year 2010, the population of the town in 2010 is $p = 3{,}500e^{(0.025)(0)}$ or $p = 3{,}500e^0$ or $p = 3{,}500$, Choice C.

5. **B.** $f(k) = 0$ implies that k is a root of $f(x)$. The roots of $f(x)$ are the x-intercepts of the graph of $f(x)$. In this case, the x-intercepts are -1 and 3. Since $k < 0$, $k = -1$, Choice B.

6. **12** You need to first find the coordinates of point B and then substitute to find k. Since $AB = 4$ and the graph of $f(x) = -x^2 + k$ is symmetric with respect to the y-axis, the coordinates of B are $(2, y)$ and the coordinates of A are $(-2, y)$. Because $AB = 4$ and the area of rectangle $ABCD = (AB)(BC) = 32$, you know that $4(BC) = 32$ or $BC = 8$ and the coordinates of point B are $(2, 8)$. Since B is a point on the graph of $f(x) = -x^2 + k$, substitute $(2, 8)$ in $f(x) = -x^2 + k$ to find that $8 = -(2)^2 + k$ or $k = 12$.

XII. Additional Topics in Math

A. Geometry of the Circle

Given a circle O with radius r and diameter d, the following are true:

- Circumference: $C = 2\pi r$ or $C = \pi d$
- Area: $A = \pi r^2$
- The length of an arc: $\dfrac{m\overset{\frown}{AB}}{2\pi r} = \dfrac{m\angle AOB \text{ (in degrees)}}{360}$

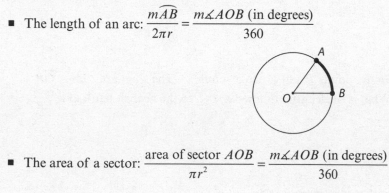

- The area of a sector: $\dfrac{\text{area of sector } AOB}{\pi r^2} = \dfrac{m\angle AOB \text{ (in degrees)}}{360}$

Practice

1. Circle O in the accompanying figure has a radius of r centimeters. The length of chord $\overline{AB}$ is also r centimeters. Which of the following is the distance between $\overline{AB}$ and point O in centimeters and in terms of r?

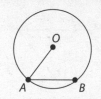

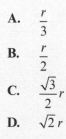

A. $\dfrac{r}{3}$

B. $\dfrac{r}{2}$

C. $\dfrac{\sqrt{3}}{2}r$

D. $\sqrt{2}\,r$

2. As shown in the accompanying figure, points H and K are on circle O. The length of radius $\overline{OH}$ is 12 inches and $m\angle HOK$ is 80. Which of the following is the area of sector HOK in square inches and in terms of π?

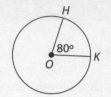

A. $\dfrac{8\pi}{3}$

B. 32π

C. 64

D. 648π

3. As shown in the accompanying figure, points P and Q are on circle O. The length of radius $\overline{OP}$ is 5 centimeters and $m\widehat{PQ}$ is 120. What is the length of minor $m\widehat{PQ}$ to the nearest tenth of a centimeter?

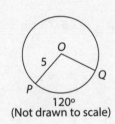

(Not drawn to scale)

A. 5

B. 5.2

C. 10.5

D. 20.9

4. In the accompanying figure of circle O, chords $\overline{MN}$ and $\overline{HK}$ are parallel, $\overline{HN}$ is a diameter, and $m\angle NHK$ is 54. What is the degree measure of minor $\widehat{MH}$?

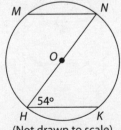

(Not drawn to scale)

A. 18

B. 27

C. 54

D. 108

5. In the accompanying figure, O is the center of the circle and $\overline{AB}$ is a diameter. If $BC = 6$ and $m\angle B = 60$, what is the length of $\overset{\frown}{BC}$?

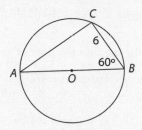

6. In the accompanying figure, there are two concentric circles with center O. If $m\angle AOB = 60$, $OD = 6$, $DB = 6$, and $\overline{OCA}$ and $\overline{ODB}$ are radii of the large circle, what is the area of the shaded region?

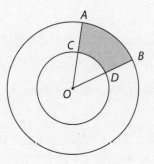

Answers

1. **C.** Let P be a point on $\overline{AB}$ such that $\overline{OP}$ is perpendicular to $\overline{AB}$. Draw $\overline{OP}$. Note that $\overline{OP}$ is the distance between $\overline{AB}$ and center O. Also, since $\overline{OA} \equiv \overline{OB}$ and $\overline{OP} \perp \overline{AB}$, $\overline{OP}$ bisects $\overline{AB}$. In addition, you have $AB = r$; therefore $AP = \dfrac{r}{2}$.

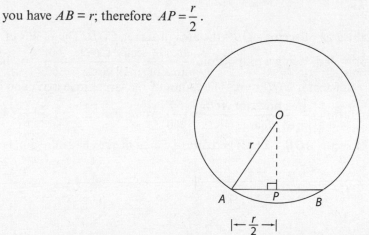

Using the Pythagorean theorem, you have $r^2 = \left(\dfrac{r}{2}\right)^2 + (OP)^2$ or $r^2 = \dfrac{r^2}{4} + (OP)^2$. Solving for OP, you

have $(OP)^2 = \dfrac{3}{4}r^2$ or $OP = \dfrac{\sqrt{3}}{2}r$, Choice C. (Note that $\triangle OAP$ is a 30°–60°–90° triangle.)

2. **B.** The area of circle O is $\pi(12)^2 = 144\pi$. To find the area of sector HOK, set up a proportion:
   $\dfrac{80}{360} = \dfrac{\text{area of sector } HOK}{144\pi}$. Thus, the area of sector $HOK = \dfrac{(80)(144\pi)}{360} = 32\pi$, Choice B.

3. **C.** The circumference of circle O is $C = 2\pi r = 2\pi(5) = 10\pi$ centimeters. To find the length of minor

   $\overparen{PQ}$ (call it l), set up a proportion: $\dfrac{120}{360} = \dfrac{l}{10\pi}$. Thus, $l = \dfrac{120(10\pi)}{360} = \dfrac{10}{3}\pi \approx 10.5$ centimeters,

   Choice C. Alternatively, you could also use the formula $S = \theta r$, where θ is in radians, and get the
   same result.

4. **D.** Since $\overline{MN}$ and $\overline{HK}$ are parallel, and $\angle NHK$ and $\angle HNM$ are alternate interior angles,

   $\angle NHK \cong \angle HNM$. Therefore, $m\angle HNM = 54$. Also, $\angle HNM$ is an inscribed angle, and

   $m\angle HNM = \dfrac{1}{2}m\overparen{MH}$. Thus, $54 = \dfrac{1}{2}m\overparen{MH}$ or $m\overparen{MH} = 108$, Choice D.

5. **2π** Diameter $\overline{AB}$ divides the circle into two semicircles. Therefore, $\angle ACB$ is inscribed in a semicircle,
   which means $m\angle ACB = 90$. In $\triangle ABC$, $m\angle A = 30$ and $\triangle ABC$ is a 30°–60°–90° triangle. In a 30°–60°–90°
   triangle, the length of the hypotenuse is twice the length of the leg opposite the 30° angle. Thus,
   $AB = 2(6)$ or 12. (The relationship among the sides of a 30°–60°–90° triangle is given in the reference
   information at the beginning of each math section on the SAT.) The circumference of the circle is 12π.
   Because $\overparen{ACB}$ is a semicircle, its length is 6π. $\angle B$ and $\angle C$ are inscribed angles, and $m\angle B = 2m\angle C$, so
   the length of $\overparen{AC}$ = twice the length of $\overparen{BC}$, and you have $2x + x = 6\pi$ or $x = 2\pi$. Thus, the length of
   $\overparen{BC}$ is 2π.

6. **18π** The area of shaded region = the area of sector AOB – the area of sector COD. The radius of the

   small circle is 6, and its area is $\pi(6)^2 = 36\pi$. Using a proportion, $\dfrac{\text{area of sector } COD}{\text{area of small circle}} = \dfrac{60}{360}$, you have

   $\dfrac{\text{area of sector } COD}{36\pi} = \dfrac{1}{6}$ or the area of sector $COD = 6\pi$. The radius of the large circle is 12, and its

   area is $\pi(12)^2 = 144\pi$. Using a proportion, $\dfrac{\text{area of sector } AOB}{\text{area of large circle}} = \dfrac{60}{360}$, you have

   $\dfrac{\text{area of sector } AOB}{144\pi} = \dfrac{1}{6}$ or area of sector $AOB = 24\pi$. Therefore, the area of the shaded region is

   $24\pi - 6\pi = 18\pi$.

B. Congruence and Similarity

When working with similar or congruent triangles, it is important to remember the following:

- If two triangles are similar, then
  (a) their corresponding angles are congruent, and
  (b) their corresponding sides are in proportion
- Methods of proving triangles are similar include:
  (a) If two angles of one triangle are congruent to two angles of another triangle, then the triangles are similar: angle-angle similarity (AA).

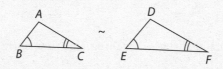

  (b) If an angle of one triangle is congruent to an angle of another triangle, and the sides including those angles are in proportion, the triangles are similar: side-angle-side similarity (SAS).

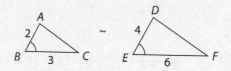

  (c) If the sides of two triangles are in proportion, then the triangles are similar: side-side-side similarity (SSS).

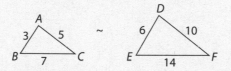

- If two triangles are congruent, then
  (a) their corresponding angles are congruent, and
  (b) their corresponding sides are congruent
- Methods of proving triangles are congruent include:
  (a) For all triangles: SSS, SAS, ASA, and AAS

  SSS: three sides of one triangle $\cong$ three sides of another triangle

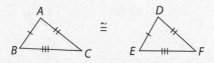

SAS: two sides and the included angle of one triangle ≅ two sides and the included angle of another triangle

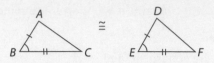

ASA: two angles and the included side of one triangle ≅ two angles and the included side of another triangle

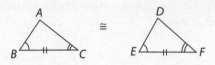

AAS: two angles and a non-included side of one triangle ≅ the corresponding parts of another triangle

(b) For right triangles: Hy-leg

Hy-leg: the hypotenuse and a leg of one right triangle ≅ the corresponding parts of another right triangle

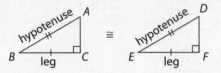

Practice

1. In the accompanying figure, $DE = 8$, $BC = 12$, and $AC = 24$. What is the length of $\overline{EC}$?

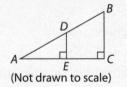

(Not drawn to scale)

   A.   4
   B.   8
   C.   16
   D.   20

2. In the accompanying figure of two overlapping triangles, the two larger triangles are similar, $\angle A \cong \angle D$, and $HE \neq HC$. Which of the following must be true?

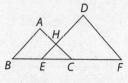

(Not drawn to scale)

   A. $\angle B \cong \angle F$
   B. $m\angle DEF \neq m\angle B$
   C. $\overline{BC} \cong \overline{EF}$
   D. $\overline{AB} \parallel \overline{DE}$

3. In the accompanying figure, $\overline{AB} \cong \overline{AC}$. Which of the following statements is NOT necessarily true?

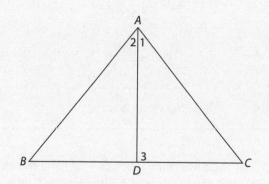

   A. $\angle B \cong \angle C$
   B. $m\angle 3 = m\angle 2 + m\angle B$
   C. $m\angle 3 = m\angle 2 + m\angle C$
   D. $\angle 1 \cong \angle 2$

4. In the accompanying figure, the two triangles are congruent, and $\angle M \cong \angle P$. If the two triangles are also scalene triangles, which of the following must be true?

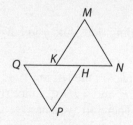

(Not drawn to scale)

   A. $\angle MKN \cong \angle PHQ$
   B. $\overline{MN} \cong \overline{PQ}$
   C. $\overline{KM} \cong \overline{QH}$
   D. $\overline{QK} \cong \overline{NH}$

5. In the accompanying figure of circle O, $\overline{PG}$ is a diameter, $\overset{\frown}{PK} \cong \overset{\frown}{HG}$, $KG = 2x - 2$, $PK = x + 6$, and $PH = 10$. What is the length of chord $\overline{HG}$?

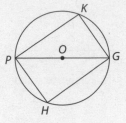

(Not drawn to scale)

6. In the accompanying figure, $\overline{MA} \parallel \overline{HD}$, $MA = 4$, $HD = 8$, $PM = x + 4$, $MH = 2x - 2$, and $PD = 2x + 4$. What is the length of $\overline{PD}$?

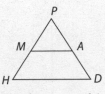

(Not drawn to scale)

Answers

1. **B.** Let x represent the length of $\overline{EC}$; therefore, $AE = 24 - x$. Note that $\triangle ADE \sim \triangle ABC$ because $\angle AED$ and $\angle ACB$ are right angles and $\angle A$ is an angle of both triangles, $\angle A \cong \angle A$; thus, $AA \sim AA$.

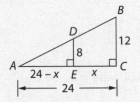

Set up a proportion of the corresponding sides, and you have $\dfrac{24 - x}{8} = \dfrac{24}{12}$ or $\dfrac{24 - x}{8} = \dfrac{2}{1}$, which has a solution of $x = 8$, Choice B.

2. **D.** The three angles of the larger triangle on the left are $\angle A$, $\angle B$, and $\angle HCE$. The three angles of the larger triangle on the right are $\angle D$, $\angle F$, and $\angle HEC$. Since the two triangles are similar, their corresponding angles are congruent. Therefore, you need to determine which angles are the corresponding angles.

Angle HEC must be congruent to one of three angles of $\triangle ABC$. Note that $HE \neq HC$; therefore, $m\angle HEC \neq m\angle HCE$. Since $\angle A \cong \angle D$, $\angle HEC$ must be congruent to $\angle B$. Also note that $\angle HEC$ and $\angle B$ are corresponding angles with $\overline{BF}$ as the transversal intersecting $\overline{AB}$ and $\overline{DE}$. Since the corresponding angles $\angle HEC \cong \angle B$, $\overline{AB} \parallel \overline{DE}$, Choice D.

3. **D.** Examine the statement in each of the four choices. Choice A, $\angle B \cong \angle C$ because the base angles of an isosceles triangle are congruent. Choice B, $m\angle 3 = m\angle 2 + m\angle B$ because the measure of an exterior angle of a triangle is equal to the sum of the measures of the two nonadjacent interior angles. Choice C, since $m\angle 3 = m\angle 2 + m\angle B$ and $\angle B \cong \angle C$, substituting $m\angle B$ with $m\angle C$ you have $m\angle 3 = m\angle 2 + m\angle C$. Regarding Choice D, in order to have $\angle 1 \cong \angle 2$, you must have sufficient information to show that $\triangle ABD \cong \triangle ACD$. Reviewing all the congruent parts of the two triangles, you have $\angle B \cong \angle C$, $\overline{AB} \cong \overline{AC}$, and $\overline{AD} \cong \overline{AD}$, which is equivalent to having a pair of congruent angles and two pairs of congruent sides. However, $\angle B$ and $\angle C$ are not the included angles, which means you could not use the theorem $SAS \cong SAS$ (side-angle-side) to prove the triangles congruent. Note that ASS (angle-side-side) is not an acceptable method for proving triangles are congruent. Thus, in this case, it is not necessarily true that $\angle 1 \cong \angle 2$, Choice D.

4. **D.** Since the two triangles are congruent and $\angle M \cong \angle P$, the corresponding sides of the two triangles are $\overline{QH}$ and $\overline{NK}$, which means $\overline{QH} \cong \overline{NK}$. Thus, subtracting $\overline{KH}$ from both sides of the equation $\overline{QH} \cong \overline{NK}$, you have $\overline{QH} - \overline{KH} \cong \overline{NK} - \overline{KH}$ or $\overline{QK} \cong \overline{NH}$, Choice D. Note that $\angle MKN$ could be congruent to $\angle PHQ$ or to $\angle PQH$, depending on how the two triangles are drawn. See accompanying figures.

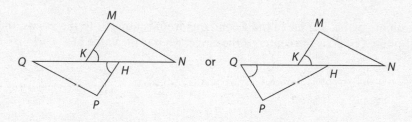

$\angle MKN \cong \angle PHQ$ or $\angle MKN \cong \angle PQH$

5. **12**

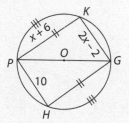

Since $\overline{PG}$ is a diameter, $\angle K$ and $\angle H$ are inscribed angles in semicircles and, thus, right angles. Also $\overparen{PK} \cong \overparen{HG}$, and, therefore, $\overline{PK} \cong \overline{HG}$. Note that $\overline{PG}$ is the hypotenuse for the right triangles $\triangle PKG$ and $\triangle GHP$. Therefore, $\triangle PKG \cong \triangle GHP$, Hy-leg $\cong$ Hy-leg. Chords $\overline{PH}$ and $\overline{KG}$ are corresponding sides; $\overline{PH} \cong \overline{KG}$. Setting $2x - 2 = 10$, you have $x = 6$. Since $PK = x + 6$, $PK = 6 + 6 = 12$. Thus, $HG = 12$.

6. **16** Note that $\angle P$ is an angle of both $\triangle PMA$ and $\triangle PHD$. Since $\overline{MA} \parallel \overline{HD}$, $\angle PMA$ and $\angle PHD$ are corresponding angles and $\angle PMA \cong \angle PHD$. Therefore, $\triangle PMA \sim \triangle PHD$. Since the corresponding sides of the two similar triangles are in proportion, you have $\dfrac{x+4}{4} = \dfrac{x+4+2x-2}{8}$ or $\dfrac{x+4}{4} = \dfrac{3x+2}{8}$. Solve the equation and obtain $x = 6$. Since $PD = 2x + 4$, $PD = 2(6) + 4 = 16$.

C. Circles in the Coordinate Plane

Equations of a circle include the following:

- $x^2 + y^2 = r^2$, center at $(0, 0)$, radius r with $r > 0$
- $(x - h)^2 + (y - k)^2 = r^2$, center at (h, k), radius r with $r > 0$
- $x^2 + y^2 + ax + by + c = 0$, where a, b, c are constants (Note that the equation may lead to degenerate cases with which the radius is zero.)

Practice

1. In the xy-plane, an equation of circle O is $x^2 + (y + 3)^2 = 25$. If $A(-4, -6)$, $B(x, y)$, and $\overline{AB}$ is a diameter of circle O, what are the coordinates of point B?

   A. $(3, 1)$
   B. $(4, 0)$
   C. $(4, 6)$
   D. $(6, 4)$

2. In an xy-coordinate plane, a circle in the second quadrant is tangent to the x-axis, the y-axis, and the line $x = -8$. If point $C(h, k)$ is the center of the circle, what is the value of $h + k$?

   A. -8
   B. -4
   C. 0
   D. 8

3. In an xy-coordinate plane, point C with coordinates $(2, 1)$ is the center of a circle and point A with coordinates $(7, 1)$ is on the circle. Which of the following could be the coordinates of point B if B is also a point on the circle?

   A. $(-7, 1)$
   B. $(1, 7)$
   C. $(4, 6)$
   D. $(6, 4)$

4. In the xy-plane, an equation of a circle is $(x - 4)^2 + (y - 12)^2 = 169$. Which of the following values is an x-intercept of the circle?

   A. -9
   B. -1
   C. 4
   D. 12

5. In the xy-plane, an equation of a circle is $x^2 + y^2 - 4x + 6y - 23 = 0$. What is the length of the radius of the circle?

6. In the xy-plane, an equation of a circle is $(x + 4)^2 + (y - 2)^2 = 100$. What is the slope of the tangent to the circle in the first quadrant at $x = 4$?

Answers

1. **B.** Note that the center of a circle is also the midpoint of a diameter of the circle. In this case, the center of circle O is $(0, -3)$. Therefore, $\left(\dfrac{-4+x}{2}, \dfrac{-6+y}{2}\right) = (0, -3)$, and you have $\dfrac{-4+x}{2} = 0$ and $\dfrac{-6+y}{2} = -3$. Thus $x = 4$ and $y = 0$. The coordinates of point B are $(4, 0)$, Choice B.

2. **C.** Draw a sketch of the coordinate plane and the line $x = -8$.

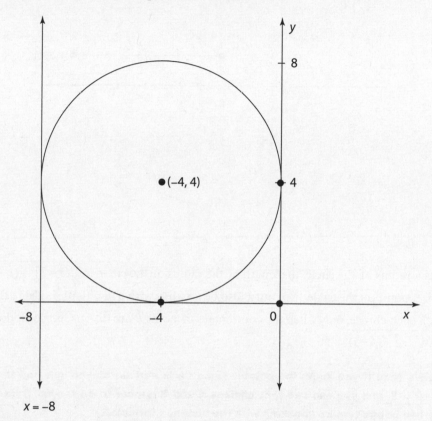

Since the circle is tangent to both axes and the line $x = -8$, its diameter must be 8, which implies the radius is 4. Therefore, the center must be 4 units from all three lines, making its coordinates $(-4, 4)$. Thus, the value of $h + k$ is $(-4) + (4)$ or 0, Choice C.

3. **D.**

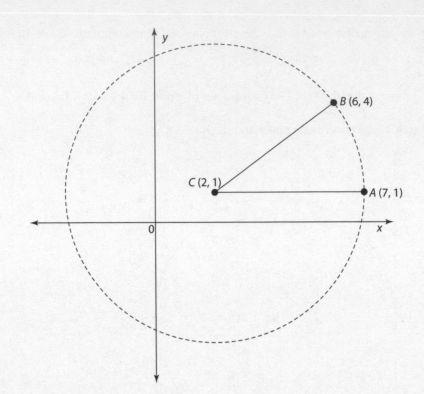

Since $\overline{CA}$ is a radius of the circle, the length of the radius of the circle is $\sqrt{(7-2)^2+(1-1)^2}=5$. Because B is a point on the circle, $\overline{CB}$ must also be a radius with a length of 5. Using the distance formula with each choice, only when the coordinates of point B are $(6, 4)$, Choice D, does the length equal 5: $\sqrt{(6-2)^2+(4-1)^2}=5$.

> **Note: You can save time if you graph the points. Since $\overline{CA}$ is horizontal, you can find the length of the radius using 7 – 2 = 5, and you can see that choices A and B appear to be too far from C to be on the circle. Now only two points require checking with the distance formula.**

4. **B.** To find the x-intercepts, set $y = 0$, and you have $(x-4)^2+(0-12)^2=169$ or $(x-4)^2+144=169$ or $(x-4)^2=25$. Solve and obtain $(x-4)=\sqrt{25}$ or $(x-4)=-\sqrt{25}$, which yields $x = 9$ or $x = -1$, respectively. Since 9 is not a value among the answer choices, the x-intercept is –1, Choice B.

5. **6** Rewrite the equation in $(x-h)^2+(y-k)^2=r^2$ form by completing the square.

   Step 1: Add 23 to both sides of the equation and obtain $x^2+y^2-4x+6y=23$.

   Step 2: Regroup as $x^2-4x+y^2+6y=23$.

Step 3: Take $\frac{1}{2}$ of –4, square $\left(\frac{1}{2}(-4)\right)^2$, and obtain 4. Take $\frac{1}{2}(6)$, square $\left(\frac{1}{2}(6)\right)^2$, and obtain 9. Add 4 and 9 to both sides of the equation: $x^2 - 4x + 4 + y^2 + 6y + 9 = 23 + 4 + 9$, or $x^2 - 4x + 4 + y^2 + 6y + 9 = 36$.

Step 4: Factor and obtain $(x - 2)^2 + (y + 3)^2 = 36$ or $(x - 2)^2 + (y + 3)^2 = 6^2$. Following the form $(x - h)^2 + (y - k)^2 = r^2$, note that the length of the radius is 6.

6. $-\frac{4}{3}$ The accompanying figure shows the tangent line to the circle at $x = 4$.

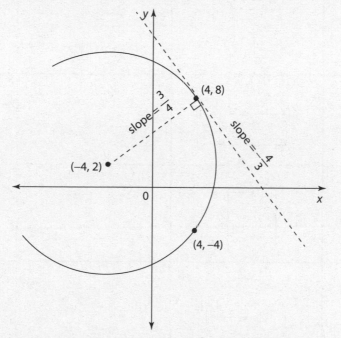

Begin by finding the y-value at $x = 4$. You have $(4 + 4)^2 + (y - 2)^2 = 100$ or $64 + (y - 2)^2 = 100$ or $(y - 2)^2 = 36$. Take the square root of both sides of the equation and obtain $y - 2 = 6$ or $y - 2 = -6$; therefore, $y = 8$ or $y = -4$. Note that there are two points on the circle at $x = 4$, namely, $(4, 8)$ and $(4, -4)$, but only $(4, 8)$ is in the first quadrant. The slope of the radius joining the center of the circle $(-4, 2)$ and the point $(4, 8)$ is $m = \dfrac{8-2}{4-(-4)} = \dfrac{3}{4}$. The tangent to the circle at $(4, 8)$ is perpendicular to the radius from the center of the circle to the point of tangency $(4, 8)$. Thus, the slope of the tangent is the negative reciprocal of $\dfrac{3}{4}$ or $-\dfrac{4}{3}$.

D. Volumes, Areas, and Perimeters

On the SAT, some questions require you to find the volume and surface areas of solids. Here are the important formulas to keep in mind. Some of these formulas also appear in the reference information at the beginning of the math section of the test.

		Volume	Surface Area
Cube		s^3	$6s^2$
Rectangular box		lwh	$2(lh + hw + lw)$
Right circular cylinder		$\pi r^2 h$	Total surface area: $2\pi r^2 + 2\pi rh$ Lateral surface area: $2\pi rh$
Sphere		$\frac{4}{3}\pi r^3$	$4\pi r^2$
Pyramid		$\frac{1}{3}$(base area)(height)	Base area + lateral surface areas
Right circular cone		$\frac{1}{3}\pi r^2 h$	Lateral: $\pi r\sqrt{r^3 + h^2}$ Total: $\pi r\sqrt{r^2 + h^2} + \pi r^2$

Practice

1. The slant height of a right circular cone is $\sqrt{61}$ and its radius is 5. What is the volume of the cone in terms of π?

   A. 15π
   B. 50π
   C. 60π
   D. 150π

2. The area of an equilateral triangle is $9\sqrt{3}$. What is its perimeter?

   A. 6
   B. 12
   C. 18
   D. 24

3. If all faces of a pyramid (including the base) are equilateral triangles, and an edge of the pyramid measures 2 centimeters, what is the total surface area, in cm^2, of the pyramid?

   A. 4
   B. $3\sqrt{3}$
   C. $4\sqrt{3}$
   D. 8

4. A sphere with a diameter measuring 3 centimeters is inscribed in a cube. What is the length of a diagonal, in centimeters, of the cube?

   A. 3
   B. $3\sqrt{2}$
   C. $3\sqrt{3}$
   D. 6

Use the following information to answer questions 5 and 6.

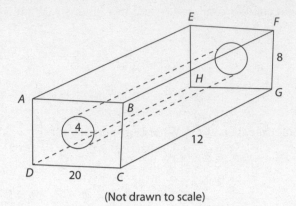

(Not drawn to scale)

As shown in the accompanying figure, a wooden rectangular block has dimensions 20 by 12 by 8 centimeters. A hole with a diameter of 4 centimeters is drilled through the block from the front surface, *ABCD*, to the back surface, *EFGH*.

5. What is the volume, to the nearest cm^3, of the rectangular block after the hole is drilled?

6. What is the total surface area, to the nearest cm^2, of the block after the hole is drilled?

Answers

1. **B.** The volume of a right circular cone is $V = \frac{1}{3}\pi r^2 h$.

(Not drawn to scale)

Find h (height) by using the Pythagorean theorem: $h^2 + 5^2 = \left(\sqrt{61}\right)^2$, which yields $h^2 + 25 = 61$ or $h = \pm 6$; in this case, $h = 6$. Therefore, $V = \frac{1}{3}\pi(5)^2(6) = \frac{1}{3}\pi(25)(6) = 50\pi$, Choice **B**.

2. **C.** Since the area of the equilateral triangle is $9\sqrt{3}$ and $A = \frac{s^2\sqrt{3}}{4}$, $\frac{s^2\sqrt{3}}{4} = 9\sqrt{3}$ or $s^2 = 4(9)$ or $s = \pm 6$.

Since s is the length of a side, it must be positive, so $s = 6$. The perimeter is $3(6)$ or 18, Choice **C**.

3. **C.** Since **all** faces of the pyramid are congruent equilateral triangles, the total surface area of the pyramid is four times the area of one of the triangles. Each edge of the pyramid is also a side of a triangle, and so the triangles are equilateral triangles with sides of length 2 centimeters. The area of each triangle is $A = \dfrac{s^2\sqrt{3}}{4} = \dfrac{(2)^2\sqrt{3}}{4} = \sqrt{3}$. The total surface area of the pyramid is, therefore, $4\sqrt{3}$ cm^2, Choice C.

4. **C.** Since the diameter of the sphere is 3 centimeters, the length of each edge of the cube, including edges $\overline{AE}$, $\overline{EH}$, and $\overline{HG}$, is 3 centimeters, as shown in the figure below.

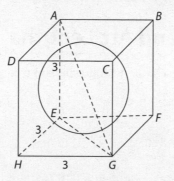

(Not drawn to scale)

To find a diagonal of the cube, you must use the Pythagorean theorem twice: first to find $\overline{EG}$ and then to find $\overline{AG}$. Since $\overline{EG}$ is a side in right triangle $\triangle EHG$, $(EG)^2 = 3^2 + 3^2 = \sqrt{18}$. Since $\overline{AG}$ is a side in right triangle $\triangle AEG$, $(AG)^2 = 3^2 + \left(\sqrt{18}\right)^2 = 9 + 18 = 27$ and $AG = \pm\sqrt{27} = \pm 3\sqrt{3}$. The length of a diagonal must be positive and is therefore $3\sqrt{3}$ centimeters, Choice C.

5. **1,769** Note that Volume of Block$_{\text{with hole}}$ = Volume of Block$_{\text{without hole}}$ − Volume$_{\text{cylindrical hole}}$.

Volume of Block$_{\text{without hole}}$ = $l \cdot w \cdot h = (20)(12)(8) = 1{,}920$ cm^3, and

Volume$_{\text{cylindrical hole}}$ = $\pi r^2 h = \pi (2)^2 (12) = 48\pi$ cm^3. Therefore,

Volume of Block$_{\text{with hole}}$ = $1{,}920 - 48\pi \approx 1{,}769.2035$ cm^3 $\approx 1{,}769$ cm^3. Note that if you use $\pi = 3.14$ instead of the π key on your calculator, then Volume of Block$_{\text{with hole}}$ $\approx 1{,}769.28$ cm^3 $\approx 1{,}769$ cm^3.

6. **1,118** Note that Surface Area of Block$_{\text{with hole}}$ = Surface Area of Block$_{\text{without hole}}$ − 2(Area of Circle) + Area of Cylindrical Hole. If Surface Area of Block$_{\text{without hole}}$ = $2(l)(w) + 2(l)(h) + 2(h)(w) = 2(20)(12)$ $+ 2(12)(8) + 2(20)(8) = 992$ cm^2, 2(Area of Circle) = $2\pi r^2 = 2\pi(2)^2 = 8\pi$ cm^2, and Area of Cylindrical Hole = $2\pi rh = 2\pi(2)(12) = 48\pi$ cm^2.

Therefore, Surface Area of Block$_{\text{with hole}}$ = $9,928\pi + 48\pi = 992 + 40\pi \approx 1,117.6637$ cm^2 $\approx 1,118$ cm^2. Note that if you use $\pi = 3.14$ instead of the π key on your calculator, then Surface Area of Block$_{\text{with hole}}$ $\approx 1,117.6$ cm^2 $\approx 1,118$ cm^2.

E. Radians, Degrees, and Arc Lengths

Given a circle O with radius r and diameter d, the following are true:

- Circumference: $C = 2\pi r$ or $C = \pi d$
- Area: A = πr^2
- 2π radians = 360° (or π radians = 180°)

  1 radian = $\left(\dfrac{180}{\pi}\right)^{\circ} \approx 57.3°$ and $1° = \dfrac{\pi}{180}$ radian ≈ 0.01745 radian

- Arc length:

  $S = |\theta|r$, S = length of $\overset{\frown}{AB}$, and $\theta = m\angle AOB$ in radian or $S = \dfrac{\left|m\angle AOB(\text{in degrees})\right|}{360} \cdot 2\pi r$

- Arc sector:

  Area of Sector $AOB = \dfrac{\left|m\angle AOB(\text{in radians})\right|}{2\pi} \cdot \pi r^2$ or $= \dfrac{\left|m\angle AOB(\text{in degrees})\right|}{360} \cdot \pi r^2$ or

  $= \dfrac{\text{length of } \overset{\frown}{AB}}{2\pi r} \cdot \pi r^2$

Practice

1. What is the radian measure of 210°?

   A. $\dfrac{\pi}{180}$

   B. $\dfrac{\pi}{210}$

   C. $\dfrac{7\pi}{6}$

   D. $\dfrac{7\pi}{3}$

2. Which of the following is the degree measure of $-\dfrac{3\pi}{4}$ radians?

   A. $-135°$
   B. $-45°$
   C. $135°$
   D. $225°$

3. The radius of a circle is 6 centimeters. To the nearest tenth of a centimeter, what is the length of the arc intercepted by a central angle of 1.4 radians?

   A. 1.5
   B. 4.2
   C. 8.4
   D. 16.8

4. What is the exact value of $\sin\left(\dfrac{\pi}{4}\right)$?

   A. 0.7071

   B. $\dfrac{\sqrt{2}}{2}$

   C. $\dfrac{\sqrt{3}}{2}$

   D. $\sqrt{2}$

5. In a circle, a central angle of 68° intercepts an arc of 4.5 centimeters. What is the length of the radius of the circle to the nearest hundredth of a centimeter?

6. The area of a sector in a circle is 4π cm^2. If the length of the radius of the circle is 4 centimeters, what is the length of the arc, to the nearest tenth of a centimeter, determined by the sector?

Answers

1. **C.** To convert from degree measure to radian, multiply the given degree measure by $\dfrac{\pi}{180}$. In this case, $210° = 210\left(\dfrac{\pi}{180}\right)$ radians $= \dfrac{7\pi}{6}$ radians. Choice C.

2. **A.** To convert from radian measure to degree, multiply the given radian measure by $\dfrac{180}{\pi}$. Therefore, $-\dfrac{3\pi}{4}$ radians $= -\dfrac{3\pi}{4} \cdot \dfrac{180}{\pi} = -135°$, Choice A. Note that the negative sign remains for both degree and radian measure of the given angle.

3. **C.**

Using the formula $S = |\theta|r$, you have $S = |1.4|(6) = 8.4$ cm, Choice C.

4. **B.** Note that $\dfrac{\pi}{4}$ radian is equivalent to $\dfrac{\pi}{4}\left(\dfrac{180}{\pi}\right) = 45°$.

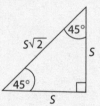

Inspecting the 45°–45°–90° triangle in the accompanying figure, you see that $\sin 45° = \dfrac{S}{S\sqrt{2}} = \dfrac{1}{\sqrt{2}} = \dfrac{1}{\sqrt{2}} \cdot \dfrac{\sqrt{2}}{\sqrt{2}} = \dfrac{\sqrt{2}}{2}$, Choice B. Note that a 45°–45°–90° triangle is in the reference information at the beginning of every math section.

5. **3.79** If you wish to use the formula $S = |\theta|r$, you must convert the degree measure of the central angle to radians. Note that $68° = 68\left(\dfrac{\pi}{180}\right) = \dfrac{17\pi}{45}$ radian. Set $4.5 = \dfrac{17\pi}{45} \cdot r$ and solve for r. Thus,

$r = (4.5)\left(\dfrac{45}{17\pi}\right) \approx 3.7916 \approx 3.79$ cm. Note that if you use $\pi = 3.14$ instead of the π key on your calculator, then $r = 3.7935 \approx 3.79$ cm. Alternatively, you could use the formula

$S = \dfrac{\left|\text{measure of central } \measuredangle \text{(in degrees)}\right|}{360} \cdot 2\pi r$. In this case, $4.5 = \dfrac{68}{360} \cdot 2\pi r$. Solve for r and obtain the same result of 3.79 centimeters.

6. **6.3** Using the formula, Area of Sector $= \dfrac{\text{length of Arc of Sector}}{2\pi r} \cdot \pi r^2$, you have $4\pi = \dfrac{S}{2\pi(4)} \cdot \pi(4)^2$ or

$4\pi = 2S$. Thus, $S = 2\pi$ cm ≈ 6.3 cm.

F. Pythagorean Theorem and Trigonometric Ratios

A right triangle has many properties involving the measurements of its sides and angles. Below is a list of these properties you need to know for the SAT:

- Pythagorean theorem
  $a^2 + b^2 = c^2$

- Trigonometric functions

  The mnemonic *SOHCAHTOA*, sometimes written as $S\dfrac{o}{h}C\dfrac{a}{h}T\dfrac{o}{a}$, may be helpful in remembering some of the trigonometric ratios:

  $$\sin A = \dfrac{\text{opp}}{\text{hyp}} \qquad \cos A = \dfrac{\text{adj}}{\text{hyp}} \qquad \tan A = \dfrac{\text{opp}}{\text{adj}}$$

  $$\csc A = \dfrac{\text{hyp}}{\text{opp}} \qquad \sec A = \dfrac{\text{hyp}}{\text{adj}} \qquad \cot A = \dfrac{\text{adj}}{\text{opp}}$$

- Reciprocal functions

  $$\csc \theta = \dfrac{1}{\sin \theta} \qquad \sec \theta = \dfrac{1}{\cos \theta} \qquad \cot \theta = \dfrac{1}{\tan \theta}$$

  $$\sin \theta = \dfrac{1}{\csc \theta} \qquad \cos \theta = \dfrac{1}{\sec \theta} \qquad \tan \theta = \dfrac{1}{\cot \theta}$$

■ Cofunctions

In radians:

$$\sin\theta = \cos\left(\frac{\pi}{2} - \theta\right) \qquad \cos\theta = \sin\left(\frac{\pi}{2} - \theta\right)$$

$$\tan\theta = \cot\left(\frac{\pi}{2} - \theta\right) \qquad \cot\theta = \tan\left(\frac{\pi}{2} - \theta\right)$$

$$\sec\theta = \csc\left(\frac{\pi}{2} - \theta\right) \qquad \csc\theta = \sec\left(\frac{\pi}{2} - \theta\right)$$

In degrees:

$$\sin\theta = \cos(90° - \theta) \qquad \cos\theta = \sin(90° - \theta)$$

$$\tan\theta = \cot(90° - \theta) \qquad \cot\theta = \tan(90° - \theta)$$

$$\sec\theta = \csc(90° - \theta) \qquad \csc\theta = \sec(90° - \theta)$$

■ Special right triangles

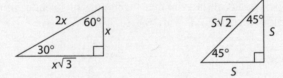

Practice

1. Starting from home, Mary drove 5 miles due east to Bill's house. She then drove 6 miles due south to Karen's house. Mary then drove 3 miles due east to Janet's house. What is the direct distance, in miles, between Mary's house and Janet's house?

   A. 4
   B. 8
   C. 10
   D. 14

2. Which of the following ratios is equivalent to tan A?

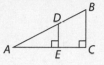

A. $\dfrac{DE}{BC}$

B. $\dfrac{DE}{AC}$

C. $\dfrac{BC}{AE}$

D. $\dfrac{DE}{AE}$

3. A 20-foot ladder is leaning against a wall of a building. The wall is perpendicular to the ground. If the ladder makes an angle of 52° with the ground, what is the distance, to the nearest tenth of a foot, from the foot of the ladder to the bottom of the wall?

A. 12.3
B. 12.4
C. 15.7
D. 15.8

4. In right $\triangle MNP$, if $\sec M = \dfrac{\sqrt{5}}{2}$, what is $\csc N$?

(Not drawn to scale)

A. $\dfrac{1}{\sqrt{5}}$

B. $\dfrac{2}{\sqrt{5}}$

C. $\dfrac{\sqrt{5}}{2}$

D. $\sqrt{5}$

5. In the accompanying figure, $\triangle HKJ$ is isosceles with $HK = HJ = \sqrt{3}$ and $KJ = 1$. What is the measure of $\angle J$ to the nearest degree?

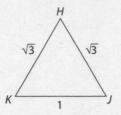

6. In the accompanying diagram, $ABCD$ is an isosceles trapezoid with $\overline{AB} \parallel \overline{DC}$. If $AB = 8$, $DC = 16$, and altitude $\overline{AE}$ has a length of 3, what is the perimeter of trapezoid $ABCD$?

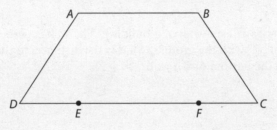

Answers

1. **C.**

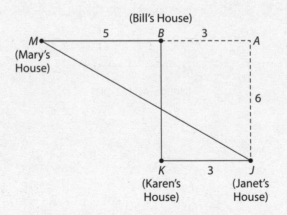

In the accompanying diagram of Mary's trip, if you extend $\overline{MB}$ to A and draw $\overline{AJ}$, $\triangle MAJ$ is a right triangle and quadrilateral $BAJK$ is a rectangle with $BA = KJ = 3$ and $BK = AJ = 6$. Since $AM = 8$, $(AM)^2 + (AJ)^2 = (MJ)^2$ or $8^2 + 6^2 = (MJ)^2$ and $MJ = 10$, Choice C.

2. **D.** Using the mnemonic SOHCAHTOA, you have $\tan = \dfrac{\text{opposite}}{\text{adjacent}}$. In this case, $\angle A$ is an angle in both right triangles, $\triangle ADE$ and $\triangle ABC$. Using right $\triangle ADE$, $\tan A = \dfrac{DE}{AE}$, and using right $\triangle ABC$, $\tan A = \dfrac{BC}{AC}$.

Both ratios are correct. Among the four given choices, Choice D is correct.

3. **A.**

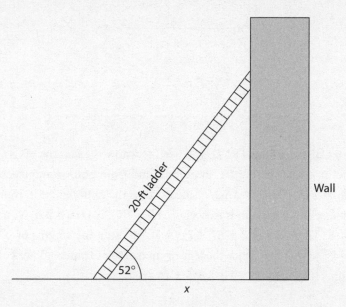

Let x be the distance from the foot of the ladder to the bottom of the wall. Applying the cosine ratio, you have $\cos 52° = \dfrac{x}{20}$. Using a calculator, you have cos 52° = 0.6157; therefore, $0.6157 = \dfrac{x}{20}$ or $x = 12.314$ feet. Thus, the distance is 12.3 feet, Choice A.

4. **C.** Since ΔMNP is a right triangle, $\angle M$ and $\angle N$ are complementary angles. Therefore, $m\angle M + m\angle N = 90$, or $m\angle N = 90 - m\angle M$. Note that sec θ and csc θ are cofunctions. Thus, sec θ = csc $(90° - \theta)$, and in this case, sec M = csc$(90° - M)$ or sec M = csc N. Thus, $\csc N = \dfrac{\sqrt{5}}{2}$, Choice C.

Alternatively, you could also use the reciprocal function relationships, namely $\sec\theta = \dfrac{1}{\cos\theta}$ and $\csc\theta = \dfrac{1}{\sin\theta}$, and the mnemonic SOHCAHTOA, to determine that $\csc N = \dfrac{\sqrt{5}}{2}$.

5. **73** Draw the altitude $\overline{HL}$ as shown in the accompanying figure.

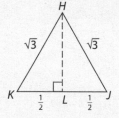

Note that $\Delta HKL \cong \Delta HJL$ (AAS); therefore, $KL = JL = 0.5$. In ΔHKL, $\cos J = \dfrac{LJ}{JH}$. Therefore, $m\angle J = \cos^{-1}\left(\dfrac{0.5}{\sqrt{3}}\right) = 73.2213$. Thus, $m\angle J \approx 73$. Note that you could also find $m\angle J$ by using the Law of Cosines; $\left(\sqrt{3}\right)^2 = \left(\sqrt{3}\right)^2 + (1)^2 - 2\left(\sqrt{3}\right)(1)\cos J$, and obtain $m\angle J \approx 73$.

6. **34**

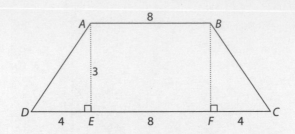

To find the perimeter of trapezoid $ABCD$, you need to know the lengths of $\overline{AD}$ and $\overline{BC}$. To start, draw a line from point A intersecting $\overline{DC}$ at point E and from point B intersecting $\overline{DC}$ at point F to form two right triangles: $\triangle ADE$ and $\triangle BCF$. Since $\overline{AD}$ is the hypotenuse in right $\triangle ADE$, $(AD)^2 = (AE)^2 + (DE)^2$. Because the trapezoid is isosceles, $AD = BC$, $\triangle ADE \cong \triangle BCF$, and $DE = FC$. And since $AB = 8$, $EF = 8$. Therefore, $DE + EF + FC = 16$, making the lengths of $\overline{DE}$ and $\overline{FC}$ both 4. Also, $(AD)^2 = 3^2 + 4^2$, so $AD = 5$. Since the legs of an isosceles trapezoid are congruent, $BC = 5$. Therefore, the perimeter of $ABCD = 5 + 8 + 5 + 16 = 34$.

G. Complex Numbers

Complex numbers are numbers that can be expressed in $a + bi$ form with a and b real numbers and i an imaginary unit. Below are some of the properties of complex numbers:

- $i = \sqrt{-1}$
  $i = i$, $i^2 = -1$, $i^3 = -i$, $i^4 = 1$
- If $a + bi = c + di$, then $a = c$ and $b = d$
- Addition: $(a + bi) + (c + di) = (a + c) + (b + d)i$
  Subtraction: $(a + bi) - (c + di) = (a - c) + (b - d)i$
  Multiplication: $(a + bi)(c + di) = (ac - bd) + (ad + bc)i$

  Division: $\dfrac{a + bi}{c + di}$

  $\dfrac{a + bi}{c + di} = \dfrac{a + bi}{c + di} \cdot \dfrac{c - di}{c - di} = \left(\dfrac{ac + bd}{c^2 + d^2}\right) + \left(\dfrac{bc - ad}{c^2 + d^2}\right)i$

- Given $a + bi$ (with $a + bi \neq 0 + 0i$):
  conjugate: $a - bi$

  multiplication inverse: $\dfrac{1}{a + bi}$ and additive inverse: $-a - bi$

  additive identity: $0 + 0i$ and multiplicative identity: $1 + 0i$

Practice

1. For $i^2 = -1$, what is the value of $2i^4 + i^3 - 3i^2 + i$?

   A. -1
   B. 1
   C. 5
   D. $-1 + 2i$

2. Given $i^2 = -1$, what is the value of $(3 - i)(3 + i)$?

   A. 5
   B. 8
   C. 10
   D. 12

3. In the complex plane as shown in the accompanying figure, point Q is a complex number. Which of the following points could be $i^3 Q$?

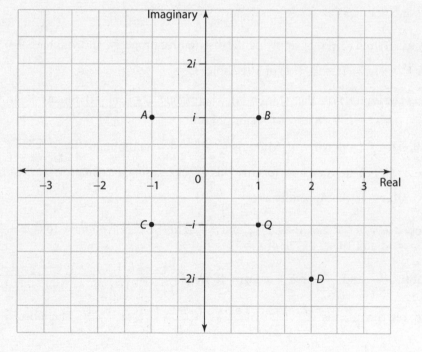

   A. A
   B. B
   C. C
   D. D

4. Which of the following is equivalent to $\dfrac{4-2i}{2-4i}$?

   A. $-i$

   B. i

   C. $\dfrac{4}{5}+\dfrac{3}{5}i$

   D. $4 + 3i$

5. Given $i^2 = -1$ and both m and n are real numbers, if $10 - mi = (m + 2n) + 4i$, what is the value of n?

6. For $i^2 = -1$, what is the value of $\dfrac{1}{1+i}+\dfrac{1}{1-i}$?

Answers

1. **C.** Since $i^2 = -1$, you have $2i^4 = 2(1)$, $i^3 = -i$, and $-3i^2 = -3(-1) = 3$. Therefore, $2i^4 + i^3 - 3i^2 + i = 2 - i + 3 + i$ or 5, Choice C.

2. **C.** Multiply $(3 - i)$ and $(3 + i)$ by applying the distributive property, and you have $9 + 3i - 3i - i^2$ or $9 - i^2$. Since $i^2 = -1$, $9 - i^2 = 9 - (-1)$ or 10, Choice C.

3. **C.** Inspecting the figure, note that Q is $(1 - i)$. Therefore, $i^3Q = i^3(1 - i)$. Since $i^3 = -i$, you have $i^3Q = (-i)(1 - i) = -i + i^2 = -i - 1 = -1 - i$, or point C.

4. **C.** The conjugate of $2 - 4i$ is $2 + 4i$. Multiply $\dfrac{4-2i}{2-4i}\cdot\dfrac{2+4i}{2+4i}$ and obtain $\dfrac{8+16i-4i-8i^2}{4+8i-8i-16i^2}=\dfrac{16+12i}{20}$ or $\dfrac{4}{5}+\dfrac{3}{5}i$, Choice C. For steps on how to solve this problem using a calculator, see "Working with Complex Numbers" in the Appendix.

5. **7** Remember: If $a + bi = c + di$, then $a = c$ and $b = d$. In this case, you have $10 = m + 2n$ and $-m = 4$. Therefore, $m = -4$ and $10 = -4 + 2n$ or $n = 7$.

6. **1** Express both $\dfrac{1}{1+i}$ and $\dfrac{1}{1-i}$ in $a + bi$ form. Rewrite $\dfrac{1}{1+i}$ as $\dfrac{1}{1+i}\cdot\dfrac{1-i}{1-i}=\dfrac{1-i}{1-i^2}=\dfrac{1-i}{1-(-1)}=\dfrac{1-i}{2}$ or $\dfrac{1}{2}-\dfrac{i}{2}$. Also, rewrite $\dfrac{1}{1-i}$ as $\dfrac{1}{1-i}\cdot\dfrac{1+i}{1+i}=\dfrac{1+i}{1-i^2}=\dfrac{1+i}{1-(-1)}=\dfrac{1+i}{2}$ or $\dfrac{1}{2}+\dfrac{i}{2}$. Therefore, $\dfrac{1}{1+i}+\dfrac{1}{1-i}=\dfrac{1}{2}-\dfrac{i}{2}+\dfrac{1}{2}+\dfrac{i}{2}$ or 1.

   An alternate solution is to add the two fractions as follows: $\dfrac{1}{1+i}+\dfrac{1}{1-i}=\dfrac{1-i+1+i}{(1+i)(1-i)}=\dfrac{2}{1-i^2}=\dfrac{2}{2}=1$.

XIII. Full-Length Practice Test with Answer Explanations

Like the actual SAT exam, this Full-Length Practice Test has five sections—Reading Test, Writing and Language Test, Math Test – No Calculator, Math Test – Calculator, and the Essay (optional). The tests are designed to measure your ability in these five areas and to predict your success in college. Each question is numbered. Choose the best answer for each question and fill in the corresponding circle on the answer sheet provided.

When you take this Practice Test, try to simulate the test conditions by following the time allotments carefully. On the actual SAT, if you finish a section before the allotted time runs out, you may not work on any other section. You may not go back to a previous section. The total time for the entire Practice Test (including the optional essay) is 3 hours and 50 minutes:

- Section 1: Reading Test: 65 minutes
- Section 2: Writing and Language Test: 35 minutes
- Section 3: Math Test – No Calculator: 25 minutes
- Section 4: Math Test – Calculator: 55 minutes
- Section 5: The Essay (optional): 50 minutes

Answer Sheet

Section 1: Reading Test

1 Ⓐ Ⓑ Ⓒ Ⓓ	21 Ⓐ Ⓑ Ⓒ Ⓓ	41 Ⓐ Ⓑ Ⓒ Ⓓ
2 Ⓐ Ⓑ Ⓒ Ⓓ	22 Ⓐ Ⓑ Ⓒ Ⓓ	42 Ⓐ Ⓑ Ⓒ Ⓓ
3 Ⓐ Ⓑ Ⓒ Ⓓ	23 Ⓐ Ⓑ Ⓒ Ⓓ	43 Ⓐ Ⓑ Ⓒ Ⓓ
4 Ⓐ Ⓑ Ⓒ Ⓓ	24 Ⓐ Ⓑ Ⓒ Ⓓ	44 Ⓐ Ⓑ Ⓒ Ⓓ
5 Ⓐ Ⓑ Ⓒ Ⓓ	25 Ⓐ Ⓑ Ⓒ Ⓓ	45 Ⓐ Ⓑ Ⓒ Ⓓ
6 Ⓐ Ⓑ Ⓒ Ⓓ	26 Ⓐ Ⓑ Ⓒ Ⓓ	46 Ⓐ Ⓑ Ⓒ Ⓓ
7 Ⓐ Ⓑ Ⓒ Ⓓ	27 Ⓐ Ⓑ Ⓒ Ⓓ	47 Ⓐ Ⓑ Ⓒ Ⓓ
8 Ⓐ Ⓑ Ⓒ Ⓓ	28 Ⓐ Ⓑ Ⓒ Ⓓ	48 Ⓐ Ⓑ Ⓒ Ⓓ
9 Ⓐ Ⓑ Ⓒ Ⓓ	29 Ⓐ Ⓑ Ⓒ Ⓓ	49 Ⓐ Ⓑ Ⓒ Ⓓ
10 Ⓐ Ⓑ Ⓒ Ⓓ	30 Ⓐ Ⓑ Ⓒ Ⓓ	50 Ⓐ Ⓑ Ⓒ Ⓓ
11 Ⓐ Ⓑ Ⓒ Ⓓ	31 Ⓐ Ⓑ Ⓒ Ⓓ	51 Ⓐ Ⓑ Ⓒ Ⓓ
12 Ⓐ Ⓑ Ⓒ Ⓓ	32 Ⓐ Ⓑ Ⓒ Ⓓ	52 Ⓐ Ⓑ Ⓒ Ⓓ
13 Ⓐ Ⓑ Ⓒ Ⓓ	33 Ⓐ Ⓑ Ⓒ Ⓓ	
14 Ⓐ Ⓑ Ⓒ Ⓓ	34 Ⓐ Ⓑ Ⓒ Ⓓ	
15 Ⓐ Ⓑ Ⓒ Ⓓ	35 Ⓐ Ⓑ Ⓒ Ⓓ	
16 Ⓐ Ⓑ Ⓒ Ⓓ	36 Ⓐ Ⓑ Ⓒ Ⓓ	
17 Ⓐ Ⓑ Ⓒ Ⓓ	37 Ⓐ Ⓑ Ⓒ Ⓓ	
18 Ⓐ Ⓑ Ⓒ Ⓓ	38 Ⓐ Ⓑ Ⓒ Ⓓ	
19 Ⓐ Ⓑ Ⓒ Ⓓ	39 Ⓐ Ⓑ Ⓒ Ⓓ	
20 Ⓐ Ⓑ Ⓒ Ⓓ	40 Ⓐ Ⓑ Ⓒ Ⓓ	

Section 2: Writing and Language Test

1 Ⓐ Ⓑ Ⓒ Ⓓ	21 Ⓐ Ⓑ Ⓒ Ⓓ	41 Ⓐ Ⓑ Ⓒ Ⓓ
2 Ⓐ Ⓑ Ⓒ Ⓓ	22 Ⓐ Ⓑ Ⓒ Ⓓ	42 Ⓐ Ⓑ Ⓒ Ⓓ
3 Ⓐ Ⓑ Ⓒ Ⓓ	23 Ⓐ Ⓑ Ⓒ Ⓓ	43 Ⓐ Ⓑ Ⓒ Ⓓ
4 Ⓐ Ⓑ Ⓒ Ⓓ	24 Ⓐ Ⓑ Ⓒ Ⓓ	44 Ⓐ Ⓑ Ⓒ Ⓓ
5 Ⓐ Ⓑ Ⓒ Ⓓ	25 Ⓐ Ⓑ Ⓒ Ⓓ	
6 Ⓐ Ⓑ Ⓒ Ⓓ	26 Ⓐ Ⓑ Ⓒ Ⓓ	
7 Ⓐ Ⓑ Ⓒ Ⓓ	27 Ⓐ Ⓑ Ⓒ Ⓓ	
8 Ⓐ Ⓑ Ⓒ Ⓓ	28 Ⓐ Ⓑ Ⓒ Ⓓ	
9 Ⓐ Ⓑ Ⓒ Ⓓ	29 Ⓐ Ⓑ Ⓒ Ⓓ	
10 Ⓐ Ⓑ Ⓒ Ⓓ	30 Ⓐ Ⓑ Ⓒ Ⓓ	
11 Ⓐ Ⓑ Ⓒ Ⓓ	31 Ⓐ Ⓑ Ⓒ Ⓓ	
12 Ⓐ Ⓑ Ⓒ Ⓓ	32 Ⓐ Ⓑ Ⓒ Ⓓ	
13 Ⓐ Ⓑ Ⓒ Ⓓ	33 Ⓐ Ⓑ Ⓒ Ⓓ	
14 Ⓐ Ⓑ Ⓒ Ⓓ	34 Ⓐ Ⓑ Ⓒ Ⓓ	
15 Ⓐ Ⓑ Ⓒ Ⓓ	35 Ⓐ Ⓑ Ⓒ Ⓓ	
16 Ⓐ Ⓑ Ⓒ Ⓓ	36 Ⓐ Ⓑ Ⓒ Ⓓ	
17 Ⓐ Ⓑ Ⓒ Ⓓ	37 Ⓐ Ⓑ Ⓒ Ⓓ	
18 Ⓐ Ⓑ Ⓒ Ⓓ	38 Ⓐ Ⓑ Ⓒ Ⓓ	
19 Ⓐ Ⓑ Ⓒ Ⓓ	39 Ⓐ Ⓑ Ⓒ Ⓓ	
20 Ⓐ Ⓑ Ⓒ Ⓓ	40 Ⓐ Ⓑ Ⓒ Ⓓ	

CUT HERE

Section 3: Math Test – No Calculator

1 Ⓐ Ⓑ Ⓒ Ⓓ
2 Ⓐ Ⓑ Ⓒ Ⓓ
3 Ⓐ Ⓑ Ⓒ Ⓓ
4 Ⓐ Ⓑ Ⓒ Ⓓ
5 Ⓐ Ⓑ Ⓒ Ⓓ
6 Ⓐ Ⓑ Ⓒ Ⓓ
7 Ⓐ Ⓑ Ⓒ Ⓓ
8 Ⓐ Ⓑ Ⓒ Ⓓ
9 Ⓐ Ⓑ Ⓒ Ⓓ
10 Ⓐ Ⓑ Ⓒ Ⓓ
11 Ⓐ Ⓑ Ⓒ Ⓓ
12 Ⓐ Ⓑ Ⓒ Ⓓ
13 Ⓐ Ⓑ Ⓒ Ⓓ
14 Ⓐ Ⓑ Ⓒ Ⓓ
15 Ⓐ Ⓑ Ⓒ Ⓓ

16.
17.
18.
19.
20.

Section 4: Math Test – Calculator

1 Ⓐ Ⓑ Ⓒ Ⓓ
2 Ⓐ Ⓑ Ⓒ Ⓓ
3 Ⓐ Ⓑ Ⓒ Ⓓ
4 Ⓐ Ⓑ Ⓒ Ⓓ
5 Ⓐ Ⓑ Ⓒ Ⓓ
6 Ⓐ Ⓑ Ⓒ Ⓓ
7 Ⓐ Ⓑ Ⓒ Ⓓ
8 Ⓐ Ⓑ Ⓒ Ⓓ
9 Ⓐ Ⓑ Ⓒ Ⓓ
10 Ⓐ Ⓑ Ⓒ Ⓓ
11 Ⓐ Ⓑ Ⓒ Ⓓ
12 Ⓐ Ⓑ Ⓒ Ⓓ
13 Ⓐ Ⓑ Ⓒ Ⓓ
14 Ⓐ Ⓑ Ⓒ Ⓓ
15 Ⓐ Ⓑ Ⓒ Ⓓ

16 Ⓐ Ⓑ Ⓒ Ⓓ
17 Ⓐ Ⓑ Ⓒ Ⓓ
18 Ⓐ Ⓑ Ⓒ Ⓓ
19 Ⓐ Ⓑ Ⓒ Ⓓ
20 Ⓐ Ⓑ Ⓒ Ⓓ
21 Ⓐ Ⓑ Ⓒ Ⓓ
22 Ⓐ Ⓑ Ⓒ Ⓓ
23 Ⓐ Ⓑ Ⓒ Ⓓ
24 Ⓐ Ⓑ Ⓒ Ⓓ
25 Ⓐ Ⓑ Ⓒ Ⓓ
26 Ⓐ Ⓑ Ⓒ Ⓓ
27 Ⓐ Ⓑ Ⓒ Ⓓ
28 Ⓐ Ⓑ Ⓒ Ⓓ
29 Ⓐ Ⓑ Ⓒ Ⓓ
30 Ⓐ Ⓑ Ⓒ Ⓓ

31. 32. 33. 34. 35. 36. 37. 38.

Section 5: The Essay

Section 1: Reading Test

65 Minutes—52 Questions

Directions: Carefully read the following passages and answer the questions that follow each passage. The questions after the pair of related passages may ask you about the relationship between the passages. Answer the questions based on the content of the passages: both what is stated and what is implied in the passages. Refer to the introductory material before each passage and any accompanying graphs and charts as needed to answer the questions.

Questions 1–13 are based on the following passages.

The first passage is an excerpt from "Civil Disobedience," an essay by nineteenth-century American author, Henry Thoreau. The second passage is from the 1825 State of the Union Address by John Quincy Adams.

Passage 1

I heartily accept the motto,—"That government is best which governs least"; and I should like to see it acted up to more rapidly and sys-
tematically. Carried out, it finally amounts to
(5) this, which also I believe,—"That government is best which governs not at all"; and when men are prepared for it, that will be the kind of government which they will have. Government is at best but an expedient; but
(10) most governments are usually, and all govern-
ments are sometimes, inexpedient. The objec-
tions which have been brought against a standing army, and they are many and weighty, and deserve to prevail, may also at last be
(15) brought against a standing government. The standing army is only an arm of the standing government. The government itself, which is only the mode which the people have chosen to execute their will, is equally liable to be
(20) abused and perverted before the people can act through it. Witness the Mexican war, the work of comparatively a few individuals using the standing government as their tool; for, in the outset, the people would not have con-
(25) sented to this measure.

This American government—what is it but a tradition, though a recent one, endeavoring to transmit itself unimpaired to posterity, but each instant losing some of its integrity? It has
(30) not the vitality and force of a single living man; for a single man can bend it to his will. It is a sort of wooden gun to the people themselves. But it is not the less necessary for this; for the people must have some complicated
(35) machinery or other, and hear its din, to satisfy that idea of government which they have. Governments show thus how successfully men can be imposed on, even impose on themselves, for their own advantage. It is excellent,
(40) we must all allow. Yet this government never of itself furthered any enterprise, but by the alacrity with which it got out of its way. *It* does not keep the country free. *It* does not settle the West. *It* does not educate. The charac-
(45) ter inherent in the American people has done all that has been accomplished; and it would have done somewhat more, if the government had not sometimes got in its way. For government is an expedient by which men would fain
(50) succeed in letting one another alone; and, as has been said, when it is most expedient, the governed are most let alone by it. Trade and commerce, if they were not made of India rubber, would never manage to bounce over the
(55) obstacles which legislators are continually putting in their way; and, if one were to judge these men wholly by the effects of their actions, and not partly by their intentions, they would deserve to be classed and punished
(60) with those mischievous persons who put obstructions on the railroads.

Passage 2

(65) The organization of the militia is yet more indispensable to the liberties of the country. It is only by an effective militia that we can at once enjoy the repose of peace and bid defiance to foreign aggression; it is by the militia that we are constituted an armed nation, standing in perpetual panoply of defense in the presence of all the other nations of the (70) earth. To this end it would be necessary, if possible, so to shape its organization as to give it a more united and active energy. There are laws establishing an uniform militia throughout the United States and for arming and (75) equipping its whole body. But it is a body of dislocated members, without the vigor of unity and having little of uniformity but the name. To infuse into this most important institution the power of which it is susceptible and (80) to make it available for the defense of the Union at the shortest notice and at the smallest expense possible of time, of life, and of treasure are among the benefits to be expected from the persevering deliberations of (85) Congress.

The condition of the various branches of the public service resorting from the Department of War, and their administration during the current year, will be exhibited in the (90) report of the Secretary of War and the accompanying documents herewith communicated. The organization and discipline of the Army are effective and satisfactory. To counteract the prevalence of desertion among the troops (95) it has been suggested to withhold from the men a small portion of their monthly pay until the period of their discharge; and some expedient appears to be necessary to preserve and maintain among the officers so much of the (100) art of horsemanship as could scarcely fail to be found wanting on the possible sudden eruption of a war, which should take us unprovided with a single corps of cavalry.

1. The author's main argument in Passage 1 is that

   A. a government must reflect the will of the majority.
   B. the democratic form of government is the most expedient in that it is both effective and inclusive.
   C. the best form of government is one that least interferes in the lives of its citizens.
   D. power in the hands of the state government is more suitable to the American character than a powerful federal government.

2. The phrase "many and weighty" (Passage 1, line 13) refers to

   A. the reasons to support the establishment of a state militia.
   B. arguments against the formation of a permanent army.
   C. objections to a government that interferes little in the everyday lives of its citizens.
   D. heated discussions of U.S. involvement in the Mexican War.

3. By using the word "expedient" (line 9) to refer to the government, the author of Passage 1 indicates his belief that the U.S. government is

   A. an effective and desirable institution.
   B. a brutal regime used to oppress.
   C. a traditionally successful organization.
   D. an unfortunate but necessary tool.

4. The word "mode" (Passage 1, line 18) most nearly means

   A. style.
   B. method.
   C. world.
   D. mannerism.

5. The repetition of the word *It* (Passage 1, lines 42–44) serves to

   A. distinguish between the entity of the governing body and the human nature of the populace.

   B. indicate the inadvisability of a military arm that does not reflect the will of the people.

   C. defend the use of force to protect the nation from foreign invasion.

   D. reinforce the constitutional insistence on a system of checks and balances.

6. The author refers to "India rubber" (Passage 1, lines 53–54) to make the point that

   A. the U.S. should engage in profitable trade with India.

   B. a comparison of the actions of the government and the actions of men reveals they are both inherently flexible.

   C. adherence to government regulations can expedite the free enterprise system.

   D. without its innate resilience, commercial trade would be thwarted by government regulations.

7. The word "vigor" (Passage 2, line 76) most nearly means

   A. life.
   B. difficulty.
   C. drive.
   D. strength.

8. The author of Passage 2 believes that the benefits of the "persevering deliberations of Congress" (lines 84–85) include all of the following EXCEPT

   A. to energize and strengthen the militia.
   B. to save money.
   C. to protect the lives of soldiers.
   D. to establish specialized, autonomous military units.

9. The author of Passage 2 acknowledges all of the following as problems of the militia EXCEPT

   A. preserving the art of horsemanship.
   B. an absence of organization and discipline.
   C. a disunity in the militia.
   D. desertion among the ranks.

10. The attitude of the author of Passage 2 toward the assertion of the author of Passage 1 that "*It* does not keep the country free" (lines 42–43) would most likely be

    A. whole-hearted agreement.
    B. qualified approval.
    C. complete disagreement.
    D. guarded ambivalence.

11. Which choice provides the best evidence for the answer to question 10?

    A. Lines 62–63 ("The organization . . . of the country.")

    B. Lines 70–72 ("To this end . . . more united and active energy.")

    C. Lines 92–93 ("The organization . . . effective and satisfactory.")

    D. Lines 93–96 ("To counteract . . . monthly pay")

12. The author of Passage 1 would most likely argue that the justification for a "perpetual panoply of defense" (Passage 2, line 68) is

    A. substantiated by the threat of foreign aggression.

    B. not meant to be taken literally.

    C. of dubious validity.

    D. driven by political expedience.

13. The authors of the two passages most strongly disagree on

    A. the effectiveness of discipline in the armed forces.

    B. the indispensability of a permanent military force in the U.S.

    C. the organizational plan of the three branches of the government.

    D. the role of the cavalry in case of a sudden attack.

Questions 14–22 are based on the following passage.

The following excerpt is from *Middlemarch*, a novel by British author George Eliot first published in 1871. Dorothea Brooke and her sister Celia are well-to-do young ladies living in an English village.

Miss Brooke had that kind of beauty which seems to be thrown into relief by poor dress. Her hand and wrist were so finely formed that she could wear sleeves not less bare of style
(5) than those in which the Blessed Virgin appeared to Italian painters; and her profile as well as her stature and bearing seemed to gain the more dignity from her plain garments, which by the side of provincial fashion gave
(10) her the impressiveness of a fine quotation from the Bible,—or from one of our elder poets,—in a paragraph of today's newspaper. She was usually spoken of as being remarkably clever, but with the addition that her
(15) sister Celia had more common-sense. Nevertheless, Celia wore scarcely more trimmings; and it was only to close observers that her dress differed from her sister's, and had a shade of coquetry in its arrangements; for
(20) Miss Brooke's plain dressing was due to mixed conditions, in most of which her sister shared. . . .

The rural opinion about the new young ladies, even among the cottagers, was gener-
(25) ally in favour of Celia as being so amiable and innocent-looking, while Miss Brooke's large eyes seemed, like her religion, too unusual and striking. Poor Dorothea! compared with her, the innocent-looking Celia was knowing and
(30) worldly-wise; so much subtler is a human mind than the outside tissues which make a sort of blazonry or clock-face for it. . . .

Yet those who approached Dorothea, though prejudiced against her by this alarm-
(35) ing hearsay, found that she had a charm unaccountably reconcilable with it. Most men thought her bewitching when she was on horseback. She loved the fresh air and the various aspects of the country, and when her eyes
(40) and cheeks glowed with mingled pleasure she looked very little like a devotee. Riding was an indulgence which she allowed herself in spite of conscientious qualms; she felt that she enjoyed it in a pagan sensuous way, and always
(45) looked forward to renouncing it. She was open, ardent, and not in the least self-admiring; indeed, it was pretty to see how her imagination adorned her sister Celia with attractions altogether superior to her own,
(50) and if any gentleman appeared to come to the Grange from some other motive than that of seeing Mr. Brooke, she concluded that he must be in love with Celia: Sir James Chettam, for example, whom she constantly considered
(55) from Celia's point of view, inwardly debating whether it would be good for Celia to accept him. That he should be regarded as a suitor to herself would have seemed to her a ridiculous irrelevance. Dorothea, with all her eagerness
(60) to know the truths of life, retained very childlike ideas about marriage.

14. The primary purpose of this passage is to

A. argue that the rural setting of the story is more appropriate than an urban setting.

B. expose the rivalry between two sisters.

C. create a character sketch.

D. explain the artistic source from which the subject of the novel will be drawn.

15. The narrator refers to "the Bible" (line 11) and "today's newspaper" (line 12) to suggest

A. the epic cadences of the Bible are far more expressive of Miss Brooke's beauty than ordinary journalistic prose.

B. the inappropriateness of the religious content of a paragraph in the local paper.

C. displeasure with modern styles, which should reflect the modesty of more ancient garments.

D. the refined and enduring simplicity of Miss Brooke's dress.

16. The word "addition" (line 14) most nearly means

    A. qualification.
    B. sum.
    C. total.
    D. completion.

17. The narrator suggests that a notable characteristic of Miss Brooke was her

    A. modesty.
    B. flirtatiousness.
    C. ostentatiousness.
    D. vanity.

18. Which choice provides the best evidence for the answer to question 17?

    A. Lines 13–15 ("She was usually spoken of as . . . more common-sense.")
    B. Lines 28–30 ("Poor Dorothea! compared with her . . . worldly wise")
    C. Lines 45–49 ("She was open, . . . to her own")
    D. Lines 59–61 ("Dorothea, with all . . . about marriage.")

19. The narrator suggests that the cottagers (line 24) found Dorothea's religious views

    A. traditional and innocent.
    B. passionate and pagan.
    C. extraordinary and remarkable.
    D. subtle and charming.

20. Which of the following statements, if true, would most undermine the narrator's point about Dorothea's attitude toward riding?

    A. She unabashedly adored riding and had no qualms about indulging in this exercise every day.
    B. She was somewhat embarrassed by the pleasure she received from riding.
    C. Horseback riding was considered too wild an activity for well-bred young women of the time.
    D. Men found Miss Brooke especially appealing when she rode with abandon.

21. According to Dorothea, any man who came to the Grange not to see Mr. Brooke was motivated by

    A. the desire to ask her father for her hand in marriage.
    B. religious zeal.
    C. interest in purchasing horses.
    D. love for Celia.

22. The word "adorned" (line 48) most nearly means

    A. decorated.
    B. admired.
    C. envied.
    D. credited.

Questions 23–36 are based on the following passage and supplementary material.

The following passage and related graphs are adapted from the U.S. Fish and Wildlife Service.

The red wolf was designated an endangered species in 1967. In 1973, the U.S. Fish and Wildlife Service began efforts to save the red wolf from extinction. Four hundred animals were captured from southwestern Louisiana and southeastern Texas from 1973 to 1980. Tests were made on the captives to distinguish red wolves from coyotes and red wolf–coyote hybrids. The 43 believed to be red wolves were sent to a breeding facility where the first litters were produced in May 1977.

(5)   The red wolf is one of the most endangered animals in the world. A shy species, red wolves once roamed about as a top predator, but aggressive predator control programs and clearing of forested habitat combined to bring the red wolf to the brink of extinction. By 1970, the entire population of red wolves was believed to be less than 100 animals confined to a small area of coastal Texas and Louisiana.

(10)   The original range of the red wolf is somewhat of a mystery. Today, the majority of researchers agree that red wolves occurred historically in the United States from south central Texas to Florida, and north to the Ohio River.

(15) According to researcher R. M. Nowak, the historic range of red wolves extended into Pennsylvania and into New England as far as south-central Maine. Nowak also suggested that red wolves might have extended histori-(20) cally into eastern Canada, blending with gray wolves to create the Algonquin wolf. Lending support to Nowak's suggestion, or otherwise to the concept of the eastern wolf, P. J. Wilson described historic museum samples labeled in (25) the late 1800s as gray wolves from New England, but found they contained new world DNA, not gray wolf DNA, a finding that some scientists interpret to be coyote-like DNA.

Post-colonial information documents the (30) presence of wolves in New England, but which wolf species occurred there historically is subject to further discussion. Physical specimens and pre-Columbian information are scarce for New England, so a combination of reasoning, (35) science, historic accounts, and minimal physical evidence potentially support the occurrence of red wolves. Occurrence of these three kinds of wolves in New England may have differed over geologic time. Yet, reasoning based (40) on the ecology of wolves and their prey leads us to believe the northeastern United States and southeastern Canada were likely a contact zone between the smaller red wolf in the south and the larger gray wolf in the north. This (45) north/south interface likely occurred where the northern edge of mixed coniferous-deciduous forest with smaller prey (white-tailed deer) met the southern edge of boreal forest with larger prey (moose, caribou, elk). Areas of overlap (50) could have brought the two wolves together in evolutionary time to form the eastern wolf, but full scientific consensus has not yet been reached regarding the eastern wolf concept.

Ongoing efforts are underway to prevent (55) extinction of the species and to restore the ecosystems in which red wolves once occurred. If the goal is to preserve the environment and be good stewards of the land, it is important to save all members of an ecosystem, including (60) predators. Predators maintain the balance and health of ecosystems by controlling overpopulations of prey species and removing unhealthy animals. The recovery population goal in the Red Wolf Recovery Program is 550 (at least (65) three wild populations, totaling 220 and 330 in captivity at 30 or more facilities). Lessons learned in the Red Wolf Recovery Program have served, and will continue to serve, as a template for recovery of other species whose (70) only hope for survival is reintroduction.

Conservation of the red wolf gene pool and associated genetic fitness are primary concerns in the red wolf recovery and species survival plan. The current red wolf captive breeding (75) program began with 14 founders. With very small populations, survival can be affected by genetic drift (random loss of genetic diversity) and inbreeding depression (increased genetic homozygosity and subsequent expression of (80) deleterious genes). Genetic diversity of less than 90 percent in founder populations can result in compromised reproduction. Gene diversity in the current captive red wolf population is approximately 89.65 percent of that in (85) the founder population. Several researchers report no inbreeding depression in the red wolf captive program. However, physical anomalies have been observed in a small number of captive and wild red wolves such as progressive (90) retinal atrophy, malocclusion, and undescended testicles. Yet, steady progress in red wolf reproductive research is being made in the captive breeding program that includes two red wolf litters produced in 1992 and 2003 via artificial (95) insemination. The captive breeding program is augmented by the adaptive management plan that involves sterilizing encroaching coyotes to prevent coyote/red wolf hybrids.

Advances in genetics and associated field (100) techniques provide new information helpful in managing wild red wolves. Research on grizzly bears has demonstrated that only a small number of individuals per generation are needed to maintain sufficient genetic diversity; red (105) wolf researchers conjecture this will be true for red wolves as well. Through the cooperative efforts of many dedicated individuals and organizations, red wolves were saved from extinction and are being restored to parts of (110) their historical range.

Figure 1: Annual Counts of Free-Ranging Red Wolves in North Carolina

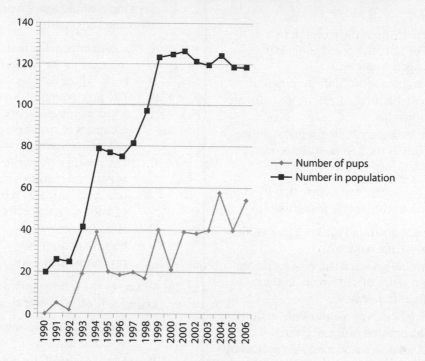

Figure 2: Numbers of Known Red Wolf Pups in the U.S.

Black: before adaptive management plan implementation
Gray: after adaptive management plan implementation

23. The passage is written from the perspective of one who is

    A. a participant in the recent debate in the field of adaptive management of endangered species.
    B. an advocate for wildlife preservation.
    C. a researcher in the field of predator/prey relationships.
    D. an evolutionary biologist investigating changes in the habits of the red wolf population.

24. Which of the following is supported by the information in the second paragraph?

    A. Researchers didn't always agree on the range of the red wolf.
    B. Historical museum samples repudiate the presence of red wolves in the northeastern states.
    C. Researchers Nowak and Wilson disagree on the reputed range of the red wolf.
    D. DNA evidence isn't a reliable indication of the presence of gray wolves in New England.

25. According to the passage, some support for the occurrence of red wolves in New England comes from all of the following sources EXCEPT

    A. historic accounts.
    B. physical evidence.
    C. archeological evidence.
    D. scientific reasoning.

26. The reference to the "north/south interface" serves to

    A. point out how unlikely it was that the red wolf was a progenitor of the eastern wolf.
    B. contrast the white-tailed deer evolution with that of the moose and caribou.
    C. postulate a reasonable explanation for contact between the red wolf and the gray wolf.
    D. calculate the ecological advantage of the coniferous-deciduous forest over the boreal forest.

27. It is reasonable to conclude that the writer of this article would agree with which of the following statements?

    A. It is unethical for human beings to interfere in the natural ebb and flow of animal populations.
    B. The production of hybrids, which occurs when members of one species mate with members of another species, is a healthy way of increasing genetic diversity.
    C. The practice of sterilizing a species to prevent its mating with another species is a valid action to prevent the extinction of endangered species.
    D. Human society has a responsibility to remove predators in an ecosystem to protect weaker prey.

28. Which of the following provides the best evidence for the answer to question 27?

    A. Lines 37–39 ("Occurrence . . . over geologic time.")
    B. Lines 54–56 ("Ongoing efforts . . . occurred.")
    C. Lines 57–60 ("If the goal is to preserve the environment . . . including predators.")
    D. Lines 95–98 ("The captive breeding program . . . hybrids.")

29. The information in the passage suggests genetic fitness is a serious issue because

    A. without genetic diversity, deleterious genes may be suppressed.
    B. without genetic diversity, red wolves may suffer from depression.
    C. genetic diversity increases the odds of hybrids when red wolves mate with coyotes.
    D. genetic homogeneity adversely affects reproductive capacity.

30. The word "deleterious" (line 80) most nearly means

    A. deleted.
    B. detrimental.
    C. delicate.
    D. dubious.

31. The word "compromised" (line 82) most nearly means

    A. negotiated.
    B. jeopardized.
    C. mediated.
    D. conceded.

32. Which of the following is most similar to the relationship between the captive breeding program and the adaptive management plan?

    A. Environmentalists try the same method of reducing pollution with two different types of incinerators.
    B. Farmers try parallel breeding experiments on two species of cows with similar results.
    C. Physicians try chemotherapy and behavior modification to reduce pain in cancer patients.
    D. Psychiatrists treat two patients with schizophrenia with the same drug and chart the changes in brain activity.

33. The reference to the grizzly bear serves to

    A. point out that genetic diversity is dependent on large populations.
    B. indicate that captive breeding programs have worked with species other than wolves.
    C. speculate on the outlook for red wolf species' survival.
    D. draw an analogy between red wolf and grizzly bear predatory habits.

34. The parenthetical information in the fifth paragraph serves to

    A. emphasize technological modernizations.
    B. demystify technical terminology.
    C. explain recent innovations.
    D. highlight confusing jargon.

35. The information in the graphs can be used to support which of the following statements about the red wolf population in North Carolina?

    A. The number of pups born every year after adaptive management plan implementation exceeded the number of pups born every year prior to adaptive management plan implementation.
    B. The number of pups born from 1989 to 1993 was greater than the number of pups born in 1994.
    C. Since the adaptive management plan implementation, there has been a steady increase in the number of pups born.
    D. In 1993 and 1994, approximately half the population of red wolves was comprised of adults.

36. What information in the passage is supported by the data in Figure 1?

    A. "the northeastern United States and southeastern Canada were likely a contact zone between the smaller red wolf in the south and the larger gray wolf in the north"
    B. "Areas of overlap could have brought the two wolves together in evolutionary time to form the eastern wolf"
    C. "physical anomalies have been observed in a small number of captive and wild red wolves"
    D. "red wolves were saved from extinction and are being restored to parts of their historical range"

Qustions 37–44 are based on the following passage.

The following passage, adapted from *The History of Modern Painting,* written in 1907 by Richard Muther, discusses the history of modern English art.

The year 1849 was made famous by a momentous interruption in the quiet course of English art brought about by the Pre-Raphaelites. A movement, recalling the
(5) Renaissance, laid hold of the spirit of painters. In all studios artists spoke a language which had never been heard there before; the most celebrated Cinquecentisti,* whose names had hitherto been mentioned with respectful
(10) awe, were referred to with a shrug as bunglers. A miracle seemed to have taken place in the world, for the muse of painting was removed from the pedestal on which she had stood for three centuries and set up in triumph upon
(15) another.

To understand fully the aims of pre-Raphaelitism it is necessary to recall the character of the age, which gave it birth.

After English art had had its beginning
(20) with the great national masters and enjoyed a prime of real splendor, it became, about the middle of the nineteenth century, the prey to a tedious disease. A series of crude historical painters endeavored to fathom the noble style
(25) of the Italian Cinquecento, without rising above the level of intelligent plagiarism. As brilliant decorative artists possessed of pomp and majesty, and sensuously affected by plastic beauty, as worshippers of the nude human
(30) form, and as modern Greeks, the Italian classic painters were the worst conceivable guides for a people who in every artistic achievement have pursued spiritual expression in preference to plastic beauty. They all went on the
(35) pilgrimage to Rome, as to a sacred spring, drank their fill in long draughts, and came back poisoned. Even Wilkie, that charming "little master," who did the work of a pioneer so long as he followed the congenial Flemish
(40) painters and the Dutch, even Wilkie lost every trace of individuality after seeing Spain and Italy. As this imitation of the high Renaissance period led to forced and affected sentiment, it also developed an empty academical tech-
(45) nique. In accordance with the precepts of the Cinquecento, artists proceeded with an affected ease to make brief work of everything, contenting themselves with a superficial *façade* effect. A painting based on dexterity of
(50) hand took the place of the religious study of nature, and a banal arrangement took the place of inward absorption.

It was to no purpose that certain painters, by imitation of the Flemish and Venetian mas-
(55) ters, made more of a return from idealism of form to colour. Their art was an imposing scene painting, borrowing drawing from Michelangelo and colour from Titian, taking the best from every one, putting it all into a
(60) pot, and shaking it together. Thus English art lost the peculiar national stamp, which it had had under Reynolds and Gainsborough, Constable and Turner. It became an insignificant tributary of the false art, which then held
(65) sway over the Continent, insincere towards nature, full of empty rhetorical passion, and bound to the most vacant routine. And as the grand painting became hollow and mannered, *genre* painting grew Philistine and decrepit. Its
(70) innocent childishness and conventional optimism had led to a tedious anecdotic painting. It repeated, like a talkative old man, the most insipid tales, and did so with a complacency that never wavered and with an unpleasant
(75) motley of color. The English school still existed in landscape, but for everything else it was dead.

A need for reform became urgent all the sooner because literature too had diverged
(80) into new lines. In poetry there was the influence of the Lake poets Wordsworth and Coleridge, who had simplicity and a direct feeling for nature, which was a reaction against the dazzling imaginative fervor of those great
(85) and forceful men of genius Byron and Shelley. In the year 1843 John Ruskin published the first volume of his *Modern Painters,* the aesthetic creed of which culminated in the tenet

(90) that nature alone could be the source of all true art.

This was the mood of the young artists who united to form the Pre-Raphaelite group of 1848. Boldly they declared war against all con- ventional rules, described themselves as begin- (95) ners and their pictures as attempts, and announced themselves to be, at any rate, sin- cere. The program of their school was truth; not imitation of the old masters, but strict and keen study of nature such as the old masters (100) had practiced themselves. They were in reac- tion against the superficial dexterity of tech- nique and the beauty of form and intellectual emptiness to which the English historical pic- ture had fallen victim; they were in reaction (105) against the trivial banality, which disfigured English *genre* painting. The end for which they strove was to be true and not to create what was essentially untrue by a borrowed idealism, which had an appearance of being sublime. In (110) opposition to the negligent painting of the art- ists of their age, they demanded slavishly faith- ful imitation of the model by detail, carried out with microscopic exactness. Nothing was to be done without reverence for nature; every (115) part of a picture down to the smallest blade or leaf was to be directly painted from the origi- nal. Even at the expense of total effect every picture was to be carried out in minutest detail. It was better to stammer than to make empty (120) phrases. A young and vigorous art, such as had been in the fifteenth century, could win its way, as they believed, from this conception alone.

Also Cinquecento: an Italian, especially a poet or an artist, of the sixteenth century

37. The primary purpose of this passage is to

   A. analyze the abstract techniques of artists who worship nature.
   B. denigrate the spirit of the Pre-Raphaelite movement in English art.
   C. explain the artistic upheaval brought about by the Renaissance.
   D. account for an artistic spirit that rejected academical technique.

38. The "spirit of painters" (lines 5–6) would most likely be supported by

   A. historical painters (lines 23–24).
   B. Wilkie (line 37).
   C. they (lines 100 and 104).
   D. decorative artists (line 27).

39. The passage suggests the author would agree with which of the following statements about English art?

   A. It had always been rather tedious and formal.
   B. It underwent a decline in originality and in depth of genuine sentiment.
   C. Unlike Greek and Italian art, it retained a noble splendor.
   D. In all genres other than landscapes, it was worthy of admiration.

40. The word "fathom" (line 24) most nearly means

   A. deepen.
   B. discover.
   C. portray.
   D. comprehend.

41. The use of the phrase "intelligent plagiarism" (line 26) suggests that

   A. the historical painters clearly understood the role of decorative art.
   B. the efforts of the Cinquecentisti deserve contempt.
   C. imitation without originality is of little value.
   D. imitative art is by definition both clever and precise.

42. In lines 34–37 ("They . . . poisoned."), the author describes the actions of those who "went on the pilgrimage to Rome" (lines 34–35) in language best described as

   A. literal.
   B. metaphorical.
   C. understated.
   D. objective.

43. In line 61, "peculiar" most nearly means

   A. weird.
   B. irregular.
   C. strange.
   D. distinctive.

44. The author mentions Wordsworth and Coleridge (lines 81–82) primarily in order to

   A. illustrate the prevalence of an aesthetic creed.
   B. exemplify the rise of English nationalism in poetry.
   C. illustrate an unusual process of reasoning.
   D. contrast the reactions of different genres to the reform movement.

Questions 45–52 are based on the following passage and the accompanying graphics.

The following passage is adapted from written text of Congressional testimony given on May 21, 2014, by Seth Shostak, Senior Astronomer at the SETI Institute in California. SETI is an acronym that stands for the Search for Extraterrestrial Intelligence.

The question of whether we share the universe with other intelligent beings is of long standing. Written speculation on this subject stretches back to the classical Greeks, and it (5) hardly seems unreasonable to suppose that even the earliest Homo sapiens gazed at the night sky and wondered if beings as clever as themselves dwelled in those vast and dark spaces. What is different today is that we have (10) both sufficient scientific knowledge and adequate communications technology to permit us to address this question in a meaningful way.

Finding extraterrestrial intelligence would calibrate humanity's place in the cosmos. (15) Beginning about 470 years ago, observation and scientific reasoning led to an accurate understanding of our place in the physical universe. The goal of SETI—the Search for Extraterrestrial Intelligence—is to learn our (20) place in the intellectual universe. Are our cognitive abilities singular, or are they simply one instance among many? Just as large sailing ships and the compass inaugurated the great age of terrestrial exploration at the end of the (25) 15th century, so too does our modern technology—coupled to a far deeper understanding of the structure of the universe than we had even two decades ago—give us the possibility to discover sentient life elsewhere. (30) SETI is exploration, and the consequences of exploration are often profoundly enlightening and ultimately of unanticipated utility. We know that our species is special, but is it unique? That is the question that SETI hopes (35) to answer.

There is, as of now, no compelling evidence for biology beyond Earth. While the widely reported claims of fossilized microbes in a Martian meteorite generated great excitement (40) in 1996, most members of the astrobiology community today consider the claims are unconvincing. Nonetheless these same astrobiologists, if asked if they think it likely that extraterrestrial life is both commonplace and (45) discoverable, would nod their heads affirmatively. They would do so largely because of what we've learned in the past two decades concerning the prevalence of life-friendly cosmic habitats. Until 1995, we knew of no plan- (50) ets around other stars, habitable or otherwise. And yes, there was speculation that such worlds might be common, but that sunny thought was only speculation.

In the last two decades, astronomers have (55) uncovered one so-called exoplanet after another. The current tally is approximately two thousand, and many more are in the offing thanks to the data from NASA's enormously successful Kepler space telescope. (60) Estimates are that at least 70 percent of all stars are accompanied by planets, and since the latter can occur in systems rather than as individuals (think of our own solar system), the number of planets in the Milky Way galaxy is about one trillion. And, the Milky Way (65) is only one of 150 billion galaxies visible to our telescopes—and each of these will have its own complement of planets. This is plentitude beyond easy comprehension.

(70) The Kepler mission's principal science objective has been to determine what fraction of this planetary harvest consists of worlds that could support life. The usual metric for whether a planet is habitable or not is to ascer- (75) tain whether liquid water could exist on its surface. Most worlds will either be too cold, too hot, or of a type (like Jupiter) that may have no solid surface and be swaddled in noxious gases. Recent analyses of Kepler data suggest (80) that as many as one star in five will have a habitable, Earth-size planet in orbit around it. This number could be too large by perhaps a factor of two or three, but even so it implies that the Milky Way is home to 10 to 80 billion (85) cousins of Earth. There is, in other words, more than adequate cosmic real estate for extraterrestrial life, including intelligent life.

Although encounters with intelligent aliens are a frequent staple of movies and television (90) (and in many blurry cell-phone "photos" of flying saucers), the idea of establishing the existence of these putative beings by traveling to their home planets is one that will remain fiction for the foreseeable future. The planets (95) that orbit the Sun may include other worlds with life (Mars, various moons of the planets Jupiter and Saturn). But they are surely devoid of any life that would be our cerebral equals. Intelligent beings—assuming they exist—are (100) on planets (or possibly large moons) orbiting other stars. Those are presently unreachable: Even our best rockets would take 100 thousand years to traverse the distance to the nearest other stellar systems. The idea that (105) extraterrestrials have come here, while given credence by approximately one-third of the populace, is not considered well established by the majority of scientists.

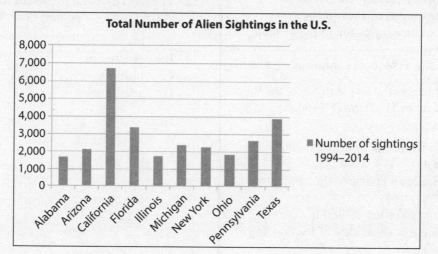

45. The primary purpose of the second paragraph is to

A. compare 15th-century exploration techniques with modern-day efforts.
B. argue that ancient speculation led to current technology.
C. justify the existence and continuation of SETI.
D. exploit the universal human desire to be superior to life on other planets.

46. As it is used in line 14, the word "calibrate" most nearly means

A. adjust.
B. rectify.
C. standardize.
D. assess.

47. The writer uses the phrase "unanticipated utility" (line 32) to indicate that

    A. imaginative musings often lead to concrete findings.

    B. previously dismissed planets can unexpectedly support life.

    C. traditionally underrated theories can eventually prove true.

    D. theoretical investigations can have inadvertent practical applications.

48. The function of the first sentence of the third paragraph (reproduced below) is to

    There is, as of now, no compelling evidence for biology beyond Earth.

    A. state a position that is in direct contradiction to the writer's position on the issue.

    B. give historical background on the current status of the investigation.

    C. serve as a qualification to the writer's main thesis.

    D. explicate a frequent confusion.

49. The writer begins the last sentence of the third paragraph (lines 51–53) with "And yes . . ." in order to

    A. affirm the presence of life-friendly habitats.

    B. anticipate an imagined thought in the readers' minds.

    C. respond to critics of SETI.

    D. provide a positive view of the ongoing speculation.

50. As it is used in line 92, the word "putative" most nearly means

    A. reputed.
    B. believable.
    C. fabled.
    D. actual.

51. The data in the graph supports which of the following textual references?

    A. Lines 13–14 ("Finding extraterrestrial intelligence . . . the cosmos.")

    B. Lines 37–42 ("While the widely reported claims . . . the claims are unconvincing.")

    C. Lines 79–81 ("Recent analyses . . . around it.")

    D. Lines 88–94 ("Although encounters . . . foreseeable future.")

52. The writer's attitude toward the information in the graph would best be described as

    A. regret.
    B. skepticism.
    C. hostility.
    D. admiration.

IF YOU FINISH BEFORE TIME IS CALLED, CHECK YOUR WORK ON THIS SECTION ONLY. DO NOT WORK ON ANY OTHER SECTION IN THE TEST.

Section 2: Writing and Language Test

35 Minutes—44 Questions

Directions: Read the following passages carefully. Then consider the underlined words and phrases or the questions asked to determine the best answer to each question. Fill in the corresponding circle on your answer sheet. Some questions may refer to a whole paragraph or to the whole passage. Some questions may refer to graphs or charts that accompany a passage.

The evidence-based Writing and Language Test tests your ability to apply your knowledge of words, phrases, and language. You will be asked to recognize correctness and effectiveness of expression, organization, and sentence structure. In each passage, questions will ask you to make language choices; some questions give you the option of NO CHANGE. Choose NO CHANGE if you think the underlined portion is best as it is. If not, carefully consider choices B, C, and D, and select the one you think is the best.

In making your selection, follow the requirements of standard written English. Carefully consider the grammar, diction (word choice), sentence construction, and punctuation of each sentence. When you make your choice, select the most effective choice, the one that is clear and precise, without any awkwardness or ambiguity.

Questions 1–12 are based on the following passage.

Adapted from *Cassell's Book of Birds* (1875) by Thomas Rymer Jones.

Flying with Ease

The muscular activity of every animal is **[1]** <u>intimate dependent</u> on the efficacy of its breathing apparatus and on the **[2]** <u>efficiency with which</u> oxygen enters the blood, which it enriches. **[3]** <u>For this respect,</u> birds surpass all living creatures, with the exception, perhaps, of insects.

The lungs of a bird are not suspended, like those of a quadruped, within a **[4]** <u>chest or thoracic cavity that is circumscribed and confined,</u> and inflated by each inspiration; rather, they are soft, porous, and highly vascular organs, through which the air passes **[5]**. The movements of the chest, upon which depend the inspiration and expiration of air, may be compared to those of a bellows continually taking in and expelling air. The framework of the chest, consisting of the ribs and of the breast-bone, is so put together that at each inspiration it can be raised, thus materially enlarging the thoracic chamber, just as the upper board of an ordinary bellows is raised for the purpose of taking in the air; **[6]** <u>but in this case the air, instead</u> of passing through a valve, rushes down the windpipe, and through the immovable, sponge-like lungs, permeating the perforations, and not only filling the entire thorax, but **[7]** <u>penetrated</u> into the interior of hollow bones.

The mechanism of expiration is equally simple; just as, when the upper board of the bellows is depressed, the air is forced out through the nozzle, so, as breast-bone returns to its former position, the inspired air is again forced through the lungs and out the windpipe. By this process it is obvious that as the vital **[8]** <u>element—oxygen, is</u> admitted to every part of the system, the blood is vitalized and temperature is raised until the heat of the bird's body is far greater than that of an ordinary quadruped, and **[9]** <u>its'</u> energy is proportionately increased. **[10]** <u>Consequently,</u> as the blood circulates through the system, it carries with it heat and life; the energies of the entire system are fired up; the muscles quiver with intense life, like a steam-engine working under high pressure. **11**

This admission of air into every part of the system serves not only to fan the vital flame and rouse the energies of the **12** bird, it also assists in giving buoyancy to its movements, bearing it upward, as the gas does a balloon. It is evident that when the air received into the body is raised to a temperature corresponding to the heat of its blood, the specific gravity of the bird is proportionately diminished, and it rises into the air almost without an effort, and even hovers in the sky with scarcely perceptible movement of its wings.

1. A. NO CHANGE
   B. dependently intimate
   C. intimate and dependent
   D. intimately dependent

2. A. NO CHANGE
   B. efficiency to which
   C. efficiency through which
   D. efficiency that

3. A. NO CHANGE
   B. In this respect,
   C. Respectively,
   D. Respectfully,

4. A. NO CHANGE
   B. circumscribed chest or thoracic cavity that is confined
   C. circumscribed chest or thoracic cavity that confines
   D. circumscribed chest or thoracic cavity

5. At this point (before the period), the writer would like to add a detail to help the reader visualize the process of the airflow. Which of the following choices best accomplishes the writer's goal?

   A. freely
   B. going through freely
   C. as through the interior of a sponge
   D. going through the organs

6. A. NO CHANGE
   B. but, in this case, the air, instead
   C. but, in this case; the air, instead
   D. but; in this case the air, instead

7. A. NO CHANGE
   B. has penetrated
   C. is penetrating
   D. penetrating

8. A. NO CHANGE
   B. element; oxygen, is
   C. element—oxygen—is
   D. element: oxygen is

9. A. NO CHANGE
   B. their
   C. it's
   D. its

10. A. NO CHANGE
    B. However
    C. In contrast
    D. While

11. At this point, the writer wants to add a concluding sentence for the paragraph that will vividly illustrate the process described in the paragraph. Which of the following choices would best accomplish this goal?

    A. This process allows birds to fly through the air without the benefit of jet fuel.
    B. By using this process, birds can overcome gravity and travel long distances above the clouds.
    C. Working very efficiently, the breathing mechanism of the bird is a miraculous invention.
    D. This process enables the falcon to plummet with tremendous velocity and the swallow to achieve its wonderful migration.

12. A. NO CHANGE
    B. bird, but it also
    C. bird, it, also
    D. bird; while it also

Questions 13–23 are based on the following passage.

Adapted from "Aboard the Underground Railroad" from the National Park Service website (nps.gov).

Escape from Slavery

The Underground Railroad refers to the effort—sometimes spontaneous, sometimes **13** highly organized, to assist persons held in bondage in North America to escape from slavery. The network provided an opportunity for sympathetic white Americans to play a role in resisting slavery, and brought together, **14** however uneasily at times, men and women of both races to begin to set aside assumptions about the other race and to work together on issues of mutual concern. At the most dramatic level, the Underground Railroad provided stories of guided escapes from the South, **15** rescuing of arrested fugitives in the North, complex communication systems, and individual acts of bravery and suffering in the quest for freedom for all.

16 In debating in Congress in 1819 and 1820 over whether Missouri should enter the Union as a slave or free state **17** have made it clear to the entire nation that the slavery issue was not going to simply evaporate in the American republic. For free blacks, the formation of the national American Colonization Society persuaded them to organize for the abolition of slavery rather than act individually. **18** The Colonization Society wanted federal government funds and moving black Americans away. The threat to free African Americans that this appeared to represent **19** called to a more organized black response and for more white allies. The era of immediate abolitionism is generally acknowledged **20** to have begun on January 1, 1831, when William Lloyd Garrison first published his abolitionist newspaper, *The Liberator*.

21 The abolitionists were mostly in the North. Many of them were part of the organized Underground Railroad that flourished between 1830 and 1861. Not all abolitionists favored aiding fugitive slaves, and some believed that money and energy should go to political action. Even those **22** of whom were not abolitionists might be willing to help when they encountered a fugitive, or they might not. It was very difficult for fugitives to know who could be trusted.

(1) Southerners were outraged that escaping slaves received assistance from so many sources and that they lived and worked in the North and Canada. (2) As a part of the Compromise of 1850, a new Fugitive Slave Act was passed that made it both possible and profitable to hire slave catchers to find and arrest runaways. (3) They worked together with local abolition societies, African American churches, and a variety of individuals to help fugitives move farther on or to find them homes and work. (4) This was a disaster for the free black communities of the North, especially since the slave catchers often kidnapped legally free blacks as well as fugitives. (5) But these seizures and kidnappings brought the brutality of slavery into the North and persuaded many more people to assist fugitives. (6) Vigilance Committees acted as contact points for runaways and watched out vigilantly for the rights of northern free blacks. (7) Those who went to Canada in the mid-nineteenth century went primarily to what was then called Canada West, now Ontario. **23**

13. **A.** NO CHANGE
    B. high organized to assist
    C. high organized—to assist
    D. highly organized—to assist

14. The writer is considering deleting the underlined portion. Should the writer make this deletion?

    A. Yes, because the underlined portion detracts from the emphasis on interracial cooperation.
    B. Yes, because the information in the underlined portion is provided elsewhere in the paragraph.
    C. No, because the underlined portion reflects the reality of the situation.
    D. No, because the underlined portion gives an example that is relevant to the paragraph.

15. A. NO CHANGE
    B. rescue of arrested fugitives in the North
    C. the arresting of escaping fugitives who fled to the North
    D. fugitives being arrested in the North

16. A. NO CHANGE
    B. In the debating in Congress
    C. In the debate in congress
    D. The debate in Congress

17. A. NO CHANGE
    B. has made
    C. made
    D. was making

18. Which of the following choices, if true, provides the most specific information on the plans of the Colonization Society?

    A. NO CHANGE
    B. The Colonization Society wanted federal government funds to pay the costs of moving black Americans away.
    C. The Colonization Society wanted federal government funds to pay the costs of moving black Americans far away to a nation in Africa.
    D. The Colonization Society wanted federal government funds to pay the costs of settling free blacks in an African colony they founded and called Liberia.

19. A. NO CHANGE
    B. called for
    C. called by
    D. called in

20. A. NO CHANGE
    B. to have began
    C. began
    D. to begin

21. Which of the following provides the most effective opening sentence for this paragraph?

    A. NO CHANGE
    B. The abolitionists, who began the movement in the North, got their name because they wanted to abolish slavery.
    C. Working behind the scenes to abolish slavery, the abolitionists were united in their efforts to remove slavery from the states.
    D. The abolitionists were divided over strategy and tactics, but they were very active and very visible.

22. A. NO CHANGE
    B. whom were
    C. who were
    D. who was

23. The best placement for Sentence 3 in this paragraph is

    A. where it is now.
    B. after Sentence 4.
    C. after Sentence 5.
    D. after Sentence 6.

Questions 24–33 are based on the following passage and supplementary material.

The following passage is based on information in the U.S. Department of Agriculture website (usda.gov).

Concern for Citrus

Citrus production in the United States has been an important part of our rich and abundant agricultural heritage **24** due to the fact of the introduction of citrus into St. Augustine, Florida, in the 1500s and the planting of the first commercial grove in 1823 by French Count Odet Philippe. Citrus production **25** has spread across the southern tier states of the United States in the 1800s with Louisiana, Texas, Arizona, and California joining Florida as citrus-producing states.

Citrus production in the United States has a colorful history with many challenges over the years. Catastrophic weather events **26** have occurred periodically and temporarily reduced citrus production. Exotic citrus pest and disease incursions **27** have effected and continue to effect citrus production in the United States, with citrus canker, citrus tristeza virus, and fruit flies being of economic importance and having significant impacts over the last 100 years.

It is noteworthy that citrus production in the United States coincides with geographic regions that are considered high-risk areas for the introduction and establishment of invasive pests and diseases. Key factors that are common to the high-risk states of Florida, California, Texas, and Arizona are climate, crop diversity, geography, urban encroachment, and international air and maritime ports, which bring in international cargo and passengers. **28** However, competition for foreign and domestic market shares and escalating agricultural land values are more recent problems, but have also **29** contributed to the escalation of citrus production. Despite past and current challenges placed on United States citrus **30** production; it has survived and is recognized as an important part of our agricultural well-being. In Florida alone, commercial citrus is a nine billion dollar a year industry with some 750,000 acres in production. In fact, the pattern of the citrus industry in Florida is a microcosm of that in the country as a whole.

In recent years, commercial citrus production in Florida has been at the forefront of many of the issues that face United States citrus production. Weather events that occurred within the 2004 and 2005 hurricane seasons, coupled with the introduction and spread of citrus canker and huanglongbing (citrus greening) in more recent years, **31** resulting in a unique combination of impacts.

Despite a 10-year monumental effort to eliminate citrus canker, a combination of program delays from legal challenges to the Citrus Canker Eradication Program (CCEP) and unprecedented hurricane activity in 2004 and 2005, the disease spread to the point that eradication was considered no longer feasible. Huanglongbing, a serious citrus disease, was detected in late 2005 in South Florida. The biology of huanglongbing, coupled with its primary insect vector, the Asian citrus psyllid, does not lend itself well to early detection nor eradication. Survey activities subsequent to huanglongbing detection in Florida revealed that the disease is well established in South Florida and is present at lower levels in an apparent gradient from south to north in the southern half of the Florida peninsula. Although two other strains of this disease **32** is known to attack citrus, they have yet to be detected in Florida or other citrus-producing areas of the U.S. **33**

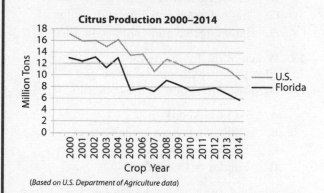

Citrus Production 2000–2014

Million Tons / Crop Year — U.S., Florida

(Based on U.S. Department of Agriculture data)

24. **A.** NO CHANGE
    B. because of the fact of its dating back
    C. dating back to the
    D. from dating to the

25. **A.** NO CHANGE
    B. spread
    C. have spread
    D. is spreading

26. The writer is considering adding the following information to the passage at this point (after *events*).

    in the form of freezes, hurricanes, and drought

    Should the writer make this addition here?

    A. Yes, because it explains the weather events that affect crops.

    B. Yes, because without it, the reader would not know that the weather events are disastrous.

    C. No, because this is a discussion of the citrus crop, and weather is not important to the writer's main point.

    D. No, because it would be better placed in the first paragraph.

27. **A.** NO CHANGE
    B. has effected and continue to effect
    C. have affected and continue to effect
    D. have affected and continue to affect

28. Which of the following most smoothly and effectively provides a transition and introduces the point of the sentence?

    A. NO CHANGE
    B. Other challenges in the form of
    C. While it is true that
    D. Similar to that are

29. After interpreting the data in the chart, which of the following changes would best clarify the sentence?

    A. NO CHANGE
    B. prevented declines in
    C. encouraged growth in
    D. contributed to instabilities in

30. **A.** NO CHANGE
    B. production—it
    C. production, it
    D. production. It

31. **A.** NO CHANGE
    B. have resulted in
    C. has resulted in
    D. resulting with

32. **A.** NO CHANGE
    B. known
    C. was known
    D. are known

33. The data in the chart supports which of the following statements from the passage?

    A. Citrus production has spread across the southern tier states of the United States in the 1800s with Louisiana, Texas, Arizona, and California joining Florida as citrus-producing states.

    B. In Florida alone, commercial citrus is a nine billion dollar a year industry with some 750,000 acres in production.

    C. In fact, the pattern of the citrus industry in Florida is a microcosm of that in the country as a whole.

    D. In recent years, commercial citrus production in Florida has been at the forefront of many of the issues that face United States citrus production.

Questions 34–44 are based on the following passage.

The following passage is based on information on the Centers for Disease Control and Prevention website (cdc.gov).

Healthy Choices

Childhood obesity is the result of eating too many calories and not getting enough physical activity. A variety of environmental factors determine whether or not the healthy choice is the easy choice for children and their parents. **34** It can be difficult for children to make healthy food choices and get enough physical activity when they are exposed to unhealthy environments in their home, child care center, school, or community.

About 55 million school-aged children are enrolled in schools across the United States, and many eat and drink meals and snacks there. **35** More than half of U.S. middle and high schools still offer sugary drinks and less healthy foods. Students have access to sugary drinks and less healthy foods at school throughout the day **36**. In addition, foods high in total calories, sugars, salt, and fat and low in nutrients are highly advertised and marketed through media **37** targeted to children and adolescents.

(1) Lack of daily, quality physical activity during and after school is a major contributor to the problem. (2) Most adolescents fall short of the recommended 60 minutes of aerobic physical activity **38** each day, regularly scheduled, quality physical education in school can help students. (3) In addition, getting to parks and recreation centers may be difficult, and public transportation may be unavailable. (4) For many children, safe routes for walking or biking to school or play may not exist. (5) Half of the children in the United States do not have a park, community center, or sidewalk in their neighborhood. **39**

Another problem is that some people have less access to markets that sell healthy, affordable food such as fruits and vegetables, especially in rural, minority, and lower-income neighborhoods. Supermarket access is associated with a reduced risk for obesity. Choosing healthy foods is difficult for parents in areas **40** that have, over abundantly, too many convenience stores and fast food restaurants that sell less healthy food.

Still another issue is that children 8 to 18 years of age spend an average of 7.5 hours a day using entertainment media, including TV, computers, video games, cell phones, and movies. Of those 7.5 hours, about 4.5 hours is dedicated to viewing TV. **41** Children's TV viewing is a contributing factor to obesity because **42** time may be taken away by it from the time children spend in physical activities, lead to increased energy intake through snacking and eating meals in front of the TV, and influence children to make unhealthy food choices through exposure to food advertisements.

There is no single or simple solution to the childhood obesity epidemic, but states, communities, and parents can take some actions to help make healthy opportunities for children, adolescents, and their families. They can provide incentives for supermarkets, farmers markets, or other retail models to establish their businesses in underserved areas, expand programs that bring local fruits and vegetables to schools, **43** putting salad bars in schools, and improve access to parks and playgrounds. **44**

34. **A.** NO CHANGE
    B. There is difficulty
    C. Difficulty is in place
    D. The difficulty is there

35. The writer would like to add a transitional word at this point to improve the coherence in the sentence. Which of the following words is the best choice to provide a smooth and effective transition?

    A. Yet, more
    B. In contrast, more
    C. Likewise, more
    D. In that case, more

36. At this point (before the period), the writer wants to add some supporting detail to provide a clearer picture of the situation in schools. Which of the following choices best accomplishes the writer's goal?

    A. in the cafeteria, which in many schools in rural areas, also functions as the auditorium.
    B. , which are often available for purchase for a student who wants to have a sugary snack or a soft drink loaded with extra calories.
    C. , which cost so much that they can also put a financial burden on families who have several children in school.
    D. from vending machines and school canteens and at fundraising events, school parties, and sporting events.

37. All of the following are acceptable replacements for the underlined portion EXCEPT

    A. pointed at
    B. aimed to
    C. focused on
    D. directed toward

38. **A.** NO CHANGE
 B. each day, regularly scheduled quality physical
 C. each day. Regularly scheduled: quality, physical
 D. each day. Regularly scheduled, quality physical

39. The writer would like to add the following statistic to the third paragraph.

 However, in 2009 only 33% attended daily physical education classes.

 Where is the best place to add the statistic?

 A. After Sentence 1
 B. Before Sentence 3
 C. After Sentence 3
 D. After Sentence 5

40. **A.** NO CHANGE
 B. that have too many abundant
 C. with too many, abundant
 D. with an overabundance of

41. **A.** NO CHANGE
 B. Childrens'
 C. Children
 D. Childrens's

42. **A.** NO CHANGE
 B. time may be taken away by viewing
 C. it may take away from the time
 D. they may take away the time

43. **A.** NO CHANGE
 B. they can put salad bars in schools
 C. to put salad bars in schools
 D. put salad bars in schools

44. At this point, the writer wants to add a concluding sentence that emphasizes the importance for children of getting physical exercise every day. Which choice is the best conclusion to accomplish this purpose?

 A. In conclusion, it is time to take action to reduce the problem of childhood obesity.
 B. The whole problem can go away if only states get involved and prevent schools from providing unhealthy choices for kids.
 C. Perhaps most important, states can provide the financial support necessary for quality, daily physical education in schools.
 D. In the future, we can avoid this problem if schools and states agree on the guidelines for what is healthy and what is unhealthy.

IF YOU FINISH BEFORE TIME IS CALLED, CHECK YOUR WORK ON THIS SECTION ONLY. DO NOT WORK ON ANY OTHER SECTION IN THE TEST.

Section 3: Math Test – No Calculator

25 Minutes—20 Questions

Directions: For questions 1–15, choose the best answer from the choices given. Use of a calculator is not permitted.

Unless otherwise indicated:

- All figures are drawn to scale.
- All figures lie in a plane.
- All variables used represent real numbers.
- The domain of a given function f is the set of all real numbers x such that $f(x)$ is a real number.

Reference

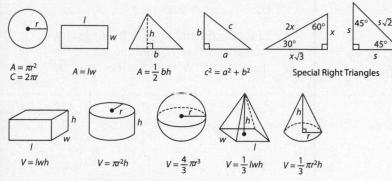

$A = \pi r^2$
$C = 2\pi r$

$A = lw$

$A = \frac{1}{2} bh$

$c^2 = a^2 + b^2$

Special Right Triangles

$V = lwh$

$V = \pi r^2 h$

$V = \frac{4}{3}\pi r^3$

$V = \frac{1}{3} lwh$

$V = \frac{1}{3}\pi r^2 h$

The complete arc of a circle measures 360°.

Also, the complete arc of a circle measures 2π radians.

The sum of the measures of the angles of a triangle is 180°.

1. If $7 - 2x$ is 6 less than $x + 1$, what is the value of $3x + 4$?

   A. 4
   B. 8
   C. 12
   D. 16

2. If $y = 2 - 2x$, what is the value of $(25^x)(5^y)$?

   A. 5
   B. 25
   C. 125
   D. 625

Use the following information to answer questions 3 and 4.

t	0	1	2	3	4
A	120	170	220	270	320

Daryn wishes to save money for a vacation. The accompanying table shows t, the number of weeks since she began saving for her vacation, and A, the amount of money, in dollars, in her savings account.

3. Which of the following equations best models the data?

   A. $A = 50t$
   B. $A = 320 - 50t$
   C. $A = 120 + 50t$
   D. $A = 120(0.5)^t$

4. What is the minimum number of weeks Daryn needs to save at this rate in order to have at least $1,000 in her savings account?

   A. 17
   B. 19
   C. 18
   D. 20

5. If $\dfrac{1}{2}\left(\dfrac{x}{y}\right) = 4$, then $\dfrac{y}{x} =$

   A. $\dfrac{1}{8}$
   B. $\dfrac{1}{2}$
   C. 1
   D. 8

6. If a and b are positive integers and $(a - b)^2 = 36$, which of the following must be true?

   A. $a^2 + b^2 < 36$
   B. $a^2 + b^2 > 36$
   C. $a^2 + b^2 = 36$
   D. $a^2 - b^2 = 36$

7. Given $i = \sqrt{-1}$, which of the following complex numbers is equivalent to $\dfrac{4 - 7i}{3 + 2i}$?

   A. $\dfrac{4}{3} - \dfrac{7}{2}i$
   B. $\dfrac{26}{5} - \dfrac{29}{5}i$
   C. $-\dfrac{2}{13} - \dfrac{29}{13}i$
   D. $-2 + 29i$

8. If $3^{n^2} \cdot 3^{2n} = 27$ and $n > 0$, what is the value of n?

   A. -1
   B. 0
   C. 1
   D. 3

9. In the accompanying circle, the length of diameter $\overline{EF}$ is 12, and the $m\angle DFE$ is twice the $m\angle DEF$. What is the length of $\overline{DF}$?

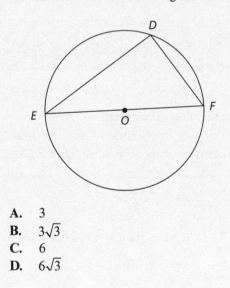

   A. 3
   B. $3\sqrt{3}$
   C. 6
   D. $6\sqrt{3}$

10. If $2 \le |x| \le 5$, which of the following number lines shows all the possible values of x?

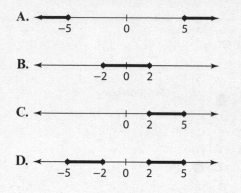

A.

      −5   0   5

B.

      −2 0 2

C.

      0 2 5

D.

  −5 −2 0 2 5

11. If $2a - 2b = 5$ and $a^2 - b^2 = 10$, what is the value of $a + b$?

  A. 4
  B. 5
  C. 10
  D. 20

12. If $pqt \ne 0$, which of the following is equivalent to $\sqrt[3]{16p^6q^5t}$?

  A. $4p^3q^2\sqrt[3]{qt}$
  B. $4p^2q\sqrt[3]{q^2t}$
  C. $8p^2q^2\sqrt{q^2t}$
  D. $2p^2q\sqrt[3]{2q^2t}$

13. If k is a constant, which of the following could be the graph of the equation $x - (k^4 + 3)y = 5$?

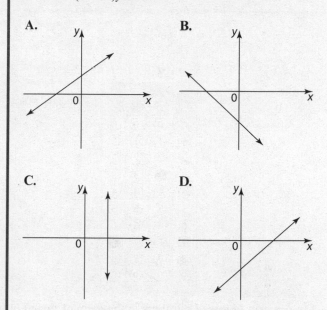

A.

B.

C.

D.

14. If b is a positive integer and $a + b = 1$ and $ab = -6$, what is the value of a?

  A. −3
  B. −2
  C. 0
  D. 2

15. Which of the following is equivalent to the expression $25p^4 - 20p^2q^2 + 4q^4$?

  A. $(5p^2 - 2q^2)^2$
  B. $(5p^2 + 2q^2)^2$
  C. $(25p^2 - 4q^2)^2$
  D. $(5p^2 - 2q^2)(5p^2 + 2q^2)$

Directions for Student-Produced Response Questions (grid-ins): Questions 16–20 require you to solve the problem and enter your answer by carefully marking the circles on the special grid. Examples of the appropriate way to mark the grid follow.

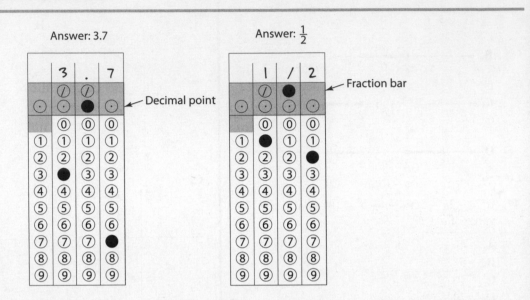

Do not grid in mixed numbers in the form of mixed numbers. Always change mixed numbers to improper fractions or decimals.

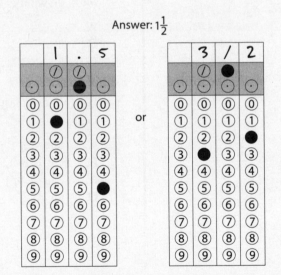

Space permitting, answers may start in any column. Each grid-in answer below is correct.

Answer: 123

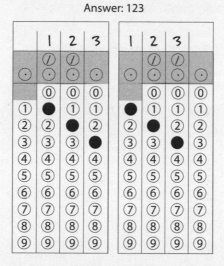

Note: Circles must be filled in correctly to receive credit. Mark only one circle in each column. No credit will be given if more than one circle in a column is marked. Example:

Answer: 258 (no credit)

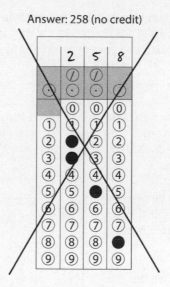

Always enter the most accurate decimal value that the grid will accommodate. For example, an answer such as .8888 . . . can be gridded as .888 or .889. Gridding this value as .8, .88, or .89 is considered inaccurate and, therefore, not acceptable. The acceptable grid-ins of $\frac{8}{9}$ are:

Answer: $\frac{8}{9}$

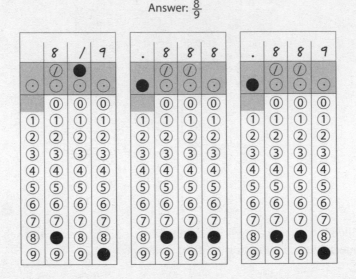

Be sure to write your answers in the boxes at the tops of the circles before doing your gridding. Although writing out the answers above the columns is not required, it is very important to ensure accuracy. Even though some problems may have more than one correct answer, grid only one answer. Grid-in questions contain no negative answers.

---

16. In the xy-plane, the point $(2, 5)$ is on the line $ax + by = 1$, which is perpendicular to another line, $2x + 3y = 7$. What is the value of b?

17. In the xy-plane, the equation of a circle is given as $x^2 + y^2 - 6x + 8y - 11 = 0$. If the point (m, n) is the center of the circle, what is the value of $m - n$?

18. Given the equation $3t^2 + 3 = 12t$, what is the product of all values of t that satisfy the equation?

19. If the ordered pair (h, k) satisfies the system of equations below, what is the value of $-h + k$?

$$\frac{1}{3}x - \frac{1}{2}y = -3$$

$$\frac{1}{6}x + 4y = 7$$

20. Given $kx + 6 < 3 + 12x$, what is the smallest integer value of k when $x = -\frac{1}{2}$?

IF YOU FINISH BEFORE TIME IS CALLED, CHECK YOUR WORK ON THIS SECTION ONLY. DO NOT WORK ON ANY OTHER SECTION IN THE TEST.

Section 4: Math Test – Calculator

55 Minutes—38 Questions

Directions: For questions 1–30, choose the best answer from the choices given. Use of a calculator is permitted.

Unless otherwise indicated:

- All figures are drawn to scale.
- All figures lie in a plane.
- All variables used represent real numbers.
- The domain of a given function f is the set of all real numbers x such that $f(x)$ is a real number.

Reference

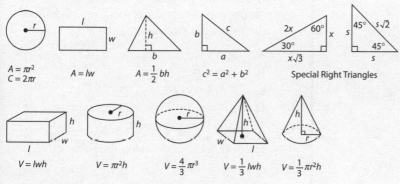

$A = \pi r^2$
$C = 2\pi r$

$A = lw$

$A = \frac{1}{2}bh$

$c^2 = a^2 + b^2$

Special Right Triangles

$V = lwh$

$V = \pi r^2 h$

$V = \frac{4}{3}\pi r^3$

$V = \frac{1}{3}lwh$

$V = \frac{1}{3}\pi r^2 h$

The complete arc of a circle measures 360°.

Also, the complete arc of a circle measures 2π radians.

The sum of the measures of the angles of a triangle is 180°.

---

1. A bacteria culture is placed in a petri dish. The bacteria grows in number as modeled by the equation $A = 20(5^t)$, where t represents the number of hours passed since the culture has been in the petri dish, and A represents the number of bacteria. Which of the following statements is the best interpretation of the number 20 in the context of the problem?

   A. The maximum number of bacteria during the first 5 hours
   B. The percent increase in the number of bacteria per hour
   C. The percent increase in the number of bacteria every 5 hours
   D. The number of bacteria placed in the petri dish initially

2. If you hire Mary's Car Service to drive you across town, you will be charged a flat fee of $10, plus $2 for each $\frac{1}{4}$ of a mile. Which of the following represents the total number of dollars that you would be charged if the trip is n miles?

   A. $2n$
   B. $10 + 2n$
   C. $10 + 4n$
   D. $10 + 8n$

297

3. The average score of four math tests is 90. If the highest score is 98, and all scores are integers with no two scores the same, what is the lowest possible score?

   A. 68
   B. 69
   C. 87
   D. 88

4. An online video service charges $4 for a monthly membership and $2 for each video game rental. In December, Amanda rented 10 video games. What is the average cost per rental for that month?

   A. $2
   B. $2.20
   C. $2.40
   D. $3

5. If a and b are constants and $x(ax + b) = 4x^2 + 2ax$ is true for all values of x, what is the value of $a + b$?

   A. 4
   B. 8
   C. 12
   D. 16

6. A recreational fishing boat charges $20 per adult and $10 per child for a 4-hour fishing trip, plus $2 per fish caught during the trip. If a family of two adults and three children went fishing on the boat, and at the end of the trip paid a total charge of $82, how many fish did the family catch?

   A. 6
   B. 12
   C. 24
   D. 41

7. Set A = {–4, –2, 0, 2, 4, 6, 8}. If Set B contains only members obtained by multiplying every member of Set A by 7, what is the average of Set B?

   A. 0
   B. 7
   C. 14
   D. 28

8. The accompanying table shows the distribution of grades on a math test for an honors class of 24 students.

Grades	Frequency
100	2
98	4
95	6
92	3
90	7
88	1
75	1

   If the mean, median, and mode of the 24 grades are x, y, and z respectively, which of the following statements is true?

   A. $x < y < z$
   B. $y < x < z$
   C. $z < x < y$
   D. $z < y < x$

9. In the xy-plane, $y = 4x + 1$ and $cx + 2y = d$ are parallel lines. What is the value of c?

   A. –8
   B. –4
   C. $-\dfrac{1}{4}$
   D. 4

10. In a math class, there are 12 girls. If 25% of the students in the class are boys, what is the total number of students in the class?

   A. 15
   B. 16
   C. 24
   D. 36

11. Given the scatterplot in the accompanying figure, which of the following could be the approximate value of its correlation coefficient?

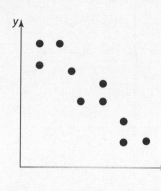

 A. −0.91
 B. −0.15
 C. 0.25
 D. 0.87

12. Given the accompanying figure, $g(x) = h(x - 2)$. What is the value of $g(3)$?

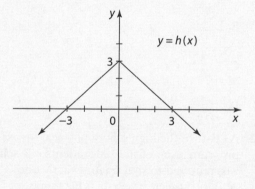

 A. 0
 B. 1
 C. 2
 D. 3

13. Two rounds of auditions were being held to select 120 students for a new chorus that was being formed. In the first round of auditions, 80 students were selected, 75% of whom were girls. If 40% of the members of the chorus had to be boys, how many boys had to be selected in the second round of auditions?

 A. 20
 B. 28
 C. 40
 D. 48

14. If a is directly proportional to b, which of the following tables could be the values of a and b?

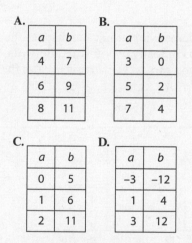

A.

a	b
4	7
6	9
8	11

B.

a	b
3	0
5	2
7	4

C.

a	b
0	5
1	6
2	11

D.

a	b
−3	−12
1	4
3	12

15. In a music class with 20 students, each student plays only the violin, plays only the cello, or plays both. If four students play both the violin and the cello and, of all the students in the class, twice as many play the violin as play the cello, how many students play only the cello?

 A. 4
 B. 6
 C. 10
 D. 12

16. If $\left|\dfrac{k}{3} - 4\right| = \dfrac{k}{3} - 4$, what is the smallest possible value for k?

   A.   −12
   B.   0
   C.   8
   D.   12

17. Given that k is an integer and if k is decreased by 25% of itself, the result is 24, what is the value of k?

   A.   18
   B.   28
   C.   32
   D.   36

18. The accompanying graph summarizes the sales of a company over 6 years. Between which two years is the increase in sales the greatest?

   A.   '11–'12
   B.   '13–'14
   C.   '14–'15
   D.   '15–'16

19. Which of the following is equivalent to $\dfrac{6x - 5}{2x - 1}$?

   A. $3x + 5$

   B. $3 - \dfrac{2}{2x - 1}$

   C. $3 + \dfrac{5}{2x - 1}$

   D. $3 + \dfrac{2}{2x - 1}$

20. Which of the following could be the equation of the graph in the accompanying figure?

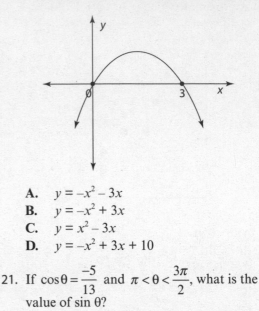

   A. $y = -x^2 - 3x$
   B. $y = -x^2 + 3x$
   C. $y = x^2 - 3x$
   D. $y = -x^2 + 3x + 10$

21. If $\cos\theta = \dfrac{-5}{13}$ and $\pi < \theta < \dfrac{3\pi}{2}$, what is the value of $\sin\theta$?

   A. $\dfrac{-12}{13}$

   B. $\dfrac{-5}{13}$

   C. $\dfrac{5}{13}$

   D. $\dfrac{5}{12}$

22. As part of the high school physical fitness program, each of the 180 students in a school was required to sign up for exactly one activity: soccer, baseball, table tennis, or volleyball. If half the students signed up for soccer, one-third signed up for baseball, and, of the remaining students, twice as many signed up for volleyball as signed up for table tennis, how many students signed up for table tennis?

   A.   5
   B.   10
   C.   15
   D.   20

23. Lara invested $3,500 today in a stock that is projected to increase its value each year by 9% over the next 10 years. Which of the following expressions represents Lara's annual balance in her investment t years from now with $0 \le t \le 10$?

   A. $3,500(.09)^t$
   B. $3,500 + (.9)^t$
   C. $3,500(1.09)^t$
   D. $3,500(1.90)^t$

24. If $\dfrac{2}{5} - \dfrac{x}{3} < 2x + \dfrac{1}{2}$, what is the value of x?

   A. $x > -\dfrac{3}{70}$

   B. $x < \dfrac{3}{70}$

   C. $x < -\dfrac{3}{50}$

   D. $x > \dfrac{27}{70}$

25. In the xy-plane, a line has a slope of $-\dfrac{1}{2}$ and passes through the point $(-6, 0)$. Which of the following points is also on the line?

   A. $(0, -6)$
   B. $(0, -3)$
   C. $(0, 3)$
   D. $(6, 0)$

26. Given $\dfrac{2v+3}{5v-2} = 4$, what is the value of v?

   A. $-\dfrac{1}{2}$

   B. $\dfrac{1}{2}$

   C. $\dfrac{5}{18}$

   D. $\dfrac{11}{18}$

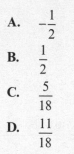

27. If $h \ne 0$, $k \ne 0$, and $h \ne k$, which of the following is equivalent to $\dfrac{\dfrac{h}{k} - \dfrac{k}{h}}{\dfrac{1}{h} - \dfrac{1}{k}}$?

   A. $-h - k$
   B. $-h + k$
   C. $h + k$
   D. $h^2 - k^2$

28. If the number of lottery tickets sold in a store doubled every hour and if, at noon, there were 800 tickets sold at the store, how many tickets were sold at the store at 8 a.m. that day?

   A.   25
   B.   50
   C.   100
   D.   200

29. If $x = 5$ in the equation below, what is the value of t?

$$t = 1 + \sqrt{t + x}$$

   A. -4
   B. -1
   C.   1
   D.   4

30. If $4x^2 - 4x + 1$ is equivalent to $\left(mx + \dfrac{h}{2}\right)^2$, what is the value of $m + h$?

   A. -4
   B. -1
   C.   0
   D.   1

Directions for Student-Produced Response Questions (grid-ins): Questions 31–38 require you to solve the problem and enter your answer by carefully marking the circles on the special grid. Examples of the appropriate way to mark the grid follow.

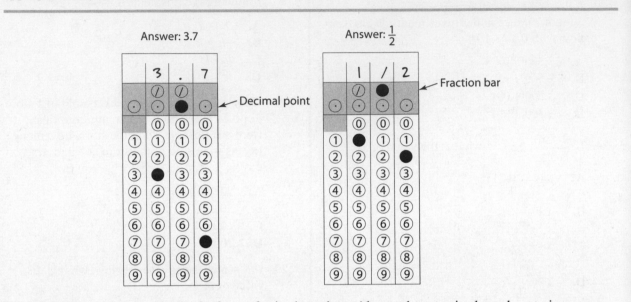

Do not grid in mixed numbers in the form of mixed numbers. Always change mixed numbers to improper fractions or decimals.

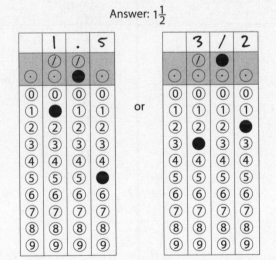

Space permitting, answers may start in any column. Each grid-in answer below is correct.

Answer: 123

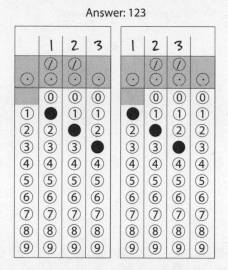

Note: Circles must be filled in correctly to receive credit. Mark only one circle in each column. No credit will be given if more than one circle in a column is marked. Example:

Answer: 258 (no credit)

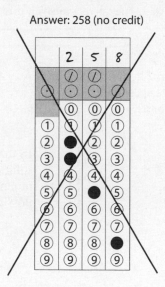

Always enter the most accurate decimal value that the grid will accommodate. For example, an answer such as .8888 . . . can be gridded as .888 or .889. Gridding this value as .8, .88, or .89 is considered inaccurate and, therefore, not acceptable. The acceptable grid-ins of $\frac{8}{9}$ are:

Answer: $\frac{8}{9}$

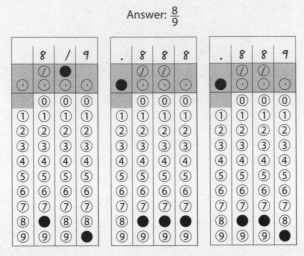

Be sure to write your answers in the boxes at the tops of the circles before doing your gridding. Although writing out the answers above the columns is not required, it is very important to ensure accuracy. Even though some problems may have more than one correct answer, grid only one answer. Grid-in questions contain no negative answers.

31. If a particle traveled 2,651 miles in 2 hours and 13 minutes, what is its average speed, to the nearest integer, in feet per second?

32. A system of inequalities is given below.

$$y \le 5$$
$$-3x + y \le -1$$

In the xy-plane, if a point (h, k) lies in the solution set of the system, what is the minimum value of h when k is the maximum possible value?

Use the following information to answer questions 33 and 34.

The scatterplot in the accompanying figure shows the number of minutes a student studied for a math quiz and the grade the student received on the quiz. The line of best fit is also shown.

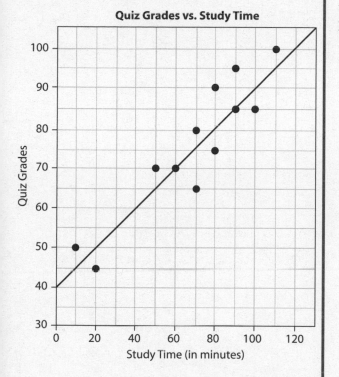

Quiz Grades vs. Study Time

33. If $g = ht + k$ is the equation of the line of best fit, where g represents a student's grade on the quiz and t represents the number of minutes the student studied for the quiz, what is the value of h?

34. If a student wished to receive a grade of no lower than 80 on the quiz, what is the minimum number of minutes he must study according to the line of best fit?

Use the following information to answer questions 35 and 36.

The tenth-grade class at Jefferson High School has 124 students. Every tenth grader is taking either physics or chemistry, but not both. The partially completed table in the accompanying figure shows the frequencies of these students taking either physics or chemistry by gender.

Frequency Table			
	Physics	Chemistry	Total
Male	28		68
Female		25	
Total			124

35. What is the total number of tenth graders at Jefferson High School taking physics?

36. The partially completed table shows the relative frequencies, to the nearest hundredth, of tenth graders at Jefferson High School taking either physics or chemistry by gender. What is the value of $x + y$?

Relative Frequency Table			
	Physics	Chemistry	Total
Male	x	0.32	
Female		y	0.45
Total	0.48		1

Use the following information to answer questions 37 and 38.

A right circular cone with a radius of 6 centimeters has a slant height of 10 centimeters, and a right circular cylinder with a radius of 9 centimeters has a height of 11 centimeters.

37. What is the maximum integer number of full cones of water that can be poured into an empty cylinder?

38. If four full cones of water are poured into the empty cylinder, what is the height, to the nearest centimeter, of the water level in the cylinder?

IF YOU FINISH BEFORE TIME IS CALLED, CHECK YOUR WORK ON THIS SECTION ONLY. DO NOT WORK ON ANY OTHER SECTION IN THE TEST.

Section 5: The Essay (Optional)

50 Minutes

Directions: You must write your essay in the space provided; you must use only the lines within the margin. You should write on every line (do not skip lines), avoid wide margins, and keep your handwriting to a reasonable size. You may write or print, but try to write as legibly as you can.

You will have 50 minutes for this section.

Read the following passage and consider the author's argument. Note how the author uses

- evidence, such as reasons, facts, or examples, to support his claim.
- logical reasoning to support and develop his ideas.
- stylistic elements such as diction and emotional appeals.

The following passage is adapted from *A Matter of Equity: Preschool in America*, a publication of the U.S. Department of Education (April 2015).

(1)   Each year, about 4 million children enter kindergarten in the United States. All parents hope their child will start school ready for success. And many parents turn that hope into action, seeking out supportive and high-quality early learning opportunities. Unfortunately, not every parent finds those opportunities, and access differs based on geography, race, and income.

(2)   As a result, too many children enter kindergarten a year or more behind their classmates in academic and social-emotional skills. For some children, starting out school behind their peers can trap them in a cycle of continuous catch-up in their learning. As a nation, we must ensure that all children, regardless of income or race, have access to high-quality preschool opportunities.

(3)   This year, as Congress seeks to reauthorize the Elementary and Secondary Education Act (ESEA), our nation is at a critical moment. Congress can honor this important legacy and moral imperative—as our nation observes ESEA's 50th anniversary—by reauthorizing a strong education law. This new law must reflect real equity of opportunity, starting with our youngest children.

(4)   Significant new investments in high-quality early education are necessary to help states, local communities, and parents close the school-readiness gaps between disadvantaged children and their more advantaged peers. Across the country, we must expand access to high-quality early learning to ensure that all children graduate from high school prepared to succeed in college, careers, and life.

(5)   Advances in neuroscience and research have helped to demonstrate the benefits of quality early education for young children and that the early years are a critical period in children's learning and development, providing the necessary foundation for more advanced skills. For example, children's language skills from ages 1 to 2 are predictive of their pre-literacy skills at age 5. A robust body of research shows that children who participate in high-quality preschool programs have better health, social-emotional, and cognitive outcomes than those who do not participate. The gains are particularly powerful for children from low-income families and those at risk for academic failure who, on average, start kindergarten 12 to 14 months behind their peers in pre-literacy and language skills.

(6)   Studies also reveal that participating in quality early learning can boost children's educational attainment and earnings later in life. Children who attend high-quality preschool programs are less likely to utilize special education services or be retained in their grade and are more likely to graduate from high school, go on to college, and succeed in careers than those who have not attended high-quality preschool programs. Research also suggests that expanding early learning—including high-quality preschool—provides society with a return on investment of $8.60 for every $1 spent. About half of the return on investment originates from increased earnings for children when they grow up.

(7)   While both states and the federal government invest in early learning, these efforts have fallen short of what is needed to ensure that all children can access a high-quality early education that will prepare them for success. Across the nation, 59% of 4-year-olds—or 6 out of every 10 children—are not enrolled in publically funded preschool programs through state preschool, Head Start, and special education preschool services. Even fewer are enrolled in the highest-quality programs. For Latino children, the unmet need is especially great. While Latinos are the fastest growing and largest minority in the U.S., they demonstrate the lowest preschool participation rate. Their participation rate is 40% compared to 50% for African-American children and 53% for white children.

(8)   Racial and socioeconomic disparities in access to high-quality early education contribute to achievement gaps that are noticeable by the time children enter kindergarten. Scores on reading and math tests were lowest for kindergartners in households with incomes below the federal poverty level and highest for those in households with incomes at or above 200% of the federal poverty level. Without access to quality preschool, African-American and Latino children, and children from low-income families are far less likely to be prepared to start kindergarten with their peers.

(9)   Providing children with quality early education experiences is not only the right thing to do for America's youngest learners, it's imperative for strengthening our nation's economy.

Write an essay in which you analyze how the author builds an argument to convince the reader that the federal government should fund preschools. Consider how the author uses evidence, such as reasons, facts, or examples, to strengthen the logic of his claim. As you write your essay, consider his reasoning and his use of stylistic elements such as word choice and appeals to emotion.

In your essay, do not explain your position on this issue; rather, analyze how the author builds his argument to accomplish his purpose.

Be sure to write only in the space provided on your answer sheet.

IF YOU FINISH BEFORE TIME IS CALLED, CHECK YOUR WORK ON THIS SECTION ONLY. DO NOT WORK ON ANY OTHER SECTION IN THE TEST.

Answer Key

Section 1: Reading Test

1. C	14. C	27. C	40. D
2. B	15. D	28. D	41. C
3. D	16. A	29. D	42. B
4. B	17. A	30. B	43. D
5. A	18. C	31. B	44. A
6. D	19. C	32. C	45. C
7. D	20. A	33. C	46. D
8. D	21. D	34. B	47. D
9. B	22. D	35. D	48. C
10. C	23. B	36. D	49. B
11. A	24. A	37. D	50. A
12. C	25. C	38. C	51. D
13. B	26. C	39. B	52. B

Section 2: Writing and Language Test

1. D	12. B	23. D	34. A
2. A	13. D	24. C	35. A
3. B	14. C	25. B	36. D
4. D	15. B	26. A	37. B
5. C	16. D	27. D	38. D
6. B	17. C	28. B	39. B
7. D	18. D	29. D	40. D
8. C	19. B	30. C	41. A
9. D	20. A	31. B	42. C
10. A	21. D	32. D	43. D
11. D	22. C	33. C	44. C

Section 3: Math Test – No Calculator

1. D (*HA*)
2. B (*PAM*)
3. C (*HA*)
4. C (*HA*)
5. A (*PAM*)
6. B (*PAM*)
7. C (*ATM*)

8. C (*PAM*)
9. C (*ATM*)
10. D (*HA*)
11. A (*PAM*)
12. D (*PAM*)
13. D (*HA*)
14. B (*PAM*)

15. A (*PAM*)
16. $\frac{1}{2}$ (*HA*)
17. 7 (*ATM*)
18. 1 (*PAM*)
19. 8 (*HA*)
20. 19 (*HA*)

(*HA*) – Heart of Algebra

(*PSDA*) – Problem Solving and Data Analysis

(*PAM*) – Passport to Advanced Math

(*ATM*) – Additional Topics in Math

Section 4: Math Test – Calculator

1. D (*PSDA*)
2. D (*HA*)
3. B (*PSDA*)
4. C (*HA*)
5. C (*PAM*)
6. A (*HA*)
7. C (*PSDA*)
8. C (*PSDA*)
9. A (*HA*)
10. B (*PSDA*)
11. A (*PSDA*)
12. C (*PAM*)

13. B (*PSDA*)
14. D (*PSDA*)
15. A (*HA*)
16. D (*HA*)
17. C (*HA*)
18. D (*PSDA*)
19. B (*PAM*)
20. B (*PAM*)
21. A (*ATM*)
22. B (*PSDA*)
23. C (*PSDA*)
24. A (*HA*)

25. B (*HA*)
26. D (*HA*)
27. A (*PAM*)
28. B (*PSDA*)
29. D (*PAM*)
30. C (*PAM*)
31. 1,754 (*PSDA*)
32. 2 (*HA*)
33. $\frac{1}{2}$ (*PSDA*)
34. 80 (*PSDA*)
35. 59 (*PSDA*)
36. 0.43 (*PSDA*)

37. 9 (*ATM*)
38. 5 (*ATM*)

(*HA*) – Heart of Algebra

(*PSDA*) – Problem Solving and Data Analysis

(*PAM*) – Passport to Advanced Math

(*ATM*) – Additional Topics in Math

Answer Explanations

Section 1: Reading Test

1. **C.** Main idea: The writer clearly states (lines 5–6), *That government is best which governs not at all.* He reiterates this point throughout the passage. Choices A and B are statements that may be true but don't state the writer's main argument. The writer doesn't distinguish between state and federal governments, so Choice D is incorrect.

2. **B.** Analyzing text structure: The phrase *many and weighty* refers to the beginning of the sentence, *The objections which have been brought against a standing army* (lines 11–13). The writer isn't referring to the establishment of the state militia (Choice A). He would disagree with Choice C, and Choice D only occurs as an example later in the passage.

3. **D.** Command of evidence: The word *expedient* suggests something convenient and practical. Throughout the passage, however, the author emphasizes his point that government interference is undesirable. Thus, while he reluctantly admits that government is a necessary tradition (lines 26–27), he would rather see men rule their own lives. He would disagree that it is desirable and successful (choices A and C). Choice B is too strongly negative.

4. **B.** Words in context: The context of the line suggests the *mode* is the method (Choice B) *which the people have chosen to execute their will.* In this context, *mode* doesn't mean style (Choice A), world (Choice C), or mannerism (Choice D).

5. **A.** Analyzing text structure: The author repeats *It* in order to show what the government does not do in contrast to what the character of the American people can do. The clue is in the next sentence: *The character inherent in the American people has done all that has been accomplished.* The other choices are incorrect because they don't refer to the specific contrast between the government and the people.

6. **D.** Determining meaning: The author points out that legislators have put obstacles in the way of trade and commerce (lines 52–56). The reference to India rubber is used to show that trade and commerce are flexible and capable of "bouncing" over the obstacles. Choice A is off-topic. Choice B is contradicted by the passage. Choice C is incorrect because it contradicts the author's point that the government regulations often hinder commerce.

7. **D.** Words in context: The context suggests that unity would make the militia stronger; thus, *strength* is the best choice. While *vigor* can mean life (Choice A) or drive (Choice C), these meanings aren't supported by the context. Choice B isn't a meaning of *vigor.*

8. **D.** Command of evidence: The author mentions choices A, B, and C as goals for the Congressional deliberations. He states that Congress should try to make the *smallest expense possible of time, of life, and of treasure* and *to infuse* power into the militia. Choice D is incorrect because the author states that one of the problems of the existing Army is that it is *a body of dislocated members, without the vigor of unity and having little of uniformity but the name.* If his goal were to create unity and uniformity, he wouldn't support the establishment of specialized, autonomous military units.

9. **B.** Command of evidence: In lines 92–93, the author states, *The organization and discipline of the Army are effective and satisfactory.* Thus, the answer is Choice B. All the other choices he mentions as problems. He thinks it is critical to *maintain among the officers so much of the art of horsemanship* (Choice A). He finds the Army is *without the vigor of unity* (Choice C). He expresses concern over *the prevalence of desertion among the troops* (Choice D).

10. **C.** Synthesis: The writer of Passage 2 strongly believes *the militia is yet more indispensable to the liberties of the country* (lines 62–63) and would completely disagree with the assertion of the writer of Passage 1. His attitude wouldn't be whole-hearted agreement (Choice A), qualified approval (Choice B), or guarded ambivalence (Choice D) because he would completely disagree, Choice C.

11. **A.** Command of evidence: The author makes the strong point that an army is *indispensable to the liberties of the country,* Choice A. None of the other choices specifically address the necessity for a militia.

12. **C.** Synthesis: The author of Passage 1 repeatedly states his objection to a standing army and would find any argument supporting the establishment of one as having questionable validity. He wouldn't agree that it was substantiated by the threat of foreign aggression (Choice A) or driven by political expedience (Choice D). Choice B is incorrect because no evidence exists that the statement is not meant to be taken literally.

13. **B.** Synthesis: The authors of the two passages most strongly disagree on the indispensability of a permanent military force in the U.S. (Choice B). The author of the first passage states, *The objections which have been brought against a standing army, and they are many and weighty, and deserve to prevail . . .* (lines 11–15), while the second author states in lines 62–63, *The organization of the militia is yet more indispensable to the liberties of the country.* All the other choices are off-topic.

14. **C.** Writer's purpose: The passage is a character study of Dorothea, Choice C. It doesn't argue about setting (Choice A), expose a rivalry (Choice B), or explain sources (Choice D).

15. **D.** Command of evidence/Inference: The narrator suggests that Dorothea's *plain garments* gave her *the impressiveness of a fine quotation from the Bible . . . in a paragraph of today's newspaper.* The comparison suggests her clothing is like the words of the Bible, simple and enduring, Choice D. The narrator isn't comparing to the cadence (rhythm) of language in the Bible to the cadence of journalistic prose (Choice A). The narrator doesn't discuss the religious content of the local paper, so Choice B is incorrect. There is no disapproval of modern styles, so Choice C is incorrect.

16. **A.** Words in context: The narrator remarks that Dorothea is very clever, but then qualifies (limits or restricts) this statement by pointing out that Celia has more common sense, Choice A. While *addition* can mean sum (Choice B) or total (Choice C), neither fits the context. Choice D is incorrect because *addition* doesn't mean completion.

17. **A.** Command of evidence/Inference: Miss Brooke is described as being unaware of her beauty and attractiveness. She is modest (Choice A). She is the opposite of flirtatious (Choice B), ostentatious (Choice C), and vain (Choice D).

18. **C.** Command of evidence: *She was open, ardent, and not in the least self-admiring; indeed, it was pretty to see how her imagination adorned her sister Celia with attractions altogether superior to her own . . . .* The excerpt in Choice C provides the best evidence that Dorothea is modest, as indicated in question 17. In these lines, she is described as *not in the least self-admiring.* In her mind, Celia is the more attractive woman. The other choices don't provide evidence of Dorothea's modesty.

19. **C.** Command of evidence/Inference: In the opinion of the rural villagers, Dorothea's eyes are *like her religion, too unusual and striking* (lines 27–28).The best match among the answer choices is Choice C, extraordinary and remarkable. Choice A is the opposite of the villager's views. There is no textual evidence that they found her views passionate or pagan (Choice B) or subtle and charming (Choice D).

20. **A.** Command of evidence/Relationships: The narrator implies that Dorothea was embarrassed by her enjoyment of riding (she had *conscientious qualms,* line 43) and *looked forward to renouncing it* (line 45). Thus, Choice A would undermine the narrator's point. All the other choices wouldn't undermine the point.

21. **D.** Command of evidence/relationships: If a man did not come to see Mr. Brooke, Dorothea *concluded that he must be in love with Celia* (lines 52–53). Choice A is incorrect because Dorothea is very modest. There is no textual evidence for choices B or C.

22. **D.** Words in context: Dorothea gave her sister credit for having *attractions altogether superior to her own* (line 49). Therefore, in context, *adorned* means credited, Choice D. It can mean decorated (Choice A), but this doesn't fit the context. It doesn't mean envied (Choice C) or admired (Choice B). (If you selected Choice B, you might be thinking of the word "adored" rather than "adorned.")

23. **B.** Point of view: The passage is written from the perspective of an advocate for wildlife preservation (Choice B) who believes *it is important to save all members of an ecosystem . . . .* The passage uses supportive language to describe the efforts to save the endangered wolves (*Lessons learned . . . have served, and will continue to serve, as a template for the recovery of other species . . .*). There is no evidence of a debate about adaptive management (Choice A). Choice C is incorrect because predator/prey relationships are a minor detail in the passage. Choice D is incorrect because the main idea is saving the wolves, not their changing habits.

24. **A.** Text structure: The second paragraph presents an overview of the "mystery" surrounding the origins of the red wolf. The statement, *Today, the majority of researchers agree . . .* suggests they didn't always agree on the range of the red wolf (Choice A). Choice B is contradicted by the information about the samples in the museum. Researchers Nowak and Wilson agree, so Choice C is incorrect. Choice D is inaccurate and vague.

25. **C.** Command of evidence: According to the passage, *a combination of reasoning, science, historic accounts, and minimal physical evidence potentially support the occurrence of red wolves.* No mention is made of archeological evidence (Choice C).

26. **C.** Text structure: The third paragraph focuses on the origin of the red wolf in northeastern states. The information postulates that the red wolf and the gray wolf met at a geographical point where smaller prey favored by the red wolf coexisted with the larger prey favored by the gray wolf (Choice C). Choice A isn't relevant or accurate. Choice B is irrelevant to the paragraph. Choice D is off-topic.

27. **C.** Command of evidence: While some might find objectionable the sterilization of a species to prevent its mating with another species, a practice designed to protect the endangered species, the writer presents this method as a useful one (Choice C). He states that it augments the captive breeding program. He wouldn't agree with Choice A because he supports the captive breeding program and the adaptive management plan. He wouldn't agree with Choice B because the sterilization of coyotes is implemented to prevent hybridization. He wouldn't agree with Choice D because he states, *it is important to save all members of an ecosystem, including predators.*

28. **D.** Command of evidence: The best evidence for the answer to question 27 is stated in Choice D: *The captive breeding program is augmented by the adaptive management plan that involves sterilizing encroaching coyotes to prevent coyote/red wolf hybrids.* The other choices don't speak to sterilization of members of a species.

29. **D.** Command of evidence: The writer discusses the importance of genetic diversity in the fifth paragraph, making Choice D correct. He states, *Genetic diversity of less than 90 percent in founder populations can result in compromised reproduction.* Choice A is incorrect because it contradicts the information in the passage. Genetic homozygosity can lead to expression rather than suppression of deleterious genes. The answer isn't Choice B because the writer never mentions that wolves can suffer from depression. Choice C is not addressed in the passage.

30. **B.** Words in context: The passage implies that expression of deleterious genes is harmful, or detrimental (Choice B), to the wolves. None of the other choices denotes harm. Deleted (Choice A) means omitted; delicate (Choice C) means fragile; dubious (Choice D) means doubtful or questionable.

31. **B.** Words in context: The information in the passage suggests that compromised reproduction is harmful to the red wolf population. In this context, *compromised* means jeopardized (Choice B). Compromise can mean negotiated (Choice A), mediated (Choice C), or conceded (Choice D), but not in this context.

32. **C.** Extended reasoning: First, you must understand the relationship between the two programs, then find an analogous relationship among the choices. The two programs present two different methods, each contributing to the accomplishment of one goal: conservation of the red wolf gene pool. Choice C offers a parallel situation of two methods being used to accomplish the same one goal: In this case, the physicians try two different methods to accomplish the one goal of reducing pain. Choice A involves only one method of reducing pollution. Choice B also presents only one method, but one that is tried on two different species. Choice D involves two different patients being treated with the same drug.

33. **C.** Writer's purpose: The writer makes the point that grizzly bears have maintained genetic diversity with a small population, and speculates that *this will be true for red wolves as well* (Choice C). Choice A contradicts the information in the passage. Choice B is incorrect because the writer never addresses captive breeding programs with any species other than red wolves. Choice D is incorrect because the writer doesn't discuss grizzly bear predatory habits.

34. **B.** Command of evidence: The parenthetical information clarifies (demystifies) technical terminology such as genetic drift and inbreeding depression (Choice B). It doesn't have anything to do with technological modernization (Choice A) or recent innovation (Choice C). It doesn't highlight confusing jargon (Choice D); it clarifies it.

35. **D.** Data interpretation: The information in Figure 1 indicates that in 1993 there were about 18 pups and about 24 adults ($42 - 18 = 24$) in North Carolina. In 1994, there were about 38 pups and about 41 adults ($79 - 38 = 41$). Thus, in 1993 and 1994, approximately half the population of red wolves in North Carolina was comprised of adults (Choice D). Choice A is incorrect because Figure 2 doesn't identify the wolf population by state. In addition, in 1994 (before adaptive management) more pups were born than in 2000 (after adaptive management). Choice B is incorrect because it refers to the total U.S. population and because it is mathematically incorrect. Choice C is incorrect because the growth hasn't been steady.

36. **D.** Data interpretation/Command of evidence: Figure 1 indicates that the numbers of red wolves, both adults and pups, are growing. This supports the writer's assertion that *red wolves were saved from extinction and are being restored to parts of their historical range* (Choice D). Nothing in Figure 1 supports the information in choices A, B, or C.

37. **D.** Writer's purpose: The writer's primary purpose is to explain the rise of the Pre-Raphaelite movement in art, which changed artistic style from an imitative, forced style (which the author calls *academical* in line 44) to a younger, more vigorous style. Thus, Choice D is correct. He doesn't denigrate them (Choice B). The main purpose isn't to analyze techniques (Choice A) or explain the artistic upheaval of the Renaissance (Choice C).

38. **C.** Command of evidence: The *spirit of painters* is the new movement of the Pre-Raphaelites, the school of thought to which "they" (lines 100 and 104) belong (Choice C). The antecedent of the

pronoun "they" can be traced back through the last paragraph to the "young artists" (line 91). The writer mentions all of the other choices as contrasts to these young artists.

39. **B.** Command of evidence/Inference: The writer describes the decline of English art from its position of *real splendor* to its falling *prey to a tedious disease,* which he characterizes throughout the third paragraph as both a decline in originality and a loss of genuine emotion, which is replaced by *forced and affected sentiment* (Choice B). If English art underwent a decline, it wasn't always tedious (Choice A), nor did it retain a noble splendor (Choice C). The writer actually admires the landscapes, so Choice D is incorrect.

40. **D.** Words in context: In context, the best choice is *comprehend* (Choice D). The context suggests the historical painters were attempting to understand the noble style of the Italian artists. They weren't trying to deepen (Choice A), discover (Choice B), or portray (Choice C).

41. **C.** Word choice: By using the phrase *intelligent plagiarism,* the author suggests that the historical painters had intelligence but no originality. They plagiarized art the way a writer might plagiarize the writings of another writer. Because the art they created merely imitated, it had little value. The word choices in lines 25–26 (*without rising above* and *plagiarism*) imply that the efforts were not commendable. The historical artists were described as crude and unable to match the style of the Italian decorative artists, so Choice A is incorrect. Choice B is incorrect because the author admires the Cinquecentisti and doesn't use the phrase *intelligent plagiarism* to refer to their work. Choice D is incorrect because it doesn't convey the negative connotations of the phrase *intelligent plagiarism* as it is used in the passage to convey superficial imitation.

42. **B.** Word choice: The language such as *pilgrimage, sacred spring, drank their fill,* and *poisoned* is metaphorical (non-literal) (Choice B). The author uses metaphorical language to describe how the English artists were ruined by their imitation of the Italian artists. It isn't literal (Choice A); they weren't literally poisoned. It isn't understated (Choice C) or objective (neutral) (Choice D).

43. **D.** Words in context: The context suggests that English art had a *distinctive* "national stamp," a clearly defined and recognizable style (Choice D). While peculiar can mean weird (Choice A), irregular (Choice B), or strange (Choice C), those choices don't fit the context.

44. **A.** Command of evidence/Relationships: The author points out that the need for reform in art had a parallel in literature: the aesthetic creed of the Lake poets Wordsworth and Coleridge, which was a shift away from *dazzling imaginative fervor* toward *simplicity and a direct feeling for nature.* There is no evidence in the passage that the poets were known for nationalistic poetry, so Choice B is incorrect. The comparison doesn't illustrate a process of reasoning, so Choice C is incorrect. Choice D is incorrect because the relationship isn't a contrast of reactions to the reform movement.

45. **C.** Writer's purpose: According to the introductory information, this passage is a written statement of a Senior Astronomer's testimony before Congress. The writer's main purpose in the second paragraph is to take a realistic look at the goals of SETI and justify its continued existence. He doesn't compare exploration techniques (Choice A), nor does he argue that the theorizing of the ancients led to current technology (although this may be a true statement) (Choice B). Choice D is incorrect because the writer states the question of our place in the universe is one of the mysteries he hopes SETI will ultimately be able to answer.

46. **D.** Words in context: The context, *Finding extraterrestrial intelligence would calibrate humanity's place in the cosmos,* suggests that humans want to figure out where and how they fit in with respect to other life in the universe. The best choice for this meaning is *assess* or evaluate (Choice D). While *calibrate*

can mean adjust (Choice A), rectify (Choice B), or standardize (Choice C), these words do not fit the context of the passage.

47. **D.** Analyzing word choice: The choice of *unanticipated utility* denotes a usefulness that wasn't expected. The writer applies this phrase to the consequences of exploration; in other words, explorers can accidentally make practical discoveries (Choice D). Choice A refers to imaginative musings rather than exploration. Choice B refers to planets, not to the practical consequences of exploration. Choice C doesn't include the sense of usefulness or practicality.

48. **C.** Command of evidence/Relationships: In this sentence, the writer presents the qualification (that no evidence of life on other planets exists at this point in time) to his testimony, justifying the continuation of SETI (Choice C). His point is that no evidence exists **now,** but that doesn't mean it will never exist. He doesn't state this as a contradiction to his position (Choice A), as historical background (Choice B), or as a frequent confusion (Choice D).

49. **B.** Analyzing meaning: The writer implies that his readers will be thinking, "But a lot of people believe there is life out there somewhere . . . " in response to his statement that *we knew of no planets around other stars.* He isn't affirming life on other planets (Choice A) or responding to critics (Choice C). The *yes* doesn't provide a positive view (Choice D); it merely acknowledges that there is and was speculation.

50. **A.** Words in context: The context suggests that the existence of the *beings* hasn't been proven (*the idea of establishing the existence of these putative beings*). They are *reputed* to exist, meaning they have the reputation of existing (Choice A). Choice B is incorrect because the context doesn't support the existence of believable beings. They could be fabled (enchanted or legendary) (Choice C), but in the context of a scientific presentation, *reputed* is the better choice. They certainly aren't actual (yet!) (Choice D).

51. **D.** Data interpretation/citing textual evidence: The data supports the textual evidence that many people claim to have seen alien spacecraft (*in many blurry cell-phone "photos" of flying saucers*), Choice D. Choice A doesn't address the sightings. Choice B refers to fossilized microbes, not sightings. Choice C refers to the findings that there may be other habitable planets.

52. **B.** Point of view: Throughout the passage, the writer is doubtful of the likelihood of finding extraterrestrial beings capable of space travel, so he would view the "sightings" with skepticism (Choice B). He wouldn't regret (Choice A) the sightings, nor would he view them with hostility (Choice C) or admiration (Choice D).

Section 2: Writing and Language Test

1. **D.** Adjective/adverb confusion: The adverb *intimately* is needed to modify the adjective *dependent.* Choice A, which uses two adjectives, is grammatically incorrect because *intimate* and *dependent* don't logically modify *activity*. Choice B incorrectly changes the meaning of the sentence. Choice C also changes the meaning by making *intimate* an adjective that modifies *activity*.

2. **A.** Idiom: The idiomatic expression is correct as written. All of the other choices are not idiomatically correct in this context.

3. **B.** Transitions: The correct transitional phrase in this context is *In this respect*. The phrase *For this respect* doesn't make sense in this sentence. Choices C and D are also illogical in this sentence.

4. **D.** Redundancy/Wordiness: The words *circumscribed* and *confined* have the same meaning in this context. To use both words is unnecessarily redundant.

5. **C.** Rhetoric: Choice C is the best answer because the analogy of a sponge allows the reader to visualize air passing through the porous organs. None of the other choices presents as clear an image.

6. **B.** Punctuation/Comma use: Commas are needed around *in this case* to set it off as an interrupter. In addition, a comma is needed after *air* to set off a contrasting statement (*instead of passing through a valve*). Choice A is missing the comma after *but*. Choices C and D incorrectly use the semicolon.

7. **D.** Parallel verb forms: The verb form *penetrating* is needed to be parallel to *filling* (*not only filling . . . but penetrating*). Choice A incorrectly uses the past tense. Choice B incorrectly uses the present perfect tense. Choice C incorrectly uses the present progressive tense.

8. **C.** Punctuation/Dash use: When a word or phrase is set off by a dash for emphasis, two dashes must be used. Choice A incorrectly uses a comma after *oxygen*. Choice B incorrectly uses a semicolon before *oxygen*. Choice D incorrectly uses a colon before *oxygen*.

9. **D.** Pronoun use: The correct pronoun for the antecedent *bird's* is *its*. Choice A is incorrect because there is no such word as *its'*. Choice B incorrectly uses the plural pronoun *their*. Choice C incorrectly uses the contraction *it's*.

10. **A.** Transitional word: The meaning here is *as a result,* so *consequently* is the correct transitional word. The other three choices are words of contrast, which is not indicated by the context.

11. **D.** Rhetoric: Choice D presents the most vivid image and appropriately uses the examples of well-known birds. Choices A and B don't present vivid images. Choice C is an example of a sentence that "tells" rather than "shows," so it doesn't present the most vivid image.

12. **B.** Sentence structure/Comma splice: Choice B corrects the comma splice by adding the correlative conjunction *but . . . also* to be parallel with the correlative conjunction *not only* in the first clause of the sentence. Choice A is not correct because it is a comma splice. Choice C is also a comma splice and adds an unnecessary comma after *it*. Choice D incorrectly uses the semicolon because the addition of *while* makes the second clause a subordinate clause.

13. **D.** Adjective/adverb confusion/Punctuation: The adverb *highly* is needed to modify the adjective *organized*. The dash is needed to set off the interrupting explanatory information (note the dash between *effort* and *sometimes*).

14. **C.** Rhetoric: The writer should include the information because *however uneasily at times* qualifies the reality of the situation of the white people and black people working together. Without it, the sentence is less honest about the tensions that existed.

15. **B.** Parallelism: The sentence sets up a series of phrases that begin with nouns. To be parallel, the phrase in question should begin with the noun *rescue* to be parallel to *escapes* and *systems*. Choice C is wordy, and Choice D includes the awkward phrasing *fugitives being arrested . . . .*

16. **D.** Sentence structure: The sentence as it is written is a fragment, as are the suggested revisions in choices B and C. These sentences need a subject. Changing the wording to *The debate in Congress* creates a more straightforward and clear sentence with the subject *debate*. In addition, Congress should be capitalized in this sentence.

17. **C.** Agreement/Tense: The passage is in the past tense, and the singular subject *debate* requires the singular form of the verb. Choice A is plural present perfect tense. Choice B is singular present perfect tense. Choice D is singular past progressive tense.

18. **D.** Rhetoric: The choice with the most specific information is Choice D. Unlike the other choices, it names the African colony (Liberia) that the Colonization Society founded.

19. **B.** Idiom: The correct idiom depends on the context. The correct idiom in this sentence is *called for* because the phrase refers to a *response*. You call *for* a response. You call someone *by* name. You call *in* an order.

20. **A.** Verb form: The correct verb form for the present perfect tense is *to have begun.* Choice B is incorrect because you never use *began* with *have.* Choice C doesn't make sense following *is generally acknowledged* (in this sentence, *acknowledged* should be followed by *to*). Choice D is an infinitive, not in the past tense.

21. **D.** Rhetoric/Organization: Choice D is the best topic sentence because it sets up the details that follow in the rest of the paragraph. Choice A only sets up location. Choice B sets up location and the origin of the name but doesn't reflect the content of the paragraph. Choice C presents inaccurate information (*working behind the scenes* and *united*).

22. **C.** Pronoun case: The nominative pronoun *who* is needed to be the subject of the verb *were.* Choices A and B incorrectly use the objective pronoun *whom.* Choice D incorrectly uses the singular form of the verb *was* rather than the plural *were,* which is needed because the antecedent of *who* is the plural noun *abolitionists.*

23. **D.** Rhetoric/Coherence: For logical coherence the sentence should be moved after Sentence 6. Placed where it is now, the sentence inaccurately implies that *They* refers to the *slave catchers.* Since *They* refers to *Vigilance Committees,* the only logical placement is after Sentence 6, which is the first mention of the Vigilance Committees.

24. **C.** Wordiness: Choices A and B are incorrect because they contain wordy expressions. Choice D is not idiomatic in this sentence. Choice C is idiomatically correct and concise.

25. **B.** Tense: The singular present perfect *has spread* (Choice A) and the plural present perfect *have spread* (Choice C) are incorrect. The past tense verb *spread* is needed because the events in the sentence occurred in the past. Choice D is the present progressive and is also incorrect to indicate events in the past.

26. **A.** Rhetoric: The information should be included because it gives further details about the weather events. Choice B is incorrect because the sentence uses the word *catastrophic* to describe the events. Choice C is incorrect because weather is important to the paragraph. Choice D is incorrect because weather is not mentioned in the first paragraph.

27. **D.** Diction/Agreement: The correct verb to mean *to influence* is *affect,* so choices A, B, and C are incorrect. The subject of the sentence is the plural noun *incursions,* so *have affected and continue to affect* is correct.

28. **B.** Rhetoric: *However* is not correct because the ideas in this sentence don't contrast with those in the previous sentence. Choice B provides transition (*Other challenges*) and introduces competition with other countries. Choice C incorrectly suggests a concession point. Choice D doesn't make sense because competition is not similar to problems in the previous sentence; it is a new challenge.

29. **D.** Data interpretation: The data on the chart shows a decline in citrus production, not an escalation. Choices A, B, and C all indicate growth. Only Choice D, *contributed to instabilities in,* matches the data on the chart.

30. **C.** Sentence structure: The sentence begins with two prepositional phrases, *Despite past and current challenges placed on United States citrus production,* which should not be followed by a semicolon (Choice A) or a period (Choice D). Choice B is incorrect because there is no logical reason for the dash here; a comma should follow the introductory prepositional phrases.

31. **B.** Sentence structure: The sentence is a fragment because it has no verb for the subject *events.* The *–ing* form of the verb *resulting* can't be used without a helping verb, so choices A and D are incorrect. Choice C incorrectly uses the singular form of the verb *has* rather than the plural *have.* Changing to *have resulted in* solves the problem.

32. **D.** Agreement/Tense: The plural subject *strains* requires the plural form of the verb *are known.* Choice A is incorrect because *is known* is singular. Choice B is incorrect because the past participle *known* needs a helping verb. Choice C is incorrect because *was known* is past tense.

33. **C.** Data interpretation: The data in the chart shows a decline in overall production in the U.S. and in Florida from 2000 to 2014. The two lines follow very similar patterns. Thus, the pattern in Florida mirrors the pattern in the whole country. (A *microcosm* is a small world or a small representation of a larger unit.) None of the other sentences in the choices refers to this similar pattern.

34. **A.** Rhetoric/Word choice: No change is needed here. Choices B, C, and D create wordiness and awkward expressions in this sentence.

35. **A.** Rhetoric/Coherence: The logical transition here is *Yet* because the writer wants to make the point that so many children eat and drink in school, **yet** the schools (which should be educating children to make good choices) provide unhealthy choices. Choice B is incorrect because there is no contrast here. Choice C is incorrect because *Likewise* (meaning in a similar manner) doesn't fit the logic of the sentence. Choice D is incorrect because *In that case* doesn't fit the logic of the sentence.

36. **D.** Rhetoric/Supporting details: Choice D provides details about where students would have easy access to unhealthy choices. These details support the point in the paragraph and provide additional details. Choice A brings in irrelevant information. Choice B repeats information already in the passage. Choice C also brings in information about the cost of snacks that is irrelevant to the main point about obesity.

37. **B.** Idiom: All of the choices are acceptable replacements except *aimed to.* The correct idiom is *aimed at.*

38. **D.** Sentence structure/Comma use: Choice A is incorrect because it is a comma splice error. Choice B is incorrect because it is a comma splice error, and it omits the comma after *regularly scheduled.* Choice C is incorrect because it uses an unnecessary colon after *Regularly scheduled.*

39. **B.** The best place to add this statistic is right after the writer makes the point that physical education in schools can help students. This statistic (following *However*) can strengthen the writer's argument. *However* makes it illogical to place this sentence after Sentence 1 because no contrast exists between these ideas. It isn't logical after Sentence 3 or Sentence 5 because the topic of these sentences is parks.

40. **D.** Redundancy: *Too many* and *abundant* mean the same thing, so only one should be used here. Choice D is the least wordy and the only choice that eliminates the redundancy.

41. **A.** Apostrophe: The correct possessive of the plural noun *children* is *children's.* Choice C omits the apostrophe. Choices B and D incorrectly add an "s" to *children* (which is already plural), and Choice D also incorrectly adds an apostrophe "s."

42. **C.** Passive voice: Choice A is written in the passive voice and is awkward, unclear, and wordy. Choice B is also written in the passive voice and is awkwardly phrased. Active voice is preferable to passive voice. Choice C uses the active form of the verb (*it may take away from the time*) and avoids awkwardness. Choice D incorrectly uses the plural pronoun *they* to refer to the singular noun *viewing*.

43. **D.** Parallelism: The sentence contains a series of phrases beginning with the infinitive form of the verb: *expand . . .*, *put . . .*, and *improve . . . .* The use of *putting* (Choice A) or *to put* (Choice C), or the addition of *they can* (Choice B) make the sentence nonparallel.

44. **C.** The only choice that directly addresses the need for more physical education on a daily basis is Choice C. Choice A is very general and doesn't specify any particular need. Choice B doesn't mention the need for exercise. Choice D is also too general and doesn't address the need for physical activity.

Section 3: Math Test – No Calculator

1. **D.** Since $7 - 2x$ is 6 less than $x + 1$, you have $7 - 2x = (x + 1) - 6$ or $7 - 2x = x - 5$, which yields $x = 4$. Therefore, $3x + 4 = 3(4) + 4$ or 16, Choice D.

2. **B.** Rewrite $(25^x)(5^y)$ as $(5^2)^x(5^y)$, which is equivalent to $(5^{2x})(5^y)$ or 5^{2x+y}. Note that $y = 2 - 2x$ is equivalent to $y + 2x = 2$. Therefore, $5^{2x+y} = 5^2$ or 25, Choice B.

3. **C.** Note that at $t = 0$, $A = 120$, which shows that Daryn had an initial amount of \$120 in her savings account. Each subsequent week, she saved an additional \$50. Thus, $A = 120 + 50t$, Choice C, is correct.

4. **C.** Set $120 + 50t \geq 1{,}000$, so you have $50t \geq 880$ or $t \geq 17.6$. Thus, Daryn needs to save at this rate for a minimum of 18 weeks, Choice C.

5. **A.** Multiply both sides of the equation by 2, and you get $\dfrac{x}{y} = 8$. But $\dfrac{y}{x}$ is the reciprocal of $\dfrac{x}{y}$. Thus, $\dfrac{y}{x} = \dfrac{1}{8}$, Choice A.

6. **B.** Since $(a - b)^2 = a^2 - 2ab + b^2$, you know that $a^2 - 2ab + b^2 = 36$ or $a^2 + b^2 = 36 + 2ab$. Because a and b are positive integers, $2ab$ is positive. Thus, $a^2 + b^2 > 36$, Choice B.

7. **C.** Multiply both the numerator and denominator of $\dfrac{4-7i}{3+2i}$ by $3 - 2i$, and you have $\dfrac{4-7i}{3+2i} \cdot \dfrac{3-2i}{3-2i}$ or $\dfrac{12-8i-21i+14i^2}{9-6i+6i-4i^2} = \dfrac{12-29i-14}{9+4}$ or $\dfrac{-2-29i}{9+4}$, which is equivalent to $-\dfrac{2}{13} - \dfrac{29}{13}i$, Choice C. (Remember that $i^2 = -1$.)

8. **C.** Rewrite the given equation as $3^{n^2} \cdot 3^{2n} = 3^3$ or $3^{n^2+2n} = 3^3$. Therefore, $n^2 + 2n = 3$ or $n^2 + 2n - 3 = 0$. Factoring, you have $(n + 3)(n - 1) = 0$, which yields $n = -3$ or $n = 1$. Since $n > 0$, $n = 1$, Choice C.

9. **C.** Since $\overline{EF}$ is a diameter, D is inscribed in a semicircle; therefore, $\angle D$ is a right angle. Thus, $\triangle EDF$ is a right triangle. Also, $m\angle DFE = 2m\angle DEF$, and the sum of their measures is $90°$. Therefore, $m\angle DFE = 60$, $m\angle DEF = 30$, and $\triangle EDF$ is a $30°$–$60°$–$90°$ triangle. Note that leg $\overline{DF}$ is opposite the $30°$ angle; therefore, $DF = \dfrac{1}{2}(12) = 6$, Choice C.

10. **D.** Rewriting $2 \leq |x| \leq 5$, you have $|x| \geq 2$ and $|x| \leq 5$. Since $|x| \geq 2$, you have $x \geq 2$ or $x \leq -2$. Also, $|x| \leq 5$, so you have $-5 \leq x \leq 5$. Thus, numbers that satisfy both conditions are $-5 \leq x \leq -2$ and $2 \leq x \leq 5$, as depicted in the number line in Choice D.

11. **A.** Because one equation has a and b while the other has a^2 and b^2, begin by factoring. Since $(a-b)(a+b) = 10$ and $2(a-b) = 5$ or $(a-b) = \dfrac{5}{2}$, you know that $\dfrac{5}{2}(a+b) = 10$ or $(a+b) = 4$, Choice A.

12. **D.** Rewrite $\sqrt[3]{16p^6q^5t}$ as $\sqrt[3]{(2)^3(2)(p^2)^3(q)^3(q^2)(t)}$. Note that $\sqrt[3]{(2)^3} = 2$, $\sqrt[3]{(p^2)^3} = p^2$, and $\sqrt[3]{(q)^3} = q$. Therefore, an equivalent expression is $2p^2q\sqrt[3]{2q^2t}$, Choice D.

13. **D.** Rewrite $x - (k^4 + 3)y = 5$ in slope-intercept form of $y = mx + b$ and you have $y = \dfrac{1}{(k^4+3)}x - \dfrac{5}{(k^4+3)}$. The slope of the line is $m = \dfrac{1}{(k^4+3)}$, and the y-intercept is $b = -\dfrac{5}{(k^4+3)}$. Note that $k^4 \geq 0$ for all real values of k; therefore, $(k^4 + 3)$ is positive for all real values of k. Thus, the slope of the line $m > 0$ and the y-intercept $b < 0$, Choice D.

14. **B.** If $a + b = 1$, then $b = 1 - a$. Substitute $b = 1 - a$ in the equation $ab = -6$. You have $a(1-a) = -6$ or $a - a^2 = -6$ or $0 = a^2 - a - 6$. Factor and you have $(a - 3)(a + 2) = 0$; therefore, $a = 3$ or $a = -2$. Since b is positive and $ab = -6$, $a = -2$, Choice B.

15. **A.** One approach to solving the problem is to expand the algebraic expression in each of the given choices. Starting with Choice A, note that $(5p^2 - 2q^2)^2 = (5p^2 - 2q^2)(5p^2 - 2q^2) = 25p^4 - 20p^2q^2 + 4q^4$, so Choice A is correct. Another approach is to factor the trinomial $25p^4 - 20p^2q^2 + 4q^4$. Note that the factors of 25 are ± 1, ± 5, and ± 25, and the factors of 4 are ± 1, ± 2, and ± 4. Using trial and error, you could obtain $(5p^2 - 2q^2)(5p^2 - 2q^2)$. You could also use a variety of different factorization methods, including one called "splitting the middle." Begin by multiplying 25 and 4, and obtain $p^4 - 20p^2q^2 + 100q^4$. Note that $p^4 - 20p^2q^2 + 100q^4 = (p^2 - 10q^2)(p^2 - 10q^2)$. Rewrite $25p^4 - 20p^2q^2 + 4q^4$ as $25p^4 - 10p^2q^2 - 10p^2q^2 + 4q^4$. Factor by grouping, and you have $5p^2(5p^2 - 2q^2) - 2q^2(5p^2 - 2q^2) = (5p^2 - 2q^2)(5p^2 - 2q^2)$ or $(5p^2 - 2q^2)^2$. In this practice test, this is a no calculator question. However, this question could also be given in a calculator section. For steps on how to solve this problem using a calculator, see "Factoring an Algebraic Expression" in the Appendix.

16. $\dfrac{1}{2}$ Rewrite $2x + 3y = 7$ in $y = mx + b$ form and obtain $y = -\dfrac{2}{3}x + \dfrac{7}{3}$, whose slope is $-\dfrac{2}{3}$. Since the two lines are perpendicular, the slope of $ax + by = 1$ is $\dfrac{3}{2}$, the negative reciprocal of $-\dfrac{2}{3}$. Also, since the slope of the line $ax + by = 1$ is $\dfrac{3}{2}$ and it passes through the point $(2, 5)$, the equation of the line $ax + by = 1$ can be written as $y - 5 = \dfrac{3}{2}(x - 2)$. Multiplying both sides of the equation by 2, you have $2y - 10 = 3x - 6$ or $3x - 2y = -4$. Dividing both sides of the equation by -4, you have $-\dfrac{3}{4}x + \dfrac{1}{2}y = 1$. Therefore $ax + by = 1$ is $-\dfrac{3}{4}x + \dfrac{1}{2}y = 1$, and $b = \dfrac{1}{2}$.

17. **7** Rewrite the given equation as $x^2 - 6x + y^2 + 8y = 11$. Take $\dfrac{1}{2}$ of the coefficient of the linear term in x, which is $\dfrac{1}{2}(-6) = -3$, and square the result, $(-3)^2 = 9$. Similarly, do the same for the coefficient of the linear term of y, and you have $\dfrac{1}{2}(8) = 4$ and $(4)^2 = 16$. Add 9 and 16 to both sides of the equation, and you have $x^2 - 6x + 9 + y^2 + 8y + 16 = 11 + 9 + 16$ or $(x - 3)^2 + (y + 4)^2 = 36$. Therefore, the center of the circle is $(m, n) = (3, -4)$ and $m - n = 3 - (-4) = 7$.

18. **1** Rewrite $3t^2 + 3 = 12t$ as $3t^2 - 12t + 3 = 0$, which is a quadratic equation in the form of $ax^2 + bx + c = 0$. The product of the roots is $\dfrac{c}{a}$. Therefore, in this case, the product of all values of t is $\dfrac{3}{3}$ or 1.

19. **8** Multiply both sides of the top equation by 6 and obtain $2x - 3y = -18$. Multiply both sides of the bottom equation by -12 and you have $-2x - 48y = -84$. Add the two new equations and obtain $-51y = -102$ or $y = 2$. Substitute $y = 2$ in either one of the original equations, say $\frac{1}{6}x + 4y = 7$, and you have $\frac{1}{6}x + 4(2) = 7$ or $x = -6$. Therefore, $(h, k) = (-6, 2)$ and $-h + k = -(-6) + 2 = 8$.

20. **19** Substitute $-\frac{1}{2}$ for x and obtain $-\frac{1}{2}k + 6 < 3 - 6$ or $-\frac{1}{2}k < -9$. Multiply both sides of the inequality by -2 and you have $k > 18$. Since k is an integer, the smallest value for k is 19.

Section 4: Math Test – Calculator

1. **D.** The number of bacteria for the first 2 hours is shown in the accompanying table.

t (hours)	0	1	2
A (number of bacteria)	$20(5^0) = 20$	$20(5^1) = 100$	$20(5^2) = 500$

   Note that in this case, $A = 20(5^t)$ is an exponential function with an initial value of 20 and A increasing by a factor of 5 per hour. Thus, the number 20 is the number of bacteria placed in the petri dish at the beginning, Choice D.

2. **D.** Because you're charged $2 for each quarter mile, the charge for each mile is $4(\$2) = \$8$, and the charge for n miles would be $8n$. The total charge, in dollars, is $10 + 8n$, Choice D.

3. **B.** That the average is 90 implies $\dfrac{\text{the sum of the four test scores}}{4} = 90$. Multiplying both sides of the equation by 4, you have the sum of the four test scores = 360. You are given that the highest score is 98. Let the other three test scores be represented as T_2, T_3, and T_4. You have $98 + T_2 + T_3 + T_4 = 360$. Since you want the lowest possible score for one of the three tests, say T_4, let the other two test scores, T_2 and T_3, be as large as possible. In this case, T_2 and T_3 must be 97 and 96. You then have $98 + 97 + 96 + T_4 = 360$. Thus, $T_4 = 360 - (98 + 97 + 96) = 69$, Choice B.

4. **C.** Renting 10 video games costs $\$4 + 10(\$2) = \$24$. The average cost per video game is $\$24 \div 10 = \$2.40$, Choice C.

5. **C.** Because you're trying to find the value of $a + b$, not the value of x, you need to try to isolate a and b. If you start by removing parentheses, you find that $ax^2 + bx = 4x^2 + 2ax$. You have two terms on the left side: one term with x^2 and one term with x. Because the right side also has exactly two terms, one term with x^2 and one term with x, you can match the terms to find that $ax^2 = 4x^2$ and $bx = 2ax$. Because $ax^2 = 4x^2$, you have $a = 4$, and because $bx = 2ax$, you have $b = 2a = 2(4) = 8$. The value of $a + b$ is $4 + 8 = 12$, Choice C.

6. **A.** Two adults and three children cost $2(\$20) + 3(\$10) = \$70$. So $\$82 - \$70 = \$12$ for the fish caught. Thus, $\dfrac{\$12}{\$2} = 6$ fish, Choice A.

7. **C.** The average of the members of Set A is $(-4 - 2 + 0 + 2 + 4 + 6 + 8) \div 7 = 2$. Because the members of Set B are 7 times the members of Set A, the average of Set B is $7(2) = 14$, Choice C.

8. **C.** Enter the data in your graphing calculator. Note that the mean $x = 92.96$, the median $y = 93.5$, and the mode $z = 90$. Thus, $z < x < y$, Choice C. See "Finding Mean, Median, Quartiles, and Standard Deviation of a Given Set of Data" in the Appendix.

9. **A.** If two lines are parallel, their slopes are equal. The line $y = 4x + 1$ is written in slope-intercept form $y = mx + b$. The slope of this line is $m = 4$. To find the slope of $cx + 2y = d$, rewrite the equation in $y = mx + b$ form. Subtract cx from both sides of the equation, and you have $2y = -cx + d$. Dividing both sides by 2, you have $y = \dfrac{-cx}{2} + \dfrac{d}{2}$. Therefore, the slope of this line is $m = -\dfrac{c}{2}$. Since the two lines are parallel, the slopes are equal. Set $-\dfrac{c}{2} = 4$ and you have $c = -8$, Choice A.

10. **B.** If 25% of the students are boys, then 75% are girls. Set up a proportion with s being the number of students in the class. You have $\dfrac{12}{75\%} = \dfrac{s}{100\%}$ or $\dfrac{12}{0.75} = \dfrac{s}{1}$ or $s = 16$, Choice B.

11. **A.** The points in the scatterplot approximate a straight line with a negative slope. The data has a strong

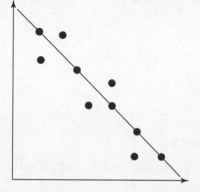

negative linear correlation. Thus, the linear correlation coefficient for the line of best fit could be –0.91, Choice A.

12. **C.** Since $g(x) = h(x - 2)$, $h(3) = h(3 - 2)$ or $g(3) = h(1)$. Looking at the graph, we have $h(1) = 2$, Choice C.

13. **B.** If 40% of the 120 chorus members must be boys, there must be a total of $(0.40)(120) = 48$ boys selected. In the first round, because 75% of the 80 students were girls, you know that 25% of the 80 students were boys; 25% of 80 is $(0.25)(80) = 20$. Because 48 boys are needed and 20 were already selected in the first round, the number of boys selected in the second round must be $48 - 20 = 28$, Choice B.

14. **D.** "Directly proportional" implies $\dfrac{a_1}{b_1} = \dfrac{a_2}{b_2}$. Only the table in Choice D satisfies this proportion: $\dfrac{-3}{-12} = \dfrac{1}{4} = \dfrac{3}{12}$.

15. **A.** Set up a Venn diagram with x representing the number of students who play only the cello and y representing the number of students who play only the violin.

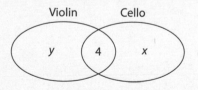

Because there are 20 students in the class, $x + y + 4 = 20$ or $x + y = 16$. Twice as many students play the violin as play the cello; thus, $y + 4 = 2(x + 4)$ or $y = 2x + 4$. Substitute $2x + 4$ for y in the equation $x + y = 16$ and solve to find that $x = 4$ and $y = 12$. The number of students who play only the cello is 4, Choice A. You could also solve the two equations by using your graphing calculator. See "Solving a System of Equations" in the Appendix.

16. **D.** The absolute value of a quantity must be greater than or equal to 0. Since $\left|\dfrac{k}{3}-4\right| = \dfrac{k}{3}-4$, which means

$\dfrac{k}{3}-4$ is either positive or zero, you have $\dfrac{k}{3}-4 \geq 0$. Solve the inequality; you have $\dfrac{k}{3}-4$ or $k \geq 12$. Thus, the smallest value for k is 12, Choice D. You could also solve the given equation using your graphing calculator. See "Solving an Equation" in the Appendix.

17. **C.** You have $k - 0.25k = 24$, and thus, $0.75k = 24$. Dividing both sides by 0.75 gives you $k = 32$, Choice C.

18. **D.** Between '15 and '16, the increase is 2 million, the greatest increase, Choice D.

19. **B.** Using long division, you have

$$\begin{array}{r} 3 \\ (2x-1)\overline{)6x-5} \\ \underline{6x-3} \\ -2 \end{array}$$

Therefore, $\dfrac{6x-5}{2x-1} = 3 - \dfrac{2}{2x-1}$, Choice B.

Alternatively, express the algebraic expression in each of the choices as a single fraction. In Choice B, you have $3 - \dfrac{2}{2x-1} = \dfrac{3(2x-1)}{2x-1} - \dfrac{2}{2x-1} = \dfrac{6x-5}{2x-1}$. Furthermore, you could also use your graphing calculator. See "Working with Equivalent Forms of an Algebraic Expression" in the Appendix.

20. **B.** For a parabola written in the form of $y = ax^2 + bx + c$, c is the y-intercept. If $a > 0$, then the parabola is concave up, and if $a < 0$, then the parabola is concave down. The parabola in the accompanying figure is concave down; therefore, $a < 0$, thus eliminating Choice C. Also, the y-intercept in the accompanying parabola is 0, which implies that $c = 0$, thus eliminating Choice D. In addition, the x-intercepts of the accompanying parabola are 0 and 3; therefore, the roots of the equation must be 0 and 3. In Choice A, let $-x^2 - 3x = 0$, and you have $-x(x + 3) = 0$, which is equivalent to $x = 0$ or $x = -3$, which are not the roots of the accompanying parabola. In Choice B, letting $-x^2 + 3x = 0$, you have $x(-x + 3) = 0$ leading to $x = 0$ or $x = 3$; therefore, the roots of the equation are 0 and 3, which means Choice B, $y = -x^2 + 3x$, could be the equation of the accompanying parabola.

21. **A.** One approach is to draw θ, as illustrated in the accompanying figure.

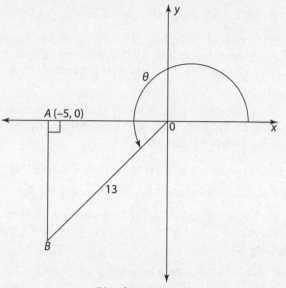

(Not drawn to scale)

Using the Pythagorean theorem, you have $5^2 + (AB)^2 = 13^2$, which is equivalent to $25 + (AB)^2 = 169$ or $(AB)^2 = 144$ or $AB = \pm 12$. Since AB is the length of a side of right $\triangle AOB$, $AB = 12$ because it must be positive; however, note that the coordinates of point B are $(-5, -12)$.

Remember the mnemonic CAST for determining the sign of a trigonometric function in each of the four quadrants. The letter A in the first quadrant indicates that all functions are positive in that quadrant. The letter S in the second quadrant indicates that only sine and cosecant are positive in that quadrant. The letter T in the third quadrant indicates that only tangent and cotangent are positive in that quadrant. And lastly, the letter C in the fourth quadrant indicates that only cosine and secant are positive in that quadrant.

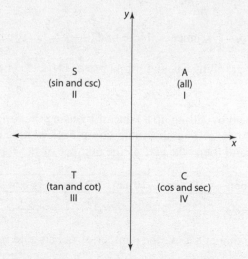

The sine ratio is negative in the third quadrant. Thus, $\sin \theta = \dfrac{-12}{13}$, Choice A.

22. **B.** Half of the students signed up for soccer, so that's $\frac{1}{2}(180) = 90$ students. One-third of the students signed up for baseball, so that's $\frac{1}{3}(180) = 60$ students. The $180 - (90 + 60) = 180 - 150 = 30$ remaining students signed up for table tennis or volleyball. Of the 30 remaining students, twice as many signed up for volleyball as signed up for table tennis. Let x be the number of students who signed up for table tennis and $2x$ be the number of students who signed up for volleyball, so $x + 2x = 30$, $3x = 30$, and $x = 10$, Choice B.

23. **C.** Note that 9% = .09. Since the value of the stock increases by 9% each year, the balance of the investment must be multiplied by a factor of 1.09. The initial investment is $3,500; therefore, the annual balance in t years is $3,500(1.09)^t$, Choice C.

24. **A.** Multiply both sides of the inequality by 30 (the LCD of 2, 3, and 5), and obtain $12 - 10x < 60x + 15$ or $-70x < 3$. Divide both sides of the equality by -70 and you have $x > -\frac{3}{70}$, Choice A. Note that when multiplying or dividing both sides of an inequality by a negative number, you switch the inequality sign. Alternatively, you could also solve the inequality by using your graphing calculator. See "Solving an Inequality" in the Appendix.

25. **B.** Using the point-slope form of an equation of a line $y - y_1 = m(x - x_1)$, you have $y - 0 = -\frac{1}{2}(x - (-6))$ or $y = -\frac{1}{2}x - 3$. Inspecting the choices, note that only the coordinates of Choice B $(0, -3)$ satisfy the equation: $-3 = -\frac{1}{2}(0) - 3$ or $-3 = -3$.

26. **D.** Multiply both sides of the equation by $5v - 2$ and you have $\left(\frac{2v + 3}{5v - 2}\right)(5v - 2) = 4(5v - 2)$ or $2v + 3 = 20v - 8$; thus, $v = \frac{11}{18}$, Choice D. You can also solve the given equation using your graphing calculator. See "Solving an Equation" in the Appendix.

27. **A.** Multiply both the numerator and the denominator of the complex fraction by hk, the LCD of the denominators h and k. You have $\dfrac{\frac{h}{k}(hk) - \frac{k}{h}(hk)}{\frac{1}{h}(hk) - \frac{1}{k}(hk)}$ or $\dfrac{h^2 - k^2}{k - h}$. Factor and obtain

$\dfrac{(h - k)(h + k)}{(k - h)} = -(h + k) = -h - k$, Choice A. Note that $\dfrac{h - k}{k - h} = -1$. You could also enter the given complex fraction into your graphing calculator and press $\boxed{\text{ENTER}}$. The calculator will simplify the fraction.

28. **B.** You can solve this problem by setting up a table or by using the formula for finding a term of a geometric sequence. To solve by setting up a table, count back in time from noon to 8 a.m. in 1-hour increments. Start with 800 and then take half of the number of tickets as you count back in time.

Noon	11 a.m.	10 a.m.	9 a.m.	8 a.m.
800	400	200	100	50

From the table you can see that at 8 a.m., the number of tickets sold was 50, Choice B.

An alternative solution is as follows. Since the number of lottery tickets sold doubled every hour, the number of tickets sold by the hour formed a geometric sequence with the ratio equal to 2. Let a_1 be the first term of the sequence representing the number of tickets sold at 8 a.m. and let a_5 be the fifth term representing the number of tickets sold at noon.

8 a.m.	9 a.m.	10 a.m.	11 a.m.	Noon
a_1	a_2	a_3	a_4	a_5

The formula for a_n (the nth term of the geometric sequence) is $a_n = (a_1)(r^{n-1})$. In this case, $a_5 = (a_1)(2^{5-1})$ or $800 = (a_1)(2^4)$, which yields $a_1 = 50$.

29. **D.** Since $x = 5$, you have $t = 1 + \sqrt{t+5}$ or $t - 1 = \sqrt{t+5}$. Squaring both sides of the equation, you have $(t+1)^2 = \left(\sqrt{t+5}\right)^2$ or $t^2 - 2t + 1 = t + 5$ or $t^2 - 3t - 4 = 0$. Factoring, you obtain $(t-4)(t+1) = 0$, which yields $t = 4$ or $t = -1$. Substituting $t = 4$ in the original equation, you have $4 = 1 + \sqrt{4+5}$ or $4 = 4$. Substituting $t = -1$, you have $-1 = 1 + \sqrt{-1+5}$ or $-1 = 3$, which is not possible. Thus, $t = 4$, Choice D. You could also solve the problem using your graphing calculator. See "Solving an Equation" in the Appendix.

30. **C.** Factor $4x^2 - 4x + 1$ and you have $(2x - 1)(2x - 1)$ or $(2x - 1)^2$. Thus, $m = 2$ and $\dfrac{h}{2} = -1$ or $h = -2$. Therefore, $m + h = 2 + (-2) = 0$, Choice C. See "Factoring an Algebraic Expression" in the Appendix.

31. **1,754** Note that 2 hours and 13 minutes is equal to $2(60) + 13$ or 133 minutes. The particle's average speed in feet per second is $\dfrac{2{,}651 \text{ miles}}{133 \text{ min}} \cdot \dfrac{1{,}760 \text{ yds}}{1 \text{ mile}} \cdot \dfrac{3 \text{ feet}}{1 \text{ yd}} \cdot \dfrac{1 \text{ min}}{60 \text{ sec}} \approx 1{,}754.045$ ft/sec $\approx 1{,}754$ ft/sec.

32. **2** Rewrite $-3x + y \le -1$ as $y \le 3x - 1$. Using your graphing calculator, graph the inequalities as shown in the accompanying figure.

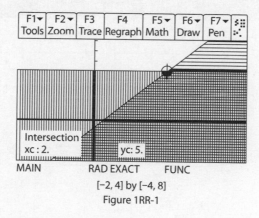

[−2, 4] by [−4, 8]

Figure 1RR-1

Note that the intersection of the lines $y = 5$ and $-3x + y = -1$ is $(2, 5)$. Also note that if (h, k) lies in the solution set of the system, the maximum possible value of k is 5. And when $k = 5$, the minimum value of h is 2.

33. $\dfrac{1}{2}$ Inspecting the line of best fit in the given figure, note that the points $(0, 40)$, $(60, 70)$, and $(90, 95)$ are all on the line. Use two of the points, say $(0, 40)$ and $(60, 70)$, and obtain the slope; slope $= \dfrac{70 - 40}{60 - 0} = \dfrac{30}{60} = \dfrac{1}{2}$. Since at $t = 0$, $g = 40$, the equation of the line of best fit is $g = \dfrac{1}{2}t + 40$, and $h = \dfrac{1}{2}$.

34. **80** The equation of the line of best fit is $g = \frac{1}{2}t + 40$. Since the student wanted a grade of 80 or higher, you have $\frac{1}{2}t + 40 \geq 80$ or $t \geq 80$. Thus, the minimum number of minutes the student must study for the quiz is 80.

35. **59** Inspecting the Total column on the right side of the table, you see that the total number of female students is equal to 124 – 68 or 56. Looking at the row labeled "Female," note that the number of female students taking physics is 56 – 25 or 31. Also note the column labeled "Physics" shows that the total number of tenth graders taking physics is 28 + 31 or 59. Please note that there are other approaches of solving the problem. A completed frequency table is shown below.

Frequency Table			
	Physics	Chemistry	Total
Male	28	40	68
Female	31	25	56
Total	59	65	124

36. **0.43** Inspecting the Total column on the right, the relative frequency of male students is 1 – 0.45 or 0.55. Looking at the row labeled "Male," the relative frequency of male students taking physics, x, is 0.55 – 0.32 or 0.23. Looking at the row labeled "Total," the relative frequency of the total number of students taking chemistry is 0.52; therefore, the chemistry column yields that $y = 0.52 - 0.32$ or $y = 0.20$. Thus, $x + y = 0.23 + 0.20 = 0.43$. Please note that there are other approaches of solving the problem. A completed relative frequency table is shown below.

Relative Frequency Table			
	Physics	Chemistry	Total
Male	0.23	0.32	0.55
Female	0.25	0.20	0.45
Total	0.48	0.52	1

37. **9**

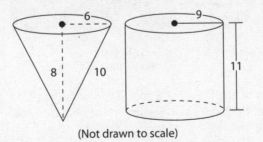

(Not drawn to scale)

Using the Pythagorean theorem, find the height of the cone: $6^2 + h^2 = 10^2$ or $h = 8$. The volume of the cone is $V_{\text{cone}} = \frac{1}{3}\pi r^2 h$; therefore, $V_{\text{cone}} = \frac{1}{3}\pi(6)^2\,8 = 96\pi$ cm^3. The volume of a right circular cylinder is $V_{\text{cylinder}} = \pi r^2 h$. In this case, $V_{\text{cylinder}} = \pi(9)^2(11) = 891\pi$ cm^3. Thus, the number of full cones of water that can be poured into an empty cylinder is $\frac{891\pi}{96\pi} \approx 9.281$, and the maximum integer number of full cones of water is 9.

38. **5**

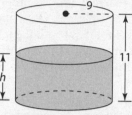

(Not drawn to scale)

The volume of four full cones of water is $4(96\pi)$ cm$^3 = 384\pi$ cm^3. Let h be the height of the water level in the cylinder. The volume of a right circular cylinder is $V_{\text{cylinder}} = \pi r^2 h$. Therefore, $\pi(9)^2 h = 384\pi$ and $h = \frac{384\pi}{81\pi} \approx 4.7407$ cm ≈ 5 cm.

Section 5: The Essay

To score your essay: First, reread your essay. Then look at the sample essays below and compare your essay to the samples provided. (*Tip:* Because grading your own essay can be difficult, ask an English teacher at your school to grade it for you, based on the rubric on pages 141–142 in Chapter VII.) The numbers after the scores indicate the essay's scores on the three categories: Reading/Analysis/Writing.

To read more sample essays with commentaries, follow this link to the College Board Official site: https://collegereadiness.collegeboard.org/sample-questions/essay.

Sample Essays

Advanced Response: 4/4/4

In this passage, the author attempts to convince the reader that the federal government should fund preschools. He accomplishes this through a variety of tactics such as using facts and statistics from scientific research, creating inferences based on this research about the importance of preschool education, and employing compelling diction to emphasize the urgency of this issue. In addition, the author successfully uses all these strategies and blends them together in order to build a strong, cohesive argument in favor of federal financial support for preschools.

To charge his argument with broad appeal and urgency, the author begins by suggesting that preschool education is not simply an issue for parents of toddlers, but one that impacts the nation as a whole. He uses facts and statistics from scientific studies about both the short-term and long-term benefits of preschool to build this strong foundation for his argument. For example, he references research that shows how children's language skills at ages 1 and 2 can predict their pre-literacy skills at age 5 and points out that preschool experience leads to "better health, social-emotional, and cognitive outcomes," a goal that appeals to all Americans. This use of diverse research studies strengthens the argument with multiple examples: Children who attend preschool are less likely to need special education; they are more likely to continue their education; they earn more money over their lifetimes. Finally, he provides statistics to prove the importance of federally funded programs to close the achievement gaps that are the result of "racial and socioeconomic disparities." Low-income families can't afford to pay for private preschool. Statistics on access to preschool show both the relatively low overall rate (about 41%) and the low individual rates, especially for Latinos, who form the largest minority in the United States. The author notes these specific groups at different points in the passage to emphasize the disparities between races.

The author continues to strengthen his argument by interpreting the scientific studies and creating inferences based on the previously stated facts. For instance, he uses the statistics that show that Latino and African-American children have less access to preschool to explain the achievement gap between the racial groups in the U.S. He cites this lack of access as one of the underlying reasons for the unpreparedness of these children compared to white children of the same age. This idea of unequal opportunities, one he references frequently throughout the passage, is the main basis for his argument. Since he states that unequal opportunity is a major reason for the learning gap, he infers that equal opportunities would make the system more equitable and help close this gap. He continues his argument with an appeal to the financial interests of society as a whole by citing statistics that show that investment in preschool is profitable for all: "a return on investment of $8.60 for every $1 spent." These inferences, based on facts and supported throughout the passage, allow the author to connect the cited facts and statistics into evidence for a cohesive and persuasive argument.

A final tool that the author employs to create a cogent argument is his use of strong and compelling diction. He chooses his words carefully to create a serious tone and a sense of urgency. He describes preschool education as critical, imperative, and necessary to the health of the nation. He refers to funded preschool as part of society's "important legacy" and "moral imperative," emotional language that underscores the seriousness and importance of this issue. In addition, by closing his argument with a double appeal—to morality ("the right thing to do") and to money ("strengthening our nation's economy")—the author pokes Americans in their most sensitive places: their hearts and their wallets.

Clearly, this author believes that the issue of federal funding for preschool is critical to improving society. Facts based on scientific research, observation and inferences based on these facts, and strong language convey the depth of his conviction. Working in conjunction, these tactics create a strong and sturdy argument, well founded in fact and delivered with confidence and passion. This author has convinced his readers of the validity and worthiness of his position that it is in the best interests of all Americans to provide all the necessary funding for all children to have access to preschool education.

Commentary:

This **Advanced** response demonstrates a clear comprehension of the source text, insightfully analyzes the article, and provides effective textual evidence to support the author's claims. The information is accurate and well organized, with a clear introduction, body, and conclusion. The writer uses transitions within paragraphs (*In addition, For example, Finally*) and between paragraphs (*continues, A final, Clearly*). The writer skillfully weaves textual references into the response, referring to statistics and using appropriate quotations to support assertions. The writer demonstrates a facility with language in the sentence variety (*Since he states that unequal opportunity is a major reason for the learning gap, he infers that equal opportunities would make the system more equitable and help close this gap.*), in the repetition of the word *"all"* three times in the last sentence and in word choice (*compelling diction to emphasize the urgency, the author pokes Americans in their most sensitive places: their hearts and their wallets*). The response is free of errors, and the tone is formal and objective.

Proficient Response: 3/3/3

Some people think that all children should be able to go to preschool, but many families, especially Latino and African-American families, can't afford to pay for preschool. According to the author of this article, the answer is the federal government. He uses many facts, some important financial statistics, and good writing to convince the reader to see his point of view.

The federal government pays for a great number of services that help many Americans with different needs. Why shouldn't the federal government also pay for preschool? It seems like it would be a solid idea for many reasons. To prove this position is reasonable, the author has information from scientific studies to back his argument. The studies that the author discusses show that preschool helps kids in their literacy learning. Kids can learn to read earlier, and this skill will help them in all parts of their education. According to the studies mentioned in the article, kids who go to preschool tend to stay in school longer. They finish high school and some go on to college. This education helps them earn more money and be healthier because they are better educated. As a result, the whole country is better off with healthier and better educated people in it. This reasonable conclusion helps strengthen the argument to convince people that the government should pay for preschool.

Another good argument to convince the government to pay for preschool has to do with money. Of course, paying for preschool for everyone is expensive, and the government already has a lot of debt. But, the author has statistics to show that spending money on preschool is not money wasted. He points out that it will be a good investment because for every dollar spent, the government will get back over eight dollars. The additional resource comes from "increased earnings for children when they grow up." This effective statistic provides evidence to back up the author's main argument that it is in the best interests of the financial health of this country to support universal preschool. By investing in kids who are young, the government gets back its investment.

Finally, this is a convincing argument because the author has a good writing style. He uses powerful language to impress the readers so they will see how true his point is. He uses phrases like "unfortunately," and "trap them in a cycle of continuous catch-up" that show how poor people are neglected. The writing makes people want to care and support his position. The article also has a good flow of ideas and is written in a way that readers can understand and relate to, especially when he explains scientific studies in everyday language. I think that most people who read this article will be convinced by this author and will write to their congressmen and ask them to fund preschool for anyone who can't afford to pay.

Commentary:

This **Proficient** response demonstrates that the writer understands the main point of the source text, interprets its sub-points, and analyzes the evidence and rhetorical style of the author. The writer uses textual evidence to support the analysis by paraphrasing source material (*According to the studies mentioned in the article, kids who go to preschool tend to stay in school longer.*) and by quoting relevant information (*"increased earnings for children when they grow up."*). The response is organized coherently with an introductory paragraph that states the main claim (*He uses many facts, some important financial statistics, and good writing to convince the reader to see his point of view.*), and a body paragraph to explicate each part of the claim. The concluding paragraph is effectively combined with the last body paragraph. The writer uses some sentence variety (*Why shouldn't the federal government also pay for preschool?*) and transitions within paragraphs (*As a result, Of course*) and between paragraphs (*Another, Finally*). The essay is free from mechanical errors, but has some repetitive wording (*healthier and better educated* in the second paragraph) and some awkward phrasing (*Kids can learn to read earlier, and this skill will help them in all parts of their education.*), but, for the most part, the language use is proficient.

Partial Response: 2/2/2

This is an impressive arguement. I agree with the author that kids should be able to go to preschool. This is very true for kids from minoritys who can fall behind and never catch up. Like the author says, "too many children enter kindergarden a year or more behind their classmates." He makes this a strong arguement.

The author says that Congress should help with paying for preschool. He gives a lot of examples. He says that kids who can't read are not as healthy and as prepared for life as kids who can read. They fall behind and can't catch up. This is a major point for his arguement and it is a good one. He says that kids who go to preschool will earn more money which is good for everyone. It is good for the kids because they will be able to buy more things to make their lives better. It is good for everyone because they will earn more money which will let them spend more and help the economy. Being that they are richer and smarter they will be better from having gone to preschool.

This author has a lot of evidence to back up what he says, it is persuasive because he has facts and numbers to prove his point. He says that 59% of 4 year olds don't go to preschool. He says that 50% of African-Americans go to preschool. He says that 53% of white children go to preschool. He says that the government should pay for preschool so more kids can go to preschool. Education is important for everyone. Not only rich people should send kids to preschool. The numbers show that he has reasons and evidence for this arguement. I agree with him so he made a good arguement.

Commentary:

This **Partial** response demonstrates some understanding of the task and the writer's main point, but contains errors in interpretation (*He says that kids who can't read are not as healthy*). The response uses textual evidence, but uses it haphazardly, quoting from the text (*"too many children enter kindergarden a year or more behind their classmates"*) and then paraphrasing the same reference (*They fall behind and can't catch up.*) in the next paragraph. The response makes an attempt to describe the use of evidence in the source text (*he has facts and numbers to prove his point*) but then merely lists the statistics without explaining their significance to the argument. The organization of the response is uneven, with a vague introduction and very little conclusion. Transitions are lacking, and sentence structure is repetitive (most sentences begin *He says*). In addition, grammatical errors (run-on sentence begins paragraph three, awkward use of *Being that*) and spelling errors (arguement, minoritys, kindergarden) detract from the quality of the writing.

Inadequate Response: 1/1/1

People expect the goverment to pay for everything, even for preschool. Why should it always be the responsibility of the goverment to pay for everything? It is enough time to learn to read in kindergarden like I did. Even though this writer says that preschool is needed for all of life, I don't agree.

The article has lots of reasons to pay for preschool. I know that some people can't pay for preschool because they might have too many kids and not enough money. The author says that mostly poor people don't go to preschool, but my parents have enough money and I didn't go to school before kindergarden. It is enough years in school without going to preschool.

The author says that people who go to preschool earn more money than people who don't go. I don't know that its true. My uncle is a construction worker who never even finhed high school but he makes alot of money. He also pay alot of taxes to the goverment so he would not want the taxes to go higher to pay for preschool for some other kids so he would disagree with this author.

This article uses alot of facts and reasons, but I don't agree with him. So if I don't agree with him, I don't think he does his purpose.

Commentary:

This **Inadequate** response demonstrates little understanding of the analytical task and little control of the conventions of standard written English. While there is an attempt to respond to the controlling idea of government-funded preschool, the writer digresses from the task. The writer substitutes his or her opinion of the claim in the source text and some personal anecdotes for analysis of the argument (reference to personal experience, and to his or her relatives). In addition, the response is rife with spelling errors (*goverment, finhed, alot, its, kindergarden*) and grammatical errors (*He also pay, I don't think he does his purpose*). While the writer does present paragraph units, the essay has no internal or external coherence, no use of transitional words or phrases, and little evidence of organization.

Score Sheet for Practice Test

Section 1: Reading Test

Section 2: Writing and Language Test

To calculate your Reading and Writing score:

1. Count the number of correct answers you got on Section 1: Reading Test. This is your raw score.
2. Using the Raw Score Conversion table, locate your raw score and match it to the number in the Reading Test score column.
3. Do the same with your Section 2: Writing Test score.
4. Add the two scores together (Reading Test score and Writing Test score).
5. Multiply that number by 10 to get your Reading and Writing score.

	Raw Score	Scaled Score
Section 1: Reading	(0–52)	(10–40)
Section 2: Writing and Language	(0–44)	(10–40)
Total of Reading and Writing Scaled Scores		(20–80)
Multiply Scaled Scores × 10		(200–800)

Reading Raw Score = Number right (Section 1) _____

Reading Scaled Score _____

Writing Raw Score = Number right (Section 2) _____

Writing Scaled Score _____

(Remember that there is no penalty for incorrect answers.)

Reading and Writing Scaled Score: _____ × 10 = _____

Note: To find your scaled score, use the following chart.

Reading and Writing Raw Score Conversion								
Raw Score	Reading Section Score	Writing Section Score	Raw Score	Reading Section Score	Writing Section Score	Raw Score	Reading Section Score	Writing Section Score
1	10	10	21	23	23	41	33	37
2	10	10	22	23	24	42	34	38
3	11	10	23	24	25	43	35	39
4	12	11	24	24	25	44	35	40
5	13	12	25	25	26	45	36	
6	14	13	26	25	26	46	37	
7	15	13	27	26	27	47	37	
8	15	14	28	26	28	48	38	
9	16	15	29	27	28	49	38	
10	17	16	30	28	29	50	39	
11	17	16	31	28	30	51	40	
12	18	17	32	29	30	52	40	
13	19	18	33	29	31			
14	19	19	34	30	32			
15	20	19	35	30	32			
16	20	20	36	31	33			
17	21	21	37	32	34			
18	21	21	38	32	34			
19	22	22	39	32	35			
20	22	23	40	33	36			

Section 3: Math Test – No Calculator

Section 4: Math Test – Calculator

	Number Right
Section 3: Math Test – No Calculator	
Section 4: Math Test – Calculator	
TOTAL (Section 3 + Section 4)	

Raw score = Number right (Section 3 + Section 4) _____

(Remember that there is no penalty for incorrect answers.)

Raw score × 2 = _____

Math scaled score range: _____

Note: To find your scaled score range, use the following chart.

Mathematics Raw Score Conversion					
Raw Score	Math Section Score	Raw Score	Math Section Score	Raw Score	Math Section Score
58	800	38	640	18	450
57	790	37	630	17	440
56	780	36	620	16	430
55	760	35	610	15	420
54	750	34	610	14	400
53	750	33	600	13	390
52	740	32	590	12	380
51	740	31	580	11	370
50	730	30	570	10	360
49	720	29	560	9	350
48	710	28	550	8	340
47	710	27	540	7	330
46	700	26	530	6	320
45	690	25	520	5	300
44	690	24	510	4	280
43	680	23	500	3	250
42	670	22	490	2	230
41	660	21	480	1	220
40	650	20	470	0	200
39	650	19	460		

Appendix: Using the TI-89 Graphing Calculator

The TI-89 graphing calculator is a versatile tool. Many of the features are useful in solving SAT math questions. For example, the TI-89 graphing calculator can be used for:

- Solving an equation
- Solving equations involving absolute values
- Solving a system of equations
- Solving an equation with a variable in the exponent
- Solving an equation involving a function
- Solving a problem involving an unusual symbol
- Evaluating algebraic expressions involving functional notations
- Working with the distance formula
- Evaluating algebraic expressions involving inequalities
- Simplifying a numerical expression
- Solving an inequality
- Factoring an algebraic expression
- Isolating a variable in an equation
- Working with complex numbers
- Finding the exact value of a trigonometric ratio
- Working with rational expressions
- Working with equivalent forms of an algebraic expression
- Finding the zeros of polynomial functions
- Solving radical equations
- Finding mean, median, quartiles, and standard deviation of a given set of data

In this appendix, we offer 20 examples of how to use the TI-89 graphing calculator to solve SAT math questions.

Solving an Equation

1. If x is a real number, how many values of x satisfy the equation $(x + 10)^2 = 25$?

   A. 0

   B. 1

   C. 2

   D. 4

TI-89 solution:

Press: | HOME | | F2 | 1

Enter: | (| x | + | 10 |) | ^ | 2 | = | 25 | , | x |)

Press: | ENTER |

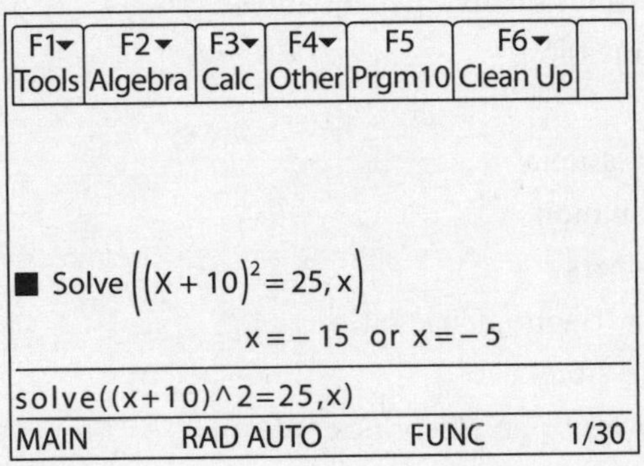

| F1▾ | F2▾ | F3▾ | F4▾ | F5 | F6▾ | |
| Tools | Algebra | Calc | Other | Prgm10 | Clean Up | |

■ Solve $\left((X + 10)^2 = 25, x \right)$

$x = -15$ or $x = -5$

solve((x+10)^2=25,x)

| MAIN | RAD AUTO | FUNC | 1/30 |

Correct Answer: **C**

Note that the function Solve(contains an open parenthesis which cannot be used as the open parenthesis for the expression $(x + 10)^2$. See figure above.

Also note that you can see an algebraic solution to this problem in Chapter XI, "Passport to Advanced Math," Section F, "Solving Quadratic Equations," question 5.

Solving Equations Involving Absolute Values

2. If n satisfies both of the equations below, what is the value of n?

$$|2n - 4| = 10$$
$$|3 - 2n| = 11$$

TI-89 solution:

Press: HOME F2 1

Enter: CATALOG A ENTER 2 x − 4) = 10 CATALOG

Select: ▷ *and* ENTER

Enter: CATALOG A ENTER 3 − 2 x) = 11 ,
x)

Press: ENTER

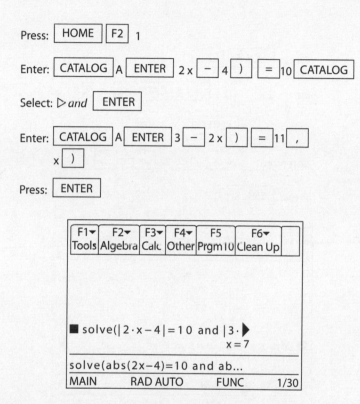

Note: It is more convenient to use the letter x instead of n, because the letter x has its own designated key while, for n, you have to first press the ALPHA key and then press n.

Correct Answer: **7**

Note that when you press CATALOG followed by pressing the letter A, the calculator will bring you to the absolute value function abs(.

Solving a System of Equations

3. If $2a - 2b = 5$ and $a^2 - b^2 = 10$, what is the value of $a + b$?

  A. 4

  B. 5

  C. 10

  D. 20

TI-89 solution:

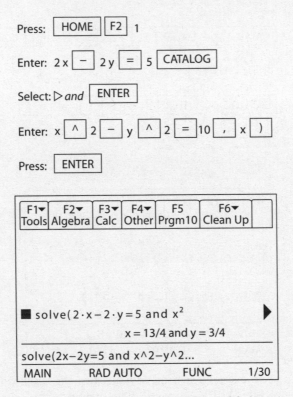

Press: HOME F2 1

Enter: 2 x − 2 y = 5 CATALOG

Select: ▷ *and* ENTER

Enter: x ^ 2 − y ^ 2 = 10 , x)

Press: ENTER

Note: It is more convenient to use the letters x and y instead of a and b, because the letters x and y have their own designated keys. In contrast, for a, you have to first press the ALPHA key and then press a, and then repeat the same procedure for b.

Correct Answer: **A**

Solving an Equation with a Variable in the Exponent

4. If $3^n + 3^n + 3^n = 9^6$, what is the value of n?

   A. 2

   B. 3

   C. 4

   D. 11

TI-89 solution:

Press: | HOME | | F2 | 1

Enter: 3 | ^ | x | + | 3 | ^ | x | + | 3 | ^ | x | = | 9 | ^ |
        6 | , | x |) |

Press: | ENTER |

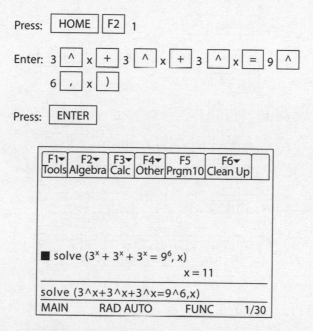

F1▾	F2▾	F3▾	F4▾	F5	F6▾	
Tools	Algebra	Calc	Other	Prgm10	Clean Up	

■ solve ($3^x + 3^x + 3^x = 9^6$, x)

$\qquad\qquad$ x = 11

solve (3^x+3^x+3^x=9^6,x)

| MAIN | RAD AUTO | FUNC | 1/30 |

Note: It is more convenient to use the letter x instead of n, because the letter x has its own designated key while, for n, you have to first press the ALPHA key and then press n.

Correct Answer: **D**

Solving an Equation Involving a Function

5. If a function p is defined as $p(x) = x^2 + 2x$, and $p(2h) = 8h$, and $h > 0$, what is the value of h?

A. -4

B. -1

C. 0

D. 1

TI-89 solution:

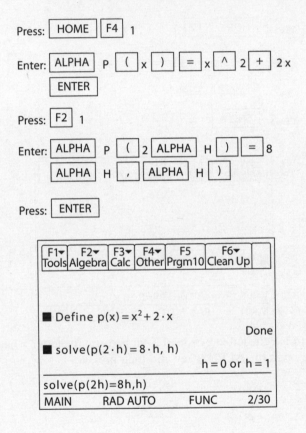

Correct Answer: **D**

Solving a Problem Involving an Unusual Symbol

6. Let $@p$ be defined as $2^p - 1$ for all integers p. What is the value of $@((@3)$?

TI-89 solution:

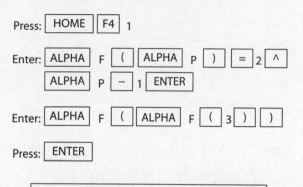

Press: HOME   F4   1

Enter: ALPHA F (ALPHA P) = 2 ^
       ALPHA P − 1 ENTER

Enter: ALPHA F (ALPHA F (3))

Press: ENTER

| F1▾ | F2▾ | F3▾ | F4▾ | F5 | F6▾ | |
| Tools | Algebra | Calc | Other | Prgm10 | Clean Up | |

■ Define f(p) = $2^P - 1$ Done
■ f(f(3))   127

f(f(3))

MAIN   RAD AUTO   FUNC   2/30

Correct Answer: **127**

Evaluating Algebraic Expressions Involving Functional Notations

7. If the function f is defined by $f(x) = 2x - 6$, which of the following is equivalent to $5f(x) + 10$?

   A. $7x + 4$

   B. $10x - 20$

   C. $10x + 4$

   D. $10x + 20$

TI-89 solution:

Press: | HOME | F4 | 1

Enter: | ALPHA | F (x) | = 2 x − 6 | ENTER |

Enter: 5 | ALPHA | F (x) | + 10

Press: | ENTER |

F1▾ Tools	F2▾ Algebra	F3▾ Calc	F4▾ Other	F5 Prgm10	F6▾ Clean Up	

■ Define f(x) = 2·x − 6   Done

■ 5·f(x) + 10   10·x − 20

5f(x) + 10

| MAIN | RAD AUTO | FUNC | 2/30 |

Correct Answer: **B**

Note that you can see an algebraic solution to this problem in Chapter IX, "The Heart of Algebra," Section C, "Applications of Linear Functions," question 1.

Working with the Distance Formula

8. In a coordinate plane, the distance between point $A(10, 5)$ and point $B(-2, b)$ is 13. If $b > 0$, what is the value of b?

TI-89 solution:

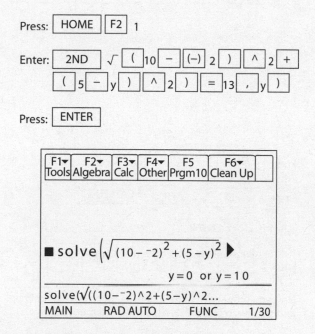

Press: | HOME | | F2 | 1

Enter: | 2ND | | √ | | (| 10 | − | | (−) | 2 |) | | ^ | 2 | + | | (| 5 | − | y |) | | ^ | 2 |) | | = | 13 | , | y |)

Press: | ENTER |

Note: It is more convenient to use the letter y instead of b, because the letter y has its own designated key while, for b, you have to first press the ALPHA key and then press b.

Correct Answer: **10**

Evaluating Algebraic Expressions Involving Inequalities

9. In the accompanying figure, four points, A, B, C, and D, are on a number line in the positions indicated. Which point has m as its coordinate if $m < m^3 < m^2$?

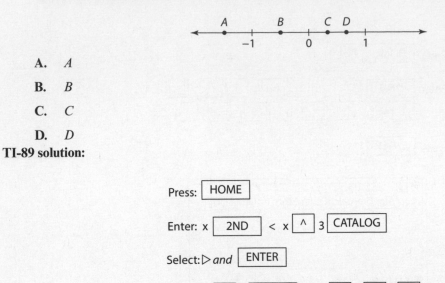

A. A

B. B

C. C

D. D

TI-89 solution:

Press: ⬛ HOME

Enter: x ⬛ 2ND ⬛ < x ⬛ ^ ⬛ 3 ⬛ CATALOG ⬛

Select: ▷ *and* ⬛ ENTER ⬛

Enter: x ⬛ ^ ⬛ 3 ⬛ 2ND ⬛ < x ⬛ ^ ⬛ 2 ⬛ | ⬛ x ⬛ = ⬛

Now you enter each of the given 4 choices, one at a time, and see which one produces a true statement.

Let A = −1.5, B = −0.5, C = 0.3, and D = 0.6.

Enter: ⬛ (−) ⬛ 0.5

Press: ⬛ ENTER ⬛

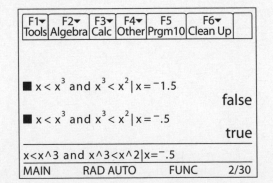

Note: It is more convenient to use the letter x instead of m, because the letter x has its own designated key while, for m, you have to first press the ALPHA key and then press m.

Correct Answer: **B**

Simplifying a Numerical Expression

10. What is the numerical value of $\dfrac{\dfrac{1}{2}+\dfrac{1}{3}}{\dfrac{1}{6}}$?

TI-89 solution:

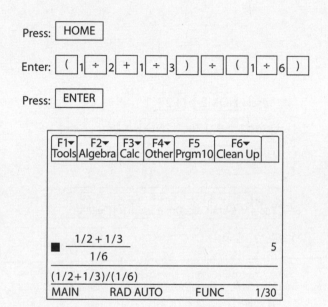

Press: | HOME |

Enter: | (|1| ÷ |2| + |1| ÷ |3|) | | ÷ | | (|1| ÷ |6|) |

Press: | ENTER |

Correct Answer: **5**

Solving an Inequality

11. For the inequality below, which of the following inequalities gives all values of x?

$$1 - 2x < 13$$

A. $x > -7$

B. $x > -6$

C. $x < 6$

D. $x < 7$

TI-89 solution:

Press: | HOME | | F2 | 1

Enter: 1 | − | 2x | 2ND | < 13 | , | x |)

Press: | ENTER |

F1▾ Tools	F2▾ Algebra	F3▾ Calc	F4▾ Other	F5 Prgm10	F6▾ Clean Up	

■ solve (1 − 2 · x < 13, x)

x > −6

solve (1−2x <13, x)

MAIN   DEG EXACT   FUNC   1/30

Correct Answer: **B**

Note that you can see an algebraic solution to this problem in Chapter IX, "The Heart of Algebra," Section B, "Linear Inequalities in One Variable," question 1.

Factoring an Algebraic Expression

12. Which of the following is equivalent to the expression $25p^4 - 20p^2q^2 + 4q^4$?

   A. $(5p^2 - 2q^2)^2$

   B. $(5p^2 + 2q^2)^2$

   C. $(25p^2 - 4q^2)^2$

   D. $(5p^2 - 2q^2)(5p^2 + 2q^2)$

TI-89 solution:

Press: HOME   F2   2

Enter: 25 ALPHA p ∧ 4 − 20 ALPHA p ∧ 2 x

    ALPHA q ∧ 2 +   4 ALPHA q ∧ 4)

Press: ENTER

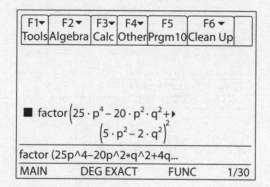

Correct Answer: **A**

Note that $\boxed{x}$ is the multiplication symbol, while x without the box represents a variable.

Also note that this problem could be given in either no-calculator or calculator section. You can see an algebraic solution to this problem in the Practice Test, Section 3, question 15.

Isolating a Variable in an Equation

13. If $ax + by + c = 0$ and $b \neq 0$, what is the value of y in terms of a, b, c, and x?

A. $\dfrac{ax - c}{b}$

B. $\dfrac{-b}{ax + c}$

C. $\dfrac{ax + c}{-b}$

D. $\dfrac{ax + c}{b}$

TI-89 solution:

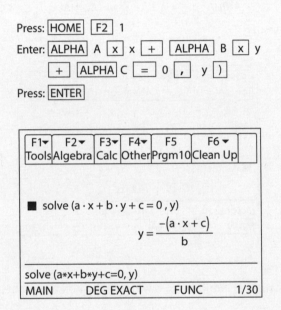

Press: [HOME] [F2] 1

Enter: [ALPHA] A [x] x [+] [ALPHA] B [x] y

[+] [ALPHA] C [=] 0 [,] y [)]

Press: [ENTER]

F1▾	F2▾	F3▾	F4▾	F5	F6▾	
Tools	Algebra	Calc	Other	Prgm10	Clean Up	

■ solve (a · x + b · y + c = 0 , y)

$$y = \frac{-(a \cdot x + c)}{b}$$

solve (a*x+b*y+c=0, y)

| MAIN | DEG EXACT | FUNC | 1/30 |

Correct Answer: **C**

Note that [x] is the multiplication symbol, while x without the box represents a variable.

Also note that you can see an algebraic solution to this problem in Chapter XI, "Passport to Advanced Math," Section E, "Isolating a Variable or a Quantity of Interest in an Equation," question 1.

Working with Complex Numbers

14. Which of the following is equivalent to $\dfrac{4-2i}{2-4i}$?

   A. $-i$

   B. i

   C. $\dfrac{4}{5} + \dfrac{3}{5}i$

   D. $4 + 3i$

TI-89 solution:

Press: HOME

Enter: (4 − 2 2ND i) ÷

(2 − 4 2ND i)

Press: ENTER

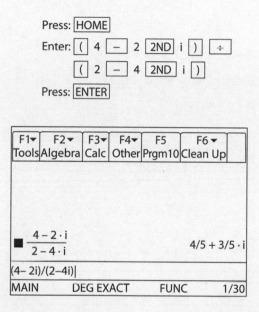

Correct Answer: **C**

Note that you can see an algebraic solution to this problem in Chapter XII, "Additional Topics in Math," Section G, "Complex Numbers," question 4.

Finding the Exact Value of a Trigonometric Ratio

15. What is the exact value of $\sin\left(\dfrac{5\pi}{4}\right)$?

    A. $-\sqrt{2}$

    B. $-\dfrac{\sqrt{2}}{2}$

    C. $\dfrac{1}{2}$

    D. $\dfrac{\sqrt{2}}{2}$

TI-89 solution:

Press: $\boxed{\text{HOME}}$

Enter: $\boxed{\text{2ND}}$ SIN 5 $\boxed{\text{2ND}}$ π $\boxed{\div}$ 4 $\boxed{)}$

Press: $\boxed{\text{ENTER}}$

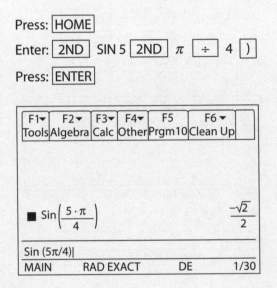

Correct Answer: **B**

Note: Since the measure of the angle is given in radian, you must set the MODE of the calculator in radian.

Working with Rational Expressions

16. If $y \neq -1$ and $y \neq 1$, which of the following is equivalent to $\dfrac{2}{y-1} - \dfrac{1}{y+1} - \dfrac{4}{y^2-1}$?

   A. $\dfrac{1}{y-1}$

   B. $\dfrac{1}{y+1}$

   C. $\dfrac{-1}{y^2-1}$

   D. $\dfrac{y-3}{y^2-1}$

TI-89 solution:

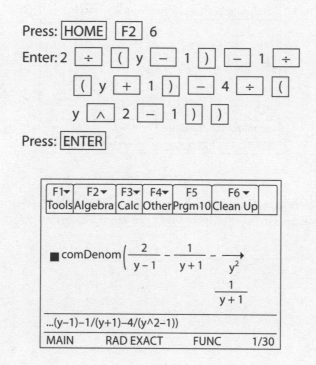

Press: | HOME | | F2 | 6

Enter: 2 | ÷ | | (| y | − | 1 |) | | − | 1 | ÷ |

     | (| y | + | 1 |) | | − | 4 | ÷ | | (|

     y | ∧ | 2 | − | 1 |) | |) |

Press: | ENTER |

Correct Answer: **B**

Note that you can see an algebraic solution to this problem in Chapter XI, "Passport to Advanced Math," Section B, "Arithmetic Operations on Rational Expressions," question 3.

Working with Equivalent Forms of an Algebraic Expression

17. If $t \neq -2$ and $\dfrac{t^2}{t+2}$ is written in an equivalent form $t - 2 + \dfrac{k}{t+2}$, what is the value of k?

TI-89 solution:

Press: HOME F2 7

Enter: t ∧ 2 ÷ (t + 2))

Press: ENTER

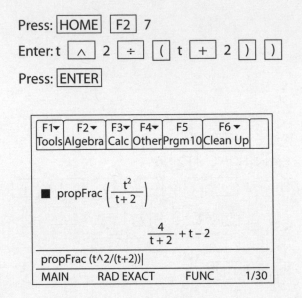

Correct Answer: **4**

Note that you can see an algebraic solution to this problem in Chapter XI, "Passport to Advanced Math," Section D, "Creating Equivalent Forms of Algebraic Expressions," question 5.

Finding the Zeros of Polynomial Functions

18. What are the zeros of $f(x) = x^3 + 2x^2 - x - 2$?

    A. 0, –1, and 1

    B. –2, 1, and 2

    C. –2, –1, and 1

    D. 0, –2, and 2

TI-89 solution:

Press: HOME F2 1

Enter: x ∧ 3 + 2x ∧ 2 − x − 2 = 0

, x)

Press: ENTER

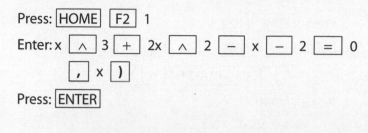

F1▼ Tools	F2▼ Algebra	F3▼ Calc	F4▼ Other	F5 Prgm10	F6▼ Clean Up	

■ solve($x^3 + 2 \cdot x^2 - x - 2 = 0$, ▶
    $x = -2$ or $x = -1$ or $x = 1$

solve $(x^3+2x^2-x-2=0, x)$

| MAIN | RAD EXACT | FUNC | 1/30 |

Correct Answer: **C**

Note that this problem could be given in either no-calculator or calculator section. You can see an algebraic solution to this problem in the Diagnostic Test, Section 3, question 7.

Solving Radical Equations

19. Which of the following is the solution set of the equation $9 + \sqrt{2n-1} = 4$?

    A. $\{-13\}$

    B. $\{-12\}$

    C. $\{13\}$

    D. $\{\ \}$

TI-89 solution:

Press: HOME F2 1

Enter: 9 + 2ND √ 2 ALPHA n − 1)

　　　　= 4 , ALPHA n)

Press: ENTER

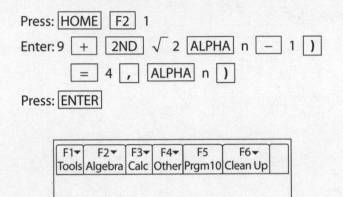

Correct Answer: **D**

Note that you can see an algebraic solution to this problem in Chapter XI, "Passport to Advanced Math," Section G, "Rational and Radical Equations," question 1.

Finding Mean, Median, Quartiles, and Standard Deviation of a Given Set of Data

20. Tommy's test grades in his math class for the first quarter are 90, 84, 80, 92, 84, and 98. Of the six grades in the first quarter, if p is the mean, q is the median, and r is the mode, which of the following inequalities is true?

    A. $r < q < p$

    B. $r < p < q$

    C. $p < r < q$

    D. $q < p < r$

TI-89 solution:

Press: HOME

Enter: 2ND { 90 , 84 , 80 , 92 ,

84 , 98 2ND } STO ▷ ALPHA ↑ L1E

Press: ENTER

Enter: 2ND MATH 6 ▷ 1

Press: ENTER ALPHA ↑ L1

Press: ENTER

Enter: 2ND MATH 6 ▷ 9

Press: ENTER

Press: ENTER

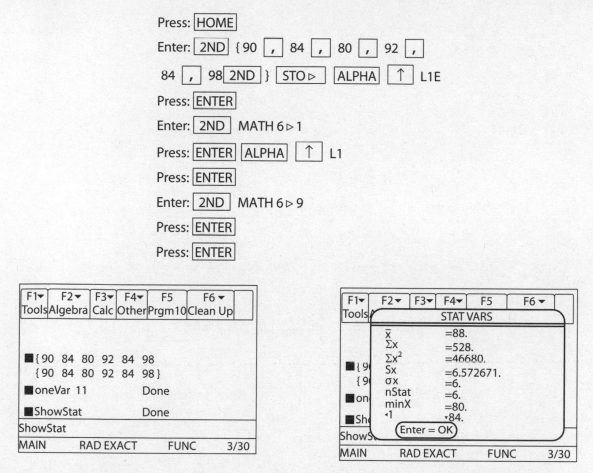

Note: $\overline{x}$ is the mean and medStat is the median. Also, depending on the model of the calculator, you might need to scroll downward to see the value of medStat.

Correct Answer: **A**

Note that you can see an algebraic solution to this problem in Chapter X, "Problem Solving and Data Analysis," Section G, "Statistics: Mean, Median, Mode, Range, and Standard Deviation," question 1.